OXFORD WORLD'S CLASSICS

THE OXFORD SHAKESPEARE

General Editor · Stanley Wells

The Oxford Shakespeare offers new and authoritative editions of Shakespeare's plays in which the early printings have been scrupulously re-examined and interpreted. An introductory essay provides all relevant background information together with an appraisal of critical views and of the play's effects in performance. The detailed commentaries pay particular attention to language and staging. Reprints of sources, music for songs, genealogical tables, maps, etc. are included where necessary; many of the volumes are illustrated, and all contain an index.

ROGER WARREN, the editor of *Pericles* in the Oxford Shakespeare, has also edited *Cymbeline* and *Henry VI, Part Two*, and co-edited *Twelfth Night* with Stanley Wells for the series.

THE OXFORD SHAKESPEARE

Currently available in paperback

The rest of the plays are forthcoming

OXFORD WORLD'S CLASSICS

WILLIAM SHAKESPEARE
AND
GEORGE WILKINS

A RECONSTRUCTED TEXT OF

Pericles, Prince of Tyre

Edited by
ROGER WARREN

on the basis of a text prepared by
GARY TAYLOR *and* MACD. P. JACKSON

OXFORD
UNIVERSITY PRESS

OXFORD
UNIVERSITY PRESS

Great Clarendon Street, Oxford OX2 6DP

Oxford University Press is a department of the University of Oxford.
It furthers the University's objective of excellence in research, scholarship,
and education by publishing worldwide in

Oxford New York

Auckland Bangkok Buenos Aires Cape Town Chennai
Dar es Salaam Delhi Hong Kong Istanbul Karachi Kolkata
Kuala Lumpur Madrid Melbourne Mexico City Mumbai Nairobi
São Paulo Shanghai Taipei Tokyo Toronto

Oxford is a registered trade mark of Oxford University Press
in the UK and in certain other countries

Published in the United States
by Oxford University Press Inc., New York

First published 2003
First published as an Oxford World's Classics paperback 2004

British Library Cataloguing in Publication Data

Data available

Library of Congress Cataloging in Publication Data

Data available

ISBN 978-0-19-281460-9 (Paperback)

3 5 7 9 10 8 6 4 2

Typeset by SNP Best-set Typesetter Ltd., Hong Kong
Printed in Great Britain by
Clays Ltd, St Ives plc

PREFACE

THIS edition of *Pericles* offers a conjectural reconstruction of the play that lies behind the corrupt text of the Quarto published in 1609. It is based on that by Gary Taylor and MacDonald P. Jackson in the Oxford Shakespeare *Complete Works* of 1986, and is greatly indebted to their ground-breaking work. In presenting the play as a collaboration between Shakespeare and George Wilkins, I have especially benefited from Mac Jackson's meticulous research in his book *Defining Shakespeare: 'Pericles' as Test Case*; this is a major contribution to scholarship, and I am most grateful to Mac Jackson for letting me see it in advance of publication. I should also like to thank Brian Vickers for allowing me to read his *Shakespeare, Co-Author* at proof stage.

I have of course reconsidered every detail of the Quarto text and of the Oxford reconstruction. Where my text differs from Oxford's, that usually reflects the practical experience of using their version in rehearsal, first at Stratford, Ontario in 1986, and then at Stratford-upon-Avon in 1989. The contribution made by the directors and actors concerned will be evident from the frequency with which they are cited. I thank them all warmly, as I do the library staff at the Shakespeare Centre and the Shakespeare Institute for their unfailing help.

I have been constantly supported by the generosity and friendship of my colleagues. Stanley Wells, general editor of the Oxford Shakespeare, has once again been a source of invaluable advice; Frances Whistler at Oxford University Press read the entire edition in draft, and her detailed responses have improved it throughout; and once more I owe a very special debt to Angie Kendall who helped prepare this edition through all its stages.

ROGER WARREN

CONTENTS

LIST OF ILLUSTRATIONS

INTRODUCTION

Preliminaries: Theatre, Text, Authors

WHEN *Pericles* was first performed by Shakespeare's company, the King's Men, at the Globe theatre in Southwark, south London, in 1607 or early 1608, it was a great popular success;[1] and it has regained much of that popularity in the modern theatre. It was first published in a Quarto edition in 1609, and reprinted in the same year, suggesting an exceptional public demand;[2] only the quartos of *Richard II* and *Henry IV Part One* in 1598 had a similar success. The play's popularity is also attested in *Pimlico*, an anonymous pamphlet of 1609:

> Amazed I stood to see a crowd
> Of civil throats stretched out so loud . . .
> So that I truly thought all these
> Came to see *Shore* or *Pericles*.[3]

It seems to have been still popular twenty years later, to judge by Ben Jonson's envious grumble about the success of a 'mouldy tale, | Like *Pericles*' after the failure of his own play *The New Inn* in 1629.[4] The Venetian ambassador saw a performance at some time between April 1607 and July 1608, after which the theatres were closed until late 1609, because of a particularly severe outbreak of plague.[5] Performances were not confined to the Globe theatre: we know of one given by a touring company in Yorkshire on 2 February 1610,[6] and another at court in 1619.[7] Of the latter, the

---

[1] The title-page of the 1609 edition states that *Pericles* was 'divers and sundry times acted by his Majesty's Servants at the Globe on the Bankside'; the date of composition is suggested by the absence of any reference to the play before 1607–8, and by numerous allusions thereafter. 'It probably made its initial impact in the first five months of 1608' (*TC*, p. 131).

[2] There were further reprints in 1611, 1619, 1630, and 1635. See p. 71 below.

[3] Sig. C1. *Shore* is a reference to Jane Shore, the King's mistress, in Thomas Heywood's *Edward IV* (*c.* 1599).

[4] *Ode to Himself*, ll. 21–2.

[5] E. K. Chambers, *William Shakespeare*, 2 vols. (Oxford, 1930), ii. 335.

[6] C. J. Sisson, 'Shakespeare Quartos as Prompt-Copies', *RES* 18 (1942), 129–43; p. 138.

[7] Chambers, *William Shakespeare*, ii. 346.

Earl of Pembroke wrote in a letter that he could not bear to see the performance 'so soon after the loss of my old acquaintance Burbage':[1] the natural deduction is that Pericles was usually played by Richard Burbage, leading actor of the King's Men. The play's popularity is summed up in the Prologue to Robert Tailor's play *The Hog hath Lost his Pearl* (1614):

> And if it prove so happy as to please,
> We'll say 'tis fortunate like *Pericles*.
>
> (ll. 31–2)

Pericles was the first of Shakespeare's plays to be revived after the Restoration, but thereafter it went into eclipse,[2] and received only sporadic revivals[3] until after the Second World War. Since then, the number of performances world-wide steadily increased until by the end of the twentieth century *Pericles* had become, if not a regular presence in the repertory, at least a frequent visitor, usually greeted with acclaim by reviewers and audiences. This introduction will draw upon the evidence provided by several of these productions in order to suggest some reasons for that enthusiasm.[4]

But if *Pericles* is a stageworthy play, it is also a tantalizing one, because of two major problems which must be briefly mentioned at the outset. First, that much-reprinted Quarto text is grossly corrupt: many passages are garbled and nonsensical, others are actually missing, one of them crucially. It is almost certainly a

[1] E. K. Chambers, *The Elizabethan Stage*, 4 vols. (Oxford, 1923), ii. 308.

[2] There was only a single production in the eighteenth century, George Lillo's adaptation *Marina*, given for a mere three performances in 1738, and only one in the nineteenth, by Samuel Phelps at Sadler's Wells theatre, London, in 1854. Or so the records suggest; but John Masefield quotes 'two managers' of 'the lesser [minor London] theatres of the mid-nineteenth century' as saying 'When ruin stares you in the face, put on *Pericles*, that will save you' (*William Shakespeare* (1954), 149). It seems astonishing that a play with two scenes, one a crucial one, set in a brothel should have been popular in the Victorian period; but maybe the eclipse in the play's popularity was less extreme than it seems. For Lillo's version, see *The Dramatic Works of George Lillo*, ed. J. L. Steffensen (Oxford, 1993), 333–87; for Phelps's, see Henry Morley's account, conveniently reprinted in Stanley Wells's anthology *Shakespeare in the Theatre* (Oxford, 1997), 92–4: this concludes that Phelps's version 'may be said to succeed only because it is a spectacle'. A preposterous adaptation by the actor-director John Coleman was a fiasco at Stratford-upon-Avon in 1900: see J. C. Trewin and T. C. Kemp, *The Stratford Festival* (Birmingham, 1953), 52–5.

[3] For example, at the Old Vic theatre, London, in 1921, and at the open-air theatre, Regent's Park, in 1939, both directed by Robert Atkins.

[4] For a sketch of major productions since the Second World War, see pp. 20–30 below.

'reported text', put together by an actor or actors who had appeared in it.[1] Moreover, since *Pericles* was not included in the First Folio of Shakespeare's works in 1623,[2] we have no adequate text by which to remedy the Quarto's deficiencies. But a prose narrative by George Wilkins, *The Painful Adventures of Pericles Prince of Tyre*, published in 1608, claimed on its title-page to be 'the true history of the play of *Pericles*, as it was lately presented by the worthy and ancient poet John Gower', i.e. that it was an account of the play given at the Globe, in which Gower is the narrator or 'Presenter', as Wilkins calls him in his list of characters. Wilkins's prose contains passages which read as if they were originally verse lines in a play, either the play reported in the Quarto text or something very close to it. By re-casting these verse 'fossils' back into blank verse, it is possible to reconstruct passages missing in the Quarto text and to emend much of its corruption. But although phrases from Wilkins have been drafted into some modern editions, the first sustained attempt to use Wilkins more extensively, in order to reconstruct what the original play might have been like, was made by Gary Taylor and MacDonald P. Jackson in the Oxford Shakespeare *Complete Works* of 1986. Here again, the theatre led the way. No production of *Pericles* known to me has ever performed the Quarto text exactly as it stands, because of its manifest defects, so directors have regularly drawn on passages from Wilkins to provide themselves with a more performable script. Following their example, and believing that merely to provide a cleaned-up reprint of the Quarto[3] is an evasion of editorial responsibility towards users of a modern edition, the text in this edition builds upon Oxford's and draws on Wilkins in an attempt to reconstruct the play that lies behind the Quarto text. This is not, therefore, a conservative edition; but in order to enable readers to judge the original for themselves, the Quarto text is reprinted unaltered in Appendix A.

[1] Since the whole theory of memorial transmission has come under fire in recent years, I have re-examined the evidence, and re-stated the case, for reported texts in my edition of *2 Henry VI* in this series, pp. 78–87.

[2] See pp. 60–1 for discussion of this omission. *Pericles* appeared for the first time in a folio edition of Shakespeare in the second issue of the Third Folio (1664).

[3] This is the declared policy of the New Cambridge edition, ed. Doreen DelVecchio and Antony Hammond (Cambridge, 1998). I have given my reasons for thinking this an inadequate approach in 'Theatrical Use and Editorial Abuse: More Painful Adventures for Pericles', *RES* 49 (1998), 478–86, and shall not therefore allude any further to this edition, except at Sc. 21.68.1–71.1, where I follow these editors in making a rearrangement necessitated by the staging.

In his brief introduction to *Pericles* in the Oxford *Complete Works*, Stanley Wells warns against allowing the textual problems to distract attention from the play's dramatic merits. Accordingly, the textual complexities are postponed to the final section of this introduction; but since in practice the play's dramatic merits cannot be entirely dissociated from its textual difficulties, or from this reconstruction's attempt to solve them, it has been necessary to alert readers to the textual situation from the outset.

The same also applies to the second initial problem, closely connected with the first, which concerns authorship. Commentators, performers, and audiences have instinctively felt that there is a discrepancy between the writing of Scenes 1–9 (Acts 1–2 in other editions) and Scenes 11–22 (Acts 3–5)[1] so marked that it points to collaborative authorship; and that while the verse in the second half of the play, even when only glimpsed through the corruption of the Quarto text, is characteristic of that in Shakespeare's late plays, the verse of the first half is unlike Shakespeare's at any stage of his career. This edition presents *Pericles* as a collaboration between Shakespeare and George Wilkins, Wilkins writing Scenes 1–9, Shakespeare Scenes 11–22.[2] The detailed evidence for Wilkins's part-authorship will be considered at the end of the introduction in order to keep the focus on the play itself; but it may be helpful at this stage to say a little about George Wilkins, his relationship with Shakespeare's theatre company, and how he might have come to be collaborating with Shakespeare on *Pericles*.

Shakespeare and George Wilkins

George Wilkins (*c.* 1575–1618) was a minor dramatist who, so far as we know, wrote only one play that was not a collaboration. This was *The Miseries of Enforced Marriage*, published in 1607 and probably performed shortly before by the King's Men. It was a popular success, and Wilkins may have attempted to follow it up by offering

[1] There are no act divisions in the Quarto text. This edition provides Scene numbers only: see the Editorial Procedures.

[2] Within this broad division, each dramatist may have contributed to scenes largely written by the other; Scene 10 (the Gower speech between the two halves of the play), for example, shows signs of the stylistic habits of both Wilkins and Shakespeare: see p. 69 below.

the company an outline or a draft of a play based on the legend of Apollonius of Tyre, the story of *Pericles*. The *Diary* or account-book of the theatrical impresario Philip Henslowe makes it clear that offering a theatre such an outline, for advance part-payment, was common in the period;[1] and Gary Taylor in the Oxford *Textual Companion* points out that 'Shakespeare, as sharer and company dramatist, must have been involved in such transactions . . . and could have decided to contribute to (or take over) a play initiated by someone else' (p. 130). It is worth emphasizing that Wilkins is not without merit as a dramatist. *The Miseries of Enforced Marriage* is an ambitiously planned play; and *Pericles*, despite its unevenness and its wandering narrative, holds together in performance since it is well constructed, each half building to an act of healing, Cerimon's revival of Thaisa in Scene 12 and Marina's of Pericles in Scene 21. If Wilkins did offer a 'plot' or outline of the play to the King's Men, the credit for its construction should go to him.

At first sight, it might seem strange for a dramatist who had just scored a success with a domestic tragi-comedy based on recent events in Yorkshire to follow it with a tale of far-flung wandering around exotic locations in the Mediterranean; but in fact Wilkins's other works, written at about the same time, show a marked interest in just such stories and locations. He contributed a share, probably the lion's share,[2] to a play written in collaboration with John Day and William Rowley, *The Travels of the Three English Brothers* (1607). The travels of Sir Thomas, Sir Anthony, and Robert Sherley in Persia were much in the news at the time; so Wilkins was combining his sense of the newsworthy, evident in *The Miseries of Enforced Marriage*, with an interest in exotic locations that is also evident in his pamphlet *Three Miseries of Barbary* (*c.* 1606) and especially in *The History of Justine* (1606), which claimed to be a new translation of the 'narration of kingdoms from the beginning of the Assyrian monarchy unto the reign of the Emperor Augustus

---

[1] On 10 August 1599, for example, Henslowe advanced money to Ben Jonson and Thomas Dekker 'in earnest of their book [i.e. play] which they be a-writing' (*Henslowe's Diary*, ed. R. A. Foakes and R. T. Rickert (2nd edn., Cambridge, 2002), 123). For examples of a scenario or 'plot' from the Jacobean period, see Brian Vickers, *Shakespeare, Co-Author* (Oxford, 2002), 21–3.

[2] See D. J. Lake, 'Wilkins and *Pericles*', *N&Q* 214 (1969), 288–91, especially p. 289.

[by] that famous historiographer Justine [Justinian]', as the title-page puts it.[1] The section on the Athenians describes the celebrated statesman Pericles, 'a man of tried virtue and experience' who 'royally gave all [his] lands and livings to the good of the whole commonwealth' (p. 20); that on the Macedonians praises a certain Lysimachus, whose 'prowess, knighthood, and experience in martial direction [were] unsurpassed', but who, like many of the rulers described by Justinian, became a tyrant and abuser of his authority (pp. 64–9), which may have provided a hint for the behaviour of Lysimachus in Scene 19 of *Pericles*; and Antiochus the Great plays a considerable role in the later stages of the work. The occurrence of all three names in both *Justine* and *Pericles* is discussed further on p. 17 below. E. A. J. Honigmann concludes that 'Wilkins's special interest in Mediterranean histories [makes it] likely that *Pericles* the play originated with Wilkins too'.[2]

Our knowledge of Wilkins himself depends primarily upon Roger Prior's painstaking research into the records of the Middlesex Sessions in the early seventeenth century, where eighteen separate law cases involved a George Wilkins (or the spelling variants Wilkinson on Wilkeson, which nonetheless, as Prior shows, clearly refer to the same man).[3] Drawing upon the Sessions records, Prior demonstrates that Wilkins was an innkeeper in Cow Cross, an area of London 'notorious as the haunt of whores and thieves . . . he was implicated in thefts and harboured whores who had stolen'; it looks very much as if his 'inn' was in fact a brothel. Several of the accusations against him concern extreme violence towards women: 'Once he kicked a pregnant woman in the belly; he beat another woman and stamped upon her so that she had to be carried home'; and this second woman was later before the courts for being a common bawd.[4] It seems quite likely that these women whom he attacked may have been in his employment as bawds or prostitutes when they had incurred his displeasure; but at any rate it comes as no surprise that Wilkins should relish a story

---

[1] Much of Wilkins's translation is plagiarized from Arthur Golding's earlier one (1564). Where I refer to Wilkins's phrasing (as at the Commentary to Sc. 2.12), I have of course checked that it is independent of Golding's.

[2] *The Stability of Shakespeare's Text* (1965), 196–7. The title-page of *Justine* merely attributes the work to 'G.W.', which *OED* takes to be G. Woodcocke; but Honigmann offers strong evidence to support the attribution to Wilkins.

[3] Roger Prior, 'The Life of George Wilkins', *SS* 25 (Cambridge, 1972), 137–52.

[4] Prior, pp. 140–1, 147, 150–1.

which dramatizes the abuse of Antiochus' daughter, the attempted prostitution of Marina, and Pericles' striking Marina at the climax of the play.[1]

In his Arden edition of *Pericles*, F. D. Hoeniger writes: 'Not a few scholars have rejected Wilkins primarily because the very idea that Shakespeare should have collaborated with such a minor dramatist near the end of his career was repugnant to them' (p. lix). He was writing before Roger Prior's evidence from the Sessions appeared: that would presumably have caused even greater repugnance. Such an attitude prompts two responses. On the personal level, Shakespeare was unquestionably acquainted with Wilkins, for both gave evidence in a court case between two French Protestant wig-makers, Stephen Belott and Christopher Mountjoy, in 1612: Shakespeare had lodged in Mountjoy's house, and both he and Wilkins were clearly friends of the Mountjoy family.[2] On the professional level, Shakespeare was a 'sharer' in his theatre company and so partly responsible for running it; Wilkins had recently written a play that proved a popular success for them; and since collaboration was frequent in the Elizabethan and Jacobean theatre, there is nothing improbable in a collaboration between Shakespeare and Wilkins.[3] They might have collaborated in various ways. Shakespeare could simply have taken over a complete play and rewritten parts of it, or completed a partly written play; but the likeliest interpretation is that Wilkins presented an outline and the writing was divided up between them; that would accord better with the evidence that the sources were consulted in both halves of the play, i.e. by both writers.[4]

In his New Penguin edition of *Pericles*, Philip Edwards writes: 'It would be curious indeed if Shakespeare had discovered, in a poor play that he started tinkering with, the kind of plot, the kind of art, the kind of theme, which he was to spend all the endeavour of the last years of his writing life trying to develop. It would be curious, but it has to be admitted it would not be

---

[1] See p. 16 below.

[2] Chambers, *William Shakespeare*, ii. 90–5.

[3] Shakespeare certainly collaborated later with John Fletcher on *The Two Noble Kinsmen* (1613–14) and probably *Henry VIII* (1613); there is strong evidence that he collaborated with Thomas Middleton on *Timon of Athens* (1605) and perhaps with other writers on earlier plays too. See *TC*, pp. 71–3, 127–8, 133–4.

[4] See Geoffrey Bullough, *Narrative and Dramatic Sources of Shakespeare*, vol. 6 (1966), 355; Brian Vickers, *Shakespeare, Co-Author*, p. 445.

impossible' (p. 41). To put the point rather more positively, Wilkins's outline of his draft may have provided Shakespeare with a stimulus for all his late work: at any rate, as Edwards remarks elsewhere, Shakespeare 'undoubtedly enters the world' of his late plays through *Pericles*.[1]

'Pericles' and Shakespeare's Other Plays

Whether or not *Pericles* is wholly by Shakespeare, it has much in common with the closely-linked group of plays—*Cymbeline, The Winter's Tale,* and *The Tempest*—which he wrote at the end of his career in 1610–11. All these plays have a particularly wide emotional range, focusing on extremes of love, hate, jealousy, grief, despair, even apparent death and resurrection, ultimately reunion, forgiveness, and reconciliation. These extremes of emotion are often dramatized by equivalent extremes of theatrical virtuosity. In *Cymbeline,* for example, the heroine Innogen apparently dies and is ritually mourned by her brothers, only to revive and find herself beside a headless corpse which she mistakes for her husband's; and later the god Jupiter descends from the heavens on an eagle's back to promise that husband and wife will ultimately be united. In *The Winter's Tale* Leontes is suddenly struck down by jealousy of his wife, and after her apparent death and his sixteen-year repentance is reunited with her when her 'statue' comes to life. In *The Tempest* Prospero's magic is dramatized by a series of elaborate theatrical shows. The narrative of these plays is far-flung in both space and time: *Cymbeline* moves between ancient Britain, classical Rome, medieval Italy, and Renaissance England (and Wales), *The Winter's Tale* between Sicilia and Bohemia, with a gap of sixteen years in the middle of the play. The action of *The Tempest* is restricted to one place, Prospero's island in the Mediterranean, and to the time it takes to perform; but by having Prospero recall and in the process re-experience the events in Naples twelve years before, the play, as it were, brings the outside world to the island itself; and by looking into 'the dark backward and abyss of time' through Prospero's eyes, it emphasizes that it is essentially about his spiritual journey. In the other two plays, too, the external journeys mirror the psychological journeys of the central characters, Innogen and Posthu-

---

[1] 'Shakespeare's Romances: 1900–1957', *SS 11* (Cambridge, 1958), 1–18; p. 5.

mus in *Cymbeline* and Leontes in *The Winter's Tale*, which are at the heart of each play and help to hold each together.

Clearly *Pericles* shares several of these features. Pericles' geographical journeys take him over most of the Mediterranean, from Antioch, Tyre, and Tarsus in the north-eastern corner to Pentapolis in North Africa to Ephesus and Mytilene on the Aegean coast (see fig. 1). Although these places still exist, or have modern equivalents, the geography of *Pericles* is as much symbolic as actual; Pericles is on a journey of discovery and self-discovery, in important respects a journey through life: seeking a wife, eventually finding one, apparently losing her in childbirth, also apparently losing his daughter and so giving way to despair, until he is ultimately reunited with both daughter and wife after fourteen years' wandering. We do not, however, see him during those fourteen years, when his place at the centre of the play is taken by his daughter Marina, whose trials—surviving an attempt on her life, kidnapped by pirates, sold to a brothel—parallel, and in some respects exceed, those of her father. So when they meet at the end of the play, the long-drawn-out process of revelation and recognition is the final stage in the journey of discovery that each has undertaken.

Crucial stages in Pericles' journey are dramatized, as in the other three plays, by a focus on emotional states: his searing grief when he believes that his wife Thaisa has died in childbirth, his despairing self-neglect when he thinks Marina too is dead, and then his ecstatic outburst when he discovers she is in fact alive, which takes him beyond his human state to make contact with the divine, as he hears the music of the spheres and the voice of the goddess Diana. The descent of the goddess herself is one of the many moments of theatrical virtuosity that *Pericles* has in common with the other late plays: Pericles solving Antiochus' riddle surrounded by the severed heads of former suitors; the tournament and dance at Pentapolis; the apparent death of Thaisa on board a storm-swept ship, and then the slow, enthralling process of her revival by Cerimon at Ephesus; the reunion of father and daughter, again on board ship; the final family reunion in Diana's temple. Certain incidents are presented in the form of mime, 'dumb shows' that look back to an older form of drama, Tudor and medieval, but which also anticipate the dramatization of Prospero's magic in *The Tempest*.

In their emphasis upon the emotional journeys of the central characters, in their use of sea and shipwreck as both destroyer and

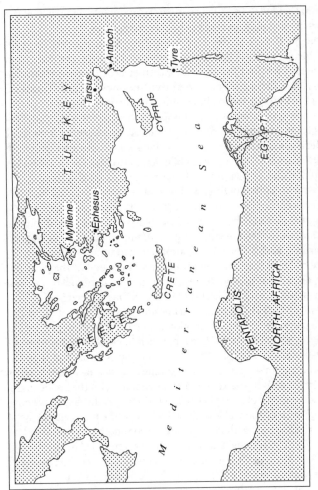

1. Map showing the principal locations of *Pericles*.

renewer, and in making the reunion of a family as important as the coming together of lovers, the late plays also mark a return to the preoccupations of Shakespeare's earlier comedies; and *Pericles* has specific connections with two of them in particular, *The Comedy of Errors* and *Twelfth Night*. The main action of *The Comedy of Errors* draws upon two farces by the Roman dramatist Plautus, but places the farcical events within a framework very different in tone, concerning a family separated by shipwreck but ultimately reunited many years later. This 'frame' story derives from the legend of Apollonius of Tyre, which also supplies the entire plot of *Pericles*. At the heart of the family reunion in *Errors* is the Abbess of a priory at Ephesus, a Christian version of the temple of Diana in which the family reunion in *Pericles* takes place. But even in the midst of the farcical events in *Errors*, the central character, Antipholus of Syracuse, is, like Pericles, on a quest, searching the cities of the Mediterranean for the twin brother from whom he was separated as a child in the shipwreck which also parted his father and mother. But as he tries to find his twin, he has a strange sensation that he is losing his own identity in the process:

> I to the world am like a drop of water
> That in the ocean seeks another drop . . .
> So I, to find a mother and a brother,
> In quest of them, unhappy, lose myself.
> (1.2.35–40)

This sensation is inevitably sharpened when he encounters a group of strangers who all seem to know him; and while these encounters are primarily farcical, it is a basic principle of farce that its situations should seem absolutely serious to those who experience them. Clifford Williams, who directed a celebrated production of *Errors* at Stratford-upon-Avon in 1962, catches the serious undertow of Antipholus' lines when he says that they represent Shakespeare's 'first steps along a road' that shows 'a man in search of his origin and his end, in search of forgiveness and reconciliation, in search of reality and identity. It is a road that Shakespeare travels and re-travels from *The Comedy of Errors* through to the last plays.'[1] If Wilkins offered the King's Men a scenario based on the story of

---

[1] Introduction to the Folio Society edition of *The Comedy of Errors* (1969), 10.

Apollonius of Tyre, it may well have seemed the more attractive to Shakespeare because he had already dramatized aspects of it earlier in his career.

In the climactic scene of reunion between Pericles and Marina, Shakespeare reworks a speech that he had placed at the emotional heart of *Twelfth Night*, where Viola obliquely declares her love for Orsino in the allegory of an invented sister who died of love:

> She pined in thought,
> And with a green and yellow melancholy
> She sat like patience on a monument,
> Smiling at grief.
>
> (2.4.112–15)

This clearly lies behind perhaps the most memorable lines in *Pericles*, in which Pericles describes Marina:

> thou dost look
> Like patience gazing on kings' graves, and smiling
> Extremity out of act.
>
> (Sc. 21.127–9)

But typically of the technique of the late plays, the language is extended and developed in its implications. Both Viola's 'sister' and Marina represent contrasting emotions, succinctly summarized in Viola's 'Smiling at grief'; but Marina goes further: her smiling patience has the capacity to convert Pericles from the extremes of violence and grief, and in this way to smile 'Extremity out of act'.

In one important respect, however, *Pericles* differs both from the earlier comedies and from the other late plays. Apart from bridging the sixteen-year gap in *The Winter's Tale* by using the device of an actor representing Time itself, the late plays move through wide distances of space and time without apology or mediation; but *Pericles* introduces the figure of the medieval poet John Gower to tell the story and to invite the audience's participation, encouraging them to use their imagination to bridge those very gaps:

> Thus time we waste, and long leagues make we short,
> Sail seas in cockles, have an wish but for't,
> Making to take imagination
> From bourn to bourn, region to region.
>
> (Sc. 18.1–4)

Precisely why was it thought so dramatically appropriate for Gower to introduce and comment on the action of *Pericles*? This question conveniently raises the topic of where the story came from.

Origins

The tale that Gower 'presents' is of great antiquity. It probably originated in a Greek romance of the fifth century AD, and it is said to be still current in oral tradition in Greece today. The earliest written version is a Latin manuscript of the ninth century, *Historia Apollonii Regis Tyri*, and the earliest surviving vernacular version is an Anglo-Saxon translation of it.[1] Among numerous other Latin versions of the tale was a twelfth-century rhymed one by Godfrey of Viterbo, *Pantheon, or Universal Chronicle*; and in the fourteenth century the story became part of a popular collection called *Gesta Romanorum*.[2] These last two works were the respective sources for the two most important retellings of the legend from the point of view of *Pericles*. As the medieval poet John Gower begins to tell the story in his long poem *Confessio Amantis* (1393, first printed in 1483 and reprinted in 1533 and 1554), he says that it comes from an old chronicle called *Pantheon* (l. 280); and much of Laurence Twine's version in his prose work *The Pattern of Painful Adventures* (1576, later editions in *c.* 1594 and 1607) is simply a translation of that in the *Gesta Romanorum*.[3]

The story of the play comes from Book 8 of *Confessio Amantis*, which John Gower devotes to 'Unlawful love', distinguishing

> What is to love in good manere,
> And what to love in other wise
> (ll. 2018–19)

—i.e. between love and lust, of which the incest at Antioch serves as a good example. The plot of *Pericles* follows Gower's narrative closely, apart from greatly developing the brothel scenes. It is unusual for Shakespeare to stick so closely to a single narrative

[1] The Anglo-Saxon version, with a modern English translation, is available in Elaine Treharne's *Old and Middle English: An Anthology* (Oxford, 2000), 234–53.

[2] Translated by C. Swan, revised by W. Hooper (1905), Tale 153, pp. 259–99.

[3] Bullough, pp. 354–5. All quotations from Gower and Twine are from Bullough's texts. The 1607 edition of Twine may have provided the spur for the composition of *Pericles*, or may have been reprinted in response to the play's success.

source, and this is one of the reasons for thinking that the outline of the play may not have originated with him but with George Wilkins. But if Gower was the principal source, the expansion and treatment of several episodes clearly show the influence of Laurence Twine's *Pattern of Painful Adventures*. Wilkins plagiarizes Twine extensively in his own *Painful Adventures of Pericles*; and Shakespeare draws on both Gower and Twine for the scene of Thaisa's revival from apparent death. In Gower, her resuscitation is the work of Cerimon himself, as in the play; but although in Twine it is done by his assistant Machaon, the detail given corresponds to much of Scene 12.77–108:

Then came Machaon unto the corpse, and pulled the clothes from the lady's bosom, and poured forth the ointment, and bestowing it abroad with his hand, perceived some warmth in her breast, and that there was life in the body. Machaon stood astonished, and he felt her pulses, and laid his cheek to her mouth, and . . . he perceived how death strived with life within her, and that the conflict was dangerous and doubtful who should prevail. . . . Then took he certain hot and comfortable oils, and warming them upon the coals, he dipped fair wool therein, and fomented all the body over therewith until such time as the congealed blood and humours were throughly resolved, and the spirits eftsoons recovered their wonted course, the veins waxed warm, the arteries began to beat, and the lungs drew in the fresh air again, and she opened her eyes and looked about. (pp. 449–50)

But when at Sc. 12.103 Thaisa speaks, Shakespeare reverts to Gower, using his exact words to express her sense of disorientation:

> Where am I?
> Where is my lorde, what worlde is this?
> (*Confessio Amantis*, ll. 1214–15)

Twine's most important contribution, however, was to the brothel scenes. In Gower, the episode is brief: the equivalent of Marina successfully pleads with the pander's servant to allow her to earn money as a teacher rather than as a prostitute. But the play's most crucial departure from Gower in these scenes is that in *Confessio Amantis* the Governor of Mytilene does not visit the brothel at all, and so does not provide the heroine with the financial means to buy herself out. It is Twine, following the *Gesta Romanorum*, who makes the Governor a key figure. When the heroine is offered for sale by the pirates, he vies with the owner of the brothel to buy her, in a kind of auction. But then the Governor thinks: 'if I should contend with the bawd to buy her at so high a price, I must needs sell other slaves to pay for her, which were both loss and shame unto me. Wherefore I will suffer him to buy her; and when he setteth her to hire, I will be the first man that shall come unto her, and I will gather the flower of her virginity, which shall stand me in as great stead as if I had bought her' (p. 456). So he goes to the brothel in disguise, as Lysimachus does in the play, where he is 'moved with compassion' and gives the heroine the money she needs to buy her way out. But Twine makes the Governor add some surprising information: he has 'a daughter at home' who may learn from the heroine's misfortunes 'that she may take heed when she cometh unto the like years, that she fall not into the like mishap'. This implies that the Governor is nearer Pericles' age than Marina's. Altogether, Twine's Governor is a complex figure: cool and calculating in working out how to have the girl most advantageously, then moved by her—yet at the same time revealing that he has a daughter. He presents, in an even more extreme form than in the play, a problem that has often worried commentators on *Pericles*, namely that the virtuous heroine marries a man who has tried to use her as a prostitute. Although the Lysimachus of the play is also a complex figure, a flippant whoremonger and regular habitué of the brothel who is initially quite prepared to use his power to force Marina to give in to him, his behaviour is arguably less reprehensible (certainly less calculating) than Twine's character, and the complicating factor of his daughter is wisely omitted altogether.[1]

Twine provides words for Marina's song, and Wilkins incorporates them in his prose narrative (see Appendix B, Passage D); this has proved useful to modern productions, since no words are given in the Quarto text at Sc. 21.68.2. Twine also follows the *Gesta Romanorum* in making the Pericles character, rejecting his daughter, kick her in the face, so that 'the blood gushed plentifully out of

---

[1] Another contributory influence on Marina's experiences in the brothel may have been the lives of Christian saints, especially that of Saint Agnes, a thirteen-year-old Christian martyr of the fourth century AD who, when she refused to worship idols, was sent naked into a brothel. I agree with Geoffrey Bullough that 'there is no reason to suppose that Shakespeare thought' Marina like early Christian saints (p. 371), but the idea of prostituting a thirteen-year-old girl, and the lurid detail of sending her to the brothel naked, may well have appealed to Wilkins, in view of his attitude to women that Roger Prior has unearthed, cited on p. 6 above.

her cheeks' (pp. 466–7). Not even Wilkins, with his apparent liking
for kicking women (see p. 6 above), goes quite this far in his narrative: Pericles in his version 'struck her on the face' so that she fell
unconscious (p. 543), and—though the Quarto provides no stage
direction—Shakespeare too probably intends Pericles to strike
Marina, as in Gower's version (ll. 1701–2); see p. 55 below.

Neither Gower nor Twine makes the hero the victor of a tournament at Pentapolis; instead, he plays tennis with the King. Both,
however, refer to 'jousts' as part of the wedding celebrations of the
hero and heroine, and Twine also to 'dancing in armour' (p. 444;
compare Sc. 7.89–90). Geoffrey Bullough notes that 'in a Greek
poem on the story printed in the sixteenth century there is a tournament at Pentapolis', so perhaps the dramatists knew some folklore variant unknown to us (p. 355); but the tournament sequence
shows the clear influence of a work almost as important to the play
as Gower or Twine: *The Countess of Pembroke's Arcadia* by Sir Philip
Sidney, printed in 1593. It is not surprising that the *Arcadia* should
have influenced both Shakespeare and Wilkins, since despite its
great length it was one of the most widely-read books of the period.
It influenced *Pericles* in both large matters and small, including the
hero's name.

In all other versions of the story, the hero is called Apollonius.
Why then did the dramatists call him Pericles? J. M. S. Tompkins
suggests that the name derives from the Athenian statesman
whose life is told in Sir Thomas North's translation of Plutarch's
Lives of the Noble Grecians and Romans (1579), and was chosen by
the playwrights because both figures are exemplars of patience.[1]
Pericles in the play, however, seems to me to show notable patience
only once, when after he thinks his wife dead he says:

> Should I rage and roar
> As doth the sea she lies in, yet the end
> Must be as 'tis.
>
> (Sc. 13.10–12)

When he shows '*a mighty passion*' on seeing Marina's tomb (Sc.
18.22.5) and subsequently descends into a comatose state from
which Marina can only draw him with great difficulty, he scarcely
exemplifies patience; *she* has to urge him to be patient (Sc.

---

[1] 'Why Pericles?', *RES* 3 (1952), 315–24.

21.134–5), and it is Marina herself, not Pericles, who is specifically said to embody patience (Sc. 21.127–9). Even Plutarch insists only once on Pericles' patience (or 'constancy', as North calls it), and that is at the moment when it fails him, at the death of his youngest son: although he strove 'to show his natural constancy . . . sorrow did so pierce his heart [that] he burst out in tears and cried amain, which they never saw him do before', and 'he kept himself close in his house, as one bewailing his late grievous loss and sorrow'.[1] The resemblance here to Pericles' reaction to Marina's death is the only moment in Plutarch's long account of the Athenian Pericles which at all recalls the play—except in the matter of names. Antiochus, Cerimon, Helicanus, Dionyza, Lychorida, Philoten, and Thaisa (though for the daughter, not the mother) come from Gower; Cleon, Aeschines, Philemon, Simonides, and Lysimachus do not, but do occur in Plutarch's *Lives*, 'all but the last two within the Life of Pericles'.[2] And since Pericles and Lysimachus are both mentioned in Wilkins's *History of Justine*, as noted on p. 6 above, it is probable that the names of these two historical figures suggested their substitution for the Apollonius and Athanagoras of the legend, polysyllabic names that would be difficult to accommodate within ten-syllable verse lines and especially within Gower's eight-syllable ones, particularly when the name of the hero occurs so frequently.[3]

The name 'Pericles', however, may just as easily have been suggested by Sidney's *Arcadia*. One of its two heroes is called Pyrocles; and the accounts of the performances of *Pericles* in 1610 and 1619 mentioned at the start of this introduction spell the title 'Perocles' and 'Pirrocles' respectively. It seems clear that these two spellings, as well as 'Pericles' and Sidney's 'Pyrocles', are all indifferent spelling variants of the same name, which could have been

---

[1] Life of Pericles, pp. 188–9. There is no complete modern edition of North's Plutarch; references are to the 1579 edition.

[2] MacD. P. Jackson, 'North's Plutarch and the Name "Escanes" in Shakespeare's *Pericles*', *N&Q* 220 (1975), 173–4; p. 174.

[3] Some of the names of places and people in *Pericles* would have conjured up for Jacobean audiences associations with the New Testament, and especially with St Paul, who came from Tarsus, preached at Corinth and Ephesus, and wrote an Epistle to Philemon. But in general, as Naseeb Shaheen points out, '*Pericles* has relatively few biblical references' (p. 686); and as Frances Whistler notes privately, the New Testament references seem to remain 'just below the surface', apart from the associations of the Temple of Diana at Ephesus, discussed on pp. 46–7 below.

suggested by North's Plutarch or by the *Arcadia* or both. But whereas there is only a slight connection between the hero of the play and the Athenian statesman, there is a very marked connection between him and both heroes of the *Arcadia*, Pyrocles and Musidorus. These two heroes suffer shipwreck together twice, and the details of these episodes certainly influenced those in *Pericles*. The *Arcadia* opens with Musidorus cast naked on the shore, like Pericles in Scene 5, and being given clothes by a shepherd as Pericles is by a fisherman. This shipwreck in *Arcadia* is described, as it were in flashback, later in the work: Pyrocles and Musidorus showed 'no point of fear' but encouraged the sailors by their example, 'putting their hands to every most painful office',[1] as we are told Pericles did, in Marina's retrospective narrative to Leonine:

> My father, as nurse says, did never fear,
> But cried 'Good seamen' to the mariners,
> Galling his kingly hands with haling ropes.
> (Sc. 15.103–5)

Like Pyrocles and Musidorus, Pericles is a 'questing hero', 'looking for adventures in the world' as he himself puts it (Sc. 7.79). Such heroes were particularly associated with medieval narratives, above all the anonymous *Sir Gawain and the Green Knight* and Malory's *Morte Darthur*, both of them drawn from Arthurian legend, the best known repository of questing heroes.

Malory's heroes in particular frequently participate in jousts and tournaments, the chief pastime of the military aristocracy in the Middle Ages. There was a significant revival of such earlier chivalric modes at the court of Elizabeth I, and later at that of James I, emulating hers. So it is no surprise to find Pyrocles and Musidorus in the *Arcadia*, and Pericles in the play, engaging in tournaments. Again and again Sidney provides elaborate descriptions of the characters' armour, horse-trappings, and devices on their shields. To take one example of many:

His armour was blue like the heaven, which a sun did with his rays . . . gild in most places. His shield was beautified with this device: a greyhound which over-running his fellow and taking the hare, yet hurts it not when it takes it. The word [motto] was, 'The glory, not the prey.' (p. 497)

---

[1] All quotations from the *Arcadia* are from Maurice Evans's Penguin Classics edition (Harmondsworth, 1977); p. 262.

2. Isaac Oliver's miniature of Edward, 1st Baron of Cherbury. In the background is Elizabethan armour like that used in Scene 6 of *Pericles*. His shield bears an 'impresa' and the motto alludes to the idea of sympathetic magic (*Magica Sympathia*).

Such descriptions provide a context for the scene at Pentapolis in which each knight formally presents his device and motto to Simonides and Thaisa (Sc. 6.16.1–50; see also fig. 2). And Sidney's Pyrocles at one point turns up for a tournament so badly equipped that he is called the 'ill-appointed' or 'ill-apparelled' knight by the onlookers, as Pericles is called 'the mean knight' when he appears similarly under-dressed after his shipwreck at Pentapolis: Pyrocles 'had neither picture nor device; his armour of as old a fashion, besides the rusty poorness, that it might better seem a monument of his grandfather's courage' (p. 165; compare Sc. 6.43.1–62.3). The jousting that follows in the *Arcadia* degenerates into a three-sided squabble, compared by Sidney to a 'matachin' or sworddance. Later the other hero, Musidorus, actually 'danced the matachin dance in armour (O, with what a graceful dexterity!)' (p. 249), as Simonides instructs the Knights to do at Sc. 7.89–90:

> Even in your armours, as you are addressed,
> Your limbs will well become a soldier's dance.[1]

However much they do so through Elizabethan and Jacobean eyes, both the *Arcadia* and *Pericles* look back to a medieval world in making their central characters questing heroes. That is why—finally to answer the question raised in the previous section—*Pericles* resurrects the medieval author, 'ancient Gower', and brings him on stage to tell his own story, often in phrasing of archaic or gnomic simplicity. But this in turn raises the further question of how far such simplicity extends into the main action of the play. Several commentators have argued that the doggerel passages in the Quarto do not derive from inaccurate reporting, but represent a deliberate attempt to evoke a folk-tale world.[2] It is true that it is possible to prise what Philip Edwards in his edition vividly calls 'a kind of lunatic sense' from some of the doggerel (p. 196); but I find it very hard to believe that the frequent absurdities in the Quarto as it stands were *deliberately* written to ape a gnomic or folklore style. I will argue below (pp. 73–80) that misrepresentation by a reporter or reporters of what the dramatists originally wrote is much the likelier explanation; but in the meantime this introduction concentrates on what matters most, and explores the play as a dramatic experience; so a brief survey of modern productions will provide a useful context for this discussion.[3]

The Modern Revival of 'Pericles'

The theatrical revival of *Pericles* after the Second World War began with two productions given under the auspices of Sir Barry Jack-

---

[1] This connection has been independently pointed out by John P. Cutts, 'Pericles in Rusty Armour', *YES* 4 (1974), 49–51. Other echoes of the *Arcadia* are noted in the Commentary.

[2] e.g. G. Wilson Knight, *The Crown of Life* (1947, reprinted 1965), 32–75; F. D. Hoeniger, 'Gower and Shakespeare in *Pericles*', *SQ* 33 (1982), 461–79; and Barbara Everett in her programme note for the National Theatre's production in 1994.

[3] This sketch is selective. Apart from the two productions sponsored by Sir Barry Jackson, I only discuss those I have seen, and whose details I could therefore verify for myself. Even among those, I exclude the merely eccentric (like that by Prospect Theatre Company in 1973, which staged the play as a floor-show in a male brothel) or the conspicuously unsuccessful (like the National Theatre's 1994 version); but I have also had to exclude, for reasons of space, several efficient productions like those by the touring company Cheek by Jowl (1984) or the Oxford Stage Company (1993), which staged *Pericles* in repertory, not with other late plays, but with *The*

son, the first in 1947 when he was in charge of what was then called the Shakespeare Memorial Theatre at Stratford-upon-Avon, and the second at his Birmingham Repertory Theatre in 1954. Both were warmly received by audiences and reviewers; but they also demonstrated that textual problems and issues of authorship cannot be dissociated from production decisions. The Stratford director, Nugent Monck, omitted Scenes 1–4 entirely, on the grounds, as Robert Speaight wryly put it, 'that the Shakespeare Memorial Theatre owed no hospitality to what Shakespeare evidently had not written';[1] and at Birmingham, Douglas Seale, realizing that the Quarto's version of the episode between Lysimachus and Marina in the brothel is both inadequate and misleading (see pp. 49–50 below), incorporated blank-verse passages from Wilkins's prose narrative into the scene, thus anticipating the decisions of most subsequent productions and the reconstruction offered in this edition. The playing of the reunion between Pericles and Marina by Paul Scofield and Daphne Slater at Stratford[2] and by Richard Pasco and Doreen Aris at Birmingham drew especial praise; but the chief significance of these two productions was that by means of very simple staging they alerted modern audiences to the sheer theatrical impact of the play, helping to explain its success with its original audiences.

Whatever the merits of the next two major productions, simplicity was not among them. The 1950s were the heyday of scenic Shakespeare, especially at Stratford, and Tony Richardson's *Pericles* there in 1958 was a notable example. Within a permanent framework suggestive of a ship at sea, the various locations 'rise before us

Comedy of Errors, so bringing together the two plays in which Shakespeare draws upon the story of Apollonius of Tyre. The BBC television production (1983), despite using a cast of actors experienced in Shakespeare, is weakened by adopting a conversational style apt for television but at odds with the overt theatricality of the writing. I have discussed it, together with a production at the Theatre Royal, Stratford East, London, in *SQ* 35 (1984), 337–8.

[1] *Shakespeare on the Stage* (1973), 245. Despite the cuts, Monck was a champion of the play; he also staged it at his Maddermarket Theatre, Norwich, in 1929 and 1931.

[2] They returned to these roles in a near-complete text given at the Rudolf Steiner Hall, London, on two Sunday evenings in 1950. This time Daphne Slater played Thaisa as well as Marina until the final scene, thus anticipating the doubling of mother and daughter in Terry Hands's 1969 production; and another innovation was a female Gower, played by Mary Morris, a fine actress who gave several memorably incisive performances in Shakespeare.

in some of the most sumptuous sets . . . ever seen at Stratford; scene after scene appears, fades behind gauzes, rises aloft, sinks to oblivion: the sky is barred with magenta and green or whirls with shooting stars', as a local reviewer, Nigel Townshend, evocatively put it (*Leamington Spa Courier*, 11 July 1958). The red-walled brothel rose up out of the floor, and as it did so, Gower climbed out, shiftily glancing round in case anyone had noticed him, so taking part in the action as well as narrating it, which he did in the guise of a boatswain telling a tall story to his fellow sailors. For all its elaboration, the design scheme did not smother individual scenes, but allowed them to make their full impact—notably in the brothel, where Angela Baddeley was a vivid Bawd; in the reunion between Richard Johnson's Pericles and Geraldine McEwan's serene Marina; and especially in Cerimon's revival of Thaisa (see fig. 3), where Anthony Nicholls, an experienced Shakespearian actor possessing both verbal and physical authority, did full justice to the magnificent verse that is evident even through the frailties of the reporting.

If the gaudy sumptuousness of this production was far removed from the simplicity of the two earlier productions, it was equally remote from Terry Hands's staging at what was by then called the Royal Shakespeare Theatre at Stratford-upon-Avon in 1969.[1] Instead of constantly-changing pictorial sets, the stage became a vast empty chamber, initially screened off by a front cloth showing Leonardo da Vinci's celebrated image of a naked man demonstrating the Vitruvian proportions of the human figure, arms and legs stretched out, palms open. This Renaissance image was the model for Ian Richardson's near-naked appearance and formalized gestures as Pericles, and provided the inspiration for the 'ritualized nakedness' of Timothy O'Brien's designs in general:[2] the actors were almost as bare as the stage itself, and together they made a stark setting for a production which aimed to give unity to a straggling narrative. Hands went further than Barry Jackson and Douglas Seale had done at Birmingham in editing and reshaping the text, drawing extensively on passages from Wilkins's narrative, especially to clarify and unify the scenes at Pentapolis, with Pericles

---

[1] Hands restaged the production at the Comédie Française, Paris, in 1974, but my account is of the Stratford version.

[2] The phrase is cited in Dennis Kennedy, *Looking at Shakespeare*, 2nd edn. (Cambridge, 2001), 240.

3. Cerimon (Anthony Nicholls, right) revives Thaisa (Stephanie Bidmead), Stratford-upon-Avon, 1958.

displaying his skills as warrior, dancer, and singer in one continuous sequence. Its climax, and the most memorable moment of the production, was the dance of courtship between Pericles and Thaisa (Sc. 7.101.1; fig. 4). This took place in complete silence, so that, as Irving Wardle put it in his review, 'one can almost believe they are moving to the music of the spheres' (*The Times*, 5 April 1969), an image of their total harmony. This connected with the moment at the end of the play when Pericles, reunited with Marina (who in this production was played by the same actress as Thaisa, Susan Fleetwood),[1] hears the music of the spheres that is inaudible

---

[1] For the reunion of mother and daughter in the final scene, Susan Fleetwood reverted to Thaisa, and another actress, Susan Sheers, substituted as Marina.

4. Pericles (Ian Richardson) dances with Thaisa (Susan Fleetwood), Stratford-upon-Avon, 1969. In the background are Simonides (Derek Smith, left) and Gower (Emrys James, right).

to the others (Sc. 21.211), and it helped to bind the two halves of the play together and give it a kind of unity. But in seeking that overall unity, Hands sacrificed the richness, and often the interest, of individual episodes that had emerged strikingly in the 1958 production: a particular victim was Cerimon's revival of Thaisa, heavily cut and scurried through as though it were merely a piece of routine narrative instead of the engrossing theatrical event that it has been in most other productions.

Hands's version was presented within the context of a Stratford season concentrating on Shakespeare's late work, the first of several such seasons in the modern theatre, where Shakespeare's late plays seem to have held an especial fascination for performers and audiences, and which have placed particular emphasis on the spiritual journeys they dramatize.[1] Introducing the 1969 season as a whole, Trevor Nunn, at the time Artistic Director of the Royal Shakespeare Company, said in his programme notes: 'Pericles is on a journey, from the bestiality of Antiochus' court to the temple of Diana. It is a metaphysical journey; rest comes only with self-knowledge'; and in another season focusing on Shakespeare's late plays, this time given by the Canadian Shakespeare Festival at Stratford, Ontario in 1986, the director Richard Ouzounian saw Pericles' journeys as a kind of odyssey in which the hero's qualities are put to the test by the stern experiences he undergoes. Particularly when seen in close proximity to *The Winter's Tale*, two main aspects of *Pericles* emerged from these productions: that its reunions and reconciliations are hard-won, and that the play is both large and small in scale, sometimes within the same scene: there is often an intimate, private scene going on within a large-scale, public one. Both points were especially evident in the Ontario production. Geraint Wyn Davies began the play as a questing hero in golden armour; he ended it in a near-animal state of despairing self-abasement, from which Kim Horsman's Marina had to work hard to draw him. This painful spiritual process seemed very close to Leontes' sixteen-year process of repentance and recovery, under Paulina's supervision, in *The Winter's Tale*. The director exploited the full resources of Ontario's large open stage for spectacular scenes like the tournament and dance at Pentapolis; but within that public world, Pericles and Goldie Semple's radiant Thaisa expressed their growing intimacy, especially when they danced together (fig. 5). In Cerimon's revival of Thaisa, attendants with flaming torches alternately advanced to surround the chest containing Thaisa's body, and retreated, first in alarm at discovering a 'corpse' inside it, and then in amazement as she revived. As they surrounded the chest with their torches, their movement focused attention on the detailed medical means that Cerimon uses to recover Thaisa. Here, particularly, large- and small-scale actions were seen to coexist. In general, however, such a large theatre and an open, thrust stage primarily emphasized the far-flung aspect of *Pericles*; but in two other modern productions, it was the intimate

---

[1] For more detailed discussion, see my *Staging Shakespeare's Late Plays* (Oxford, 1990).

5. Pericles (Geraint Wyn Davies) dances with Thaisa (Goldie Semple),
watched by Simonides (William Needles), Stratford, Ontario, 1986.

and psychologically intense aspects of the play that dominated,
somewhat at the expense of its spectacle.

To describe the original Other Place at Stratford-upon-Avon as a
studio theatre would be an exaggeration. It was merely a corru-
gated iron storage shed minimally converted for performance use.[1]
In such a confined space, spectacle was out of the question, and
had to be replaced by imaginative suggestion. But partly because of
its very limitations, it encouraged immediate rapport between
actors and audience and great intensity of performance. Ron
Daniels's *Pericles* there in 1979 used a circular acting area with a
wooden post from which a single rope, stretched across the acting

---

[1] It was closed in 1989 for safety reasons, and replaced with a purpose-built
version nearby.

space, could be used by the actors to evoke storm and shipwreck. Costumes were of the simplest: Arab robes for many of the characters, a skimpy black shift for Antiochus' daughter, and an identical white one when the actress reappeared as Marina—a significant piece of doubling (see p. 36 below). At the start of the play, Gower was asleep, leaning against that wooden post: it was as if he was dreaming the action, using his own imagination as much as encouraging ours (fig. 7). And although Ron Daniels's text was essentially Terry Hands's adaptation of 1969, he achieved with ease the unity that Hands had had to strain for.

Daniels made the most of the intimate conditions to throw a spotlight on the human emotions so powerfully dramatized in the play. It was almost literally a spotlight, since strong overhead lighting focused Pericles' grief-stricken farewell to the 'dead' Thaisa, her revival by Cerimon, and especially Marina's conversion of Lysimachus in the brothel, where the two characters were placed on a mattress in the centre of the circle (fig. 6): she won him over, not only by her pleading (strengthened by additions from Wilkins's version of the scene), but by her enchanting tenderness and unaffected innocence. Julie Peasgood handled the meeting with her father with the same touching directness, and Peter McEnery caught both the pain and the ecstasy of the 'great sea of joys rushing upon' him as he was reunited with her. This simple staging reached to the heart of the play, and communicated more securely than any other I have seen its presentation of love, joy, and restoration of the lost in a reunion hard-won but all the more valued for that reason.

David Thacker's production at the Swan Theatre, Stratford-upon-Avon, in 1989 stood somewhere between the intimacy and directness of Daniels's version and the more elaborate earlier ones, just as the Swan itself occupies a middle position between The Other Place on the one hand and the Royal Shakespeare Theatre or the open stage at Stratford, Ontario on the other. It resembles the latter in its mock-Elizabethan thrust stage and gallery, but it has the advantages of modest size, intimacy, and good acoustics. Thacker made the most of its qualities to stage the play almost as simply as Daniels had done; but an unusual feature of his production was his decision to cast an actress as Cerimon. Helen Blatch brought to the part a combination of compassionate humanity and priestly authority, which had the interesting effect of revealing the kinship

6. Marina (Julie Peasgood) pleads with Lysimachus (Peter Clough), The Other Place, Stratford-upon-Avon, 1979.

between Cerimon's revival of Thaisa and Paulina's restoring Hermione's 'statue' to life in *The Winter's Tale*, a point to which I will return later in this introduction.[1] In a virtuoso piece of doubling, Helen Blatch went on to play the Bawd in brothel scenes that were positively Hogarthian in their fetid realism; by having one actress play parts so different, Thacker emphasized the way in which *Pericles*, like Shakespeare's other late plays, brings together contrasting extremes: here, they were juxtaposed in a single performer.

This production drew some interesting opinions from reviewers about the play itself. Irving Wardle, for example, wrote of Nigel Terry's Pericles: 'torn screaming from the coffin of Thaisa, he is deeply impressive; and his final transformation carries the emotional weight of Greek tragedy'; Wardle then commented on the play's technique: 'This is the kind of shock this play makes: setting out [in Gower's speeches] to distance the events, and then project-

---

[1] See pp. 46–7 below.

ing them point-blank with tremendous force' (*The Times*, 14 September 1989). When the production transferred to London, Benedict Nightingale provided an admirable summary of the play as a whole: 'This is a fairy story with emotional truth at its core' (*The Times*, 16 April 1990). But he also pointed out a difficulty with the final scenes of reunion: 'you cannot feel [their] full force . . . because you have not felt the full force of the emotions that put [Pericles] there'. That remark brings us back to the unevenness of the play, and to the problem that Pericles' early career, and especially his wooing and marrying Thaisa, is far less fully dramatized than his grief for her 'death' and his ultimate reunion with her and with his daughter, whether that discrepancy arises from divided authorship or textual corruption or, as I believe, both. As far as the second problem is concerned, David Thacker, like Richard Ouzounian in Ontario, had the advantage of access to the conjectural reconstruction of the Quarto text in the Oxford *Complete Works*. The advantages were reciprocal, since those rehearsals and performances, by trying out many of Oxford's proposals, put the reconstruction to the practical test, and the modifications made to it in the present edition have taken account of those experiences.[1]

The first production to be based entirely on the Oxford reconstruction, somewhat cut but essentially unaltered, was Adrian Noble's for the Royal Shakespeare Company in 2002. This was given at the Roundhouse, north London, and subsequently at Stratford-upon-Avon, as part of another season of Shakespeare's late plays. The Roundhouse, a former locomotive shed, is as its name implies a circular building; for *Pericles*, the audience surrounded a large circular wooden platform raised up upon several steps so that characters could make entrances from inside it—as if, for example, from below the deck of the ship in Scene 11. The Roundhouse is also a very tall building, so Noble exploited its height: the heads of the former suitors at the start of the play, and the goddess Diana at the end, were suddenly dropped on ropes from the roof at alarming speed. The production's aim, according to the theatre's publicity, was to bring out the Greek and Turkish origins of the story: so the actors wore enveloping robes, turbans, and fezzes; in the brothel, customers lounged on cushions smoking

[1] A detailed account of the rehearsal process of both productions is given in Chapter 5 of my *Staging Shakespeare's Late Plays*.

hookahs; suspended over the entire acting space was a multitude of oriental lamps; and the casting was multiracial.

The Oxford text proved its value in providing a secure basis for the production, especially in a very successful Pentapolis sequence, where the 'new' material, derived from Wilkins's prose narrative, fleshes out the Pericles/Thaisa relationship which is under-written in the Quarto text. It had the interesting consequence of making this relationship, rather than the Pericles/Marina one, the core of the play. Responding to Oxford's restoration of a song for Pericles (Scene 8a), Noble developed this into a duet between Pericles and Thaisa (Ray Fearon and Lauren Ward); Pericles began it resting on cushions on the central platform; then her voice joined his in the distance. The melody recalled Solveig's song from Grieg's incidental music to *Peer Gynt*; the lyric was about the influence of the various winds upon human fortunes, and culminated in the refrain 'I will carry you home'. Later, this was the song that Marina sang to Pericles in Scene 21, and it became the unifying feature of the production. This emphasis on the Pericles/Thaisa relationship helped to intensify his grief for her apparent death in Scene 11; her revival by Cerimon—a notably strong, clearly-spoken performance by Jude Akuwudike—was the climax of the first half; and the family reunion in Diana's temple was not the anti-climax it often seems in performance (see p. 58 below). The temple itself was powerfully suggested by subtle lighting and ritual movement; and Thaisa's tenderly wondering question 'Are you not Pericles?' (Sc. 22.52) was able to build upon the relationship they had successfully created at Pentapolis earlier on. Michael Billington reported that 'the audience went wild at the end' (*Guardian*, 8 July 2002), underlining that this play can prove as popular with modern audiences as with Jacobean ones. Taking its cue from the varying achievements of these very different stagings, this introduction will attempt to explore its theatricality a little further.

Ancient Gower

> To sing a song that old was sung
> From ashes ancient Gower is come . . .
>
> (Sc. 1.1–2)

Shakespeare and Wilkins place their story of Pericles within a frame. John Gower, the author of the principal source of the play, is brought back from the dead ('from ashes') to tell or to re-tell his story. So he is 'ancient' in a double sense: an old man, and also a representative of an earlier, 'antique' world. Both dramatists had used the device of a 'presenter' before, Shakespeare in the Chorus of *Henry V*, Wilkins in the figure of Fame in his collaboration with John Day and William Rowley, *The Travels of the Three English Brothers*. All three presenters encourage the audience to use their imaginations to assist the performers; but Gower is closer to Fame in *The Travels* than to the Chorus in *Henry V*. True to their function as presenters, Fame and Gower introduce, narrate, clarify the basic narrative. Introducing the dumb show at Sc. 10.14, for example, Gower says 'What's dumb in show, I'll plain with speech'; similarly, Fame in *The Travels* comments upon the final dumb show:

> To those that need further description
> We help their understandings with a tongue.
> (Epilogue, 14–15)

In other words, the presenters in *Pericles* and *Travels* offer essentially the same view of event and character as the rest of the play does, whereas *Henry V* establishes a sophisticated tension between the view of Henry presented by the Chorus and the impression given by the play as a whole. The Chorus introduces the idealized Harry of tradition, while the rest of the play modifies that impression by placing it within a wider perspective, setting, for example, the initial claim to France within a context of ecclesiastical self-interest, or showing the King ruthlessly ordering the killing of the French prisoners at Agincourt because they are a military encumbrance.

But although Gower is not dramatized with this degree of subtlety, he is differentiated from the main action of the play by the language he is given to speak. Whereas Fame in *The Travels* and the Chorus in *Henry V* use the same iambic pentameter (ten syllables per line) as the other characters, Gower at first speaks octosyllabic couplets (eight syllables per line), the verse form used by the historical John Gower in his *Confessio Amantis*. The aim is clearly to recreate the medieval 'feel' of the poem, and to this end his speeches contain deliberate archaisms, for example using the '-en' form of verbs in imitation of medieval Midlands English, as at Sc. 5.20 ('killen') and 35 ('perishen').[1] But of course the play does not

---

[1] Other archaizing touches are noted in the Commentary as they occur.

attempt to correspond too closely to medieval English: the Jacobean theatre audience needed to understand what Gower was talking about. Irving Wardle nicely summarizes the effect when he describes Gower as 'speaking in not too outlandish middle English' (*The Times*, 5 April 1969).

In any case, there are stylistic variations within Gower's speeches which help to modify too strict a 'medieval' impression. Although his first four speeches are largely in octosyllabics, Scene 18 is in iambic pentameters; Scene 20 is not only in iambics but in quatrains rather than the couplets of all the other choruses; Gower's speech introducing Scene 22 reverts to his original octosyllabics, as if the play is preparing to end in the 'medieval' idiom in which it began—but then his moralizing epilogue is surprisingly in iambics. The significance of these variants is not always apparent. They may reflect divided authorship, a possibility discussed further on p. 69 below. Or perhaps, having firmly established Gower as a medieval figure early on, either dramatist or both decided that greater flexibility in handling the later choruses would be more dramatically effective. Even in the earlier speeches, where the medievalisms are most apparent, Gower slips from time to time into iambic pentameter, and there does seem to be a clear dramatic reason for this, neatly illustrated at the first moment at which his narration gives way to the arrival on stage of the characters whom he has been describing. The octosyllabic verse in which he has been speaking modulates into a couplet in iambic pentameter, the 'norm' for verse in the main body of the play, as if Gower is providing a bridge between his 'medieval' style and their 'contemporary' Jacobean idiom:

> What now ensues, to the judgement of your eye
> I give my cause, who best can justify.
>
> (Sc. 1.41–2)[1]

After this couplet, the Quarto text, and this edition, give Gower an exit; but in Terry Hands's production at Stratford-upon-Avon in 1969, he remained on stage throughout the play. Benedict Nightingale described the effect: 'in the original text, Gower is a link-man

[1] For other examples of the flexible transition from Gower's speeches to the action they introduce, see the Commentary to Sc. 5.39–40 and to Sc. 15.50.1.

... Emrys James is rather the gloating Prospero, magic rod in hand, both impresario of the action and a participant himself' (*New Statesman*, 11 April 1969; see fig. 4). But his omnipresence tended to reduce the other characters to puppets: this was taking the integration of Gower into the action—part of Hands's unifying of the play—rather far. Most other directors, even when like Hands they have kept Gower on stage more or less throughout, have sought ways of reflecting how his 'medievalisms' distinguish him from the other characters. Taking their cue from a rather literal interpretation of his opening line, several have had the role sung, wholly or in part, and often in a musical style that sharply differentiated Gower from the verse spoken by the others. A good example of this was the casting of Edric Connor, known as a ballad singer as much as an actor, at Stratford-upon-Avon in 1958 (fig. 7). Nigel Townshend vividly evoked his technique: 'he murmurs confidentially, declaims, chants, sings outright of the splendours' (*Leamington Spa Courier*, 11 July 1958). What he did not do, however, was to tell the story clearly and comprehensibly, as several reviewers complained, reminding the actor that the primary task of a narrator is to narrate. But the problem was probably one of execution rather than of basic conception. The part had originally been intended for the celebrated American actor-singer Paul Robeson; had he been allowed to come to England, his sonorous bass voice and clear diction might have made a very different impression;[1] and the effect that his warm personality might have had was suggested by that of the most persuasive Gower in my experience, Rudolph Walker at Stratford-upon-Avon in 1989 (fig. 7). Unsupported by elaborate stage devices, indeed by any devices at all, he simply walked on to the empty stage of the Swan Theatre and started talking to the audience, drawing them into the world of the play with his expansive, friendly personality and his ability to deliver Gower's pseudo-medievalisms with maximum clarity but minimum fuss. It seems that the less strain that is put on this part, the more effective it is: the medievalisms sufficiently distinguish the teller from the tale without needing further directorial interference.

[1] Robeson was denied an exit visa by the American State Department because of his openly declared sympathy with the 'Communist' ideals of the Russian-dominated 'Eastern bloc' to which America was at that time implacably opposed. He was eventually allowed to play Othello at Stratford the following year.

(a)

(b)

7. Images of Gower: (a) the frontispiece of Wilkins's *Painful Adventures*, 1608; (b) Edric Connor at Stratford-upon-Avon, 1958; (c) Griffith Jones at The Other Place, 1979; (d) Rudolph Walker at the Swan Theatre, Stratford, 1989.

(c)

(d)

Antioch and After

Pericles' journey through life, or the questing hero's quest, begins at Antioch. Both at the start and at the end of the play Pericles is faced with a riddle, each dealing in, or using the language of, incest. In Scene 1, the answer to Antiochus' riddle is a sexual relationship between a father and his daughter; in Scene 21, the apparent impossibility that a father's 'buried' daughter stands before him leads to the paradox that a daughter gives birth, new life, to her own father: 'O come hither, | Thou that begett'st him that did thee beget' (Sc. 21.183–4). In a sense, Pericles' journey is from the one to the other. Antiochus' riddle does not seem very difficult, and it is surprising that none of the earlier suitors was able to solve it. Is this simply an example of the folk-tale origins of the story, a 'given' into which we should not enquire too closely, as F. D. Hoeniger suggests in his Arden edition? 'We must accept the convention that the riddle was difficult, even if its verses seem translucent to us' (p. lxxxii). Perhaps; but a searching production can suggest something more interesting than that. At Stratford, Ontario in 1986, it emerged that the problem was not to solve the riddle so much as to find a way of telling so formidable an antagonist as Antiochus. Here Pericles won his stay of execution by taking Antiochus downstage, out of earshot of the court, so avoiding shaming him in front of them. This interpretation emphasized the tactful evasiveness of phrases like 'Few love to hear the sins they love to act' and 'if Jove stray, who dares say Jove doth ill? | It is enough you know' (Sc. 1.135, 147–8). Pericles expounds the riddle without doing so in so many words; he preserves his life, in short, by displaying the tact that is one of the skills of a prince and statesman.

A different interpretation of Pericles' behaviour at Antioch is that by engaging with Antiochus' daughter and with the riddle that protects her, he is somehow culpable. It is true that, despite being surrounded by the decapitated heads of former suitors who, as Antiochus puts it, 'with dead cheeks advise thee to desist' (l. 82), he nonetheless rashly goes ahead—but then rashness is a characteristic of questing heroes, and another way of putting it is that he shows 'faithfulness and courage' (l. 106). But some commentators take a darker view, arguing that by showing desire for Antiochus' daughter, Pericles has, as it were by association, become contaminated by her incest, and that his misfortunes later in the play are his punishment.[1] Some support for this view might be found in the loaded sexuality of the language with which he reacts to the discovery of the incest—'touch the gate', 'fingered to make man his lawful music', 'being played upon' (ll. 123–7; see the Commentary)—but this is the expression of disgust rather than desire. The attempt to find Pericles guilty arises from a desire to motivate the 'painful adventures' that he subsequently endures; but the play surely doesn't work like that. True to the medieval tradition of Fortune's wheel, raising a man up one minute only to dash him down the next, Gower emphasizes the sheer arbitrariness of what happens to Pericles: 'fortune, tired with doing bad, | Threw him ashore to give him glad' (Sc. 5.37–8), or 'fortune's mood | Varies again' (Sc. 10.46–7); and Pericles himself says that he is

> A man whom both the waters and the wind
> In that vast tennis-court hath made the ball . . .
> (Sc. 5.99–100)

But he has good fortune as well as bad: after he has been shipwrecked and cast up naked on the shore at Pentapolis, his armour is discovered tangled in the fishermen's nets, and he comments:

> Thanks fortune, yet that after all thy crosses
> Thou giv'st me somewhat to repair my losses.
> (Sc. 5.160–1)

So he is able to participate in the tournament at Pentapolis, and to fall in love with and marry a very different kind of princess from Antiochus' daughter.

Before that, however, comes his encounter with his councillor Helicanus back at home in Tyre (Scene 2). His opening soliloquy reflects understandable fear both of Antiochus' revenge on him personally and of what Antiochus' 'hostile forces' and 'th'ostent of war' can inflict on his subjects,

> Which care of them, not pity of myself . . .
> Makes both my body pine and soul to languish.
> (Sc. 2.24–32)

In other words, he shows another quality of the prince, concern for his subjects, as he showed tact at Antioch. But in the following

---

[1] e.g. Wilson Knight, *The Crown of Life*, pp. 37–9, and, more intemperately, John P. Cutts, 'Pericles' "Downright Violence"', *Shakespeare Studies* 4 (1968), 275–93.

dialogue, Helicanus criticizes Pericles for his melancholy and retiredness.[1] After an initial angry outburst at Helicanus' outspokenness, suggesting that he has the potential for such tyrannical behaviour as Antiochus shows towards *his* councillor Thaliart in the immediately preceding scene (Sc. 1.205–8), Pericles again displays his princely qualities by accepting criticism and asking advice from a man whom he rightly calls 'Fit councillor and servant for a prince' (Sc. 2.55–69). It is interesting that Pericles' state of melancholy retirement, from which he has to be roused by Helicanus' vigorous criticism, anticipates the much greater melancholy of the comatose state into which he falls at the end of the play, and from which Marina has to arouse him with such difficulty. If *Pericles* is a collaboration, the collaborators took some trouble to bind the various parts of the play together.

Pentapolis

When Pericles arrives at the court of Pentapolis, he finds a world that is the polar opposite of Antioch; but the differences are emphasized by initial, superficial similarities. In the preliminary Fishermen scene, we are told that King Simonides 'hath a fair daughter, and tomorrow is her birthday, and there are princes and knights come from all parts of the world to joust and tourney for her love' (Sc. 5.147–9). So, as at Antioch, there is a king with a beautiful daughter who attracts, as Gower said of Antiochus' daughter, 'many princes . . . To seek her as a bedfellow' (Sc. 1.32–3). But instead of being surrounded as at Antioch by the severed heads of the other suitors, Pericles at Pentapolis finds himself participating with his rivals in a fully-fledged chivalric ritual.

The scenes at the court of Pentapolis offer great theatrical potential; but in the Quarto it remains latent, and productions have used inventive staging, and some textual borrowings from the fuller version in Wilkins's prose narrative, in order to realize that potential, and in the process to bring out the significance of the sequence as a whole. I suggested that Pericles participates in a fully-fledged chivalric ritual—but that is clearer in Wilkins's prose version than in the Quarto. In Scene 6, Simonides and Thaisa watch a formal parade of the knights who are to compete in the tournament: the

[1] For a discussion of the textual modifications made to Scene 2 in this edition, see pp. 76–8 below.

mottoes on their shields are read out by Thaisa and commented upon by Simonides. At least, in Wilkins's narrative they are; in the Quarto, some of the questions and answers are omitted, to no obvious dramatic purpose. Several productions, even before the appearance of the Oxford reconstruction, drew on Wilkins's narrative, so that the full ritual nature of the scene is sustained, rather than pointlessly fragmented. This is a simple example of the way in which the potential of the scene has to be 'realized' textually and theatrically, to some extent to be 'dug out', as it were.

But what about the tournament for which Scene 6 forms such an elaborate preparation? At the end of the scene, Simonides announces: 'We will withdraw | Into the gallery', and the Quarto's stage directions then read:

> *Great shouts, and all cry 'The mean knight!'*
> *Enter the King and Knights from tilting.*[1]

Editors interpret this as implying an exit for Simonides and Thaisa to watch offstage jousting, with cries from within which indicate that the 'mean knight'—Pericles in his rusty armour—has triumphed, followed by the reappearance of Simonides, Thaisa, and the knights to begin a new scene. This may be right, though it leaves an awkwardly empty stage; and it directly conflicts with the evidence of most modern productions, which have presented the tournament on stage. In response to this, the present edition proposes that Simonides and Thaisa play Scene 6 at ground level, then 'withdraw | Into the gallery' (i.e. the upper level of the Jacobean stage) to watch a tournament performed on the main stage below. I do not imply that horses were crashing around the Globe stage or should be on a modern one, although 'hobby-horses' (a horse's head and body suspended from the actor's shoulders, with a surcoat concealing the actor's own legs) were certainly used in masques of the period and may have been here; but no doubt the King's Men were as capable of contriving an exciting and spectacular combat between Pericles and the other knights as modern companies are. If so, the ritual of Scene 6 achieves its natural climax in the tournament itself; after Pericles' triumph, the King and Thaisa enter by descending from the gallery to greet the knights, fresh '*from tilting*', to begin the new scene.

[1] See Appendix A, ll. 788–90.

Scene 7 is concerned with feasting and especially with dancing. To rouse Pericles from his melancholy during the feast, Simonides calls for 'a soldier's dance' (l. 90). Once more, the Quarto's laconic stage direction needs interpreting. There has been dispute about what '*They dance*' (Appendix A, l. 888) implies. It has been suggested that ladies are present, and that they dance with the knights. At l. 95, Simonides says to Pericles 'here's a lady [i.e. Thaisa] that wants breathing too': 'too' may mean 'like the other ladies who have been dancing', but may equally mean 'as well as you men'; and most performances interpret the 'soldier's dance' as an all-male one, a 'matachin' or sword-dance (see p. 19 above), followed by a dance for Pericles and Thaisa alone, where again the Quarto's '*They dance*' (Appendix A, l. 897) is ambiguous.[1] The style of each dance would then be radically different, the military music of the first contrasting with the sensuousness of the second, whose dramatic importance would be emphasized by the contrast. For what the second dance represents is nothing less than the dawning love of Pericles and Thaisa. In the Quarto text, they have very few lines with which to express this; but the Quarto's '*They dance*' offers a theatrical opportunity for Pericles and Thaisa to declare their love, not in words, but in the traditional symbolism of the dance which, as Sir Thomas Elyot puts it, 'betokeneth concord'.[2]

After an intervening scene back in Tyre (Scene 8), the Quarto's final scene at Pentapolis contains a conversation in which Simonides thanks Pericles for his 'sweet music this last night' (Sc. 9.24); but in the Quarto, as Gary Taylor observes, 'Pericles has been offered no opportunity to perform this music. A playwright might perhaps use such a reference as a *substitute* for the performance itself . . . but Simonides' words are more plausibly interpreted as referring to an episode shown on stage. . . . Wilkins [in his prose narrative] devotes a page to describing such an episode' (*TC*, p. 558). The Oxford *Complete Works* reconstructs from this an entire short scene, followed in this edition (8a). What is the dramatic advantage of this procedure? At Sc. 7.78, Pericles says that his education was 'in arts and arms'. If the audience *sees* his prowess—not only as a dancer, as in the Quarto, but as a warrior

---

[1] See J. H. Long, 'Laying the Ghosts in *Pericles*', *SQ* 7 (1956), 39–42.
[2] *The Governor* (1531), Book I, Scolar Press reprint (Menston, 1970), fo. 82v.

too, in an onstage tournament—and *hears* him sing, as in this edition and in most productions, then his claim is substantiated. He is, in short, the Renaissance complete or universal man. That is the argument for letting the audience see the tournament and hear the song.

In Scene 9, once again, Wilkins's narrative gives a fuller account than the Quarto does, and if followed has the great advantage of allowing Thaisa the extended statement of her love for Pericles (ll. 77–87) that she is denied in the Quarto. It is true that she has the opportunity to express this attraction by non-verbal means in her dance with Pericles in Scene 7, but most actresses have taken advantage of the additional material from Wilkins when it has been made available to them. It is important that the audience should gain as strong an impression as possible of the relationship between Thaisa and Pericles if they are to feel the full impact upon him of her apparent death in childbirth in Scene 11, and the 'new' speech helps to achieve that. There is, however, a compensating drawback. The verse derived from Wilkins's narrative is at best vigorous and serviceable, and the more of it that is introduced the greater the risk of intensifying the stylistic contrast between Scenes 1–9 (largely by Wilkins) and Scenes 11–22 (largely by Shakespeare). The 'new' speech for Thaisa has the advantage of helping to place her love for Pericles where it needs to be, at the centre of the play, but the disadvantage of emphasizing the sheer discrepancy in expressive quality between that statement of love and Pericles' lament for her apparent death (Sc. 11.55–63). Even so, I think that on balance the dramatic advantages outweigh the stylistic disadvantages, and I have therefore followed Oxford and included a reconstruction of the lines in the text of this edition.

Ephesus: Language and Theatricality

Whatever their views about authorship or textual reporting, most commentators recognize that the language of Scenes 11 and 12, which take place at or near Ephesus, is different in kind from anything that has preceded it. The contrast can be simply demonstrated by setting the language with which Pericles evokes the storm in Scene 11 against that in which he responded to the earlier storm in Scene 5, which runs:

> Yet cease your ire, you angry stars of heaven!
> Wind, rain, and thunder, remember earthly man
> Is but a substance that must yield to you . . .
> [The sea] Washed me from shore to shore, and left my breath
> Nothing to think on but ensuing death.
>
> (Sc. 5.41–7)

The verse here is functional enough, as long as there is nothing better to compare it with; but the rhythm is plodding, the comparison—'earthly man | Is but a substance'—mechanical, and the couplet in ll. 46–7 characteristically lame. The difference is audible in the very first line of Scene 11, where Pericles invokes Neptune: 'Thou god of this great vast rebuke these surges . . .'. 'Vast' is used of the sea in the earlier storm scene—'that vast tennis-court' (Sc. 5.100)—and again, the comparison is serviceable, vivid even. But the word, used in Scene 5 conventionally as an adjective, becomes a noun in Scene 11, and in this typically Shakespearian use of one part of speech for another evokes the huge, desolate expanse of the sea. In the next lines, Pericles turns from Neptune, god of the sea, to Aeolus, god of the winds, and implores him to 'bind them in brass' (l. 3). In Homer's *Odyssey*, Aeolus' island was surrounded by walls of brass, and Shakespeare borrows the detail to create a powerful alliterative phrase which gives a sense of the sheer strength needed to control the violent wind. The phrase is striking, specific, and concrete, unlike the conventional list 'Wind, rain, and thunder' of the earlier storm scene. More alliteration conjures up the noise of the thunder—'deaf'ning dreadful thunders' (l. 5)— and another specific, concrete phrase the lightning: 'nimble sulphurous flashes' (l. 6). Here Shakespeare brings together words that he uses in similar contexts elsewhere (see the Commentary), 'nimble' to evoke the suddenness of the flashes of lightning, 'sulphurous' to suggest the smell that was thought to accompany them. After a phrase which summarizes the sheer malevolent violence and noise—'Thou stormest venomously. | Wilt thou spit all thyself?'—there is a breathtakingly precipitous drop to lines about utter silence:

> The seaman's whistle
> Is as a whisper in the ears of death,
> Unheard.
>
> (ll. 7–10)

It is typical of Shakespeare to express something in terms of its opposite: the deafening noise of the tempest by the deafness of death. Unlike the style of the preceding scenes, there is no padding, no decoration: every word contributes to conjuring up the impact of the storm for the theatre audience. The language does an extraordinary amount of work.

This applies particularly to Pericles' farewell to Thaisa, whose apparently dead body he is forced to throw overboard, and not even in a proper coffin but in a chest: he

> Must cast thee, scarcely coffined, in the ooze,
> Where for a monument upon thy bones
> And aye-remaining lamps, the belching whale
> And humming water must o'erwhelm thy corpse,
> Lying with simple shells.

(ll. 59–63)

Here again, the quality of the language evokes the physical circumstances, the 'belching' (spouting—but perhaps also suggesting that strange, deep, moaning sound that whales make) and the boom ('humming') of deep water as it envelops Thaisa's body, which will then become a part of the 'ooze' and mud of the sea-bed, 'Lying with simple shells'. Both in its poetic quality and in its specific detail, this speech is characteristic of Shakespeare's late plays, and particularly of the scene in *Cymbeline* where Innogen's brothers, believing her dead, give her funeral rites in verse of haunting beauty. Here, too, there is a reference to the ooze of the sea-bed, and then the body is imagined as becoming a part of the natural world, covered with flowers and 'furred moss' (4.2.205–30). In neither play is the character who is mourned actually dead: the focus is upon the love and grief of the mourner. But the impact of both scenes goes further than that, conjuring up an extraordinary sense of a character hovering between life and death, one of the most potent, recurring features of Shakespeare's late plays. That sense is much developed in the scene that follows.

Thaisa is revived in Scene 12 by the knowledge and skill of Cerimon, whose attitude to life is expressed in verse of great power and authority:

> I held it ever
> Virtue and cunning were endowments greater
> Than nobleness and riches. Careless heirs

43

> May the two latter darken and dispend,
> But immortality attends the former,
> Making a man a god.
>
> (Sc. 12.23–8)

Because of that last phrase in particular, and because of his learning in general, Cerimon has often been likened to Prospero in *The Tempest*, but the differences are at least as significant as the similarities. Cerimon refers to his 'secret art' (Sc. 12.29), Prospero to his 'secret studies' (*The Tempest* 1.2.77); but Cerimon's 'secret art' is the study of medicine which allows him to cure people, Prospero's is of a magic which enables him physically to control the other characters and to bring his enemies into his power. They have in fact radically different attitudes to the natural world. Cerimon's 'secret art' gives him insight into 'the disturbances | That nature works, and of her cures' (Sc. 12.34–5): he co-operates with nature, curing nature's ills by nature's means. But Prospero's 'secret studies' have been of a 'rough magic' which gives him a terrifying power, the full extent of which is only suggested at the moment when he abandons it. Far from co-operating with the natural world like Cerimon, he has dominated it and thrown it into chaos: he has 'set roaring war' between sea and sky, caused eclipses, and torn up trees by the roots. All these 'achievements' of his magic are negative and violent; but the climactic one is the most frightening:

> graves at my command
> Have waked their sleepers, oped, and let 'em forth
> By my so potent art.
>
> (5.1.48–50)

He has brought back the dead. Where Prospero is godlike in thus assuming the prerogatives of God, Cerimon's learning which makes 'a man a god' is of a quite different kind. Prospero's ability to revive the dead usefully serves by contrast to focus the boundaries of Cerimon's 'secret art'. He has only been on stage for a few moments before we learn that his power over life and death has its limits:

> Your master will be dead ere you return.
> There's nothing can be ministered in nature
> That can recover him.
>
> (Sc. 12.6–8)

It is a subtle dramatic touch that the scene in which Cerimon is to be successful in reviving Thaisa should start with an admission of failure. On a simple moment-to-moment narrative level, it increases the tension of the scene: will he save her or not? More important, it emphasizes that the agent of recovery is human, not divine. Thaisa does not need to be resurrected because she is not in fact dead; and it surely enhances the impact of her recovery if it is the work of a fallible human being rather than a magician.

The tension of the scene is implicit in the comments which Cerimon and the others make about the strangeness of the chest in which Thaisa has been laid: its heaviness, its seals, and the sweet smells of the spices that come from it as the lid is wrenched open to reveal its amazing contents. Both the opening of the chest and then the gradual resuscitation of Thaisa take up a considerable amount of stage time, far more than it takes simply to read through the scene. It is a slow, difficult, and dangerous process, and it could go wrong at any time, with fatal results for Thaisa, as Cerimon emphasizes at l. 107, and as Laurence Twine points out in the passage from his *Pattern of Painful Adventures* cited on p. 14 above: Cerimon's pupil 'perceived how death strived with life within her, and that the conflict was dangerous and doubtful who should prevail'. In the play it is Cerimon, not his assistant, who realizes that Thaisa is still alive—'They were too rash | That threw her in the sea' (ll. 77–8)—and it is he who is the focus of her recovery, although his servant Philemon is needed to help him, supplying him with the 'boxes in my closet', fire-warmed cloths to help restore her circulation, and inhalant from a 'vial' to help her breathe. These practical medical details are combined with music—the medicines help her physically, the music spiritually—until she starts to move: and the moment at which she does so is expressed in some of the finest poetry in the play:

> This queen will live. Nature awakes, a warmth
> Breathes out of her. She hath not been entranced
> Above five hours. See how she 'gins to blow
> Into life's flower again.

> > (ll. 90–3)

That exquisite final phrase in particular underlines that for all Cerimon's skill, Thaisa's recovery is a natural process.

When David Thacker at Stratford-upon-Avon in 1989 had

8. A female Cerimon (Helen Blatch) revives Thaisa (Sally Edwards), Swan
Theatre, 1989.

Cerimon played by a woman (fig. 8), the character took on even
more complex dimensions than usual. Philanthropist, herbalist,
priestess of Diana, she suggested a parallel not with Prospero in *The
Tempest* but with Paulina in *The Winter's Tale*, who also combines
several different roles: physician, psychiatrist, priestess, and coun-
sellor to Leontes. One especially interesting connection emerged.
When Paulina is about to restore Hermione's 'statue' to life, she
deliberately raises the suggestion of black magic in order decisively
to banish it. Bringing a stone statue to life might be thought
'unlawful business', 'assisted | By wicked powers'; by contrast,
Paulina's 'spell is lawful' because Hermione is not in fact dead
(5.3.90–105). In the ancient world (and in the Bible), Ephesus was
not only the site of the temple of Diana, but also had a reputation
for black magic (Acts of the Apostles 19: 13–19); and in dramatiz-
ing Cerimon's revival of Thaisa, Shakespeare can draw on that reputation to emphasize the strangeness of the episode in the reaction
of the onlookers: 'Is not this strange? | Most rare' (Sc. 12.104).
Cerimon, like Paulina, co-operates with nature, not necromancy;

but that strangeness, combined with the powerful language, dramatic tension, and music, can suggest, as Philip Edwards says in his edition, 'a near-miracle' (p. 30). Some have interpreted such scenes in Shakespeare's late plays as resurrection myths;[1] I find such views extravagant and misleading, but I can understand how they can be suggested by the potent atmosphere of a scene like this.

Now to Marina—and Mytilene

The climax of each half of the play is an act of healing, Cerimon's revival of Thaisa and Marina's of Pericles. After leaving his baby daughter in the care of Cleon and Dionyza in Scene 13, Pericles does not reappear, apart from the dumb show in which he is shown Marina's 'tomb' (Sc. 18.22.1–5), until his climactic reunion with her in Scene 21. The second half of the play focuses on Marina. Gower bridges the fourteen-year gap during which she grows up by urging us 'Now to Marina bend your mind', and by providing a portrait of her virtues (Sc. 15.5–35). When she appears, it is to strew her nurse Lychorida's grave with flowers:

> The yellows, blues,
> The purple violets and marigolds
> Shall as a carpet hang upon thy grave
> While summer days doth last.
>
> (Sc. 15.66–9)

The freshness and delicacy of Marina's language help to characterize her directness, integrity, and innocence, as the similar flower-speeches of Arviragus at *Cymbeline* 4.2.219–30 and Perdita at *Winter's Tale* 4.4.73–129 characterize theirs; but her qualities are put to a much sterner test, surviving an attempt on her life only to be sold to a brothel at Mytilene. It is important to be clear about the precise threat that the brothel-keepers present to Marina—and also that she presents to them. As so often in Shakespeare, the issues are far from simple black-and-white ones.

The brothel scenes are written in a characterful, colloquial prose, at once matter-of-fact and humorous, that is closely related to the language with which Shakespeare dramatizes the sexual

---

[1] For a brief account of these, and judicious criticism of them, see Philip Edwards, 'Shakespeare's Romances: 1900–1957', *SS 11* (Cambridge, 1958), 1–18; pp. 11–12.

underworld of bawds, pimps, and their clients in *Measure for Measure*. The humour of that play has been aptly characterized by A. P. Rossiter as 'case-hardened jesting about syphilis',[1] and it applies to these scenes in *Pericles*, too, especially to a remark about one of their clients—'The poor Transylvanian is dead that lay with the little baggage. . . . she quickly pooped him, she made him roast meat for worms' (Sc. 16.20–3)—and another who 'brought his disease hither; here he does but repair it' (Sc. 16.104–5). But these brothel scenes have proved surprisingly resistant to wholly successful theatrical realization. Prior to the twentieth century, they were regarded with embarrassment; since then, the temptation has been to go too far in the opposite direction, either overdoing the sexual innuendoes (which are less emphatic than in *Measure for Measure* and some other plays), or overstating the moral corruption that the brothel is thought to represent. In fact, the tone of these scenes is commercial. The Pander, the Bawd, and Bolt are running a business, one that is in trouble, as their opening exchanges make clear. The threat they present to Marina is not that they are wicked people, but that they have invested good money in her, and expect a return for it; and she finally escapes, not by arousing their sympathy, but by buying her way out with the gold that Lysimachus gives her in Scene 19. This unromantic, hard-headed pragmatism, both of the dramatist and the heroine, is one of the finest things in the play. It also, perhaps, makes it easier for an audience to participate in Marina's spiritual journey than in her father's, since her opponents are real people, not bogeymen like Antiochus.

Even before Marina arrives, the brothel-keepers are lamenting their lack of economic success. In a brilliant thumbnail sketch, the Pander is looking forward to retirement, memorably conveyed at Stratford-upon-Avon in 1979 by Jeffery Dench's rueful tone as he lamented that his profession was 'no calling', no vocation (Sc. 16.36). The brothel scenes worked especially well in that production, where the inhabitants were unexaggerated, human beings not monsters. It is surely significant in this connection that the word 'sin', which is a favourite of Wilkins and occurs 36 times in Scenes 1–9, does not occur in the Shakespearian scenes at all.[2] Sin

---

[1] *English Drama from Early Times to the Elizabethans* (1950), 146–7.
[2] D. J. Lake, 'Wilkins and *Pericles*', *N&Q* 214 (1969), 288–91; p. 290.

does not seem to be the primary emphasis. The point is neatly made at the end of the first brothel scene, when Marina invokes the goddess of chastity to help her:

> MARINA
> Diana aid my purpose!
> BAWD What have we to do with Diana?
>   (Sc. 16.140–1)

This is not primarily an encounter between purity and corruption, but is rather a wonderful moment of sheer incomprehension: Marina's patron goddess is simply an irrelevance to the Bawd, and the tone and rhythm of her question create one of the funniest moments in the play.

But of course Marina's predicament is no laughing matter; and although she is in danger from the bawds because her behaviour confronts them with commercial ruin, the greatest threat comes not from these tough professionals but from their principal client, the governor Lysimachus. It seems symptomatic of the problems facing interpreters of this play that what is in some respects the most crucial scene (certainly as far as Marina is concerned) should exist only in an obviously mutilated form in the Quarto text. The problems focus on the character of Lysimachus himself and on Marina's response to him. Lysimachus' behaviour and personality constitute a principal (perhaps *the* principal) puzzle of the play. From the tone of easy familiarity in his opening conversation with the brothel-keepers (Sc. 19.28–46), it is clear that he is one of their regular customers; yet at the end of his scene with Marina he says, in the Quarto text, 'For me be you thoughten, that I came with no ill intent, for to me the very doors and windows savour vilely' (Appendix A, ll. 1906–7). This odd remark, implying that he was merely carrying out a governor's responsibility by investigating the red-light district, seems at complete variance with his earlier sexual jesting with the bawds. Shortly before this, after Marina has pleaded with him in two short speeches, he says 'I did not think thou couldst have spoke so well, ne'er dreamt thou couldst' (Appendix A, ll. 1890–1901). Two brief speeches hardly seem enough to arouse such amazement and admiration in the sexual predator that we have seen in the early part of the scene. Philip Edwards certainly thinks so, and draws an important contrast with Wilkins's version of the scene in his prose narrative: in the Quarto, after what is really only a passionate and inarticulate cry, he is marvelling at her *eloquence*. . . . An affecting cry is not what the age called eloquence. What we need is amplification of these ejaculations into really persuasive arguments—and Wilkins . . . supplies just that very eloquence that is needed; we are given finely phrased, finely argued appeals which have all the power required to amaze, shame and convince Lysimachus. Moreover, these appeals carry striking verse-rhythms. Surely they must represent parts of the scene omitted in the Quarto's report.[1]

Wilkins not only extends the Quarto's version of the scene; he significantly modifies its view of Lysimachus. Instead of the lame (and lamely phrased) 'be you thoughten, that I came with no ill intent', Wilkins's Lysimachus says quite the opposite: 'I hither came with thoughts intemperate, foul and deformed, the which your pains so well hath laved that they are now white' (Appendix B, Passage C). This passage, which is virtually in blank verse, actually fits much better with the earlier part of the scene in the Quarto: instead of the patently unconvincing claim that he meant no harm, Wilkins's Lysimachus admits that he came to the brothel to have intercourse with a virgin (see p. 52 below), but that Marina has converted him. It also completely solves the problem of the inconsistency and contradictoriness of Lysimachus' character in the Quarto, as well as providing a much more dramatic confrontation between Lysimachus and Marina, which becomes a conversion scene.

In order to convert a tough, predatory whoremonger who also has the power of a governor to enforce his will, Marina needs stronger arguments than the few lines of the Quarto; as Edwards intimates, she needs in essence Wilkins's version of the scene. There are traces of the arguments given by Wilkins in Marina's first brief speech in the Quarto:

> If you were born to honour, show it now;
> If put upon you, make the judgement good
> That thought you worthy of it.
>
> (Sc. 19.108–10)

The first part of Marina's extended pleading in Wilkins, too, is about the use and abuse of honour and of a governor's power. Marina urges Lysimachus not to allow his governor's authority

[1] 'An Approach to the Problem of *Pericles*', *SS* 5 (Cambridge, 1952), 25–49; p. 44.

over others to lead him to 'misgovern much yourself' (Sc. 19.107) and so to rob her of her honour as well as disgracing his own (ll. 113–17). She then turns the argument from the more general issues to her own particular situation. Addressing him as 'My yet good lord' (l. 127), she neatly modifies the conventional phrase 'My good lord' to give it additional, sharper meaning: he will be her 'good lord' so long as he doesn't take unfair advantage of her. Her language gains in intensity and vividness as it reflects more intimately her personal predicament:

> Suppose this house—
> Which too too many feel such houses are—
> Should be the doctor's patrimony and
> The surgeon's feeding, follows it that I
> Must needs infect myself to give them maintenance?
> (ll.129–33)

And she concludes with a passionate plea to him to kill rather than deflower her. After such pleading, Lysimachus' 'I did not think thou couldst have spoke so well' makes perfect sense, as it fails to do in the Quarto.

Wilkins's version has been put to the practical test of performance. Almost every modern production has inserted some of Marina's lines from Wilkins into its playing text, and most have also adopted Wilkins's view of Lysimachus as a converted rake rather than using his Quarto excuse of having had 'no ill intent'. Perhaps because of the very need to wrestle with the textual problems, and so to probe even more deeply than usual in rehearsal into the meaning of the scene, Lysimachus has been notably well played in modern productions. Two performances in particular illuminated the scene in contrasting ways. At Stratford-upon-Avon in 1979, Marina's pleas were as usual strengthened with additions from Wilkins, but Lysimachus' excuse that he came 'with no ill intent' was retained; its transparent untruth didn't seem unconvincing because of Peter Clough's sensitive handling of it. Ashamed at what he had tried to do, moved by her pleas and her tenderness, he fabricated a shame-faced explanation in order to excuse his behaviour and to apologize to her; and there was a strong sense of their love being born in the process. The 'moral' objection that a virtuous heroine should not love, and marry, a man who tried to use her as a prostitute simply fell away.

Joseph Ziegler's Lysimachus at Stratford, Ontario in 1986 was a much tougher operator. He made no attempt to soften the chilling flippancy about sexual disease in his opening exchanges with the brothel-keepers: ' 'Tis the better for you that your resorters stand upon sound legs. How now, wholesome iniquity have you, that a man may deal withal and defy the surgeon?' (ll. 31–4). It was evident that he expected, as in the past, to be provided with a virgin, thus avoiding the risk of infection run by the other 'resorters' of the brothel; and when left alone with Marina, he ruthlessly manhandled her on to cushions on the floor. His questions to her at ll. 71–91 were small talk, the merest prelude to intercourse, as his brisk, impatient 'Come, bring me to some private place. Come, come' (l. 102) made abundantly clear. Kim Horsman's Marina needed every syllable of eloquence if she was to convert him—needed, in short, the arguments in Wilkins's version. Her achievement seemed the greater when this dangerous opponent was converted. Ziegler's incisive delivery both of the earlier flippant jokes and then of his admission of guilt valuably emphasized how Lysimachus moves from one extreme to the other. Those extremes, of course, come from Wilkins's account of the scene, but they are absolutely characteristic of Shakespeare's juxtaposition of such extreme contrasts in his late plays. Faced with such strong theatrical and textual evidence, this edition at lines 92–156 adopts Wilkins's version of the scene rather than the Quarto's, casting what Philip Edwards calls the 'striking verse-rhythms' in Wilkins's prose back into verse lines, and incorporating them into the text.[1]

The Lysimachus/Marina episode is especially crucial because of its repercussions. Marina's experiences in dealing with Lysimachus have a direct bearing upon her subsequent encounters with Bolt *and with Pericles*. No sooner has she fought off Lysimachus than she is faced with another dangerous predator. But whereas she used one kind of eloquence, argument, with Lysimachus, she uses a

---

[1] Hence the verse quotations from Wilkins in the preceding paragraphs. My reconstruction sticks closely to Wilkins even when this results in rough rather than regular blank verse. Oxford's reconstruction here is more regular and shorter (approximating to ll. 94–133, 151–6), but it seems to me that if Wilkins's version of the scene is to be followed, it is preferable to include most of it, rather than to use some passages and not others. Performers can then choose the material they find most useful. The whole of Wilkins's scene is reproduced in Appendix B, so that users of this edition can see how the reconstruction was made, and if necessary modify it in rehearsal and performance.

more abrasive kind with Bolt. In the Quarto, her exchange with Bolt is actually longer than her pleading with Lysimachus—further evidence, surely, that something is missing from the latter. It is also much more acrimonious. She turns on Bolt with extraordinary ferocity:

> Thou damnèd doorkeeper to every coistrel
> That comes enquiring for his Tib . . .
> . . . what thou professest a baboon, could he speak,
> Would own a name too dear.

$$(ll. 213-27)$$

But whereas Lysimachus hardly replies to her, Bolt answers her directly:

What would you have me do? Go to the wars, would you, where a man may serve seven years for the loss of a leg, and have not money enough in the end to buy him a wooden one? (ll. 218–21)

It may be going too far to argue, with E. M. W. Tillyard, that in this exchange it is Bolt 'rather than Marina who catches our sympathy',[1] but Bolt certainly gives a good account of himself, especially in the face of Marina's invective. Writing of Susan Fleetwood's performance at Stratford-upon-Avon in 1969, Hilary Spurling observed that 'Marina, for all her stainless, miracle-working chastity, has a rough tongue and a shrewd knowledge of the world' (*Spectator*, 11 April 1969). If so, that knowledge has been gained through the painful experiences she has endured; her roughness with Bolt no doubt expresses a character pushed almost to breaking-point. And at that point, she abruptly switches from abuse to a practical solution: 'Here's gold for thee.' At her wits' end, she tackles the brothel on its own hard terms, and makes Bolt the business proposition of ll. 228–33. After all the storms and traumas, the brothel sequence ends as it began, with the emphasis not on morality or immorality, but on money.

The Music of the Spheres: Pericles and Marina

The reunion of Pericles and Marina is often singled out for special praise by commentators, who point out its resemblance, both in impact and in verbal detail, to the reunion between King Lear and

---

[1] *Shakespeare's Last Plays* (1938), 23.

Cordelia.[1] But it is not infallible in performance. The gradual, painful process of mutual recognition takes a long time to play, and it is crucial, as always in drama, to capture and maintain an inevitable rhythm; otherwise the scene seems too long and can lose its grip. There are two dangers. It is important not to anticipate the sublime ending in the distinctly prosaic beginning. The other danger is emotional generalization: the language is extremely specific and often, again, prosaic; the entire scene is structured upon a series of questions.

One reason why the Lysimachus/Marina scene just discussed is so vital is that Marina's experiences with Lysimachus and Bolt colour the start of her encounter with Pericles. Something even of that scene's commercial basis carries over into this one, which is also set up as a business arrangement. Marina is brought to Pericles not because, as in Laurence Twine's version, Lysimachus is aware of a relationship between Pericles and Marina, but because of her gifts as a teacher and communicator, for which she will be paid (Sc. 21.64–5). There is no hint that Pericles might be anything more to her than a client, and there is even a suggestion, in Lysimachus' allusion to her 'choice attractions' (Sc. 21.36), that her physical attractiveness might be used to appeal to Pericles: this echo, in a minor key, of her ordeal in the brothel serves to emphasize that Marina, who has had to fight hard to win over Lysimachus, is faced with the task of converting another threatening male presence. The comatose state into which Pericles has allowed himself to fall should not be under-estimated or sentimentalized. He is in a condition of physical degradation—unkempt, unwashed (Sc. 18.27–8)—and, still more important, of spiritual degradation. It is from this self-consigned pit that Marina has to raise him, and she must be aware that the process is going to be even more difficult than converting Lysimachus.

John P. Cutts suggests that Marina's song 'begins to soften the shores of Pericles' flint', and that it anticipates his hearing the music of the spheres later.[2] But if that happens, it does so only in a very subliminal way, since on the face of it, Pericles has neither 'marked' her music nor looked at her (Sc. 21.69). Perhaps a connection has been made. Another, stranger, one follows. Left alone

[1] See the Commentary to Sc. 21.134, 143, and 202.
[2] See p. 37, n. 1; p. 291.

with Pericles, Marina tries to communicate verbally: 'Hail sir; my lord, lend ear'; but his reply is only an inarticulate cry of rage, 'Hum, ha!', and Wilkins is surely right to say that he strikes her, as the character does in all the previous versions (with a greater or lesser degree of violence; see p. 16 above, and the Commentary to l. 73). The dramatic gain is that, however violently, father and daughter achieve some kind of contact, which the music may or may not have begun. Marina's phrase at l. 85, 'something glows upon my cheek', may be, as J. C. Maxwell says in his edition, 'a reference to the blow' (p. xvi), not misplaced as he thinks, but direct and dramatically relevant. For Marina has to decide whether to persist or not; and the temptation to abandon someone who appears to present a yet more violent challenge than Lysimachus and Bolt must be great. In a wider sense, the combination of extremes here, music and physical attack, is typical of Shakespeare's late plays: violence in the very act of reunion recurs, for example, when Posthumus strikes the disguised Innogen at *Cymbeline* 5.6.229.

Marina's decision to stay is crucial: Pericles begins to speak. At Stratford, Ontario in 1986 in particular, the effort seemed great. This is, after all, a man who has not spoken to anyone for three months (Sc. 21.18–19). The words came with difficulty, almost dredged up from within himself, separated by pauses: 'My fortunes (*pause*), parentage (*pause*), good parentage (*pause*)'; and then the questions began: 'To equal mine? Was it not thus? What say you?' (ll. 87–8). This is the start of the barrage of questions that underpins the scene—'what countrywoman? | Here of these shores?', 'Where do you live?', 'Where were you bred?', 'What were thy friends?' and so on—but it is not for another forty lines that he asks the crucial question: 'Thy name, my most kind virgin?' (l. 130). He has already noted the similarity to Thaisa (ll. 92, 97–103, 114–15), but it is as if he has been so crushed by his experiences that he fears the pain of raising his hopes only to have them dashed. The turning-point of the scene comes when he moves from his own self-absorption to acknowledge her qualities:

> thou dost look
> Like patience gazing on kings' graves, and smiling
> Extremity out of act.

> (ll. 127–9)

As so often when Shakespeare is writing on peak form, the image is closely integrated into the dramatic situation. She *has* gazed on a king's grave in the sense that he was dead to the world; and she has smiled 'extremity out of act' by drawing him from the extremity of his earlier violence to his gentler behaviour at this point. When he asks her name and invites her to sit by him (ll. 130–1), another decisive development in the process of his recovery has been made, and a new stage in the scene reached.

But this recovery is far from secure. When he hears her name he has another dangerous outburst:

> O I am mockèd,
> And thou by some incensèd god sent hither
> To make the world to laugh at me.
>
> (ll. 132–4)

It is almost too much for him to believe. Marina, alarmed, manages to calm him somewhat, but then that obsessive questioning begins again (ll. 139–58), which results in more of the truth coming out. Even then, Pericles seems to hover between joy and madness. His psychological journey is difficult and dangerous, and the progress of the scene recalls the dangerous physical process of Thaisa's revival by Cerimon in Scene 12, in which any relapse would have been fatal. The conflicting emotions which Pericles is experiencing are expressed in the lines in which, even as he speaks of his ecstasy, he asks Helicanus to strike him, to cause him pain, so as to keep him in touch with reality, or at any rate with the harsh reality that he has often endured up to this point:

> O Helicanus, strike me, honoured sir,
> Give me a gash, put me to present pain,
> Lest this great sea of joys rushing upon me
> O'erbear the shores of my mortality
> And drown me with their sweetness!
>
> (ll. 179–83)

The gashing, pain, and mortality in these lines seem to be essential to the experience of joy and sweetness, an interrelation of pleasure and pain that is central to the dramatization of emotional states in Shakespeare's late plays.

The complexity of what Pericles is experiencing is developed in the paradoxical phrase he uses next: 'O come hither, | Thou that

begett'st him that did thee beget' (ll. 183–4). As has often been
pointed out, it is impossible when hearing these lines not to think
back to Antiochus' riddle and to the incest with which the play
began. The possibility of incest has been fleetingly raised earlier in
the scene, where Pericles dwells at length upon Marina's physical
resemblance to Thaisa (ll. 97–103): he is clearly drawn to this
stranger who recalls his apparently dead wife.[1] Any potential
danger passes when he realizes who Marina is; but the paradoxical
language keeps it before us. A daughter is to give birth to her own
father; more than that, she is to fulfil the father's role in the relationship. *OED* glosses 'beget': 'To procreate, to generate: usually
said of the father, but sometimes of both parents'—but its examples all suggest male begetting (*v*. 2). Pericles' phrase goes even further than Antiochus' riddle, where his daughter was not only wife
and child but also mother (Sc. 1.112): Marina is father, too. The
implications are considerable, and should not be undervalued. By
making Pericles express himself in a paradox that recalls Antiochus' riddle, Shakespeare binds the events of the play together: it
has come full circle, but in a way that replaces physical incest with
spiritual rebirth, expressed later in the scene by Pericles' receptiv-
ity to the divine when he hears the music of the spheres and the
voice of Diana. The values of the goddess of chastity are at the fur-
thest remove from those of Antioch; yet in one of her forms Diana
was Lucina, the goddess of childbirth,[2] so it is appropriate that she
should appear in person at the end of the scene and thus reinforce
the rebirth that Marina has brought about in her father. But also,
reminding the audience of incest in the very act of ecstatic reunion
is characteristic of the technique of Shakespeare's late plays,
which regularly emphasize the dangers and darkness out of which
the joys of reunion emerge: the principle seems to be that the further you go into the dark and the more risks you run, the more
overwhelming the compensating joy that is experienced.

[1] In Robert Greene's *Pandosto* (*c*. 1588), the source of *The Winter's Tale*, the
equivalent of Leontes attempts to seduce his daughter, unaware of her identity;
when he realizes who she is, he commits suicide. All that remains of this in *The
Winter's Tale* is Leontes' wry remark to Florizel about Perdita, 'I'd beg your precious
mistress', and Paulina's lightly reproving reaction, 'my liege, | Your eye hath too
much youth in't' (5.1.222–4); but *Pandosto* may have supplied a hint for the scene in
Pericles.

[2] See the Commentary to Sc. 1.51. It is interesting that Lucina's—i.e. Diana's—
influence is even acknowledged by Antiochus himself.

It follows that the actor of Pericles needs to encompass the extremes both of joy and pain in this demanding scene. When Robert Speaight writes of the 'agonized ecstasy' with which Ian Richardson played the scene at Stratford-upon-Avon in 1969,[1] he catches in a single phrase what this climax requires, an experience so intense for Pericles that it seems like a kind of divine madness in which he reaches a higher plane of existence, dramatized by his hearing the music of the spheres. It was traditionally believed that as the heavens moved they made a music so perfect that it was inaudible to mortal ears;[2] so the fact that Pericles *can* hear it is a poetic way of expressing the extreme spiritual state to which Marina has brought him during the scene—a journey, one might say, from her earthly music, which made little or no impact, to the heavenly music he now experiences. Sometimes in performance the audience hears the music, sometimes not. If they do not, that emphasizes the traditional belief and the rarefied state of mind Pericles has achieved. If they do, audible music acts as a theatrical externalization of that state of mind, and prepares the audience for his vision of Diana, whom they do see and hear.

The descent of the play's presiding goddess is in one way a surprise, a great *coup de théâtre*; in another, it has been prepared for by the many occasions on which she has been invoked: for example, by Pericles at Sc. 11.10–14; by Marina during her ordeal in the brothel (Sc. 16.140); and by Thaisa after she has been revived by Cerimon (Sc. 12.102–3). It is to bring about the reunion of Pericles and Thaisa that Diana appears at this point, and their reunion takes place in her temple at Ephesus. It is a short scene, and can seem perfunctory after the intensity of the gradual recognition of father and daughter in the preceding scene.[3] The dramatic problem is that it is impossible to give equal weight to the reunion of father and daughter and of husband and wife, as Shakespeare recognized when he came to write *The Winter's Tale*. By keeping the father/daughter meeting there offstage, reported by three

---

[1] *Shakespeare on the Stage* (1973), 293.

[2] This idea is beautifully expressed at *The Merchant of Venice* 5.1.63–5:

> Such harmony is in immortal souls,
> But whilst this muddy vesture of decay
> Doth grossly close it in, we cannot hear it.

[3] But see p. 30 above for a staging that reversed this process.

9. Diana's temple, Stratford-upon-Avon, 1947. Centre, back to camera, is
Paul Scofield as Pericles.

gossiping gentlemen, he was able to throw all the emotional weight
on the reunion of husband and wife in the concluding statue
scene.

In that respect, as in others, *Pericles* prepares for subsequent
plays in which the effects are achieved more securely. But it would
be seriously misleading to imply that *Pericles* is only (or even princi-
pally) of interest as a play that anticipates later successes. However
great the problems arising from textual corruption or from divided
authorship, to which this introduction must now turn, *Pericles* is a
play that has succeeded in communicating with modern audiences
as it obviously did with its original ones: in a production that I
have not so far mentioned,[1] by René Dupuy at Paris in 1957,

[1] Partly because I could find out so little about it. It is described tantalizingly
briefly in the 'International Notes' of *SS 12* (Cambridge, 1959), 111; and Jacques
Noël's design for the Antioch scene is reproduced in *Stage Design Throughout the
World Since 1950*, ed. René Hainaux (1964), 96. Antiochus' turban and upturned
shoes suggest a touch of the Arabian Nights; even the heads on poles have an airy
lightness about them, familiar from Noël's elegant designs for *The Winter's Tale* at
Stratford-upon-Avon in 1960.

the intensity of the father/daughter reunion left one reviewer with 'an invincible feeling of the mystery of human destiny and condition'.

Authorship

The most common reaction to *Pericles* is vividly summarized in the review of Tony Richardson's 1958 production that I have cited twice before in this introduction. Commenting on the programme's attribution of the whole play to Shakespeare, Nigel Townshend wrote: 'our ears are soon telling us otherwise. What? This hotch-potch of inchoate scenes; this wavering, uncertain tone, lurching in an instant from solemn banalities to sheer absurdity; this pancake-flat verse? . . . But at last the change comes, with the great storm at the beginning of Act III [Scene 11]. When it is over, the changed movement and density of the verse is unmistakable'; and as proof of this change he cited Cerimon's lines at Scene 12. 23–9, to which I shall return in a moment. Perhaps he is a trifle hard on the first nine scenes, but he surely conveys impressionistically what most people feel when watching or working on the play, and in particular about the drastic change of style in the middle. Gary Taylor in the *Textual Companion* to the Oxford Shakespeare puts it more analytically: 'By *c.* 1606–8, Shakespeare's poetic style had become so remarkably idiosyncratic that it stands out—even in a corrupt text—from that of his contemporaries, and approximately the last three-fifths of the play (Sc. 10–22) betray clear evidence of his presence. Equally clearly, Sc. 1–9 show little or no evidence of Shakespearian authorship' (p. 130).

The external evidence of the early editions is contradictory. The title-page of the Quarto text attributes the play to William Shakespeare, yet *Pericles* was not included in the First Folio of Shakespeare's plays in 1623. It must be admitted straight away that no entirely convincing explanation has ever been advanced for this omission. It might have been excluded because Heminges and Condell, the two members of Shakespeare's company who were responsible for compiling the First Folio, knew that Shakespeare did not write the whole play; or for insuperable copyright reasons; or because they could not provide a satisfactory text. The last explanation can be rejected at once: since *Pericles* was one of the most popular plays of the period, and was still being performed by

Heminges and Condell's own company, the King's Men, when the Folio was being prepared, they must have had access to an adequate text. Were they, then, prevented from using it because of complications over copyright, as was apparently the case with *Troilus and Cressida*?[1] It seems unlikely. On 20 May 1608, *Pericles* was entered in the Stationers' Register by Edward Blount, thus stating his entitlement to print it, and he was one of the syndicate who published the First Folio. The publisher of the 1609 Quarto text was not Blount but the less reputable Henry Gosson; his text seems to have been an unauthorized publication, not only because the chaotic copy from which it was evidently printed suggests that it was obtained surreptitiously, but also because there is no record of any transfer of printing rights from Blount to Gosson in the Stationers' Register. So the existence of the Quarto should not have raised copyright problems, unless the Folio syndicate faced difficulties that are unknown to us. That leaves collaborative authorship. But even this raises difficulties, since Heminges and Condell included in the Folio other collaborative plays, if modern scholars are correct in regarding *Henry VIII* or *All is True* as a collaboration between Shakespeare and John Fletcher, and *Timon of Athens* one between Shakespeare and Thomas Middleton.[2] Nevertheless, the least implausible of the various theories is that *Pericles* was excluded from the Folio because Heminges and Condell knew that Shakespeare was responsible for only part of it.[3]

The play's exclusion from the Folio, then, *may* provide support for the widespread view that *Pericles* is a collaboration between Shakespeare and another dramatist. Of the various candidates that have been put forward, good reasons have been advanced for only two: John Day and George Wilkins. F. D. Hoeniger in his Arden edition argued the case for Day, but most of the shared ideas, images,

---

[1] See *TC*, p. 425.

[2] A possible way round this is to argue that *Henry VIII* was included to conclude the history 'cycle' in the Folio; that *Timon* was not originally intended for inclusion, only being added to replace *Troilus* when copyright problems arose; and that the early plays about which doubts concerning Shakespeare's sole authorship are sometimes still entertained, the *Henry VI* plays and *Titus Andronicus*, were written so far back in Shakespeare's career that Heminges and Condell themselves were not clear about their authorship. For further discussion, see *TC*, pp. 70–4, 501–2.

[3] As they excluded *The Two Noble Kinsmen*, published in 1634 and attributed to Shakespeare and Fletcher, and the now lost play *Cardenio*, apparently another collaboration between the two.

and phrases that he cites between *Pericles* and Day's works are, as Hoeniger himself admits, commonplaces of the time.[1] The evidence for George Wilkins is of a quite different kind. It was first advanced by the German scholar Nicolaus Delius in 1868.[2] He detected two different styles in the play, contrasting the unevenness of Scenes 1–9, which oscillate unpredictably between blank verse and rhymed, moralizing *sententiae*, with the economy of Scenes 11–22, especially Cerimon's revival of Thaisa, where there is 'not one word too many, but each word hitting its target'. He proposed Wilkins as the author of the first half, noting that both Wilkins's *Miseries of Enforced Marriage* and *Pericles* Scenes 1–9 contain 'a mixture of prose, blank verse and rhymed verse without any detectable reason for the mixture'. He also pointed out that Wilkins's prose 'novel' *The Painful Adventures of Pericles* is constructed so as to follow the form of the play, and shares the characters' names as the sources do not; and he proposed that Wilkins had written a complete play which Shakespeare partly rewrote. Although I think an outline likelier than a complete play (see p. 5 above), Delius seems to me to get everything else right; and his analysis of Wilkins's style has been carried further by several twentieth-century scholars. H. Dugdale Sykes made an impressionistic case for Wilkins that drew substantially, though not exclusively, on verbal parallels;[3] these are dangerous as evidence of authorship because they can so easily be a matter of imitation, conscious or unconscious. But some of Sykes's (and Delius's) other evidence has been confirmed and refined by E. A. J. Honigmann,[4] D. J. Lake,[5] and especially by MacDonald P. Jackson,[6] who uses a vast array of computer-based tests both to establish the extreme unlikelihood that Shakespeare wrote Scenes 1–9 at any stage of his career, and to show that those scenes have much in common with

[1] Arden edition, pp. 171–80. The one verbal connection that isn't a commonplace—see the Commentary to Sc. 5.74–5—can be explained as one dramatist borrowing from another, especially since Day and Wilkins collaborated on *The Travels of the Three English Brothers* (1607). D. J. Lake drives further nails into Day's coffin in 'Rhymes in *Pericles*', *N&Q* 214 (1969), 139–43; p. 140.

[2] N. Delius, 'Ueber Shakespeare's Pericles, Prince of Tyre', *Shakespeare Jahrbuch* 3 (1868), 175–204. It is discussed, and some of it translated, by Brian Vickers, *Shakespeare, Co-Author*, pp. 293–5. Vickers's translation is cited here.

[3] *Sidelights on Shakespeare* (Stratford-upon-Avon, 1919), 150–76.

[4] *The Stability of Shakespeare's Text* (1965), 193–9.

[5] See the articles cited on pp. 5, 64, and in note 1 above.

[6] *Defining Shakespeare: 'Pericles' as Test Case* (Oxford, 2003).

Wilkins's other work. Those tests include versification, rhymes, 'function' words which are so frequently used as to constitute an author's unconscious habits, and quirks of style such as uncommon uses of the relative pronoun 'which'. In his New Penguin edition of *Pericles*, Philip Edwards objects that 'much of the energy and time spent on the subject of "Who wrote *Pericles*?" has been wasted, because the language of the Quarto . . . is the language of the pirates who got the text together' (p. 33). But it turns out that Wilkins's stylistic habits 'show through' the reporting of the first nine scenes as it is generally agreed that Shakespeare's do through the remainder. In what follows, I have had to compress Jackson's meticulously compiled data into a few examples, hoping that I have not distorted his arguments in the process.

Versification. Dugdale Sykes pointed out that in *The Miseries of Enforced Marriage* Wilkins 'not only mingles blank verse and prose but introduces riming lines into his blank verse. We find the same thing in Acts I and II [Scenes 1–9] of *Pericles*'.[1] This is especially noticeable in the Fishermen episode (Scene 5), where several of Pericles' longer speeches end with a rhyming couplet (ll. 111–17, 159–73, 175–82). At first sight, this may seem unremarkable: Shakespeare himself often moves between verse and prose in his works, and will conclude a blank verse speech with a rhyming couplet to 'clinch' its point. It is the frequency and the particular way in which Wilkins intermingles blank verse and rhyme that set him apart. D. J. Lake refined Sykes's point by drawing attention to two features: first, Wilkins's habit of moving out of blank verse into an outburst of rhyming couplets; second, and even more striking, his habit of throwing a single unrhymed line into an otherwise rhyming passage. Another Wilkins characteristic is the use of assonantal rather than perfect rhyme, as in the 'sung . . . come' of Gower's opening couplet. This is sometimes said to be an 'archaizing effect' apt to a medieval poet; but apart from the fact that few medieval poets use such assonantal rhymes (the historical Gower uses none in his *Confessio Amantis*), they occur in the dialogue of *Pericles* as well as in Gower's speeches, and, most tellingly of all, in both *The Miseries of Enforced Marriage* and in the scenes of *The Travels of the Three English Brothers* usually attributed to Wilkins, where no archaic effect can be intended. And although some of

[1] Sykes, *Sidelights on Shakespeare*, p. 156.

Wilkins's rhymes are of commonplace words, others are more striking. In Scene 7 of *Pericles*, for example, Thaisa says:

> He may my proffer take for an offence,
> Since men take women's gifts for impudence.
>
> (ll. 66–7)

Wilkins uses the same rhyme at *Miseries* ll. 1129–31:

> Who once doth cherish sin begets his shame,
> For vice being fostered once, comes impudence,
> Which makes men count sin custom, not offence,

a passage which also makes a similar point to Gower's 'By custom what they did begin | Was with long use accounted no sin' (Sc. 1.29–30). The various connections involving rhyme between *Pericles* Scenes 1–9 and Wilkins's other work are the more significant because, as D. J. Lake says, 'we can expect rhymes to resist a reporter's corruptions', since they are in themselves an actor's aid to memory.[1]

Uncommon uses of 'which'. E. A. J. Honigmann draws attention to Wilkins's partiality in his other work for beginning phrases with 'the which', or using 'which' as a relative adjective, qualifying an immediately following noun.[2] 'The which', in particular, amounts almost to a stylistic 'tic'. It occurs twice, together with the adjectival use of 'which', in a short passage that concludes Scene 4, where Pericles relieves the famine at Tarsus:

> CLEON
>
> *The which* when any shall not gratify,
> Or pay you with unthankfulness in thought,
> Be it our wives, our children, or ourselves,
> The curse of heaven and men succeed their evils!
> Till when—*the which* I hope shall ne'er be seen—
> Your grace is welcome to our town and us.
>
> PERICLES
>
> *Which welcome* we'll accept, feast here a while,
> Until our stars that frown lend us a smile.
>
> (Sc. 4.99–106, my italics)

Delius and Dugdale Sykes identified another Wilkinsian characteristic, the *omission* of 'which' as a relative pronoun, for example

---

[1] 'The *Pericles* Candidates—Heywood, Rowley, Wilkins', *N&Q* 215 (1970), 135–41; p. 136.

[2] See p. 62, n. 4.

'flattery is the bellows blows up sin' (Sc. 2.44) instead of 'which blows up sin'. Sykes detected over twenty instances of this in *Miseries* and fourteen in the first nine scenes of *Pericles*; Shakespeare's use of it is much less frequent, though it occurs at Sc. 21.77–8 and 175–6.

Quirks of style. Commentators who think that Shakespeare wrote the whole play often suggest that he is deliberately adopting a naïve, 'gnomic' style,[1] but such 'gnomic' writing, generalizing and moralizing, and including the *sententiae* to which Delius draws attention, is more generally characteristic of Wilkins's known writing. When Wilkins uses figurative expressions, they generally take the form of rough and ready similes, cued by 'like', quite different from the metaphorical boldness of Shakespeare's late style; and although Shakespeare's own writing thrives on the use of extreme contrasts (see pp. 55–7 above), Wilkins's use of antithesis is quite different. He often begins by saying what something is not, before saying what it is, as at *Miseries* ll. 251–4:

> To be a wife is to be dedicate
> Not to a youthful course, wild and unsteady,
> But to the soul of virtue, obedience,
> Studying to please and never to offend.

Wilkins versus Shakespeare. Having isolated the main features of Wilkins's style, it may be helpful to analyse how they are used in an extended speech from the first half of the play, Pericles' soliloquy reacting to his discovery of Antiochus' incest (Sc. 1.164–85), and to set that directly against a characteristic speech from the second half, Cerimon's statement of his values just before he revives Thaisa (Sc. 12.23–39). It will be helpful to have each speech before us. Here, first, is Pericles:

> How courtesy would seem to cover sin
> When what is done is like an hypocrite,   165
> The which is good in nothing but in sight.
> If it be true that I interpret false,
> Then were it certain you were not so bad
> As with foul incest to abuse your soul,
> Where now you're both a father and a son   170
> By your uncomely claspings with your child—

---

[1] See p. 20, n. 2.

> Which pleasures fits a husband, not a father—
> And she an eater of her mother's flesh
> By the defiling of her parents' bed,
> And both like serpents are, who though they feed   175
> On sweetest flowers, yet they poison breed.
> Antioch farewell, for wisdom sees those men
> Blush not in actions blacker than the night
> Will 'schew no course to keep them from the light.
> One sin, I know, another doth provoke;   180
> Murder's as near to lust as flame to smoke.
> Poison and treason are the hands of sin,
> Ay, and the targets to put off the shame.
> Then lest my life be cropped to keep you clear,
> By flight I'll shun the danger which I fear.   185

This speech shows Wilkins's habitual mingling of blank verse and rhyme. The second and third lines contain an assonantal rhyme 'hypocrite . . . sight'; the blank verse of the next eight lines is followed by rhyming couplets, but these are characteristically interrupted by a single unrhymed line (177) and then by two unrhymed lines at 182–3. The bold, effective opening line is followed by the less striking 'like an hypocrite' which does not add much information to the first. Wilkins's familiar 'The which' opens the third line, 'Which pleasures' line 172, and the omitted relative occurs at 'those men [who] | Blush not' (ll. 177–8). The habit of saying what something is not emerges in the fifth line. As the couplets begin, 'And both like serpents are' introduces a 'gnomic', and traditional, comparison likening Antiochus and his daughter to the deceptiveness of snakes. Lines 180–1 demonstrate what Jackson calls Wilkins's typical 'process of accretion' (p. 164). There is no inevitable connection between murder and lust: the lines simply accumulate crimes suitable to evil men. They also relate to a phrase in *Miseries*: 'As near as . . . sin to sin' (l. 2272). This 'process of accretion' applies to the speech as a whole: the lines are almost all end-stopped, so the implied slight pause at the end of each one deprives the speech of a sense of forward momentum: one point is simply added to another, without much sense of development. It should be emphasized that this is not a *bad* speech. Actors can, and do, use it to communicate directly with the audience, and that is important at this early stage of the play, if the actor of Pericles is to take the audience with him on his long journey. To that extent, it is serviceable enough; but it is a completely different *kind* of speech, in terms of dramatic writing, from Cerimon's, to which we now turn:

> I held it ever
> Virtue and cunning were endowments greater
> Than nobleness and riches. Careless heirs   25
> May the two latter darken and dispend,
> But immortality attends the former,
> Making a man a god. 'Tis known I ever
> Have studied physic, through which secret art,
> By turning o'er authorities, I have,   30
> Together with my practice, made familiar
> To me and to my aid the blest infusions
> That dwells in vegetives, in metals, stones,
> And so can speak of the disturbances
> That nature works, and of her cures, which doth give me   35
> A more content and cause of true delight
> Than to be thirsty after tottering honour,
> Or tie my treasure up in silken bags
> To please the fool and death.

The most noticeable difference between this speech and Pericles' is surely its continuity and development, the impression it gives of a man 'thinking through' the speech. This sense of flow is achieved by the setting of the sense units against the verse units so characteristic of late Shakespearian verse, with consequent mid-line pauses. Whereas Pericles' speech merely adds one point to another, Cerimon's moves logically from one to the next. His disregard for worldly possessions in favour of learning in his first sentence is developed in his second by examples of the consequences of each, the squandering of the possessions by those who inherit them, contrasted with the 'immortality' that achievements in learning may bring. This naturally leads into Cerimon's description of the medical skills that he has acquired, occupying the second half of the speech, which is one continuous sentence, effortlessly sustained by the strong blank-verse rhythms, and building to a climax which contrasts the genuine pleasure he obtains from his art with a pursuit of worldly honour and wealth which will simply be taken away at death. So the end of the speech returns to, reinforces and develops, the beginning. The language goes hand-in-hand with the verse structure. The contemptuous 'Careless heirs' and the sinister 'darken and dispend' are emphatically placed at the end of lines, so that the verse structure is marked even though the sense continues into the next line. The rewards that learning brings are, conversely, stressed by being placed at the *start* of line 28, and by the use primarily of weighty monosyllables: 'Making a *man* a *god*.' His 'secret art' is placed emphatically at the end of the line (29), and the natural means on which he draws for his cures are specifically, concretely stated: 'the blest infusions | That dwells in vegetives, in metals, stones' (32–3); there is a correspondingly emphatic concreteness in his reference to the 'silken bags' which he disowns, and in the bite of the final phrase with which he dismisses the wisdom of the world: 'To please the fool and death.' This is masterly dramatic writing: an entire character stands revealed in seventeen strongly fashioned lines. It is also characteristic of much of the writing in the second half of the play, and it contrasts radically with that in the first half, of which Pericles' speech is a fair example, taking twenty-two lines to make only a few points. These are not simply speeches for different characters; they are the work of different writers. And the overwhelming evidence assembled by Jackson makes it clear that Scenes 1–9 are the work of George Wilkins.

But if so, why did Wilkins apparently need to rely on his memory when compiling his prose *Painful Adventures*, and to pad it out with extended borrowings from Laurence Twine's? Although such borrowings occur throughout *Painful Adventures*, they are particularly extensive in the second half, which is not surprising if Wilkins was reporting scenes written by Shakespeare rather than himself. But why did he not copy out the first nine scenes as mechanically as he did Twine's, if he had written them? Gary Taylor provides a simple explanation:

once [a] play was purchased by a theatrical company they became sole owners. . . . Moreover, for a collaborative play Wilkins may not even have possessed, afterwards, his own foul papers [manuscript]. A fair copy would need to be made for use by the company; Shakespeare . . . may have made this copy himself (thus enabling him to smooth any joins between the two shares, or to revise his partner's work as he saw fit). . . . Wilkins might have found himself, in 1608, without a written text even of his own portion of the play [and so have been] forced to rely upon his memory, supplemented by lazy plagiarism of Twine. He would obviously know the parts of the play he had written himself much better than he knew Shakespeare's share; verbal resemblances between [his narrative] and Q are sporadic and casual in the second half of the play, but much more sustained and detailed in the first half. (*TC*, pp. 557–8)

This account may also provide an explanation of how what some commentators consider 'Shakespearian' lines or images (for example, the 'blind mole' passage at Sc. 1.143–5) seem to crop up in scenes that otherwise show no sign of Shakespearian authorship: they may have been the result of Shakespeare's revision of Wilkins's work.

Such revision might also help to account for some of the stylistic variations in Gower's speeches noted on p. 32 above. The Gower chorus between the 'Wilkins' scenes and the 'Shakespearian' ones (Scene 10) contains echoes of *A Midsummer Night's Dream* 5.2.1–36 at ll. 1–11; but ll. 31–2 contain an assonantal rhyme ('moon . . . doom') characteristic of Wilkins. The numerous archaisms in the speech could derive from either dramatist. This speech as a whole may be regarded as transitional, one dramatist taking over from, and perhaps revising the work of, the other. Wilkins's assonantal rhymes virtually disappear from Gower's later speeches, with the notable exception of 'run . . . dumb' and 'soon . . . doom' in the opening and closing couplets of his introduction to Scene 22. This might indicate composition by Wilkins, or that Shakespeare is imitating his collaborator's characteristic habit. But if Wilkins *did* write the speech, that may suggest that elsewhere in the second half of the play, Shakespeare revised or replaced existing Gower speeches by Wilkins. However that may be, in the later Gower speeches, as Jackson observes,

the dramatized Gower himself draws on a late-Shakespearian wordstock . . . but fails to do so in the choruses to [Scenes 1–9]. The association of the rare-word vocabulary of the later Gower choruses with Shakespeare's late plays is in itself instructive: it shows that even when consciously adopting an alien and archaic voice Shakespeare still used a vocabulary most closely linked to the plays of the late period within which *Pericles* [Scenes 11–22] were written. (pp. 48–9).

The possibility that Wilkins might have contributed to the second, largely Shakespearian, half of the play is also suggested by a computerized test developed by Jackson that I have not mentioned so far. The Chadwyck/Healey electronic database 'Literature Online' 'enables scholars to search virtually the whole corpus of early modern English drama', and Jackson shows how it can be used to isolate and identify recurrent turns of phrase and verbal collocations characteristic of the usage of individual dramatists (pp. 193–217). By subjecting the Quarto text of *Pericles*, Wilkins's *The Miseries of Enforced Marriage*, and *The Tempest* to this scrutiny, Jackson establishes that Scenes 1–9 'have 304 linkages with Wilkins, 102 with Shakespeare, giving percentages of 75 for Wilkins and 25 for Shakespeare', whereas Scenes 10–22 'have 177 linkages with Wilkins, 274 with Shakespeare, giving percentages of 39 with Wilkins and 61 with Shakespeare'. In short, this test supports the division of authorship suggested by all the other evidence adduced so far. It produces, however, one anomaly: the two brothel scenes, 16 and 19, 'have below 50 per cent of their linkages with Shakespeare'. As Jackson observes, there may be explanations other than authorship for this surprising figure. The brothel scenes are largely in prose, and 'it is possible that Shakespeare's prose is more "Wilkinsian", less distinctively "Shakespearian", than his verse', or that textual corruption might have 'shift[ed] the wording' towards Wilkins; 'but we should also admit the possibility that Wilkins contributed to the brothel scenes, and to [Scene 19] in particular' (pp. 204–6).

There is an obvious temptation to link these scenes with what we know about Wilkins himself, summarized at the start of this introduction: he himself ran an inn that was probably also a brothel, and this experience may have contributed to the commercial tone of the brothel scenes; on the other hand, the content and rhythm of those episodes is also very close to the equivalent scenes in *Measure for Measure*, as suggested on p. 48 above. Perhaps, as part of the collaboration between the two dramatists, Wilkins sketched out these scenes, in which he may have had a particular interest, and Shakespeare revised them. But any sign of Wilkins in the brothel scenes as they appear in the Quarto raises the possibility that in the longer version of the Lysimachus/Marina scene in his prose narrative, where verse rhythms are so clearly audible through the prose, he might be reporting verse of his own composition rather than Shakespeare's. I have argued earlier that Marina's extended conversion of Lysimachus in Wilkins is a much more powerful episode than the Quarto's brief and perfunctory episode, and that the fuller scene as reconstructed in this edition is a pivotal one because of its implications for the reunion of Pericles and Marina that follows; but we should beware of attributing any powerful writing in the play automatically to Shakespeare, and in any case the two dramatists took some trouble to make their contributions cohere, as suggested on p. 38 above. Jackson concludes that 'certainty about the brothel scenes is not attainable', but that there are at least 'grounds for believing that writing by both Wilkins and Shakespeare is present' in them (pp. 232, 212).

Otherwise, however, the numerous tests applied by Jackson leave no room for doubt that the first nine scenes of *Pericles* cannot be early work by Shakespeare, while the rest of the play consistently tests as typical of Shakespeare's dramatic writing of about 1607, thus confirming a division long ago established by commentators responding simply to issues of dramatic and poetic style. As Jackson concludes, the intermingling of blank verse and rhyme, the liking for assonantal rhyme, the uncommon uses of 'which', the particular use of antithesis (what a thing is *not*), the moralizing, the accumulated rather than developed speeches, 'all these combine to form a style that appears in *Pericles* [Scenes 1–9], *The Miseries of Enforced Marriage*, Wilkins's share of *The Travels of the Three English Brothers*, and nowhere else in English Renaissance drama' (p. 169).[1] If so, this has clear implications for an editor of the play. In the first nine scenes, 'the aim must be to present an authentic Wilkinsian text', just as it is to present a Shakespearian one later. So the work that Jackson has done in familiarizing us with Wilkins's style is directly relevant to the main editorial task: 'the establishment and elucidation of the play' (p. 189); and it has influenced the commentary of this edition.

The Text: Corruption and Reconstruction

The Quarto edition of *Pericles* printed in 1609 is the sole surviving early text of the play. Subsequent quartos—a second published in 1609, then others in 1611, 1619, 1630, and 1635—derive from it, with only minor modifications, and so does the text printed in the second issue of the Third Folio in 1664, the first time that the play

---

[1] These and other characteristics of Wilkins are noted in the Commentary at the places where they are particularly noticeable.

appeared in a folio edition of Shakespeare's works.[1] The problem presented by that single text is trenchantly summarized by Philip Edwards in his edition: 'When . . . we talk about *Pericles* as it was acted by Shakespeare's company in its heyday, we are talking about a hidden play, a play concealed from us by a text full of confusion and with a clumsiness and poverty of language unrivalled in the Shakespeare canon' (p. 8). The Quarto's defects are of various kinds: numerous nonsensical individual phrases; passages of more general feebleness, amounting almost to doggerel; chaotic mislineation (including printing verse as prose and vice versa); and missing passages, especially in Scenes 2 and 19.[2]

Two principal theories have been advanced to account for the 'confusion' and 'poverty of language' of the Quarto text: that it is a collaboration, and that it is a 'reported' text, put together from memory by an actor or actors who had appeared in it.[3] The one explanation does not necessarily exclude the other, since the Quarto could be reporting a collaboration, as I believe it is, with the stylistic characteristics of George Wilkins glimpsed through the filter of the reporters' memories in Scenes 1–9, and those of the late Shakespeare in Scenes 11–22. E. K. Chambers thought that the Quarto text was a report,[4] but the first thoroughgoing analysis was made by Philip Edwards.[5] He argued that the stylistic discrepancy between the two halves of the play could be attributed to the different techniques of two reporters, one re-casting Scenes 1–9 into new verse of his own composition, the other attempting to reproduce Scenes 11–22 more accurately. His general thesis that the different techniques of two reporters might be 'the *sole* cause of the difference in literary value between the two halves of the play', with its corollary that Shakespeare might have written it all,[6] has not met with general acceptance;[7] even so, Edwards's analysis of

[1] The printing of the Quarto was divided between the shops of William White and Thomas Creede, as Peter Blayney pointed out in *The Texts of 'King Lear' and Their Origins*, Vol. 1 (Cambridge, 1982), p. 258. (Vol. 2 has not appeared.)

[2] The entire Quarto text is reproduced in Appendix A. References are to the through line numbers in this Appendix. Quotations have been modernized since the original spelling is irrelevant to the argument.

[3] For reported texts, see p. 3, n. 1.

[4] Chambers, *William Shakespeare*, i. 521.

[5] 'An Approach to the Problem of *Pericles*', *SS* 5 (Cambridge, 1952), 25–49.

[6] See previous note; pp. 45–6.

[7] Gary Taylor assembles the evidence against it in 'The Transmission of *Pericles*', *PBSA* 80 (1986), 193–217; pp. 194–7.

the textual problems of individual scenes remains valuable, especially his account of the Lysimachus/Marina exchange, cited on p. 50 above. He also identified, and distinguished between, the compositors who set up the text; his attributions have been confirmed, with slight modification, by Gary Taylor and MacDonald P. Jackson, who comment: 'The division of work on Q between (certainly) two printers and (probably) three compositors provides the strongest possible evidence that the deficiencies of the text—present in the work of both printers—originate in the manuscript copy, not in the process of printing.'[1]

As they also say, however, *some* of the errors in Q may derive from compositorial misreading of the manuscript copy. For example, at Sc. 13.29, 'Unscissored shall this hair of mine remain', the obvious emendation 'Unscissored' for Q's nonsensical 'unsistered' (l. 1361) was made by George Steevens as early as 1793, long before the principle of the reported text had even been suggested.[2] But ll. 785–6 in the Quarto present a different kind of error. Simonides is made to say

> Opinion's but a fool, that makes us scan
> The outward habit, by the inward man.

This puts the idea the wrong way round: Simonides must mean that you can't judge the inward man by his exterior (specifically, Pericles by his rusty armour). The correct sense can, in this instance, be simply restored by changing 'by' to 'for', as in this edition (Sc. 6.59–60). It *might* be a compositorial error; but it is much likelier to be a slip by a reporter who was roughly remembering the rhyming couplet but not what it meant.

As for the Quarto's mislineation of prose and verse, Scenes 1–9 are reasonably well aligned as verse, but in Scene 5 the Fishermen's prose is also set out as if it were verse. In Scene 11 the verse is fairly accurately aligned, but from Scene 12 verse is either chaotically misaligned or printed as prose. Gower's speeches are on the whole properly set out as rhyming couplets (or quatrains in Scene 20). Is the mislineation the fault of the compositors or their copy? Unfortunately the answer is not clear-cut. When the prose in the

---

[1] *TC*, p. 556. The compositors' stints are indicated in the diplomatic reprint of Q prepared by Taylor and Jackson and reproduced in Appendix A.

[2] Steevens is supported by Wilkins's narrative—not known to Steevens because not rediscovered until 1857—which also reads 'unscissored' at this point.

Fishermen scene is set as 'verse', this must be an error on the part of a particular compositor, as Philip Edwards suggests,[1] since if the copy was put together by reporters, the actors must have known that the scene was largely in prose, especially if, as I shall propose later, the reporters probably played two of the fishermen. But error by a particular compositor will not explain the misalignment of several subsequent scenes, because they were set by different compositors. There, the responsibility must lie with those who supplied the copy. The reasonable standards of verse-as-verse in Scenes 1–9, sustained in Scene 11 but not thereafter, can be explained by the fact that Wilkins's regular verse, with its frequent rhyming (always a help to memory) would have been much easier to recall than the freer, rhythmically complex verse of late Shakespeare. What seems to have happened is that the reporter or reporters made an effort to get the verse right in Scene 11, but then concentrated on getting down on paper what they could remember of the lines, regardless of how it should be set out. Sometimes, the rhythm of the original is so strong that the correct lineation can easily be restored: compare, for example, the layout of Cerimon's speech at Appendix A, ll. 1247–61 with that at Sc. 12.23–39 of this edition, based on the re-lineation by Edmond Malone; but it is difficult to rearrange many other passages into anything like regular verse lines. As the editors of the Oxford Shakespeare observe:

Such mislineation suggests that we [are] dealing with a reported text, and this supposition is reinforced by many other features. Metrically, Q as it stands—even allowing for normal compositorial error—can hardly belong to any period of Shakespeare's career; it shows the same kind of rhythmical disorganization evident in memorial texts. It also often repeats itself verbally. (p. 556)

A simple example of such repetition is the frequent use of 'come' or 'come, come', a verbal 'filler' often encountered in such texts. Dionyza uses 'come' or 'come, come' four times in ll. 1469–85, the Bawd 'come' at ll. 1578, 1609, 1625, 1671, and 1682. It seems less likely that the Bawd and Dionyza were intended to share the same verbal 'tic' than that some at least of those repetitions originate with a reporter who was struggling to recall the lines.

Another category of corruption involves, not single words or phrases, but a more general feebleness, where Q seems to approxi-

[1] Edwards, 'Problem', pp. 30–1.

mate, rather than represent, the original, and to which straightforward emendations like those cited above cannot restore good sense. The opening scene at Antioch presents several examples, especially in the exchange between Antiochus and Pericles at ll. 96–112 (Sc. 1.73–89). Antiochus says that the heads of the executed suitors

> with dead cheeks, advise thee to desist
> For going on death's net, whom none resist.

'For' in the second line is easily corrected to 'From', but I have no idea what 'going on death's net' means, if indeed it means anything at all: is death imaged as a hunter spreading nets to trap human beings? (The line is usually cut in modern performances.) A little earlier in the speech, Antiochus says that 'desert' must gain his daughter,

> And which without desert, because thine eye
> Presumes to reach, all the whole heap must die.

Greater care is needed in dealing with this kind of passage than with obviously wrong but easily corrected words like 'unsistered' cited above. In his edition Philip Edwards says of these lines that 'the use of *the whole heap* to refer to the body of a human being is so absurd that we assume there is corruption here' (p. 142); but in his play *The Miseries of Enforced Marriage* George Wilkins uses an expression similar to this use of 'heap' in the phrase 'Make a consumption of this pile of man' (l. 946); and he uses 'the highest heap' to mean 'the greatest amount' in his prose *Painful Adventures of Pericles* (p. 502). So 'the whole heap' may be the correct reading, absurd or otherwise, but glimpsed through a tissue of feeble phrases which suggest that a reporter is mangling Wilkins here as he mangles Shakespeare elsewhere. In his reply, Pericles says that

> death remembered should be like a mirror,
> Who tells us, life's but breath, to trust it error.

Edwards comments that the first line 'seems to be a compression of the idea that if you look at a skull or "death's-head" . . . you realize that you are looking at your own image in a mirror', but that the second line 'is a weak patching to make up a rhyme'; and he concludes that there is 'better poetry behind the lines of the Quarto than there is in them' (p. 37)—almost a definition of a reported text.

If some at least of the errors so far discussed might be laid at the door of the compositors, they cannot be responsible for another category of corruption, major omissions in the text. Scene 2 offers a comparatively straightforward example of this and of other evidence for reporting. The difficulties focus on these lines in the Quarto (ll. 279–83 in Appendix A):

FIRST LORD

    Joy and all comfort in your sacred breast.

SECOND LORD

    And keep your mind till you return to us peaceful and comfortable.

HELICANUS

    Peace, peace, and give experience tongue,

    They do abuse the King that flatter him . . .

The phrase 'till you return to us' cannot be right: Pericles has just returned from Antioch and does not decide to depart—secretly— until later in the scene. A reporter is clearly anticipating what is to happen, and the phrase is accordingly omitted in this edition. A more serious problem is that nothing in the lords' innocuous greeting suggests the flattery of which Helicanus accuses them. Something is obviously missing. Fortunately, in this case, it is possible to supply the deficiency from another source.

I said at the start of this section that the Quarto was the sole surviving text of the play. That statement requires modification. As I mentioned at the beginning of the introduction, George Wilkins's narrative *The Painful Adventures of Pericles* contains 'verse fossils' embedded within its prose, some of which repeat lines of *Pericles* almost verbatim.[1] The natural deduction is that Wilkins is reporting a play; and although it has sometimes been argued, because of differences between *Pericles* and *The Painful Adventures*, that he may have been reporting an earlier version, economy of hypothesis encourages the view that he is reporting the same play that Q is reporting, of which, as argued in the previous section, he was part-author: the variants are explicable as Wilkins's tendency to decorative expansion for the reader's benefit, or as passages demonstrably plagiarized from Laurence Twine's own *Painful Adventures*. But if Wilkins *is* reporting the same play as Q, then his account is of great value, since, as the Oxford editors put it, 'two reports are obviously better than one' (*TC*, p. 557). And it provides

---

[1] e.g. Sc. 7.77–81; Bullough, p. 510.

the material missing in Scene 2, in the form of criticism by Helicanus of Pericles' behaviour.

In his prose narrative, Wilkins says that Helicanus 'boldly began to reprove' Pericles,

and not sparingly told him, he did not well so to abuse himself, to waste his body there with pining sorrow, upon whose safety depended the lives and prosperity of a whole kingdom, that it was ill in him to do it, and no less in his council to suffer him, without contradicting it. (p. 501)

The blank verse rhythms are so clearly audible in this passage that it is a straightforward matter to translate the 'prose' here into verse, and to convert reported speech back into direct speech. After Helicanus' line 'Peace, peace, and give experience tongue' (l. 282; Sc. 2.36), the Oxford *Complete Works* inserts six lines in which Helicanus vigorously criticizes Pericles for his retiredness:

> You do not well so to abuse yourself,
> To waste your body here with pining sorrow,
> Upon whose safety doth depend the lives
> And the prosperity of a whole kingdom.
> 'Tis ill in you to do it . . .

Helicanus then turns to the lords and criticizes them in turn:

> and no less
> Ill in your council not to contradict it.
> (Sc. 2.37–42)

This leads so seamlessly into the next line from the Quarto—'They do abuse the King that flatter him'—that it is hard not to feel that the lines derived from Wilkins's narrative, or something very like them, were originally part of the scene. Helicanus' criticism of the other lords now makes perfect sense: it is because they fail to criticize Pericles for his withdrawn state that he calls them flatterers. Minimal textual restoration thus restores a valuable relationship to the play, and prepares for Helicanus' role as regent of Tyre in Scene 8, which otherwise intrudes awkwardly into the Pentapolis sequence, for which reason it is often cut in performance. If Scene 2 is also omitted or abbreviated in the mistaken belief that it is irrecoverably corrupt (as at Stratford-upon-Avon in 1969 and 1979), Helicanus himself is virtually written out of the play. But productions that have used the Oxford reconstruction of the scene have been able to present the character with his role not only retained but enhanced and clarified: he then becomes the 'figure of truth, of faith, of loyalty' described by Gower in his epilogue (Sc. 22.114). The six lines inserted by Oxford are therefore included in the present edition.

Drawing on Wilkins's prose account to fill a lacuna in Scene 2, and so to make sense of a badly reported scene, is a simple matter of inserting a mere six lines. But the other scene in which material seems missing from the Quarto is more complicated and raises additional problems. I have argued on pp. 49–52 above that the encounter between Lysimachus and Marina in the brothel in Scene 19 is of central importance to the play as a whole but that, because it exists in an obviously truncated and contradictory form in the Quarto, the textual issues cannot be separated from the dramatic ones; and that Wilkins's version provides a dramatically more satisfactory report than the Quarto does, and is therefore usually followed in performance. But if Wilkins's version is so superior, why does Q present such a truncated version, and how did it come about?

The question is the more crucial because Gary Taylor has argued that the principal reporter was the boy actor who had played Marina, probably doubling Lychorida and perhaps also Antiochus' daughter. As Taylor points out, 'A boy who doubled Lychorida-Marina must have been the company's star boy at the time, at the height of his powers'; but if his voice broke in 1608, he would have been in serious trouble when trying to find work as a hired man, since plague closed the theatres in July 1608 to late 1609. 'One of the few liquid assets such a boy possessed would have been his memory of popular plays (like *Pericles*).'[1] Taylor's argument that the actor of Marina may have been the reporter is supported, for example, by the fact that the line which the Quarto text gives for the entry of Thaisa at l. 1037 (the equivalent of Sc. 9.62 in this edition)—'here comes my daughter, she can witness it'—appears to have been contaminated by the reporter's memory of the cue for Desdemona's first entry in *Othello*, a role which as the leading boy of the company he would presumably have played: 'Here comes the lady. Let her witness it' (1.3.169). Unable to recall the precise line, because not on stage either as Marina or as Lychorida, the boy

---

[1] 'The Transmission of *Pericles*', p. 216.

actor draws on another of his roles, a habit familiar from other reported texts. Taylor also argues that there was a second reporter, a hired man who probably played small parts, perhaps a Fisherman in Scene 5 and the Pander in Scenes 16 and 19. I would only add the suggestion that *both* reporters may have appeared in the Fishermen scene, the hired man as the First or Second Fisherman, the boy actor as the Third, who seems characterized as younger and less experienced than the others, ordered about by both of them, and the butt of their jokes because of his patched and threadbare clothing (Sc. 5.52–8). If both reporters were in this scene and in the brothel scenes—the boy as Marina, the hired man as the Pander—that would explain why the prose in those scenes seems in general accurately reported.

Taylor also thinks that the boy actor may have been apprenticed to the senior company actor who must have played Gower: that could have given him access to the 'roll' or scroll on which Gower's part was written, which might explain why Gower's speeches are reasonably well reported and why their lineation is on the whole satisfactory. The mistakes in Gower's part might well be compositorial, arising from misreading of the boy's illegible copying of Gower's 'roll', which would nevertheless have provided the correct lineation.

If the actor of Marina/Lychorida was the principal reporter, that accounts for the fact that Scene 11 and the Pericles/Marina reunion are better reported than most other scenes. But it also intensifies the acute difficulty that the Lysimachus/Marina scene is so truncated and unsatisfactory in the Quarto, since presumably the actor of Marina reported roughly what he had played, and so cannot have performed Wilkins's version of the scene. To get round this difficulty, Taylor initially argued, unconvincingly, that Q's version is actually superior to Wilkins's, but after reconsidering the evidence proposed that Q's truncated version was a response to censorship.[1] Marina's speeches in Wilkins are an attack on the way in which a governor can abuse his authority and pervert justice: Wilkins's 'account is extremely objectionable, politically; Q's is entirely innocuous' (*TC*, p. 559). If that is what happened, a

---

[1] Taylor's change of mind, and consequent adoption of Wilkins's version of the scene into the Oxford reconstruction, was partly in response to evidence provided by Stratford, Ontario's 1986 production, an example of the co-operation between scholarship and theatre characteristic of the Oxford Shakespeare.

powerful dramatic encounter has been emasculated, reduced to an ineffective and contradictory one. That is the argument for attempting to reconstruct it, as in this edition.

The reconstruction of this and other scenes here is not offered in the belief that it is possible to recover the original scenes exactly as written, simply that Wilkins's prose narrative gives a more adequate idea of certain episodes than the Quarto does. This edition accordingly adopts the following procedure. Where the Quarto makes reasonable sense, it is followed. Where it does not, or where the 'verse-fossils' in Wilkins's narrative offer more plausible readings, the text is reconstructed by re-casting those verse-fossils back into blank verse. This reconstruction is in practice very close to that in the Oxford Shakespeare *Complete Works*,[1] and where there are major differences (e.g. in Sc. 7 and especially Sc. 19), my decisions have been influenced by the practical use of Oxford's reconstruction in rehearsal and performance, so that this edition has been even more influenced than my earlier ones in this series by theatrical considerations. In that respect, the reconstruction carries to its logical conclusion my argument that in *Pericles* textual and theatrical issues are interdependent.

[1] Where this reconstruction differs significantly from Oxford's, this is noted in the commentary or in Appendix C.

EDITORIAL PROCEDURES

My procedure in this reconstruction of *Pericles*, and its relation to that offered in the Oxford *Complete Works* of 1986, is described at the end of the Introduction. In its details, this edition follows the editorial procedures established for the series by Stanley Wells and summarized in Gary Taylor's Oxford Shakespeare edition of *Henry V* (1982), pp. 75–81. In accordance with them, all quotations are modernized, even when they are taken from editions using old spelling, since, as Taylor says, 'if modernizing is valid for Shakespeare's text it is equally valid for passages quoted only to illuminate that text'. Old spelling is reserved for the diplomatic reprint of the Quarto text of *Pericles* in Appendix A and for citations from it in Appendix C; long 's' and ligatures are retained in Appendix A but not in Appendix C. Stage directions that a speech is delivered 'to' a character are editorial, as are 'asides' except for those at Sc. 9.72 and 100, which are in the Quarto text.

Since the Quarto is reprinted in full and without any alteration in Appendix A, thus enabling any change made in the present edition to be easily identified, collations in the normal sense become superfluous; in their place, Appendix C acknowledges the first editor to introduce each emendation, prior to Oxford's reconstruction. There are no act or scene divisions in the Quarto. F3 introduced them at Scenes 5 and 18, Malone at Scenes 5, 10, and 15. The latter have become traditional, but they are misleading. Not all Gower's speeches suggest 'act' divisions, as the Chorus speeches in *Henry V* might be thought to do, and since several of his speeches overlap with the following scene (for example in Scenes 1, 5, and 15), the traditional divisions have been abandoned and the scenes renumbered as in the Oxford edition.

My treatment of elisions in verse differs from Oxford's. The Quarto text is inconsistent in indicating these; for example, it elides 'adventurous' at Sc. 1.78 / Appendix A, l. 101, but not at Sc. 8.50 / Appendix A, l. 961, although the rhythmic requirements are the same in each case. Oxford's policy is to introduce elisions where this will regularize a verse line; I have gone in the opposite direction, usually spelling the words concerned in full, since I believe that it is perfectly possible to pronounce the complete word in such cases without destroying the rhythm.

References in the commentary to proverbs are to R. W. Dent's *Shakespeare's Proverbial Language: An Index* (Berkeley, 1981). The identification of biblical allusions is greatly indebted to Naseeb Shaheen's *Biblical References in Shakespeare's Plays* (Newark, Delaware, 1999) and normally follows the Geneva Bible of 1560. Quotations from classical works are from the Loeb editions. References to plays by other sixteenth- and seventeenth-century dramatists are to the Revels editions, unless otherwise stated, and those to other works by Shakespeare to the Oxford *Complete Works*, Compact Edition (1988).

I have adopted punctuation lighter than that required by strictly grammatical modern usage, in order to preserve the shape and rhythm of the verse lines as much as possible.

Abbreviations and References

The following references are used in the introduction, commentary, and Appendix C. The place of publication is London, unless otherwise specified.

EDITIONS OF SHAKESPEARE

Q, Q1	The First Quarto of *Pericles*, 1609
Qa	Uncorrected state of Q1
Qb	Corrected state of Q1
Q2	The Second Quarto, 1609
Q3	The Third Quarto, 1611
Q4	The Fourth Quarto, 1619
Q5	The Fifth Quarto, 1630
Q6	The Sixth Quarto, 1635
F3	The Third Folio (second issue, 1664)
F4	The Fourth Folio, 1685
Alexander	Peter Alexander, *Works* (1951)
Boswell	James Boswell, *Plays and Poems*, 21 vols. (1821)
Bullen	A. H. Bullen, *Works*, 10 vols. (1904–7)
Cambridge	W. G. Clark and W. A. Wright, *Works*, The Cambridge Shakespeare, 9 vols. (Cambridge, 1863–6)

Collier	J. P. Collier, *Works*, 8 vols. (1842–4)
Collier 2	J. P. Collier, *Comedies, Histories, Tragedies, and Poems*, 6 vols. (1858)
Deighton	Kenneth Deighton, *Pericles*, The Arden Shakespeare (1907)
Delius	Nicolaus Delius, *Works*, 3rd edn. (Leipzig, 1872)
Dyce	Alexander Dyce, *Works*, 6 vols. (1857)
Dyce 2	Alexander Dyce, *Works*, 9 vols. (1864–7)
Edwards	Philip Edwards, *Pericles*, The New Penguin Shakespeare (Harmondsworth, 1976)
Globe	W. G. Clark and W. A. Wright, *Works* (1864)
Grant White	Richard Grant White, *Works*, 12 vols. (1857–66)
Hoeniger	F. D. Hoeniger, *Pericles*, The Arden Shakespeare, 2nd series (1963)
Hudson	H. N. Hudson, *Works*, 11 vols. (1851–6)
Hudson 2	H. N. Hudson, *Works*, 20 vols. (1880–1)
Malone	Edmond Malone, *Pericles*, in *Supplement to the Edition of Shakespeare's Plays Published in 1778* (1780)
Malone 2	Edmond Malone, *Plays and Poems*, 10 vols. (1790)
Maxwell	J. C. Maxwell, *Pericles*, The New Shakespeare, 2nd edn. (Cambridge, 1969)
Norton	Stephen Greenblatt (general editor), *The Norton Shakespeare Based on the Oxford Edition* (New York, 1997)
Oxford	Stanley Wells, Gary Taylor, John Jowett, and William Montgomery, *Complete Works* (Oxford, 1986 ; Compact Edition, 1988)
Ridley	M. R. Ridley, *Pericles*, The New Temple Shakespeare (1935)
Round	P. Z. Round, *Pericles*, in Henry Irving and F. A. Marshall, *Works*, 8 vols. (1887–90)
Rowe	Nicholas Rowe, *Works*, 6 vols. (1709)
Rowe 2	Nicholas Rowe, *Works*, 2nd edn., 6 vols. (1709)
Rowe 3	Nicholas Rowe, *Works*, 8 vols. (1714)
Schanzer	Ernest Schanzer, *Pericles*, The Signet Classic Shakespeare (New York, 1965) ; also conjectures cited in Hoeniger
Singer	S. W. Singer, *Dramatic Works*, 10 vols. (1826)
Singer 2	S. W. Singer, *Dramatic Works*, 10 vols. (1856)
Sisson	C. J. Sisson, *Complete Works* (1954)
Staunton	Howard Staunton, *Plays*, 3 vols. (1858–60)
Steevens	George Steevens and Isaac Reed, *Plays*, 15 vols. (1793)
Tonson	Jacob Tonson (publisher), *Pericles* (1734)

OTHER ABBREVIATIONS

Abbott	E. A. Abbott, *A Shakespearian Grammar*, 2nd edn. (1870)
Arcadia	Sir Philip Sidney, *The Countess of Pembroke's Arcadia* (Harmondsworth, 1977)
Brooks	H. F. Brooks, conjectures cited in Hoeniger
Bullough	Geoffrey Bullough, *Narrative and Dramatic Sources of Shakespeare*, vol. 6 (1966)
Charlemont	The Earl of Charlemont, conjectures cited in Malone
Confessio Amantis	John Gower, *Confessio Amantis*, in G. Bullough, *Narrative and Dramatic Sources of Shakespeare*, vol. 6 (1966)
Dent	R. W. Dent, *Shakespeare's Proverbial Language : An Index* (Berkeley, 1981)
Edwards, 'Problem'	Philip Edwards, 'An Approach to the Problem of *Pericles*', *SS* 5 (Cambridge, 1952), 25–49
Elze	Karl Elze, *Notes on Elizabethan Dramatists* (1880, 1884, 1886)
Farmer	Richard Farmer, notes cited in Malone (1780)
Jackson	MacDonald P. Jackson, *Defining Shakespeare : 'Pericles' as Test Case* (Oxford, 2003)
Kinnear	B. G. Kinnear, *Cruces Shakespearianae* (1883)
Mason	John Monck Mason, *Comments on the Last Edition of Shakespeare's Plays* (1785)
Miseries	George Wilkins, *The Miseries of Enforced Marriage*, ed. Glenn H. Blayney, Malone Society Reprints (Oxford, 1964)
Nashe, *Works*	Thomas Nashe, *Works*, ed. R. B. McKerrow, revised F. P. Wilson, 5 vols. (Oxford, 1958)
N&Q	*Notes and Queries*
OED	*The Oxford English Dictionary*, 2nd edn., 20 vols. (Oxford, 1989)
Onions	C. T. Onions, *A Shakespeare Glossary*, 2nd edn., with enlarged addenda (Oxford, 1953)
PBSA	*The Papers of the Bibliographical Society of America*
Percy	T. Percy, notes cited in Malone and Steevens
RES	*Review of English Studies*
Schmidt	Alexander Schmidt, *Shakespeare Lexicon*, 3rd edn., 2 vols. (Berlin, 1902 ; Dover reprint, New York, 1971)
Shaheen	Naseeb Shaheen, *Biblical References in Shakespeare's Plays* (Newark, Delaware, 1999)
SQ	*Shakespeare Quarterly*

SS	*Shakespeare Survey*
TC	Stanley Wells, Gary Taylor, John Jowett, and William Montgomery, *William Shakespeare : A Textual Companion* (Oxford, 1987)
Theobald	Lewis Theobald, unpublished marginalia in copies of Q4 (Folger) and Q6 (University of Pennsylvania)
Travels	John Day, William Rowley, and George Wilkins, *The Travels of the Three English Brothers*, in *Three Renaissance Travel Plays*, ed. Anthony Parr, Revels Plays Companion Library (Manchester, 1995)
Twine	Laurence Twine, *The Pattern of Painful Adventures*, in G. Bullough, *Narrative and Dramatic Sources of Shakespeare*, vol. 6 (1966)
Tyrwhitt	Thomas Tyrwhitt, notes cited in Malone (1780)
Vaughan	H. H. Vaughan, annotations in a copy of Steevens's 1793 edition, cited in Maxwell
Walker	W. S. Walker, *A Critical Examination of the Text of Shakespeare*, ed. W. N. Lettsom, 3 vols. (1860)
Wilkins, *Painful Adventures*	George Wilkins, *The Painful Adventures of Pericles* (1608), in G. Bullough, *Narrative and Dramatic Sources of Shakespeare*, vol. 6 (1966)
Williams	Gordon Williams, *A Glossary of Shakespeare's Sexual Language* (1997)
Wilson	J. Dover Wilson, conjectures cited in Maxwell
YES	*Yearbook of English Studies*

Pericles, Prince of Tyre

THE PERSONS OF THE PLAY

John GOWER, the Presenter
PERICLES, Prince of Tyre

At Antioch

ANTIOCHUS, the King
His DAUGHTER
THALIART, a lord
MESSENGER

At Tyre

HELICANUS ⎫
          ⎬ two grave councillors of Tyre
AESCHINES ⎭
Three LORDS

At Tarsus

CLEON, the Governor
DIONYZA, his wife
LEONINE, her servant
A LORD
MARINA, Pericles' daughter
Three PIRATES

At Pentapolis

SIMONIDES, the King
THAISA, his daughter
Three FISHERMEN, his subjects
Five KNIGHTS, suitors of Thaisa
A MARSHAL
Two LORDS
Two GENTLEMEN
Pages
LYCHORIDA, Thaisa's nurse

On board ship

The MASTER

A SAILOR

At Ephesus

CERIMON, a lord

PHILEMON, his servant

Two other SERVANTS

Two GENTLEMEN

At Mytilene

LYSIMACHUS, the Governor

A PANDER

A BAWD, his wife

BOLT, their servant

Two GENTLEMEN

SAILOR of Tyre

SAILOR of Mytilene

GENTLEMAN of Tyre

LORD of Mytilene

Maid, Marina's companion

DIANA, goddess of chastity

There is no list of characters in the Quarto text ; this one expands and modifies that given in George Wilkins's prose narrative (see Introduction, p. 3).

Pericles, Prince of Tyre

Sc. 1 *Enter Gower*

GOWER

To sing a song that old was sung
From ashes ancient Gower is come,
Assuming man's infirmities
To glad your ear and please your eyes.
It hath been sung at festivals,   5
On ember-eves and holy-ales,
And lords and ladies in their lives
Have read it for restoratives.
The purchase is to make men glorious,
Et bonum quo antiquius eo melius.   10
If you, born in these latter times
When wit's more ripe, accept my rhymes,

Sc. 1.0.1 *Gower* John Gower (?1330–1408) was a contemporary of Chaucer, who told the story of this play in his poem *Confessio Amantis* (see Introduction, pp. 13–14). The metre of Gower's speeches, for most of the play in eight syllables rather than the ten of the main action, imitates that of the historical Gower.

1 **sing a song** *Song* could mean any kind of metrical composition, e.g. a poem, not necessarily sung (*OED sb.* 2a); hence the phrase can imply 'tell a tale'.
old of old. Gower emphasizes that this is a traditional story.

1–2 **sung . . . come** This assonantal, rather than perfect, rhyme was a regular habit of George Wilkins, who probably wrote Scenes 1–9. See Introduction, pp. 62–5.

2 **From ashes** i.e. from the dead (perhaps echoing the 'ashes to ashes' of the Christian burial service)

3 **Assuming man's infirmities** taking on frail human condition. Shaheen points out that *infirmities* occurs frequently throughout the Geneva Bible in this sense.

4 **glad** make glad (*OED v.* 2. *arch.*)

6 **ember-eves** evenings before periods of religious fasting ('ember-days') begin

6 **holy-ales** i.e. church-ales, festivals. Q's 'holidays' does not rhyme; Stanley Wells suggests privately that this might be another Wilkinsian assonance (see the note to ll. 1–2), but Theobald's conjecture is usually adopted, though the phrase is not recorded elsewhere. Maxwell suggests that 'Whitsun-ales' would make a better balance with 'ember-eves', and *OED* cites 'This is a Tale │ Would befit our Whitson-ale' of 1614 (*Whitsun* 1).

8 **for restoratives** as medicine

9 **purchase** profit, gain
make men glorious i.e. the story of Pericles will reflect credit on the achievements of men, or on this particular man

10 *Et . . . melius* 'And the older a thing is, the better it is' (a proverbial saying (Dent 038) which picks up the emphasis upon an 'old', well-established story from l. 1)

11 **latter** more recent

12 **wit's more ripe** intelligence is superior (than in the historical Gower's fourteenth century—but perhaps with an ironic glance at the fashionable emphasis on *wit* in the poetry that was being written (e.g. by John Donne) at the time of *Pericles*)

And that to hear an old man sing
May to your wishes pleasure bring,
I life would wish, and that I might   15
Waste it for you like taper-light.
This' Antioch, then: Antiochus the Great
Built up this city for his chiefest seat,
The fairest in all Syria.
I tell you what mine authors say.   20
This king unto him took a fere
Who died, and left a female heir
So buxom, blithe, and full of face
As heaven had lent her all his grace,
With whom the father liking took,   25
And her to incest did provoke.
Bad child, worse father, to entice his own

---

13 **that** i.e. if

14 **to your wishes** as you would wish

16 **Waste . . . light** use it up for your benefit,
as a candle is consumed while giving people light (perhaps with a hint of a tale told
in winter)
Waste consume (as at *As You Like It*
2.7.134: 'we will nothing waste (i.e. eat)
till you return')
like taper-light Proverbial: 'A candle
lights others and consumes itself' (Dent
C39).

17–18 **This' . . . seat** As Gower moves from
his personal introduction to describe
the scene and events of his story, he
temporarily changes from octosyllabic to
what Maxwell calls 'halting decasyllabic
metre', perhaps anticipating the iambic
pentameter which is the norm for the
main action.

17 **This'** this is
Antioch The capital of Syria was in fact
built in 300 BC, before the birth of Antiochus the Great. The name of the town is
stressed on the first syllable, that of the
King on the second.
Antiochus the Great (223–187 BC)
'ruled the Asian empire inherited by his
forefathers from Alexander the Great'
(Edwards). He is conflated with his son
Antiochus IV Epiphanes in the account of
his death (Sc. 8.1–13), which derives from
the apocryphal biblical book of the Mac-

cabees, 2: 9, and Willem Schrickx has
shown that Antiochus IV was established
as an embodiment of sacrilegious opposition to true religion, especially by dramatists who worked for the Jesuit theatre
('*Pericles* in a Book-List of 1619', *SS 29*
(Cambridge, 1976), 21–32).

18 **chiefest seat** capital. The phrase comes
not from John Gower's account, but from
Laurence Twine's (Bullough, p. 426). See
Introduction, p. 14.

20 **mine authors** It was characteristic of
medieval authors to appeal to the authority of older writers, as John Gower does in
his *Confessio Amantis*, ll. 279–81, 1160,
and 1554 and as the theatrical Gower does
in ll. 1 and 10 of this speech.
mine my. *Mine* is often used instead of
'my' before a vowel, as here, to allow
greater fluency of delivery (Abbott 237).

21 **fere** wife (*OED sb.*[1] 2). Q's 'peer' (= 'mate')
is sometimes retained, but *OED*'s only
earlier example of this sense is from
c. 1330, and *fere* is intelligible if old-
fashioned—presumably why it is used
here.

23 **buxom** lively
blithe cheerful
full of face Probably 'beautiful', but perhaps 'full-faced, florid' (*OED*, *face*, *sb.* 3),
'bonny'.

24 **As** as if
his its

To evil should be done by none.
By custom what they did begin
Was with long use accounted no sin.   30
The beauty of this sinful dame
Made many princes thither frame
To seek her as a bedfellow,
In marriage pleasures playfellow,
Which to prevent he made a law   35
To keep her still, and men in awe,
That whoso asked her for his wife,
His riddle told not, lost his life.
So for her many a wight did die,
   ⌈*The heads of former suitors are revealed*⌉
As yon grim looks do testify.   40

28 **should** that should. The omission of the relative 'that' is a stylistic characteristic of George Wilkins. See Introduction, p. 64.

29–30 **By custom . . . sin** Both the idea and the phrasing occur in Wilkins's *Miseries of Enforced Marriage* ll. 1129–31: 'Who once doth cherish sin begets his shame, | For vice being fostered once, comes impudence, | Which makes men count sin custom, not offence.' Both perhaps elaborate the proverb 'Custom makes sin no sin' (Dent C934).

30 **accounted** considered. Editors sometimes modify Q's 'account'd' to 'account', presumably for euphony and to ensure a regular verse line; but it is perfectly possible to sound the *ed* and to maintain the rhythm. Wilkins's prose version supports Q.

32 **frame** direct their course, go (*OED v.* 5d)

33–4 **bedfellow, playfellow** Such repetitions at the end of successive lines are characteristic of Wilkins's style.

35 **Which to prevent** This use of *Which* is characteristic of Wilkins; the whole phrase occurs in his *Miseries of Enforced Marriage*, l. 356.

36 **To . . . awe** 'to keep her still [i.e. always] to *himself*, and to deter others from demanding her in marriage' (Malone)

37 **whoso** whoever

38 **His riddle told not** if he could not solve the riddle

39 **wight** person. This is a rather old-fashioned (originally Anglo-Saxon) word, much used by Pistol (*Henry V* 2.1.58, *Merry Wives* 1.3.19, 33), and in Shakespeare's Sonnet 106 to evoke the 'fairest wights' of antique chronicles (1–2); it is probably intended to give a touch of quaint antiquity to a medieval story-teller.

40 **yon grim looks** This presumably refers to the severed heads of the unsuccessful suitors, hence the inserted stage direction in the previous line. But how were they *revealed*? In his prose version, Wilkins says that they were placed 'upon the top of his castle gate' (p. 495), but this detail was borrowed from Twine's account (p. 427), rather than necessarily reflecting a contemporary staging—i.e. that the heads were displayed on the balcony of the Jacobean stage. Surely the most effective way to display them, as in most modern performances, is to have them carried on poles by Antiochus' *followers* (l. 42.2), in which case perhaps Antiochus and Pericles should also enter at this point, rather than after Gower's exit, as at Stratford-upon-Avon in 1979, when the *grim looks* were interpreted as those of Antiochus himself.

yon those (an abbreviation of 'yonder', and one of Wilkins's favourite words). See, for example, ll. 77 and 80.

What now ensues, to the judgement of your eye
I give my cause, who best can justify.   *Exit*

> *Flourish. Enter King Antiochus, Prince Pericles, and*
> *followers*

ANTIOCHUS

Young Prince of Tyre, you have at large received
The danger of the task you undertake.

PERICLES

I have, Antiochus, and with a soul   45
Emboldened with the glory of her praise
Think death no hazard in this enterprise.

ANTIOCHUS Music!

> *Music sounds*

Bring in our daughter, clothèd like a bride
Fit for th'embracements even of Jove himself,   50
At whose conception, till Lucina reigned,
Nature this dowry gave to glad her presence:
The senate-house of planets all did sit,

41–2 **What . . . justify** 'As for what follows, I commit my theme to the judgement of your eyes—you who can best confirm the truth of my account (since seeing is believing)' (Maxwell). The change from eight-syllable to ten-syllable lines here has caused editors to suspect textual corruption, but may simply be intended to ease the transition from Gower's pseudo-medieval idiom to the normal blank verse of Jacobean drama, representing 'ordinary' speech.

42.1 **Flourish** The standard term for a fanfare automatically accompanying royal entrances, though here added editorially.

Pericles For a discussion of the name, see Introduction, pp. 16–18.

42.2 **followers** Oxford substitutes a phrase from Wilkins's prose narrative, 'lords and peers in their richest ornaments'. Wilkins may be describing what happened on stage, but he may equally be expanding the narrative imaginatively for the benefit of readers, so here as in most other stage directions, I have normally avoided filling out Q with descriptive phrases from Wilkins. In any case, it does not seem to me desirable to tie a modern edition down too closely to any one particular staging, even if that may have been the original.

43 **Tyre** 'an ancient Phoenician trading city on an island off the coast of Syria' (Edwards)

at large received heard in detail

47 **hazard** (excessive) risk

50 **Fit . . . Jove himself** *Jove* or Jupiter, king of the Roman gods, was famous for his affairs with mortal women, so *embracements* has distinctly sexual overtones.

51 **till Lucina reigned** until the goddess of childbirth allowed her to be born. *Lucina* was an alternative name for Diana, primarily the goddess of chastity, whose attributes nonetheless included supervising childbirth (see, for example, Horace, *Carmen Saeculare*, ll. 13–16): she is evoked in that capacity at Sc. II.10–12.

52 **dowry** This 'appears to be that during the time between her conception and her birth the planets were in the most auspicious conjunctions' (Maxwell). See the note to l. 53.

to glad her presence to make her appear delightful

53 **The senate-house of planets** It was a Renaissance commonplace that the heavens influence our dispositions; but the specific phrase comes from Sidney's *Arcadia* (1593) 2.6: 'The senate house of the planets was at no time so set for the decreeing of perfection in a man' (p. 258).

sit hold council, sit in session

In her their best perfections to knit.
    Enter Antiochus' Daughter

PERICLES

See where she comes, apparelled like the spring,   55
Graces her subjects, and her thoughts the king
Of every virtue gives renown to men;
Her face the book of praises, where is read
Nothing but curious pleasures, as from thence
Sorrow were ever razed, and testy wrath   60
Could never be her mild companion.
You gods that made me man, and sway in love,
That have inflamed desire in my breast
To taste the fruit of yon celestial tree
Or die in the adventure, be my helps,   65
As I am son and servant to your will,
To compass such a boundless happiness.

ANTIOCHUS

Prince Pericles—

PERICLES

That would be son to great Antiochus.

---

54 **In her ... knit** Steevens conjecturally rearranged Q's line to provide a rhyme, in keeping with Wilkins's characteristic alternation of rhyme and blank verse. See Appendix C.

55 **apparelled like the spring** dressed like Flora, goddess of spring (as Perdita is at *Winter's Tale* 4.4.1–3, 9–10), presumably wearing a robe decorated with flowers, as in Samuel Daniel's masque *The Vision of the Twelve Goddesses* (1604) ll. 94–5, and most famously in Botticelli's painting, *Primavera* (*c.* 1482)

56 **Graces her subjects** with Graces for her subjects. The three Graces (personifications of Beauty, Chastity, and Sensuality) were more usually the *subjects* of Venus, goddess of Love (as at Spenser's *Faerie Queene* (1596), 6.10.15, where they are 'handmaids of Venus'), than of Flora; but Flora, Venus, and the Graces all appear together in Botticelli's *Primavera* (see previous note).

56–7 **her thoughts ... men** The idea, clumsily put or reported, seems to be that her thoughts dwell on the kingliest form of every renowned human virtue.

57 **gives** which gives (an ellipsis characteristic of Wilkins's style)

58 **Her ... praises** Comparison of the face to a book is common in Renaissance writers, including both Shakespeare (e.g. *Romeo* 1.3.83–94) and Wilkins (e.g. *Miseries* ll. 341–3, 957–9, 2703–4).

59 **curious** exquisite

59–61 **as ... companion** 'as if sorrow were permanently blotted out (from her face) and anger were incompatible with her mildness' (Norton)

62 **sway** influence me

64–5 **To taste ... adventure** These lines imply a comparison (made specific by Antiochus at ll. 70–2) between the *adventure* of Pericles and one of the labours of Hercules, who was required to pluck the golden apples from a tree in the garden of the Hesperides, guarded by a dragon.

66 **As** as surely as

67 **compass** encompass, achieve

69 **son** son-in-law

ANTIOCHUS

Before thee stands this fair Hesperides,   70
With golden fruit, but dangerous to be touched,
For death-like dragons here affright thee hard.
Her heaven-like face enticeth thee to view
Her countless glory, which desert must gain;
And which without desert, because thine eye   75
Presumes to reach, all the whole heap must die.
Yon sometimes famous princes, like thyself
Drawn by report, adventurous by desire,
Tell thee with speechless tongues and semblance pale
That without covering save yon field of stars   80
Here they stand martyrs slain in Cupid's wars,
And with dead cheeks advise thee to desist
From going on death's net, whom none resist.

PERICLES

Antiochus, I thank thee, who hath taught
My frail mortality to know itself,   85

70–2 **Before ... hard** Antiochus picks up Pericles' hint at ll. 64–5 (see note), and represents his daughter as the garden of the Hesperides.

72 **death-like dragons** Oxford's inserted stage direction, '*He gestures towards the heads*', equates the *dragons* with the decapitated heads of the former suitors; but surely Antiochus' threat is more general: if Pericles attempts to win this particular *golden fruit*, and fails, the *death-like dragons*, his attendants, corresponding to the dragon who guarded the tree in the garden of the Hesperides, will kill him.

73 **heaven-like face** By transposing Q's 'face like heaven', Oxford provides much better sense, and 'a rhetorically attractive parallelism' with *death-like* in l. 72 (*TC*, p. 561).

74 **countless** Perhaps a reference to the stars, after *heaven* in the previous line, and possibly anticipating (or being confused with) the *countless eyes* of l. 116 (see the note); or perhaps just 'inestimable'.

76 **whole heap** entire body. Jackson points out that Wilkins uses *heap* in his contribution to *The Travels of the Three English Brothers*, 'sweep their several nations to a heap' (Sc. 2.182), where 'the notion of the combined peoples as a "heap", as of swept-up dust, perhaps throws some light

on the thinking behind Antiochus' words: ... at death man is reduced to a heap of inanimate dust' (p. 146). And see Introduction, p. 75.

77 **sometimes** once, former. 'Shakespeare has both "sometimes" and "sometime" in this sense' (Deighton), and 'sometime' might be clearer for a modern audience.

78 **adventurous** Q's 'adventrous' suggests a three-syllable pronunciation which makes the line regular; but it is perfectly possible to pronounce the complete word without destroying the rhythm.

79 **semblance** appearance. Oxford emends to 'semblants' on the grounds that 'a concrete plural seems required to match "princes", "tongues", "martyrs" and "cheeks"' (*TC*, p. 561). But *semblance* in this sense occurs elsewhere in Wilkins's share of the play (Sc. 4.70) and in Shakespeare (*Errors* 5.1.350, *2 Henry VI* 3.2.162, with, as in this line, *pale*), so I retain Q.

pale (either the pallor of death, or because they are now mere skulls)

81 **Cupid** god of love

83 **going on death's net** Obscure. See Introduction, p. 75.

going on venturing onto

And by those fearful objects to prepare
This body, like to them, to what I must;
For death remembered should be like a mirror
Who tells us life's but breath, to trust it error.
I'll make my will then, and as sick men do,   90
Who know the world, see heaven, but feeling woe
Grip not at earthly joys as erst they did;
So I bequeath a happy peace to you
And all good men, as every prince should do;
My riches to the earth from whence they came,   95
(*To the Daughter*) But my unspotted fire of love to you.
(*To Antiochus*) Thus ready for the way of life or death,
I wait the sharpest blow, Antiochus.

ANTIOCHUS

Scorning advice, read the conclusion then,
⌈*He angrily throws down the riddle*⌉
Which read and not expounded, 'tis decreed,   100
As these before thee, thou thyself shalt bleed.

DAUGHTER (*to Pericles*)

Of all 'sayed yet, mayst thou prove prosperous;
Of all 'sayed yet, I wish thee happiness.

PERICLES

Like a bold champion I assume the lists,
Nor ask advice of any other thought   105
But faithfulness and courage.
⌈*He takes up and reads aloud*⌉ *the riddle*
I am no viper, yet I feed

---

87 **must** i.e. face (inevitable death)
88 **For . . . mirror** By looking at the skulls of the unsuccessful suitors, Pericles is looking into a mirror which acts as a reminder (*death remembered*) of his own mortality.
89 **Who** which
life's but breath Proverbial (Dent B641.1).
90–2 **as sick . . . did** Probably: as dying men, with experience of the world, catch a glimpse of heaven, they do not grasp (*grip*) at earthly pleasures as they formerly (*erst*) did.
99 **conclusion** riddle. A rare usage: *OED*'s only other example (*sb*. 7b) is from Gower's *Confessio Amantis*, so this is probably a deliberately archaizing touch.

99.1 *He . . . riddle* Suggested by Wilkins's prose account (p. 498).
102–3 **'sayed** who have assayed (made the attempt)
yet so far
104 **assume** enter
lists enclosed combat area for tournaments
105–6 **Nor . . . courage** A borrowing from Sidney's *Arcadia*: 'asking advice of no other thought but of faithfulness and courage' (p. 471).
107 **viper** The popular belief that a young viper ate its way out of its mother's womb is also used by Wilkins at *Miseries* l. 1378, but it was a literary commonplace.

On mother's flesh which did me breed.
I sought a husband, in which labour
I found that kindness in a father.   110
He's father, son, and husband mild;
I mother, wife, and yet his child.
How they may be and yet in two,
As you will live resolve it you.
Sharp physic is the last. ⌈*Aside*⌉ But O you powers   115
That gives heaven countless eyes to view men's acts,
Why cloud they not their sights perpetually
If this be true which makes me pale to read it?
      ⌈*He gazes on the Daughter*⌉
Fair glass of light, I loved you, and could still,
Were not this glorious casket stored with ill.   120
But I must tell you now my thoughts revolt,
For he's no man on whom perfections wait
That knowing sin within, will touch the gate.
You are a fair viol, and your sense the strings

---

110 **kindness** (a) affection (b) close relationship

111 **father, son, and husband mild** A blasphemous echo of 'Father, Son and Holy Ghost', the three persons of the Holy Trinity that make up the one person of God, presumably evoked to blacken Antiochus further.
   son Perhaps because he usurps the position of a son-in-law, as the Daughter usurps the mother's in the next line.

113 **How . . . two** how there may be six persons within only two

115 **Sharp . . . last** the last phrase ('solve the riddle or die') is sharp medicine (perhaps with a play on the sharpness of the executioner's axe)
   Aside Although ll. 119–28 refer to 'you' and 'your', i.e. Antiochus' Daughter, it is likelier that this speech is a reflection about her rather than a direct address to her, hence Oxford's stage direction at l. 118.1. See the note to l. 123.

115–16 **powers | That gives** Plural subjects with singular verbs, and vice versa, are common in the writing of the period (Abbott 333).

116 **eyes** (i.e. the stars). Perhaps biblical in

origin: 'the eyes of the Lord' (Ecclesiasticus 23: 19).

117 **Why . . . sights** why don't they cover their eyes

119 **glass of light** 'a glass vessel with a candle in it' (Bullough, p. 360). Like the candle, the princess's outward beauty should radiate (inward) light, but instead conceals darkness (i.e. evil), as the next line specifies.

120 **glorious . . . ill** (like the deceptive golden casket at *Merchant* 2.7.61–3 which should contain Portia's portrait, but instead contains 'a carrion death'—i.e. a skull)

122 **he's . . . wait** As Maxwell says, 'probably just a mannered expression for' Malone's gloss 'he's no honest man'.

123 **touch the gate** Sexual slang for 'penetrate' (Williams, pp. 139, 311). Compare *Winter's Tale* 1.2.416–17: 'touched his queen | Forbiddenly'; and 1.2.198–9: 'other men have gates, and those gates opened, | As mine, against their will.' If this gloss is correct, the lines are unlikely to be addressed directly to the Daughter.

124 **viol** stringed instrument, ancestor of the modern violin and cello
   sense sensual nature (Onions)

Who fingered to make man his lawful music,   125
Would draw heaven down and all the gods to hearken,
But being played upon before your time,
Hell only danceth at so harsh a chime.
⌈*He turns to the Daughter*⌉
Good sooth, I care not for you.

ANTIOCHUS

Prince Pericles, touch not, upon thy life,   130
For that's an article within our law
As dangerous as the rest. Your time's expired.
Either expound now, or receive your sentence.

PERICLES

Great King,
Few love to hear the sins they love to act.   135
'Twould braid yourself too near for me to tell it.
Who has a book of all that monarchs do,
He's more secure to keep it shut than shown,
For vice repeated, like the wandering wind,
Blows dust in others' eyes to spread itself;   140
And yet the end of all is bought thus dear,
The breath is gone, and the sore eyes see clear
To stop the air would hurt them. The blind mole casts

---

125 **fingered** (a) played upon (the viol); (b) fondled genitally (the Daughter) (Williams, p. 125)

lawful (i.e. for a husband, not for a father)

126 **Would . . . hearken** the music made by the Daughter would (a) lure the gods to come down and listen and (b) arouse them sexually

128 **Hell . . . chime** only the devils would dance at so discordant a sound. Unlike the *lawful music* of l. 125, which would accompany the dance which was traditionally an image of sexual concord and of marriage (compare Pericles and Thaisa at Sc. 7.101.1), the Daughter now only makes music fit for a dance of death.

128.1 *He . . . Daughter* Something must motivate Antiochus' 'touch not' at l. 130. Perhaps it is Pericles' increasing agitation as he develops the sexually-charged language of ll. 121–8, but some impulsive movement towards the Daughter seems needed. At Stratford, Ontario in 1986, Pericles in his revulsion went to strike

her; perhaps this was going too far in so dangerous a court, but it certainly gave Antiochus something to react to.

129 **Good sooth** in truth, truly

130 **upon** if you value, at the risk of

133 **expound** explain (i.e. solve the riddle)

136 **braid** upbraid, reproach (*OED v.*[2] *Obs.*)
    near closely, intimately

137 **Who** whoever

139–43 **For . . . them** Another confused and probably corrupt passage. The general sense is probably: 'For with the breath used to speak word of others' sins, one blows irritating dust in the eyes of the offenders. But the consequence is merely the speaker's death, since the offenders nevertheless see well enough to stop the news-spreading breath' (Norton). The idea is much more concisely and vividly put in the 'blind mole' image that follows.

140 **to spread** in spreading

143 **would** which would

143–5 **The blind mole . . . for't** This image combines practical horticulture—mole-

---

Copped hills towards heaven to tell the earth is thronged
By man's oppression, and the poor worm doth die for't.   145
Kings are earth's gods; in vice their law's their will,
And if Jove stray, who dares say Jove doth ill?
It is enough you know, and it is fit,
What being more known grows worse, to smother it.
All love the womb that their first being bred;   150
Then give my tongue like leave to love my head.

ANTIOCHUS (*aside*)

Heaven, that I had thy head! He has found the meaning.
But I will gloze with him.—Young Prince of Tyre,
Though by the tenor of our strict edict,
Your exposition misinterpreting,   155
We might proceed to cancel of your days,
Yet hope, succeeding from so fair a tree
As your fair self, doth tune us otherwise.
Forty days longer we do respite you,
If by which time our secret be undone,   160
This mercy shows we'll joy in such a son.
And until then your entertain shall be

hills damage lawns, so gardeners kill the moles—with the idea that in piling up the earth the mole is aspiring towards heaven; compare Middleton's *A Game at Chess* (1624): 'the blind mole . . . in the casting his ambitious hills up | Is often taken, and destroyed i'th' midst | Of his advancèd work' (4.5.41–4). Pericles adds the slant that the mole is broadcasting man's secret wickedness, and is killed for saying so—as he fears he himself will be killed if he broadcasts the truth about Antiochus.

143 **casts** throws up

144 **Copped** heaped up, formed into a tumulus (*OED, ppl. a.* 2b)
tell tell that
thronged burdened, weighed down (*OED ppl. a.* 2a)

145 **poor worm** i.e. the mole. The alternative interpretation, that a *worm* is killed as the mole thrusts up the earth, spoils the parallel between the mole and Pericles

himself. *Poor worm* is an affectionate expression, as at *Tempest* 3.1.31, where Prospero uses it of the love-sick Miranda.
for't for saying so

147 **if . . . ill** who dares accuse Jupiter, king of the gods, of doing wrong (as, Pericles implies, he cannot accuse Antiochus)

148–9 **it is fit . . . it** it is best to conceal something which would become worse because exaggerated by repetition

152 **head** (i.e. Pericles' death)

153 **gloze** dissemble, gloss over

154 **tenor** terms

155 **Your exposition misinterpreting** since your interpretation of the riddle is wrong

156 **cancel of** cut short (i.e. kill you)

157 **hope . . . tree** such promise emerging from such noble stock

158 **tune . . . otherwise** make us change our mind

159 **respite** grant

160 **secret be undone** riddle is solved

161 **joy** rejoice

162 **entertain** entertainment

As doth befit your worth and our degree.

⌈*Flourish.*⌉ *Exeunt all but Pericles*

PERICLES

How courtesy would seem to cover sin

When what is done is like an hypocrite,   165

The which is good in nothing but in sight.

If it be true that I interpret false,

Then were it certain you were not so bad

As with foul incest to abuse your soul,

Where now you're both a father and a son   170

By your uncomely claspings with your child—

Which pleasures fits a husband, not a father—

And she an eater of her mother's flesh

By the defiling of her parents' bed,

And both like serpents are, who though they feed   175

On sweetest flowers, yet they poison breed.

Antioch farewell, for wisdom sees those men

Blush not in actions blacker than the night

Will 'schew no course to keep them from the light.

One sin, I know, another doth provoke;   180

Murder's as near to lust as flame to smoke.

Poison and treason are the hands of sin,

Ay, and the targets to put off the shame.

Then lest my life be cropped to keep you clear,

---

163 **your … degree** It is likely that the original had a rhyme for Antiochus' exit, which Oxford's emendation duly provides, modifying Q's 'our honour and your worth', and drawing on Steevens's conjecture 'our honour, your degree'. **degree** rank

164–85 See the Introduction, pp. 65–7, for an analysis of the hallmarks of George Wilkins's style in this speech.

164 **How courtesy would seem** Proverbial: 'Full of courtesy, full of craft' (Dent C732).

seem to behave deceitfully in order to

166 **The which** which

sight outward appearance

171 **uncomely** unlovely. Delius's conjectural emendation of Q's 'untimely' is supported by Wilkins's narrative (p. 500).

172 **pleasures fits** See the note to ll. 115–16.

177 **men** men who

179 **'schew … light** not shrink from (eschew) taking any action to avoid their crimes being known

180 Proverbial: 'Every sin brings in another' (Dent S467.1).

183 **Ay** Yes. *OED* says that 'ay' appeared suddenly about 1575, of unknown origin. It was usually spelt 'I' (as in the Quarto text here), which indicates the pronunciation. It survives in English dialects and regional accents.

targets shields

put off deflect

184 **cropped** cut down, harvested

clear free from blame

By flight I'll shun the danger which I fear.   *Exit*   185
    Enter King Antiochus

ANTIOCHUS
He hath found the meaning, for the which we mean
To have his head. He must not live
To trumpet forth my infamy, nor tell the world
Antiochus doth sin in such a loathèd manner,
And therefore instantly this prince must die,   190
For by his fall my honour must keep high.
Who attends us there?
    Enter Thaliart

THALIART   Doth your highness call?

ANTIOCHUS
Thaliart, you are of our chamber, Thaliart,
And to your secrecy our mind partakes
Her private actions. For your faithfulness   195
We will advance you, Thaliart. Behold,
Here's poison, and here's gold.
We hate the Prince of Tyre, and thou must kill him.
It fits thee not to ask the reason. Why?
Because we bid it. Say, is it done?   200
THALIART My lord, 'tis done.
    Enter a Messenger hastily
ANTIOCHUS Enough. Let your breath cool yourself, telling
your haste.

---

186 **the which** Oxford's emendation of Q's
'which' restores the metre (*He hath* is
the equivalent of one syllable) and 'produces an idiom characteristic of Wilkins'
(*TC*, p. 561), as does the quibble *meaning/
mean*.

192 **Thaliart** Oxford follows the spelling both
of the sources and of Wilkins, the probable author of this section, rather than Q's
'Thaliard' where 'aural confusion of d/t
would be easy' (*TC*, p. 561)—and even Q
has 'Thaliart' at l. 550 / Sc. 5.23, in a
speech which may derive from the actor's
written part (see Introduction, p. 79).
Antiochus' caressing repetitions of the
name as he persuades his chamberlain to
murder Pericles recall the technique
of King John persuading Hubert to kill
Prince Arthur (*King John* 3.3.19–28).

193–5 **of our chamber . . . actions** The relationship of king and chamberlain was

suggested by Gower: 'his privy councillor'
(*Confessio Amantis* l. 512) and by Twine:
'the only faithful and trusty minister of
my secrets' (p. 429). Thaliart therefore
balances Helicanus in the next scene: an
evil confidant of an evil king versus a
virtuous confidant of a virtuous one.
Compare *Winter's Tale* 1.2.237–9, where
Leontes says that he has trusted Camillo
with 'all the near'st things to my heart, as
well | My chamber-counsels'.

194 **partakes** communicates
199 **fits** befits
201.1 **hastily** From Wilkins's prose account,
but in any case obvious from Antiochus'
reaction. The Messenger is so hasty that
he cuts in on Antiochus' answer to
Thaliart, 'Enough'.
202–3 **Let . . . haste** i.e. cool your hot haste
by using your breath to tell me your
urgent news

MESSENGER My lord, Prince Pericles is fled.   ⌈*Exit*⌉
ANTIOCHUS (*to Thaliart*) As thou wilt live, fly after, and like   205
    an arrow shot from a well-experienced archer hits the
    mark his eye doth level at, so thou never return unless
    thou say Prince Pericles is dead.
THALIART My lord, if I can get him within my pistol's
    length, I'll make him sure enough, so farewell to your   210
    highness.   ⌈*Exit*⌉
ANTIOCHUS
    Thaliart, adieu. Till Pericles be dead
    My heart can lend no succour to my head.
                    Exit. ⌈*The heads are removed*⌉

Sc. 2   *Enter Pericles, distempered, with his Lords*
PERICLES
    Let none disturb us.   *Exeunt Lords*
                 Why should this change of thoughts,
    The sad companion, dull-eyed melancholy,
    Be my so used a guest as not an hour
    In the day's glorious walk or peaceful night,

204–11 Arguing in part from the parallel phrases *Prince Pericles is fled/dead* (ll. 204, 208), Oxford coaxes this passage into a kind of verse, but like most other editors, I think it better to follow Q and treat it as prose. Nor is it hard to find a theatrical reason for the shift to prose. With the Messenger's hasty entry, even cutting in on a conversation between Antiochus and Thaliart, the scene accelerates as Antiochus in panic despatches Thaliart with speed, only reverting to verse with a rhyming couplet to conclude the scene. And when Thaliart reappears in Scene 3, he resumes in the prose which he has used as he departs here.

207 **level** aim

209–10 **pistol's length** range of a pistol's shot. The weapon is more appropriate to the seventeenth century than to legendary times, but such anachronisms are common in the drama of the period.

210 **sure** secure (and so unable to do you harm—i.e. kill him: *OED a.* and *adv.* 3). For the idea, compare Hubert's assurance to King John: 'I'll keep him [Arthur] so |

That he shall not offend your majesty' (3.3.64–5).

211 *Exit* In view of the haste of the scene, it seems best for Thaliart to leave at once, and for Antiochus to call his farewell after him.

213 **My . . . head** i.e. I shall have no peace of mind

213.1 *The . . . removed* (unless they have already been carried off by Antiochus' attendants at l. 163.1)

Sc. 2.0.1–1 *Enter . . . Exeunt Lords* Pericles' entry *distempered*, agitated, is suggested by Wilkins's prose account ('distemperature', p. 501): it explains why he enters with his court but then dismisses them at once. For parallel examples of a ruler entering with attendants but dismissing them in order to be private, compare *1 Henry IV* 3.2.1–3 and *Two Gentlemen* 3.1.1–2.

1 **change of thoughts** i.e. from his usually serene frame of mind (Deighton)

3 **used a** customary
   as that

4 **day's glorious walk** the movement of the sun

The tomb where grief should sleep, can breed me quiet?   5
Here pleasures court mine eyes, and mine eyes shun
    them,
And danger which I feared's at Antioch,
Whose arm seems far too short to hit me here.
Yet neither pleasure's art can joy my spirits,
Nor yet care's author's distance comfort me.   10
Then it is thus: the passions of the mind,
That have their first conception by misdread,
Have after-nourishment and life by care,
And what was first but fear what might be done
Grows elder now, and cares it be not done.   15
And so with me. The great Antiochus,
'Gainst whom I am too little to contend,
Since he's so great can make his will his act,
Will think me speaking though I swear to silence,
Nor boots it me to say I honour him   20
If he suspect I may dishonour him.
And what may make him blush in being known,
He'll stop the course by which it might be known.
With hostile forces he'll o'erspread the land,
And with th'ostent of war will look so huge   25

---

8 **Whose** i.e. the King's
  far too short Plays on the proverb
'Kings have long arms' (Dent K87) and
on various biblical sayings, e.g. 'Is the
Lord's hand shortened?' (Numbers 11:
23).
9 **joy** bring joy to
10 **care's author's distance** the fact that
the cause of my sorrow is far away. Q's
'the other's distance' makes sense, but
Oxford's emendation is supported by
another Wilkins line, 'the author of my
care' (*Miseries* l. 888); and experience of
its use in rehearsal and performance
shows that the greater concreteness of
Oxford's line, contrasted with Q's vague-
ness, gives the actor more to hold on to in
a speech containing much pedestrian
verse. See the note to l. 91 for a comparable example.
11–12 **the passions . . . misdread** the mental
turmoil originally born out of fear
12 **misdread** fear, perhaps specifically fear of

evil, though this is *OED*'s only example of
this sense for *misdread* as a noun; but *OED*
cites 'misdreaded' and 'misdreading'
from *The History of Justine* (1606) by G. W.
(whom they take to be G. Woodcocke,
though it is almost certainly George
Wilkins: see Introduction, p. 6); so *misdread* may be another Wilkinsism. Interestingly, both uses in *Justine* occur in
contexts involving Antiochus.
13 **Have . . . care** are reinforced by anxiety
14 **but** only
15 **Grows elder** i.e. develops
  cares is anxious that
18 **can** that he can
  make his will his act do whatever he
wants to
20 **boots it** is it any help to
20–3 **honour him / dishonour him, being
known / be known** This kind of jingling
repetition is characteristic of Wilkins.
25 **ostent** display, ostentation. Tyrwhitt's
conjectural emendation of Q's meaning-

Amazement shall drive courage from the state,
Our men be vanquished ere they do resist,
And subjects punished that ne'er thought offence,
Which care of them, not pity of myself,
Who am no more but as the tops of trees   30
Which fence the roots they grow by and defend them,
Makes both my body pine and soul to languish,
And punish that before that he would punish.
> *Enter all the Lords, among them old Helicanus, to*
> *Pericles*

FIRST LORD
Joy and all comfort in your sacred breast!
SECOND LORD
And keep your mind peaceful and comfortable.   35
HELICANUS
Peace, peace, and give experience tongue.
(*To Pericles*) You do not well so to abuse yourself,
To waste your body here with pining sorrow,
Upon whose safety doth depend the lives
And the prosperity of a whole kingdom.   40
'Tis ill in you to do it, and no less
Ill in your council not to contradict it.
They do abuse the King that flatter him,
For flattery is the bellows blows up sin;

less 'the stint' catches the formidable
appearance of Antiochus' military might,
leading into the 'amazement' of their
opponents in the next line.

26 **Amazement** terror
28 **offence** that they had done wrong
30 **Who am I** who am
   no more but as merely like
31 **fence** protect
32–3 **languish** / **punish** An assonant
   rhyme characteristic of Wilkins's
   style.
33 **And punish . . . punish** By his self-
   lacerating anxieties, Pericles is already
   punishing the very person that Antiochus
   wants to punish.
33.1 **Helicanus** In the *Confessio Amantis*, l.
   583, 'Hellican' is merely a citizen of Tyre.
   His characterization as a wise old council-

lor (Wilkins calls him 'old': p. 501) is the
invention of the dramatists.
35 **mind** After this Q adds 'till you return to
   us', which must be a mistake, the reporter
   anticipating a decision that is not made
   until l. 120. This edition therefore follows
   Oxford in omitting the phrase.
   comfortable cheerful
36 **give experience tongue** let the experienced speak
37–42 **You. . . it** These lines are reconstructed
   by Oxford from Wilkins's prose version to
   fill an obvious gap in Q. See Introduction, p.
   77. After criticizing both Pericles' pining
   sorrow (l. 38), which we have seen and
   heard in his soliloquy, and the other Lords'
   failure to rebuke him for it, they lead naturally into Helicanus' next Q line, 'They do
   abuse the King that flatter him' (l. 43).
44 **blows up** which inflames

The thing the which is flattered, but a spark,   45
To which that wind gives heat and stronger glowing;
Whereas reproof, obedient and in order,
Fits kings as they are men, for they may err.
When Signor Soothe here does proclaim a peace
He flatters you, makes war upon your life.   50
    ⌈*He kneels*⌉
Prince, pardon me, or strike me if you please.
I cannot be much lower than my knees.

PERICLES

All leave us else; but let your cares o'erlook
What shipping and what lading's in our haven,
And then return to us.   *Exeunt Lords*
                Helicanus, thou   55
Hast movèd us. What seest thou in our looks?

HELICANUS An angry brow, dread lord.

PERICLES

If there be such a dart in princes' frowns,
How durst thy tongue move anger to our face?

HELICANUS

How dares the plants look up to heaven from whence   60
They have their nourishment?

PERICLES

Thou know'st I have power to take thy life from thee.

HELICANUS

I have ground the axe myself, do you but strike the blow.

---

46 **that wind** i.e. the bellows. Q's 'spark' probably mistakenly echoes the previous line; Edwards notes that editors 'usually read "blast", which seems strong for a bellows'.

49 **Signor Soothe** 'Master Flattery'. *OED* records this and Richard II's 'words of sooth' (3.3.135) under *Sooth sb.* 8: 'Associated with senses of the verb SOOTHE: Blandishment, flattery'. So it seems better to follow Maxwell and spell 'Soothe' (which also makes the pronunciation clear) than Q's and other editions' 'sooth', which confusingly suggests 'truth'.
proclaim a peace (as the Second Lord did at l. 35)

53 **All leave us else** everyone else leave us
cares watchfulness
o'erlook keep an eye on

54 **What shipping** Pericles needs information about any ships from Antioch.
lading cargo
haven harbour

56 **movèd** angered

57 **dread** revered, held in awe (Onions). A standard phrase of respect for a king, not necessarily a comment on the present anger of this one.

58 **dart** arrow (i.e. danger)

59 **durst** dare

63 **do you but** all you have to do is

PERICLES ⌈*lifting him up*⌉

Rise, prithee rise, sit down, thou art no flatterer,

I thank thee for it, and heaven forbid   65

That kings should let their ears hear their faults hid.

Fit councillor and servant for a prince,

Who by thy wisdom makes a prince thy servant,

What wouldst thou have me do?

HELICANUS   To bear with patience

Such griefs as you do lay upon yourself.   70

PERICLES

Thou speak'st like a physician, Helicanus,

That ministers a potion unto me

That thou wouldst tremble to receive thyself.

Attend me, then. I went to Antioch,

Where as thou know'st, against the face of death   75

I sought the purchase of a glorious beauty

From whence an issue I might propagate,

As children are heaven's blessings: to parents, objects;

Are arms to princes, and bring joys to subjects.

Her face was to mine eye beyond all wonder,   80

The rest—hark in thine ear—as black as incest,

Which by my knowledge found, the sinful father

Seemed not to strike, but smooth. But thou know'st this,

'Tis time to fear when tyrants seems to kiss;

Which fear so grew in me I hither fled   85

Under the covering of a careful night,

Who seemed my good protector, and being here

Bethought me what was past, what might succeed.

---

66 **hear . . . hid** hear words that gloss over their faults

68, 71–2 The idiom '[thou] makes', rather than 'thou mak'st', and 'Thou . . . ministers' rather than 'Thou minister'st', is probably chosen for greater fluency in delivery. 'Thou . . . makes' occurs at *Othello* 5.2.68–9.

73 **receive** swallow (*OED v.* 6)

74 **Attend** listen, pay attention to

76 **purchase** acquisition

78 A line is clearly missing in Q between ll. 77 and 79. Oxford's conjectural line draws upon Wilkins's *Miseries* ll. 2674–5:

'Heaven . . . blessed you with children, | And at heaven's blessings, all good men rejoice'. For a full discussion, see *TC*, p. 563.

78 **objects** (of affection)

79 **Are arms** i.e. give additional strength to

83 **smooth** flatter

84 **tyrants seems** See the note to Sc. 1.115–16.

85 **hither** here

86 **careful** watchful

88 **succeed** follow

I knew him tyrannous, and tyrants' fears
Decrease not, but grow faster than the years. 90
And should he doubt—as doubt no doubt he doth—
That I should open to the listening air
How many worthy princes' bloods were shed
To keep his bed of blackness unlaid ope,
To lop that doubt he'll fill this land with arms, 95
And make pretence of wrong that I have done him,
When all for mine—if I may call—offence
Must feel war's blow, who spares not innocence;
Which love to all, of which thyself art one,
Who now reproved'st me for't—

HELICANUS   Alas, sir— 100

PERICLES

Drew sleep out of mine eyes, blood from my cheeks,
Musings into my mind, with thousand doubts,
How I might stop this tempest ere it came,
And finding little comfort to relieve them,
I thought it princely charity to grieve them. 105

HELICANUS

Well my lord, since you have given me leave to speak,
Freely will I speak. Antiochus you fear,
And justly too I think you fear the tyrant,
Who either by public war or private treason
Will take away your life. 110

---

89 **fears** threats of danger (*OED sb.*[1] 5c)

91 **doubt—as doubt no doubt** suspect, as
have no doubt. For Q's limping line (see
Appendix A, l. 332), Oxford substitutes
this conjecture by H. F. Brooks, cited
by Hoeniger, who comments: 'This is
good metre, and the rhetoric is typically
Elizabethan'; he compares *Love's Labour's
Lost* 1.1.77, 'Light, seeking light, doth
light of light beguile', where 'of light' is
accidentally omitted in F2. The repeated
'doubts'—far from facing the actor with a
tongue-twister—help him to 'anchor' the
line, giving it a bite and edge in another
passage of humdrum verse, as the experience of rehearsal and performance has
shown.

92 **open** reveal

94 **unlaid ope** undisclosed

95 **lop that doubt** destroy that fear

97 **all** all people, everyone
mine . . . offence my offence, if I may call
it that

98 **who** which

100 **now** just now

105 **grieve them** Q5's reading is almost
certainly correct, since it provides a
characteristic Wilkinsian rhyme with
'relieve them' in the previous line. But it
makes the sense difficult to grasp, as the
reporter of Q clearly found when he read
'grieve for them'. *OED v.* 8(b) gives examples of *grieve* used transitively for 'grieve
for'.

Therefore, my lord, go travel for a while,
Till that his rage and anger be forgot,
Or destinies do cut his thread of life.
Your rule direct to any; if to me,
Day serves not light more faithful than I'll be.   115
PERICLES
I do not doubt thy faith.
But should he in my absence wrong my liberties?
HELICANUS
We'll mingle our bloods together in the earth
From whence we had our being and our birth.
PERICLES
Tyre, I now look from thee then, and to Tarsus   120
Intend my travel, where I'll hear from thee,
And by whose letters I'll dispose myself.
The care I had and have of subjects' good
On thee I lay, whose wisdom's strength can bear it.
I'll take thy word for faith, not ask thine oath;   125
Who shuns not to break one will sure crack both.
But in our orbs we'll live so round and safe
That time of both this truth shall ne'er convince:
Thou showed'st a subject's shine, I a true prince'.

Exeunt

113 **destinies . . . life** The three mythological
Fates were thought to end a person's
life by cutting a *thread* which represented
it.
114 **direct** assign
117 **should he** what if he should
liberties royal rights, prerogatives
(Schmidt)
121 **Intend** direct
122 **dispose myself** direct my actions
126 **Who . . . both** anyone who breaks
his word will surely break an oath as
well
127 Editors speculate that a line is missing
here, but 'Wilkins is demonstrably fond of
placing a single unrhymed line between
couplets' (*TC*, p. 563). Those editors' sus-
picions were no doubt partly fuelled by

the extreme feebleness of the couplets on
either side, especially the concluding
one, suggesting corruption; Maxwell, for
example, says that 'it has taken the
author (or reporter) all his time to achieve
the wretched [final] couplet'. I suspect
that Wilkins's verse has been misrepre-
sented by a reporter, as Shakespeare's has
been later.
orbs spheres (moving concentrically
round each other)
live so round move in such a perfect circle
128 **time . . . convince** time shall never dis-
prove this truth about us both
129 **shine** shining example
a true prince' (the example) of a
true prince. For *prince'*, compare Sc.
5.21.

Sc. 3 *Enter Thaliart alone*

THALIART So this is Tyre, and this the court. Here must I kill
King Pericles, and if I do it and am caught I am like to be
hanged abroad, but if I do it not, I am sure to be hanged
at home. 'Tis dangerous. Well, I perceive he was a wise
fellow and had good discretion, that being bid to ask what   5
he would of the King, desired he might know none of his
secrets. Now do I see he had some reason for't, for if a
king bid a man be a villain, he's bound by the indenture
of his oath to be one. Husht, here comes the lords of Tyre.
        Enter Helicanus and Aeschines, with other lords

HELICANUS

You shall not need, my fellow peers of Tyre,   10
Further to question of your King's departure.
His sealed commission left in trust with me
Does speak sufficiently he's gone to travel.

Sc. 3 There seem to be two layers of writing
in this scene. Thaliart's prose speech at
the start, his tone wry and ironic, is more
strongly fashioned and effective than
much of the verse so far (especially when
a necessary restoration at ll. 2–3 is made)
or of the verse that follows it; and his later
lines 25–6 sound to me like prose rather
than irregular verse (they also refer back
to the subject matter of his opening
soliloquy, and continue its tone). But the
rhythms of Helicanus' speeches make it
clear that they are verse, mistakenly
printed as prose in Q. And as there is
no trace of Thaliart's prose speeches in
Wilkins's narrative, it is possible that the
scene was originally a verse conversation
between Helicanus and Thaliart, to which
a more developed version of Thaliart's
ironic personality was added in prose (by
Shakespeare?), without any adjustment
of the verse. For this reason, I have not
attempted to force Thaliart's speeches
into verse (e.g. at l. 26) unless the verse
rhythms positively demand this.

2–4 **and if . . . home** Q merely reads 'and if I
do it not, I am sure to be hanged at home',
but as Maxwell says, '*sure* to be hanged *at
home*' reads like 'one side of an antithesis'. So Oxford conjecturally supplies
the other side; for detailed discussion, see
TC, p. 563.

2 **like** likely

3 **abroad** in a foreign country

4–7 **wise . . . secrets** The *wise fellow* was the
poet Philippides, the king Lysimachus
(see Sc. 19.25 and note). The anecdote
probably came from Plutarch's *Lives of the
Noble Grecians and Romans* in North's
translation of 1579 (Life of Demetrius,
p. 947), the main source for *Antony
and Cleopatra* and *Coriolanus*, written at
roughly the same time as *Pericles*. This
source is especially likely if, as conjectured
above, Shakespeare rather than Wilkins
was responsible for the characterization of
Thaliart.

8 **indenture** contract between master and
servant

9 **Husht** Quiet! In his Italian/English dictionary, *A World of Words* (1598), John Florio
glosses '*citto*' as 'a word to bid children
hold their peace, as we say "Whust,
husht"' (cited at *OED int.*[1]).

9.1 *Aeschines* The name of an Athenian ora-
tor, mentioned in Plutarch's Life of Pericles, where the dramatist[s] presumably
found it. If so, Wilkins's form *Aeschines* is
likelier to be correct than Q's 'Escanes',
though Q indicates the pronunciation,
with the stress on the first
syllable.

11 **question of** call in question

12 **sealed** (with the royal seal)

THALIART (*aside*) How? The King gone?

HELICANUS

    If further yet you will be satisfied   15

    Why, as it were unlicensed of your loves,

    He would depart, I'll give some light unto you.

    Being at Antioch—

THALIART (*aside*)   What from Antioch?

HELICANUS

    Royal Antiochus, on what cause I know not,

    Took some displeasure at him—at least he judged so—   20

    And doubting lest that he had erred or sinned,

    To show his sorrow he'd correct himself;

    So puts himself unto the shipman's toil,

    With whom each minute threatens life or death.

THALIART (*aside*) Well, I perceive I shall not be hanged now,   25

    although I would.

    But since he's gone, the King's ears it must please

    He scaped the land to perish on the seas.

    I'll present myself.—Peace to the lords of Tyre.

HELICANUS

    Lord Thaliart of Antioch is welcome.   30

---

16 **unlicensed of your loves** without your
loving consent. The King has departed
without consulting his privy council, or
cabinet.

21 **doubting lest** fearing that
erred or sinned The phrasing may
have been suggested by the 'general
confession' during Morning and Evening
Prayer in the Book of Common Prayer
(1559), 'We have erred and strayed from
thy ways like lost sheep', especially in a
context of showing sorrow (l. 22).

22 **he'd correct** he wanted to punish

23 **puts . . . toil** undergoes the rigours of a
sea-journey

25-6 Thaliart's aside seems to be in prose; he
then moves into verse as he prepares to
join in the conversation of the lords of
Tyre.

26 **although I would** (have been; see ll. 2–4)

27 **King's ears it** Dyce's conjectural emendation of Q's nonsensical 'King's seas' is the
more plausible since 'it' 'could have been
omitted easily, because it falls between
two Q prose lines' (*TC*, p. 563: see Appen-

dix A, ll. 399–400).

29-30 Between these lines, Oxford inserts
'Lord Thaliart am I, of Antioch' on the
grounds that it 'is suspicious that Helicanus knows who Thaliart is without an
introduction; suspicion is compounded
by Q's omission of the speech-prefix. . . .
Eyeskip, or reporter omission, would have
been easy' (*TC*, p. 563). On the other
hand, there is no reason why a minister
of one country should not recognize a
minister from another, even if he is a
murdering minister. Moreover, at
Stratford-upon-Avon in 1958, Helicanus
detected Thaliart's presence, and delivered the information about Pericles'
departure as much for his benefit as for
the councillors' (if I have remembered
correctly after forty years); after all, they
have been expecting visitors from Antioch
(Sc. 2.54 and first note). So since it is possible to make theatrical sense of Q as it
stands, I omit Oxford's extra line.

30-1 **of Antioch, From King Antiochus** 'Q's
repetition—"from *Antiochus* . . . welcome

THALIART

From King Antiochus I come
With message unto princely Pericles,
But since my landing I have understood
Your lord's betook himself to unknown travels.
Now my message must return from whence it came.   35

HELICANUS

We have no reason to desire it,
Commended to our master, not to us.
Yet ere you shall depart, this we desire:
As friends to Antioch, we may feast in Tyre.   *Exeunt*

Sc. 4   *Enter Cleon, the Governor of Tarsus, with*
           Dionyza his wife, and others

CLEON

My Dionyza, shall we rest us here,
And by relating tales of others' griefs,
See if 'twill teach us to forget our own?

DIONYZA

That were to blow at fire in hope to quench it,
For who digs hills because they do aspire   5
Throws down one mountain to cast up a higher.
O my distressèd lord, even such our griefs are;

| From him . . . come"—is suspicious, and a reporter could easily have confused an initial indication of place (of Antioch) with a subsequent indication of person (from Antiochus)' (*TC*, p. 563).

36, 38 **desire, desire** Oxford emends the first to 'enquire', which is what it implies, presumably assuming erroneous anticipation of the second (which is confirmed by the need for a rhyme). But the repetition may be the point: Helicanus doesn't *desire* to know the contents of the message, but does *desire* to entertain Thaliart, as a visiting ambassador, and so diplomatically to maintain good relations with Antioch.

Sc. 4.0.1 *Cleon* His name is not actually mentioned in the dialogue until Sc. 11.75. It is a common classical name, but it may have been suggested by North's translation of Plutarch's Life of Pericles, where Cleon is mentioned as an antagonist of Pericles.

1–20 There has been a great deal of threadbare verse in the play so far, whether the responsibility is Wilkins's or a reporter's or both, but these are especially impoverished lines, even when Oxford's improvements are taken into account. And since they give no information that is not provided more effectively later in the scene, most productions omit them and begin at l. 21, 'This' Tarsus o'er which I have the government', which at least makes a strong and informative opening, telling the audience who Cleon is and where.

4 **That . . . quench it** Proverbial: 'Do not blow the fire thou wouldst quench' (Dent F251).

5 **who** whoever
  digs 'endeavours to lessen by digging' (Deighton)
  aspire rise high (*OED v.* 5)

Here they're but felt and seen with midges' eyes,

But like to groves, being topped they higher rise.

CLEON   O Dionyza,   10

Who wanteth food and will not say he wants it,

Or can conceal his hunger till he famish?

Our tongues our sorrows dictate to sound deep

Our woes into the air, our eyes to weep

Till lungs fetch breath that may proclaim them louder,   15

That if heaven slumber while their creatures want,

They may awake their helps to comfort them.

I'll then discourse our woes, felt several years,

And wanting breath to speak, help me with tears.

DIONYZA   As you think best, sir.   20

CLEON

This' Tarsus o'er which I have the government,

A city o'er whom plenty held full hand,

For riches strewed herself even in the streets,

Whose towers bore heads so high they kissed the clouds,

And strangers ne'er beheld but wondered at,   25

Whose men and dames so jetted and adorned

8–9 **Here . . . rise** Gary Taylor in Oxford replaces Q's meaningless 'mischiefs' with *midges*: 'it is not clear why their griefs [l. 7] should be "but" felt or seen with the eyes of misfortune . . . or how the line contrasts with groves which grow higher by being topped. *Midges*, by contrast, are a suitable image of smallness' (*TC*, p. 564): their *griefs* remain small when viewed by the tiny *midges' eyes*, but increase when compared to the groves which grow through being pruned—and which seem bigger still when viewed through the *midges' eyes*.

13–17 **Our tongues . . . them** The general sense is that the more they declare their woes, the more hope there is of awaking the sleeping heavens to give them comfort.

13 **our sorrows dictate** Q's line lacks a verb (see Appendix A, l. 424). 'Of proposals for the missing verb, "dictate" seems superior to "force" or "cease", because of its double meaning: "command" but also "read aloud" ' (*TC*, p. 564).

19 **wanting** when I lack

20 **As you think best, sir** This is Oxford's emendation of Q's 'I'll do my best, sir' which 'has Dionyza ludicrously respond to Cleon's rhetoric as though it were a literal request. The reporter must have misunderstood' (*TC*, p. 564).

21 **This'** this is. If Q's *This* is treated as an adjective describing *Tarsus*, Cleon's ll. 21–9 lack a verb. *This' Tarsus* on the other hand corresponds to Gower's *This' Antioch* at Sc. 1.17. Dionyza obviously doesn't need to be told where she is, but the audience does, and the phrase launches a celebration of the city's former abundance and enviable prosperity.

22 **plenty . . . hand** As Deighton noted, the image is that of abundance poured by hand out of the cornucopia, the classical 'horn of plenty'.

23 **riches strewed herself** *Riches* is regarded as a feminine singular noun, i.e. 'wealth', as at Shakespeare's Sonnet 87.6: 'that riches . . .'.

25 **but wondered at** without admiring

26 **jetted** strutted
    adorned (themselves)

Like one another's glass to trim them by;
Their tables were stored full to glad the sight,
And not so much to feed on as delight.
All poverty was scorned, and pride so great   30
The name of help grew odious to repeat.

DIONYZA O 'tis too true.

CLEON

But see what heaven can do by this our change.
Those mouths who but of late earth, sea, and air
Were all too little to content and please,   35
Although they gave their creatures in abundance,
As houses are defiled for want of use,
They are now starved for want of exercise.
Those palates who, not yet two summers younger,
Must have inventions to delight the taste   40
Would now be glad of bread and beg for it.
Those mothers who to nuzzle up their babes
Thought naught too curious are ready now
To eat those little darlings whom they loved.
So sharp are hunger's teeth that man and wife   45
Draw lots who first shall die to lengthen life.
Here weeping stands a lord, there lies a lady dying,
Here many sink, yet those which see them fall
Have scarce strength left to give them burial.
Is not this true?   50

DIONYZA

Our cheeks and hollow eyes do witness it.

CLEON

O let those cities that of plenty's cup

---

27 **glass to trim them by** mirror by which to dress themselves (i.e. one person acted as a mirror of fashion for another)

31 **The name . . . repeat** i.e. that it became hateful even to mention the possibility of needing help. A clumsy way of saying that they became complacent in their well-being.

33 **see . . . change** see how heaven shows its power by our change of fortune

37 **defiled** fallen into decay
want lack

40 **inventions . . . taste** novelties to titillate the appetite

42–4 **Those . . . loved** Perhaps suggested by Nashe's account of a famine in his *Christ's Tears over Jerusalem* (*Works*, ii. 69–71).

42 **nuzzle** bring up, nourish

43 **curious** choice

46 **to lengthen life** (by eating the other)

47 **Here . . . dying** This line is based on Wilkins's prose account: 'here stands one weeping, and there lies another dying' (p. 503). Q's line (see Appendix A, l. 459) 'means no more than "lords and ladies stand around weeping"' (*TC*, p. 564).

52 **plenty's cup** See the note to l. 22.

And her prosperities so largely taste
With their superfluous riots, heed these tears!
The misery of Tarsus may be theirs.   55
    Enter a ⌈fainting⌉ Lord of Tarsus ⌈slowly⌉
LORD Where's the Lord Governor?
CLEON   Here.
Speak out thy sorrows which thou bring'st in haste,
For comfort is too far for us to expect.

LORD
We have descried upon our neighbouring shore
A portly sail of ships make hitherward.   60

CLEON
I thought as much.
One sorrow never comes but brings an heir
That may succeed as his inheritor,
And so in ours. Some neighbouring nation,
Taking advantage of our misery,   65
Hath stuffed these hollow vessels with their power
To beat us down, the which are down already,
And make a conquest of unhappy men,
Whereas no glory's got to overcome.

LORD
That's the least fear, for by the semblance   70
Of their white flags displayed they bring us peace,
And come to us as favourers, not as foes.

CLEON
Thou speak'st like him's untutored to repeat:
Who makes the fairest show means most deceit.
But bring they what they will, what need we fear?   75

---

54 **superfluous riots** extravagant self-
   indulgence
   tears lamentations
55.1 *fainting ... slowly* These details are
   from Wilkins's prose account (p. 503).
57 **in haste** He is to speak his news quickly;
   he has entered slowly.
59 **descried** observed
60 **portly sail** majestic fleet (with billowing
   sails)
   make hitherward come in this direction
62–3 **One ... inheritor** Proverbial (Dent
   M1012).
66 **stuffed ... power** filled these ships with
   their army

68 **unhappy** luckless, wretched
69 **Whereas ... overcome** whom there is no
   glory to be had by overcoming
   Whereas where
70 **least fear** least of our worries
   semblance appearance
73 **him's untutored to repeat** him who hasn't
   been taught to recite the following maxim
74 **Who ... deceit** Proverbial (Dent C732).
75 **what they will** Steevens eliminated Q's
   next phrase (see Appendix A, l. 488), to
   provide a regular line.

Our grave's the lowest, and we are half-way there.
Go tell their general we attend him here
To know for what he comes, and whence he comes,
And what he craves.

LORD   I go, my lord.   *Exit*

CLEON

Welcome is peace, if he on peace consist;   80
If wars, we are unable to resist.

> *Enter ⌈the Lord again conducting⌉ Pericles with*
> *attendants*

PERICLES (*to Cleon*)

Lord Governor, for so we hear you are,
Let not our ships and number of our men
Be like a beacon fired t'amaze your eyes.
We have heard your miseries as far as Tyre,   85
Since entering your unshut gates have seen
The widowed desolation of your streets;
Nor come we to add sorrow to your hearts,
But to relieve them of their heavy load;
And these our ships, you happily may think   90
Are like the Trojan horse was fraught within
With bloody veins importing overthrow,
Are stored with corn to make your needy bread,
And give them life whom hunger starved half dead.

ALL OF TARSUS

The gods of Greece protect you, and we'll pray for you!   95

---

76 **grave's** Oxford's emendation for Q's 'grounds'. There is a similar (presumed) error at *Hamlet* 4.5.38, where F and Q1 read 'grave', Q2 'ground'.

77 **attend** await

79 **craves** desires

80 **on peace consist** stand on (i.e. come in) peace (*OED v.* 4c)

84 **beacon fired** Bonfires were lit as alarm signals in Jacobean England.
amaze alarm

85 **as far** (away)

86–7 **Since ... streets** Oxford expands Q's 'And seen the desolation of your streets' with details from Wilkins's narrative, which add to the sense of abandonment (*unshut gates*) and desolation.

89 **load** burden (of sorrow)

90 **you happily** which you haply (perhaps)

91 **was** which was
fraught loaded, filled. Q's 'stuffed' was probably caught from l. 66 above; Wilkins's narrative supports *fraught* (p. 503).

92 **With ... overthrow** The *bloody veins* of the Trojan horse are the Greek soldiers concealed inside it, planning the *overthrow* of Troy.

93 **needy bread** The *need* is transferred from the starving citizens to the bread that will feed them. Or it may mean 'make bread (for) your needy'.

PERICLES Arise, I pray you, rise.

We do not look for reverence but for love,

And harbourage for ourself, our ships and men.

CLEON

The which when any shall not gratify,

Or pay you with unthankfulness in thought,   100

Be it our wives, our children, or ourselves,

The curse of heaven and men succeed their evils!

Till when—the which I hope shall ne'er be seen—

Your grace is welcome to our town and us.

PERICLES

Which welcome we'll accept, feast here a while,   105

Until our stars that frown lend us a smile.   *Exeunt*

Sc. 5   *Enter Gower*

GOWER

Here have you seen a mighty king

His child, iwis, to incest bring;

A better prince and benign lord

Prove awe-full both in deed and word.

Be quiet then, as men should be,   5

Till he hath passed necessity.

I'll show you those in trouble's reign,

Losing a mite, a mountain gain.

The good in conversation,

To whom I give my benison,   10

---

97 **reverence** respect (signalled by their kneeling), or perhaps stronger: the *reverence* offered to a god

99–106 For the distinctive features of Wilkins's style in these lines, see Introduction, p. 64.

99 **gratify** Either 'grant' or 'show gratitude for'.

100 **in thought** i.e. even in thought

102 **succeed** (may it) inevitably follow

Sc. 5.2 **iwis** indeed. Ultimately derived from OE *gewis*, it is probably intended as an archaism thought appropriate to Gower.

4 **Prove** Q's 'That will prove' 'seems wrong not only metrically, but in its shift of tense' (*TC*, p. 565).
awe-full awe-inspiring

5 **Be quiet . . . be** Is he urging a potentially restless audience to concentrate on the play?

6 **he** (Pericles)
passed necessity experienced extreme hardship (*OED*, *necessity*, *sb.* 11); or perhaps *necessity* means 'the suffering that is his lot' (Norton)

8 **mite** tiny particle (something very small)

9 **good** good man (i.e. Pericles)
in conversation Editors gloss 'in his behaviour' (*OED* 6), but may not *conversation* have its modern meaning (available at the time: *OED* 7), and the whole phrase mean 'the good man I have been talking about'?

10 **benison** blessing

Is still at Tarsus where each man
Thinks all is writ he speken can,
And to remember what he does
His statue build to make him glorious.
But tidings to the contrary   15
Are brought your eyes. What need speak I?
  Dumb show. Enter at one door Pericles talking with
  Cleon, all the train with them. Enter at another door a
  gentleman with a letter to Pericles. Pericles shows the
  letter to Cleon. Pericles gives the messenger a reward.
  Exeunt with their trains Pericles at one door and Cleon
  at another
Good Helicane that stayed at home,
Not to eat honey like a drone
From others' labours, for that he strive
To killen bad, keep good alive,   20
And to fulfil his prince' desire
Sent word of all that haps in Tyre:
How Thaliart came full bent with sin
And hid intent to murdren him,

---

12 **writ** i.e. Holy Writ, the truth of the gospel
he speken can that he (Pericles) speaks.
Grant White's emendation of Q's 'spoken'
restores a 'medievalism' comparable to
those at ll. 20, 24, 28, 35, and 36.

13 **remember** commemorate

14 **make him glorious** glorify his deeds

15 **to the contrary** adverse

16.1 *Dumb show* Mime, associated with earlier, and particularly medieval, drama,
though also used extensively in *The Travels
of the Three English Brothers* (1607), of
which Wilkins was part-author.

16.1–2 *at one door, at another door* The
two doors set in the back wall of the
Elizabethan and Jacobean stage.

16.2 *train* attendants

16.4 Q says that at this point Pericles knights
the messenger. It seems an excessive
reward for bringing at best dubious news,
and was probably confused with the
dumb show at Sc. 10.14.4, where a messenger brings the obviously good news
that Antiochus is dead and that it is safe
for Pericles to return to his kingdom, for
which a knighthood seems a reasonable
reward. This edition therefore transfers
the knighting to the later scene.

17–18 **home / drone** The assonance is typical
of Wilkins.

18–19 **to eat ... labours** A very common
proverbial image (Dent D612.1); the belief
that the drone (male bee) eats the honey
of the hive is from folklore rather than
natural history.

19 **for that** in that, because

20 **killen** kill. An archaism, derived from OE
and ME (Abbott 332; *OED, kill, v.*). The *-en*
form, derived from the form of verbs
in Midlands English, also occurs at ll.
12 ('speken'), 24 ('murdren'), and 35
('perishen').

23 **bent with** determined upon

24 **hid intent** This is Q's original reading, but
after some copies were printed, *hid* was
changed to 'had'. Both make sense: *hid
intent* means 'concealed purpose'; 'had
intent' was what Thaliart came to do.
murdren Q's original reading was 'murdred', the corrected version (see the previous note) 'murder'; Maxwell suggests
that 'murdred' was a misreading of an
archaic 'murdren' (hence the present
reading), comparable with 'killen' (l. 20)
and 'perishen' (l. 35).

And that in Tarsus was not best 25
Longer for him to make his rest.
He deeming so put forth to seas,
Where when men been there's seldom ease,
For now the wind begins to blow;
Thunder above and deeps below 30
Makes such unquiet that the ship
Should house him safe is wrecked and split,
And he, good prince, having all lost,
By waves from coast to coast is tossed.
All perishen of man, of pelf, 35
Ne aught escapend but himself,
Till fortune, tired with doing bad,
Threw him ashore to give him glad.
⌈*Enter Pericles wet*⌉
And here he comes. What shall be next
Pardon old Gower; this 'longs the text. *Exit* 40
⌈*Thunder and lightning*⌉

26 **make his rest** stay
27 **deeming so** i.e. thinking that Helicanus was right
28 **been** are (an archaic form: *OED*, *be*, *v*. 1h)
30–1 **deeps ... Makes** See the note to Sc. 1.115–16.
31–2 **the ship | Should** the ship that should. The omitted 'that' and the assonantal rhyme *ship/split* are by now familiar Wilkins trademarks.
35 **perishen** perished. See the note to l. 20.
    pelf possessions
36 **Ne aught escapend** nothing escaping. 'In OE and often still in ME, present participles ended in *ende*' (Hoeniger), but perhaps *escapend* should be emended to *escapen* (= escaped) to match the other archaisms at ll. 20, 24, 28, and 35.
38 **glad** gladness, happiness
38.1 **Enter Pericles wet** In all the sources for this scene (Gower, Twine, and Sidney's *Arcadia*), the hero is naked, the better to swim to safety. Sidney emphasizes the beauty of the hero's naked body: 'though he were naked, nakedness was to him an apparel' (1.1; p. 64); compare the Master Fisherman's appreciative 'a handsome fellow!' (ll. 120–1) as he wraps Pericles in his own gown. As Oxford says, 'complete

nudity is unlikely on the Jacobean stage' (*TC*, p. 565); at *History of Lear* Sc. 11 (3.4).58–9, Edgar 'reserved a blanket, else we had been all shamed'. But in modern performance, the more naked Pericles is the better, since, as with Lear, this emphasizes his destitute state.
39–40 **What ... text** 'Don't expect old Gower to tell you what happens next; that belongs to the main action of the play.' These lines emphasize the fluid way in which Gower's choruses and the acted scenes interweave; compare Sc. 1.40 and note. For this reason, Pericles' entrance is moved to before these lines (see *And here he comes*) rather than after them, as in Q.
40.1 **Thunder and lightning** In the Jacobean theatre, thunder 'could be imitated either by the battering of drums or by the rolling of stones or cannonballs down a thunder run. ... The call for lightning would make its customary demands upon the theatre's pyrotechnics experts' (Stanley Wells, 'Staging Shakespeare's Apparitions and Dream Visions', the first Globe Theatre lecture, Globe Education (1990), 5–6).

PERICLES

Yet cease your ire, you angry stars of heaven!
Wind, rain, and thunder, remember earthly man
Is but a substance that must yield to you,
And I, as fits my nature, do obey you.
Alas, the seas hath cast me on the rocks,   45
Washed me from shore to shore, and left my breath
Nothing to think on but ensuing death.
Let it suffice the greatness of your powers
To have bereft a prince of all his fortunes,
And having thrown him from your watery grave,   50
Here to have death in peace is all he'll crave.

Enter two Fishermen: one the Master, the other his
man

MASTER ⌈*calling*⌉ What ho, Pilch!

SECOND FISHERMAN ⌈*calling*⌉ Ha, come and bring away the
nets.

MASTER ⌈*calling*⌉ What, Patchbreech, I say!   55

⌈*Enter a Third Fisherman with nets to dry and repair*⌉

THIRD FISHERMAN What say you, master?

MASTER Look how thou stirr'st now. Come away, or I'll
fetch thee with a wanion.

THIRD FISHERMAN Faith, master, I am thinking of the poor
men that were cast away before us even now.   60

41–204 The verse spoken by Pericles alter-
nates with the prose spoken by the fishermen. The verse seems of better quality
than in Sc. 4, but it may simply be better
reported—perhaps because one or more
of the fishermen made the report (see
Introduction, p. 79).

51.1 Q simply says '*Enter three fishermen*', but
Wilkins's narrative differentiates between
'the master fisherman' (p. 507) and the
other two; hence the speech prefixes in
this edition.

52, 55 **Pilch, Patchbreech** Both the Master
and the Second Fisherman seem to be
calling to the same person, who answers
at l. 56; so *Pilch* and *Patchbreech* cannot be
the names of the Second and Third Fishermen, but must be nicknames for the
Third, alluding to his clothes. *Pilch* means
'a leathern or coarse woollen outer garment' (*OED sb.* 1), *Patchbreech* 'patched
trousers'. The names were suggested by

Twine's description of the (single) fisherman, who had 'a filthy leathern pelt upon
his back' (p. 434). Oxford incorporates
this into the stage direction at l. 55.1.

53 **bring away** bring here

55.1 **with nets to dry and repair**—which had
been damaged in the storm, as Wilkins's
narrative makes clear: the fishermen
'had also suffered in the former tempest,
and . . . were come out from their homely
cottages to dry and repair their nets'.
They were 'busied about their work' during the subsequent scene with Pericles
(p. 506).

57 **how . . . now** how slowly you're moving,
i.e. get on with it
Come away hurry up

58 **fetch** beat (*OED v.* 8a)
with a wanion with a vengeance (a colloquial oath)

60 **before us** before our very eyes

MASTER Alas poor souls, it grieved my heart to hear what
    pitiful cries they made to us to help them when, welladay,
    we could scarce help ourselves.

THIRD FISHERMAN Nay master, said not I as much when I
    saw the porpoise how he bounced and tumbled? They say   65
    they're half fish, half flesh. A plague on them, they ne'er
    come but I look to be washed. Master, I marvel how the
    fishes live in the sea.

MASTER Why, as men do a-land: the great ones eat up the
    little ones. I can compare our rich misers to nothing so   70
    fitly as to a whale: a plays and tumbles, driving the poor
    fry before him, and at last devours them all at a mouthful.
    Such whales have I heard on o'th' land, who never leave
    gaping till they swallowed the whole parish: church,
    steeple, bells, and all.   75

PERICLES (*aside*) A pretty moral.

THIRD FISHERMAN But master, if I had been the sexton, I
    would have been that day in the belfry.

MASTER Why, man?

THIRD FISHERMAN Because he should have swallowed me   80
    too, and when I had been in his belly I would have kept
    such a jangling of the bells that he should never have left

---

62 **welladay** alas

65 **the porpoise . . . tumbled** (proverbially
    regarded as anticipating a storm; Dent
    P483)

67 **washed** soaked (by a storm)

69 **as men do a-land** The phrase occurs in
    Wilkins's share of *The Travels of the Three
    English Brothers* (Sc. vi.27).
    a-land on the land

69–70 **the great . . . little ones** Proverbial—
    'The great fish eat the small' (Dent
    F311)—also used in John Day's *Law Tricks*
    (?1604; published 1608), Malone Society
    Reprint (1950), ll. 275–8, and in Middle-
    ton and Dekker's *The Roaring Girl* (1611)
    3.3.140–2.

71 **fitly** aptly
    a he. *OED*, *he, pers. pron.* says that collo-
    quial 'tonelessness' produced *a*, which
    'long prevailed in representations of
    familiar speech, as in the dramatists'.

72 **fry** small fish

73 **on** of. *On* and *of* were often used inter-
    changeably in the period (Abbott 175).

73–4 **leave gaping** close their mouths

74–5 **swallowed . . . all** Also occurs in John
    Day's *Law Tricks* (see note to ll. 69–70), ll.
    584–6. See p. 62, note 1.

76 **pretty** neat
    moral 'story or device conveying a moral
    lesson' (Maxwell)

77 **sexton** church officer in charge of
    bell-ringing

78 **belfry** bell tower of a church

79 **MASTER** Q's speech-prefix '2.' (i.e. the Sec-
    ond Fisherman) must be wrong, since the
    Third is talking to his 'master', who is the
    First Fisherman. There seems to be gener-
    al muddle over the speech-prefixes here,
    since what is obviously the Third Fisher-
    man's reply is given to '1.', both in the
    catchword and in the prefix itself. This slip
    is likely to be the compositor's, especially
    if, as suggested in the Introduction (p. 79),
    two of the Fishermen were played by the
    actors who reported the text for Q.

till he cast bells, steeple, church, and parish up again. But
if the good King Simonides were of my mind—

PERICLES (*aside*) Simonides?   85

THIRD FISHERMAN We would purge the land of these drones
that rob the bee of her honey.

PERICLES (*aside*)

How from the finny subject of the sea
These fishers tell the infirmities of men,
And from their watery empire recollect   90
All that may men approve or men detect!
⌈*Coming forward*⌉ Peace be at your labour, honest
    fishermen.

SECOND FISHERMAN 'Honest', good fellow, what's that? If it
be a day fits you, scratch't out of the calendar, and
nobody look after it.   95

PERICLES

May see the sea hath cast upon your coast—

SECOND FISHERMAN What a drunken knave was the sea to
cast thee in our way!

---

83 **cast** threw up, vomited. Perhaps alluding
to the biblical story of Jonah and the
whale: 'Jonah was in the belly of the fish'
(Jonah 1: 17), but 'it cast out Jonah upon
the dry land' (Jonah 2: 10).

84 **King Simonides** See the note to Sc. 6.0.1.

86–7 **drones . . . honey** See the note to ll.
18–19.

88 **finny subject** fin-bearing subjects (of a
state), i.e. fishes; *subject* is probably a col-
lective singular, but Wilkins's narrative
has 'finny subjects' (p. 506), which may
be correct.

90 **recollect** collect, gather (*OED v.*[1] 1) information (that will enable them to draw
conclusions about)

91 **All . . . detect** everything that may commend men or criticize them
detect expose (in wrong-doing)

92 **honest** Probably less a condescending
comment on their integrity than a conventional greeting, as at *Dream* 3.1.176:
'Your name, honest gentleman?' This
greeting then becomes the starting-point
for the Second Fisherman's facetious jok-
ing that follows. See the next note.

93–5 **If . . . it** Obscure. The stumbling-block
is *day*, which has led some editors to suspect that the word must have occurred in
Pericles' greeting (e.g. 'Peace be at your
labour, honest fishermen, and good time
of day') for the Second Fisherman to pick
up. Then it might mean, as M. R. Ridley
suggests, 'if the day is one that fits the
poor bedraggled creature you are, away
with it from the calendar and no one will
miss it'. The antagonistic tone, sustained
in the Second Fisherman's next speech,
may suggest that *he* at any rate (see the
previous note) thinks that Pericles' use of
'honest' is condescending.

96 **May** you may. A common ellipsis in the
period (Abbott 399).
see . . . sea A characteristic Wilkinsian
jingle: compare 'meaning / mean' (Sc.
1.186), 'honour him / dishonour him'
(Sc. 2.20–1).

96, 98 **cast** Either 'vomit', like the whale of l.
83, or just 'throw up', like the mole of Sc.
1.143.

PERICLES

    A man whom both the waters and the wind

    In that vast tennis-court hath made the ball   100

    For them to play upon, entreats you pity him.

    He asks of you that never used to beg.

MASTER No, friend, cannot you beg? Here's them in our

    country of Greece gets more with begging than we can

    do with working.   105

SECOND FISHERMAN Canst thou catch any fishes, then?

PERICLES I never practised it.

SECOND FISHERMAN Nay then, thou wilt starve, sure; for

    here's nothing to be got nowadays unless thou canst fish

    for't.   110

PERICLES

    What I have been, I have forgot to know,

    But what I am, want teaches me to think on:

    A man thronged up with cold, my veins are chill,

    And have no more of life than may suffice

    To give my tongue that heat to ask your help,   115

    Which if you shall refuse, when I am dead,

    For that I am a man, pray see me burièd.

        ⌈*He falls down*⌉

MASTER 'Die', quotha? Now, gods forbid't an I have a gown

    here! ⌈*To Pericles, lifting him up from the ground*⌉ Come

    put it on, keep thee warm. Now afore me, a handsome   120

    fellow! Come, thou shalt go home, and we'll have flesh for

---

99–101 **A man . . . play upon** This is a common metaphor to express the helplessness
of man, but Wilkins probably derived it
from *Arcadia* 5.5: men 'are but like tennis
balls, tossed by the racket of the higher
powers' (p. 817). If so, he made good use
of it, since Pericles' image of himself as a
tennis-ball bounced about the *vast tennis-
court* of the sea is an effective one.

102 **never used** has not been accustomed

104 **Greece** Pentapolis is in fact 'a country of
Africa consisting of five cities' (Steevens),
though the dramatist clearly imagines
that it is in Greece.

109–10 **fish** for get by corrupt means (as well
as the more obvious meaning)

113 **thronged up** overwhelmed, numbed

117, 167 **For that** because

118 **quotha** indeed (literally 'says he')
    an if, so long as
    gown Perhaps specifically, as Maxwell
    suggests, a sea-gown, defined by Cotgrave
    in 1611 as 'a coarse, high-collared and
    short-sleeved gown, reaching down to the
    mid-leg'. If so, the Master Fisherman is
    better dressed than the third one is (see
    the note to ll. 52, 55).

119 **lifting . . . ground** This detail is from
Wilkins's narrative, p. 507.

120 **afore me** on my word (a mild oath)

121–2 **flesh, fish** Meat was eaten on cele-
bratory church holidays, unlike the
fish eaten on penitential church fast-
days.

holidays, fish for fasting-days, and moreo'er puddings
and flapjacks, and thou shalt be welcome.

PERICLES I thank you, sir.

SECOND FISHERMAN Hark you my friend, you said you could   125
not beg?

PERICLES I did but crave.

SECOND FISHERMAN But crave? Then I'll turn craver too, and
so I shall scape whipping.

PERICLES Why, are all your beggars whipped, then?   130

SECOND FISHERMAN O not all, my friend, not all; for if all
your beggars were whipped I would wish no better office
than to be beadle. But master, I'll go draw up the other
nets.   *Exit with Third Fisherman*

PERICLES (*aside*)

How well this honest mirth becomes their labour!   135

MASTER Hark you sir, do you know where ye are?

PERICLES Not well.

MASTER Why, I'll tell you. This is called Pentapolis, and our
king the good Simonides.

PERICLES 'The good Simonides' do you call him?   140

MASTER Ay sir, and he deserves so to be called for his
peaceable reign and good government.

PERICLES

He is a happy king, since from his subjects

---

122 **puddings** large sausages (as in modern 'black pudding')

123 **flapjacks** pancakes

125, 136, 186 **Hark you** pay attention

126–8 **beg, crave** This ironical exchange depends upon using different words to describe the same thing, as the Fisherman emphasizes by saying that if he *turns craver* he will escape whipping, the standard Elizabethan punishment for beggars, on a verbal technicality. The effectiveness of the exchange surely doesn't depend upon Pericles having *actually* used the word *crave*, as Oxford implies by changing Q's 'ask' to 'crave' at l. 115.

130–2 **your, your** Pericles uses *your* in the sense of 'those in your country'; the Fisherman uses the colloquial idiom, virtually 'the' (*OED* 5b, citing e.g. *Hamlet* 5.1.166–7: 'your water is a sore decayer of your whoreson dead body').

131–3 **if all . . . beadle** Beadles were minor parish officials, often assigned to inflict corporal punishment; the Fisherman would like the job since if all the beggars were whipped, he would be kept busy and so presumably earn more money.

133–4 **But master . . . nets** Oxford has the Master interrupt here—'Thine office, knave'—to motivate the next line, but it is enough for the Second Fisherman to realize that he is rambling: it is as if he is saying 'I know, I know!' before he leaves to get on with his job.

other nets This is from Wilkins's prose narrative (p. 507); unlike Q's 'the net', it usefully makes clear that not all the nets were damaged in the storm and needed repairing: some are still being used, and Pericles' armour is caught in one of them (ll. 155–8).

135 **becomes** befits, suits

He gains the name of good by his government.
How far is his court distant from this shore?   145
MASTER Marry sir, half a day's journey. And I'll tell you, he
    hath a fair daughter, and tomorrow is her birthday, and
    there are princes and knights come from all parts of the
    world to joust and tourney for her love.
PERICLES
Were but my fortunes answerable   150
To my desires I could wish to make one there.
MASTER O sir, things must be as they may, and what a man
    cannot get himself, he may lawfully deal for with his
    wife's soul.
        Enter the other two Fishermen drawing up a net
SECOND FISHERMAN Help, master, help! Here's a fish hangs   155
    in the net like a poor man's right in the law; 'twill hardly
    come out. Ha, bots on't, 'tis come at last, and 'tis turned
    to a rusty armour.
PERICLES
An armour, friends? I pray you let me see it.
Thanks fortune, yet that after all thy crosses   160
Thou giv'st me somewhat to repair my losses,
And though it was mine own, part of my heritage
Which my dead father did bequeath to me
With this strict charge even as he left his life:
'Keep it, my Pericles; it hath been a shield   165

---

146 **Marry** (a mild oath, originally 'by the
    Virgin Mary')
148–9 **there are . . . her love** The situation at
    Pentapolis is initially set up as a parallel to
    that at Antioch, where 'many princes'
    come to win the princess (Sc. 1.32–4). It is
    not specifically stated that Thaisa is to be
    the prize for the victor of the tournament,
    though that is surely suggested by *tourney
    for her love* and, later, 'wilt thou tourney
    for the lady?' (l. 183).
150 **answerable** equivalent. *TC* points out
    that Wilkins's 'answerable' is a more
    apt, less common word than Q's 'equal':
    '*answerable* occurs only three times in
    Shakespeare; *equal* fifty seven times' (p.
    566).
151 **make one** participate in the tournament
152 **things . . . may** A rueful acceptance of
    what is inevitable, the sentiment was

proverbial: 'Men must do as they may
(can), not as they would' (Dent M554).
152–4 **what . . . soul** if a man cannot earn
    money himself, he may do so by arrang-
    ing to prostitute his wife, at the cost of her
    soul. Oxford inserts *himself* and *with* to
    make the sense clearer.
153 **lawfully** Evidently ironic in tone,
    and possibly a specific reference to the
    doctrines of a religious sect satirized in
    The Family of Love (1607) attributed to
    Middleton, but probably by Lording Barry
    (see Jackson, p. 116).
156 **like . . . law** i.e. it will never be resolved
    (hence the next phrase)
157 **bots on't** a plague upon it. *Bots* was a dis-
    ease of horses.
158, 159 **armour** i.e. suit of armour
160 **crosses** misfortunes

'Twixt me and death', and pointed to this brace,
'For that it saved me, keep it. In like necessity,
The which the gods forfend, the same may defend thee.'
It kept where I kept, I so dearly loved it,
Till the rough seas that spares not any man   170
Took it in rage, though calmed have given't again.
I thank thee for't. My shipwreck now's no ill,
Since I have here my father gave in's will.
MASTER What mean you, sir?
PERICLES
    To beg of you, kind friends, this coat of worth,   175
    For it was sometime target to a king.
    I know it by this mark. He loved me dearly,
    And for his sake I wish the having of it,
    And that you'd guide me to your sovereign's court,
    Where with it I may appear a gentleman.   180
    And if that ever my low fortune's better,
    I'll pay your bounties, till then rest your debtor.
MASTER Why, wilt thou tourney for the lady?
PERICLES
    I'll show the virtue I have learned in arms.
MASTER Why, d'ye take it, and the gods give thee good on't. 185

---

166 **brace** Literally a mailed protection, cov-
    ering the arm, it hardly seems enough to
    save Pericles' father from death, which is
    presumably why Onions suggests that it
    may mean 'coat of armour', the part
    standing for the whole.
168 **forfend** avert, prevent. Q reads *protect
    thee*, but Oxford's emendation, as well as
    making better grammatical sense, pro-
    duces a jingle—*forfend/defend*—typical of
    Wilkins, following his characteristic 'The
    which'.
169 **kept** remained
171 **calmed have** A condensed phrase: 'now
    that the seas have become calmed again,
    they have . . .'.
172 **now's** now is
173 **my father** what my father
    in's in his

175 **coat of worth** The armour will be *of
    worth* because it acts as a protection for
    him.
176 **sometime** once
    target Literally 'light shield', hence 'pro-
    tection'.
182 **pay your bounties** repay your acts of
    generosity
184 **virtue . . . arms** the knightly skill that I
    have learned. *Learned* is Oxford's emenda-
    tion, from Wilkins's prose version, which
    paraphrases Q except for that one word:
    'he would show the virtue he had learned
    in arms' (p. 508). Q reads 'borne' which
    may be correct, but might equally be the
    reporter drawing upon the familiar
    phrase 'bearing arms' (*OED, bear, v.*[1] *str.*
    6a).
185 **on't** of it, from it

SECOND FISHERMAN Ay, but hark you, my friend, 'twas we
    that made up this garment through the rough seams of
    the waters. There are certain condolements, certain
    vails. I hope sir, if you thrive, you'll remember from
    whence you had this.   190
PERICLES Believe't, I will.
    By your furtherance I am clothed in steel,
    And spite of all the rapture of the sea
    This jewel holds his building on my arm.
    Unto thy value I will mount myself   195
    Upon a courser whose delightsome steps
    Shall make the gazer joy to see him tread.
    Only, my friend, I yet am unprovided
    Of a pair of bases.
SECOND FISHERMAN We'll sure provide. Thou shalt have my   200
    best gown to make thee a pair, and I'll bring thee to the
    court myself.
PERICLES
    Then honour be but equal to my will,
    This day I'll rise, or else add ill to ill.   *Exeunt*

186–90 **'twas . . . this** Running through this
speech is a metaphor from tailoring. The
armour is seen as a *garment*, its *seams* created by their pulling it out of the sea. *Vails*
are tailors' 'remnants', pieces of material
left over after making a garment (*OED sb.*[1]
6).

188 **condolements** Since this means 'an
expression of grief or sympathy', it is
probably intended as a malapropism on
the Second Fisherman's part, perhaps
confused with 'dole', meaning share or
portion. This word is mocked as an affectation in Dekker's *Patient Grissel* 2.1.97–
8: 'the magnitude of my condolement
hath been elevated the higher' (*Works*, ed.
F. Bowers, 4 vols., i. (Cambridge,1953)).
The Second Fisherman has been characterized as one who aspires to verbal wit:
see the note to ll. 126–8; here he seems to
have over-reached himself.

189 **vails** tips, gratuities (*OED sb.*[1] 4), as well
as the meaning glossed in the note to ll.
186–90.

192 **furtherance** assistance

193 **rapture** violent seizure. Wilkins's narrative (see the next note) confirms that Q's

'rupture' is an error.

194–6 **This jewel . . . courser** Pericles appears to be saying that he still has a valuable jewel (a bracelet?) on his arm, with
which he will buy a horse. It seems very
awkward that two valuable items worn
on the arm (the jewel and the brace of l.
166) have both survived the storm, and
one might suspect textual muddle did
Wilkins's narrative not confirm Q: 'which
horse he provided [bought] with a jewel,
whom all the raptures of the sea could not
bereave from his arm' (p. 508).

194 **building** place

195 **Unto thy value** He addresses the jewel:
he will sell it and buy a horse.

196 **courser** 'A large, powerful horse ridden
in . . . a tournament' (*OED sb.*[2] 1).

199 **pair of bases** A kind of skirt, split in two,
worn with armour.

200–2 If Q is correct in giving this speech to
the Second Fisherman, he has been
converted from his earlier antagonism
towards Pericles to complete support for
him; but the tone sounds more like the
helpful Master Fisherman (compare ll.
118–23).

Sc. 6 ⌈*Flourish.*⌉ *Enter King Simonides and Thaisa, with*
Lords in attendance, ⌈*and sit on two thrones*⌉

SIMONIDES

Are the knights ready to begin the triumph?

FIRST LORD

They are, my liege,

And stay your coming to present themselves.

SIMONIDES

Return them we are ready; and our daughter,

In honour of whose birth these triumphs are,   5

Sits here like beauty's child, whom nature gat

For men to see, and seeing, wonder at.   ⌈*Exit one*⌉

THAISA

It pleaseth you, my royal father, to express

My commendations great, whose merit's less.

SIMONIDES

It's fit it should be so, for princes are   10

A model which heaven makes like to itself.

As jewels lose their glory if neglected,

Sc. 6.0.1 *Simonides* This name for the King is unique to the play (in *Confessio Amantis* Gower calls him Artestrates), and probably comes from North's translation of Plutarch's *Lives*, where he is a Greek poet of the sixth century BC. The stress falls on the first and fourth syllables.

Thaisa This is Gower's name for Marina in *Confessio Amantis*; he does not give the equivalent of Thaisa a name at all, but Twine calls her Lucina, an alternative name for Diana in her capacity as goddess of childbirth (see the note to Sc. 1.51); so the link between the character and the goddess, so important in the play, also existed before it.

0.2 *and sit on two thrones* This edition is usually reluctant to impose a specific mode of staging on the text itself, but Oxford's stage direction is adopted here because placing Simonides and Thaisa at stage level facilitates an exit at the end of the scene which allows the possibility of an onstage tournament (see the note to ll. 61–2). If the tournament is offstage, C. J. Sisson's treatment is preferable, placing Simonides and Thaisa on the upper level,

which 'represents a pavilion or gallery for the King and his Court [mentioned by Wilkins, p. 508]. The lists are behind the stage, unseen. The gallery looks out one way upon the Knights passing over the main stage, and the other way to the lists' (*New Readings in Shakespeare*, 2 vols. (Cambridge, 1956), ii. 292).

1,5 **triumph** tournament. Usually associated with the knightly combats of the middle ages, tournaments survived into the seventeenth century. See Introduction, pp. 18–19.

3 **stay** await

4 **Return** answer
and and that
daughter Q's 'daughter here' was probably influenced by 'here' in l. 6.

6 **gat** got, conceived

8–9 **to express . . . great** to praise me greatly

11 **A model . . . itself** This alludes to the doctrine of the divine right of kings, whereby the king was considered God's representative on earth.

12 **As jewels . . . neglected** For the idea, compare the neglected wife Adriana in *The*

So princes their renown, if not respected.
'Tis now your honour, daughter, to entertain
The labour of each knight in his device.   15
THAISA
Which to preserve mine honour, I'll perform.
⌈*Flourish.*⌉ *The first knight passes by* ⌈*richly armed,*
and his page before him, bearing his device on his shield,
delivers it to the Lady Thaisa⌉
SIMONIDES
Who is the first that doth prefer himself?

Comedy of Errors who compares her state to 'the jewel best enamellèd' which 'Will lose her beauty'. She continues with the common phrase about gold being tested by being rubbed on a touchstone—'Yet the gold bides still | That others touch' (2.1.108–10)—which forms the basis of the fifth knight's emblem in this scene: 'gold that's by the touchstone tried' (l. 41).

14 **honour** honourable duty. Oxford adopts Steevens's conjecture 'office', but surely *honour* needs to be mentioned for Thaisa to refer back to it in l. 16 and to cue the witty play on preserving her honour in that line.

14–15 **entertain . . . his device** accept what each knight has worked so hard to present as his emblem

14 **entertain** accept, receive (*OED v.* 12)

15 **device** emblem (image painted on his shield)

16.1–60 The formal parade of the knights displaying their shields with painted 'impresas' or emblems, and explanatory mottoes, does not occur in earlier versions of the story. It may have been suggested by the involvement of Shakespeare's company, the King's Men, with the ritual surrounding Jacobean tournaments. On 31 March 1613, payments were made to Shakespeare for composing an 'impresa' for Lord Rutland's appearance at a tournament celebrating King James's Accession Day, 24 March 1613, and to Richard Burbage, leading actor of the King's Men and probably the original Pericles,

'for painting and making it' (Chambers, *William Shakespeare,* ii. 153). Perhaps, then, this episode is the work of Shakespeare (and Burbage?), which Wilkins reports in his prose narrative. If he had composed it, it would be hard to explain why he gets the knights in the wrong order and the emblems confused (assuming that Q gets them right). In other respects, however, he provides a fuller account of the scene, so this edition draws on his narrative to fill gaps in Q.

16.1–22 **The first knight . . . of** you The stage directions here are based on Wilkins's narrative. Since in a ritual scene like this the action is identical for the remaining knights, the initial stage directions are not repeated, but replaced with the abbreviation that each knight *passes by, as before.*

16.3 **delivers . . . Thaisa** The detail of Oxford's direction is taken from Wilkins's narrative, where each 'device' is 'by the knight's page delivered to the Lady, and from her presented to the King her father' (p. 509). Oxford's direction that Thaisa actually takes the shield and hands it to the King to comment on seems unbelievably clumsy (and if they are on the upper level, physically impossible). Surely Wilkins's 'delivered' implies that the page holds up the shield so that Thaisa can see it and then moves 'from her' to 'present' it to the King; this simple procedure would work wherever Simonides and Thaisa are placed on the stage, and keep the ritual on the move.

17 **prefer** present

THAISA

A knight of Sparta, my renownèd father,
And the device he bears upon his shield
Is a black Ethiope reaching at the sun.   20
The word, *Lux tua vita mihi.*
⌈*The page presents it to the King*⌉

SIMONIDES

He loves you well that holds his life of you.
⌈*Exit the page with the first knight.*⌉
⌈*Flourish.*⌉ *The second knight passes by, as before*
Who is the second that presents himself?

THAISA

A prince of Macedon, my royal father,
And the device he bears upon his shield   25
Is an armèd knight that's conquered by a lady:
The motto thus: *Piùe per dolcezza che per forza.*

SIMONIDES

You win him more by lenity than force.
⌈*Flourish.*⌉ *The third knight passes by, as before*
And what's the third?

THAISA   The third of Antioch,

And his device a wreath of chivalry: 30
The word, *Me pompae provexit apex.*

19–21 **the device ... *mihi*** H. Green shows
that all the devices except Pericles' own
either literally cite or allude to existing
emblems and mottoes familiar in the period (*Shakespeare and the Emblem Writers*
(1870), 156–86). Alan R. Young suggests
that Pericles' emblem and motto may
have been suggested by those on the
shields used in Elizabethan court jousts
and hung in a special gallery at Whitehall
('A Note on the Tournament Impresas in
Pericles', *SQ* 36 (1985), 453–6).

20 **Ethiope** (used loosely in the period
to describe a black African, as at *Two
Gentlemen* 2.6.25–6 where Silvia's beauty
'Shows Julia but a swarthy Ethiope')

21 **word** motto
Lux* ... *mihi your light is life to me
(Latin)

22 **holds ... of** receives his life from

27 ***Piùe* ... *forza*** Q reads: 'The motto thus in
Spanish. *Pue Per doleera kee per forsa*',
which, as Edwards tartly remarks, is
'not in Spanish or any other known
language' ('Problem', p. 27); the nonsensical 'in Spanish', which does not
occur in Wilkins's prose version, 'probably expresses no more than the reporter's
own confusion' (*TC*, p. 567), so it is
omitted here. The best way to make sense
of the motto is to render it in Italian, as
this edition does, following Hoeniger and
Oxford. It means 'more by gentleness
("lenity") than force', as Simonides
comments in the next line (from Wilkins's
prose version).

30 **wreath** chaplet or garland of oak or bay
leaves awarded as a mark of victory (*OED
sb.* 11)

31 ***Me* ... *apex*** the summit of glory has led
me on (Latin)

SIMONIDES

Desire of renown he doth devise,

The which hath drawn him to this enterprise.

⌈*Flourish.*⌉ *The fourth knight passes by, as before*

What is the fourth?

THAISA   A knight of Athens with

A burning torch that's turnèd upside down: 35

The word, *Qui me alit me extinguit.*

SIMONIDES

Which shows that beauty hath this power and will,

Which can as well inflame as it can kill.

⌈*Flourish.*⌉ *The fifth Knight passes by, as before*

And who the fifth?

THAISA   The fifth, a prince of Corinth,

Presents an hand environèd with clouds,   40

Holding out gold that's by the touchstone tried:

The motto thus: *Sic spectanda fides.*

SIMONIDES

So faith is to be looked into.

⌈*Flourish.*⌉ *The sixth knight, Pericles, in a rusty*
armour, who, having neither page to deliver his shield
nor shield to deliver, presents his device unto the Lady
Thaisa

And what's the sixth and last, the which the knight
himself

With such a graceful courtesy delivereth?   45

32–3 **Desire . . . enterprise** From Wilkins ('the desire of renown drew him to this enterprise' (p. 509)), expanded by Oxford to produce two verse lines.

32 **devise** 'represent by art' (*OED v.* 5d)

34 **of Athens** From Wilkins (where he is the fifth knight); Q does not identify the fourth knight.

35 **A burning . . . down** An emblem linked to the proverbial 'A torch turned downward is extinguished by its own wax' (Dent T443).

36 ***Qui . . . extinguit*** Who feeds me extinguishes me (Latin). Echoed by Shakespeare at Sonnet 73.12, 'Consumed with that which it was nourished by'.

39 **a prince of Corinth** From Wilkins, where 'he is the second knight, bearing the third knight's device', but 'Corinth is the only

location specified in [Wilkins] which remains for Q's fifth knight. Moreover, Corinth had a reputation for wealth . . . so the gold of the emblem is unusually appropriate' (*TC*, p. 567).

41 **touchstone** Black quartz against which gold is rubbed to test its purity. A proverbial test of fidelity—'As the touchstone tries gold, so gold tries men' (Dent T448)—as Simonides comments (from Wilkins).

42 *Sic spectanda fides* (translated by Simonides in the next line)

43.1–4 This direction is substantially from Wilkins, and as Pericles has no shield, his *device* must be an actual 'withered branch' (l. 47), with the motto tied on, as often in performance.

THAISA

He seems to be a stranger, but his present is
A withered branch that's only green at top.
The motto, *In hac spe vivo.*

SIMONIDES   'In that hope I live.'

From the dejected state wherein he is
He hopes by you his fortunes yet may flourish.   50

FIRST LORD

He had need mean better than his outward show
Can any way speak in his just commend,
For by his rusty outside he appears
To have practised more the whipstock than the lance.

SECOND LORD

He well may be a stranger, for he comes   55
Unto an honoured triumph strangely furnished.

THIRD LORD

And on set purpose let his armour rust
Until this day, to scour it in the dust.

SIMONIDES

Opinion's but a fool, that makes us scan
The outward habit for the inward man.   60
            ⌈*Flourish*⌉
But stay, the knights are coming. We will withdraw

---

46 **present** offering

48 **'In that hope I live.'** Wilkins's translation
of the motto here replaces Q's phrase 'A
pretty moral', which, as Oxford says, is a
suspiciously literal repeat of Pericles'
comment at Sc. 5.76.

51–2 **He . . . commend** his inner purpose had
better be nobler than anything his outward appearance can say in his favour

54 **practised . . . whipstock** used the handle
of a whip (i.e. he appears more like
someone driving a farm-cart than like a
knight)

55–6 **stranger, strangely** (playing upon the
meanings 'foreigner' and 'bizarrely')

56 **furnished** equipped

57 **on set purpose let** deliberately allowed

58 **scour . . . dust** Armour was rolled in sand
to prevent it from rusting.

59–60 **Opinion's . . . man** general opinion
superficially judges a man's inward
nature by his external appearance

59 **scan** examine, scrutinize

61–2 **We will . . . gallery** What does this
imply? If Simonides and Thaisa are
already on the upper level of the Jacobean
stage, then they must depart to watch the
tournament from some (offstage) *gallery*,
as editors usually assume. But if, as in
Oxford and this edition, they are seated
at ground floor level, they can exit and
reappear on the upper level, which leaves
open the possibility of their watching
onstage combat (as in most modern productions). For further discussion, see
Introduction, p. 39. If two thrones were
used earlier in the scene, they could simply have been moved into the 'discovery
space' at the back of the stage, and
brought out again for the banquet that
follows in Scene 7.

Into the gallery.
⌈*Exeunt Simonides and Thaisa to the gallery to watch*
the tournament.⌉
Great shouts and all cry 'The mean knight!'

Sc. 7 ⌈*A stately banquet is brought in.*⌉ *Enter King Simonides*
and Thaisa, ⌈*from above, meeting*⌉ *a Marshal*
⌈*conducting*⌉ *Pericles and the other Knights from tilting*

SIMONIDES
Knights,
To say you're welcome were superfluous.
To place upon the volume of your deeds
As in a title-page your worth in arms
Were more than you expect, or more than's fit,   5
Since every worth in show commends itself.
Prepare for mirth, for mirth becomes a feast.
You are princes, and my guests.
THAISA (*to Pericles*)   But you, my knight and guest,
To whom this wreath of victory I give,
And crown you king of this day's happiness.   10
PERICLES
'Tis more by fortune, lady, than my merit.
SIMONIDES
Call it by what you will, the day is yours,

62.3 *mean* poor, ill-equipped

Sc. 7.0.1–3 The banquet and the Marshal are
from Wilkins's prose account, but both
are required by Q's dialogue. If the staging suggested by this edition is followed
and Simonides and Thaisa have watched
onstage tilting from the gallery above,
they descend while their thrones are
brought forward and the banquet
brought on; they then greet the knights,
fresh *from tilting,* who are presented to
them by the Marshal. The proposed
staging has the merit of continuity and
simplicity.

1 **Knights** Oxford may be right to omit this
greeting on the grounds that it is 'extrametrical and superfluous: bad quartos
often translate stage action into dialogue'
(*TC*, p. 567). On the other hand, the vigorous monosyllable may help to call the
gathering to attention, and to launch a
tricky (and textually shaky) scene more

effectively.

2–6 **To say . . . itself** Simonides' tone is that
of the after-dinner speaker who praises
his guests' achievements by saying
there's no need to do so since they speak
for themselves.

3–4 **To place . . . arms** Their military
achievements are imagined as a book,
with an elaborate title-page advertising its
contents, as in most seventeenth-century
books (equivalent to modern publishers'
blurbs).

4 **title-page** This line antedates *OED*'s first
reference, which is to 1613.

6 **in show** in practice (by being shown in
action)

7 **becomes** suits

8 **you** you are. Thaisa singles out Pericles as
her particular guest, whereas Simonides
in the previous phrase welcomes
everyone.

And here I hope is none that envies it.
In framing artists art hath thus decreed,
To make some good, but others to exceed.   15
You are her laboured scholar. (*To Thaisa*) Come, queen
   o'th' feast—
For daughter, so you are—here take your place.
(*To Marshal*) Marshal the rest as they deserve their
   grace.

KNIGHTS

We are honoured much by good Simonides.

SIMONIDES

Your presence glads our days; honour we love,   20
For who hates honour hates the gods above.

MARSHAL (*to Pericles*) Sir, yonder is your place.

PERICLES   Some other is more fit.

FIRST KNIGHT

Contend not, sir, for we are gentlemen
Have neither in our hearts nor outward eyes
Envied the great, nor shall the low despise.   25

PERICLES

You are right courteous knights.

SIMONIDES   Sit, sir, sit.

⌈*The Marshal seats Pericles opposite the King and
Thaisa, but he eats nothing*⌉

(*Aside*) By Jove I wonder, that is king of gods,

---

14 **framing** shaping
   artists Oxford adopts Malone's conjectural emendation of Q's 'an artist'
   because 'the plural is not only more metrical, but better agrees with "some" and
   "others"' (*TC*, p. 567). This scene seems
   especially badly reported (and, perhaps,
   not very well written in the first place),
   and several rhythmically defective lines,
   like this one, benefit from emendation.

16 **laboured** one on whom *art* (l. 14) has
   taken particular pains
   queen o'th' feast Compare Perdita, who is
   'mistress o'th' feast' at *Winter's Tale*
   4.4.68.

18 **Marshal** organize, place at the table
   as . . . grace according to their merit

21 **who** whoever

22 **yonder . . . place** i.e. the place of honour
   opposite the King and Thaisa, as Wilkins's
   account makes clear (p. 510), hence Pericles' modest reply.

23 **Contend not** don't argue

24 **Have** who have

26.2 *eats nothing* This detail is from Twine
   (p. 436), but is appropriate to Pericles'
   melancholy state on which Simonides
   comments at l. 53.

27 **gods** As Oxford says of Q's 'thoughts',
   'this is not an obvious attribute for Jove,
   and suspiciously anticipates' the next
   line. If Simonides swears by Jupiter as
   'king of gods', his oath appropriately
   balances Thaisa's at l. 29: 'By Juno, that
   is queen of marriage', i.e. they both swear
   by the principal attribute of both deities.

These cates distaste me, he but thought upon.
THAISA (*aside*)

By Juno, that is queen of marriage,
I am amazed all viands that I eat   30
Do seem unsavoury, wishing him my meat.
(*To the King*) Sure he's a gallant gentleman.
SIMONIDES

He's but a country gentleman.
He's done no more than other knights have done.
He's broken a staff or so, so let it pass.   35
THAISA (*aside*)

To me he seems like diamond to glass.
PERICLES (*aside*)

Yon king's to me like to my father's picture,
Which tells me in what glory once he was—
Had princes sit like stars about his throne,
And he the sun for them to reverence.   40
None that beheld him but like lesser lights
Did vail their crowns to his supremacy;

28 **cates** delicacies
  distaste are unappetizing. As Maxwell
  says, Q's 'resist' 'has to be given an
  unparalleled sense', 'repel', as *OED v.* 4
  does. Collier's conjecture 'distaste',
  however, was frequent in the seventeenth
  century, as *OED* demonstrates.
  he but thought upon i.e. contemplating
  Pericles distracts him from eating
30–1 **I am . . . meat** The *eat/meat* rhyme and
  the defective rhythm in Q (see Appendix
  A, ll. 822–3) suggest that a phrase is missing, which Oxford's *I am amazed* supplies.
  It is suggested by Wilkins's narrative:
  'both King and daughter at one instant
  were so struck in love' (p. 510). Oxford
  adds that it 'seems dramatically appropriate that Thaisa herself should express
  some astonishment at so sudden an infat-
  uation' (*TC*, p. 568).
30 **viands** items of food
33 **but . . . gentleman**—with the dismissive
  implication 'only a country bumpkin'.
  Simonides begins the process of concealing his approval of Pericles, much developed in Scene 9, perhaps initially to
  discover what Thaisa's feelings are.
35 **staff** lance

36 **diamond** The line is regular if this word is
  three syllables.
  to compared to. For the idea, compare
  Marlowe, *Hero and Leander* 1.213–14: 'her
  you surpass | As much as sparkling dia-
  monds flaring glass.'
37–47 Pericles' soliloquy contains many of
  the hallmarks of Wilkins's style: his liking
  for *Yon* (l. 37), *Where now* (l. 43), and *The
  which* (l. 44); the omitted 'who' at l. 39;
  and the movement during the speech
  from blank verse to rhyming couplets, but
  with a single non-rhyming line inserted
  between them (l. 45). See the next note.
39–40 **Had . . . reverence** Wilkins is fond of
  using the stars surrounding the sun and
  moon as images of majestic power: compare Sc. 1.74, 80, and 116 (heaven's
  'countless eyes'), and his share of *The
  Travels of the Three English Brothers*, where
  the Persian empire is compared to 'The
  silver moon and those her countless eyes |
  That like so many servants wait on her'
  (Sc. ii.192–3).
42 **vail . . . supremacy** lower their crowns
  (i.e. bow) in submission to him. Compare
  Marlowe, *Tamburlaine*, Part One, 1.2.195:
  'vail to us as lords of all the lake.'

Where now his son's a glow-worm in the night,
The which hath fire in darkness, none in light;
Whereby I see that time's the king of men;   45
He's both their parent and he is their grave,
And gives them what he will, not what they crave.
SIMONIDES What, are you merry, knights?
⌈THE OTHER KNIGHTS⌉
Who can be other in this royal presence?
SIMONIDES
Here with a cup that's stored unto the brim,   50
As you do love, full to your mistress' lips,
We drink this health to you.
⌈THE OTHER KNIGHTS⌉   We thank your grace.
SIMONIDES
Yet pause a while. Yon knight doth sit too melancholy,
As if the entertainment in our court
Had not a show might countervail his worth.   55
Note it not you, Thaisa?
THAISA   What is't to me, my father?
SIMONIDES
O attend, my daughter: princes in this
Should live like gods above, who freely give
To everyone that come to honour them.
And princes not doing so are like to gnats   60
Which make a sound, but killed, are wondered at.
Therefore to make his entertain more sweet,
Here bear this standing-bowl of wine to him.

---

43 **Where** whereas
43–4 **glow-worm . . . light** i.e. a glow-worm
   that only has any light in the darkness,
   but pales completely in the light of day
45 **king of** ruler over. Perhaps *king* is used
   here in a similar sense to Sc. 1.56, i.e. as
   something ultimate.
51 **full** Oxford's emendation of Q's 'fill',
   which makes the phrase marginally less
   clumsy: the cup is *stored . . . full* to be
   drunk as a toast to each knight's mistress
   (Thaisa, to whom they are all suitors). For
   Oxford's interpretation of the phrase as
   an elaborate conceit (the cup is as full as
   they are of love), see *TC*, p. 568.

55 **might** that might
   countervail equal
60–1 **like to gnats . . . at** i.e. they make a
   sound but when you have killed them you
   are amazed at how small they are. A
   wretched couplet that might arouse suspicion about the reporting, though the
   assonantal rhyme *gnats/at* is typical of
   Wilkins.
62 **entertain** entertainment (as at Sc. 1.162,
   which supports this emendation of Q's
   'entrance')
63 **bear** Dover Wilson's conjectural emendation of Q's 'say we drink', cited in
   Maxwell, is supported by Wilkins's narra-

THAISA

  Alas, my father, it befits not me

  Unto a stranger knight to be so bold.   65

  He may my proffer take for an offence,

  Since men take women's gifts for impudence.

SIMONIDES

  How? Do as I bid you, or you'll move me else.

THAISA (*aside*)

  Now by the gods, he could not please me better.

SIMONIDES

  And further tell him we desire to know   70

  Of whence he is, his name and parentage.

    ⌈*Thaisa bears the cup to Pericles*⌉

THAISA

  The King my father, sir, has drunk to you,

  Wishing it so much blood unto your life.

PERICLES

  I thank both him and you, and pledge him freely.

THAISA

  And further he desires to know of you   75

  Of whence you are, your name and parentage.

PERICLES

  A gentleman of Tyre, my name Pericles,

---

tive: 'he made his daughter rise from her seat to bear it to him' (p. 510), and by the action of the scene; moreover, Simonides has already drunk to all the knights at l. 52.

  standing-bowl bowl with its own legs or base

66–7 **offence/impudence** A favourite Wilkins rhyme: see the quotation in the note to Sc. 1.29–30.

68 **move** anger

72–3 Between these lines, Q gives Pericles the phrase 'I thank him', which, as Maxwell observes, is 'a pointless interruption, perhaps due to the reporter', since Pericles repeats his thanks at l. 74; Thaisa's speech flows better uninterrupted.

73 **Wishing . . . life** It was popularly believed

that wine replenished the supply of blood.

77–84 **A gentleman . . . shore** It is dramatically very clumsy that Thaisa has immediately to report Pericles' words verbatim, or nearly. (In Wilkins's prose account, Thaisa has no speech at all.) Moreover, her speech in Q is notably irregular, suggesting misreporting. In my view, Oxford exacerbates the problem by *expanding* both speeches, and increasing the repetitions; so I have left Pericles' Q speech unemended, and, taking a hint from 'sour misfortune's book' (*Romeo* 5.3.82), have attempted to improve the rhythm of Thaisa's l. 83 (compare Appendix A, l. 877).

77 **A gentleman** Pericles conceals the fact that he is *King* of Tyre for reasons of self-

My education been in arts and arms,
Who looking for adventures in the world,
Was by the rough seas reft of ships and men,   80
And after shipwreck driven upon this shore.

THAISA

He thanks your grace, names himself Pericles,
A gentleman of Tyre, whom sour misfortune,
Bereft of ships and men, cast on this shore.

SIMONIDES

Now by the gods I pity his mishaps,   85
And will awake him from his melancholy.
Come gentlemen, we sit too long on trifles,
And waste the time which looks for other revels.
Even in your armours, as you are addressed,
Your limbs will well become a soldier's dance.   90
I will not have excuse with saying this,
'Loud music is too harsh for ladies' heads',
Since they love men in arms as well as beds.
            The Knights dance

---

protection, as Marina conceals her identity later in the play. It is a folklore tradition that revealing your identity places you in another person's power, and Pericles has good reason to be wary of foreign kings with attractive daughters.

78 **been** has been
    in arts and arms This is an important phrase for the interpretation of the Pentapolis sequence as a whole: Pericles claims that he has been trained as the Renaissance complete man, and during the Pentapolis scenes he shows his expertise as a warrior (Sc. 6), a dancer (Sc. 7), and a singer (Sc. 8a). For further discussion, see Introduction, pp. 40–1.

80 **reft** bereft, deprived

85 **mishaps** Q's 'misfortune' was probably caught from l. 83, and Wilkins has 'mishaps' (p. 510). It was 'normally strongly accented on the second syllable' (*TC*, p. 568), as here.

86–7 Between these lines Oxford inserts a seven-line speech, based on the verse-rhythms in Wilkins's narrative, in which Simonides tries to cheer Pericles up by presenting him with 'a goodly milk-white steed' and 'golden spurs' as a prize for

winning the tournament (p. 510). But unlike Oxford's other major inserts (e.g. Sc. 2.37–42), it is not actually *needed* because of a lacuna in the text, and has not been adopted by any production that has used the Oxford reconstruction. Simonides' wish to arouse Pericles from his melancholy leads naturally into the proposal of revelling and dancing, so Oxford's insert is not followed in this edition.

87 **sit** dwell (as if sitting in council)

89 **addressed** dressed

90 **Your limbs** (inserted by Oxford to complete the line)
    soldier's dance Probably a sword-dance, if it is performed by the knights alone. See the next notes.

92 **Loud music** Probably the clang of the knights' armour and (if the previous note is correct) their swords.
    ladies' heads This may imply that other *ladies* are present, and that they dance, but Simonides' phrase *ladies' heads* may be no more than a sexual *double-entendre* (= 'maidenheads'), of which there are several in the following lines.

93 **arms**   armour   (with   sexual *double-entendre*)

So this was well asked, 'twas so well performed.
Come, here's a lady that wants breathing too.   95
(*To Pericles*) And I have heard, sir, that the knights of
    Tyre
Are excellent in making ladies trip,
And that their measures are as excellent.

PERICLES

In those that practise them they are, my lord.

SIMONIDES

O that's as much as you would be denied   100
Of your fair courtesy.
    They dance
Unclasp, unclasp.
Thanks gentlemen, to all; all have done well,
(*To Pericles*) But you the best.—Lights, pages, to conduct
These knights unto their several lodgings.—Yours, sir,   105
We have given order should be next our own.

PERICLES I am at your grace's pleasure.

SIMONIDES

Princes, it is too late to talk of love,
And that's the mark I know you level at.

---

94 **So . . . asked** just as 'it was a happy inspiration on my part to ask it' (Maxwell)

95 **breathing** exercise

96 **sir** (moved by Oxford from the previous
line in Q, where it spoils the rhythm, to
this one, where it helps it)
the This emendation of Q's 'you' is
required for 'their' and 'those' in ll. 98–9;
TC conjectures a misreading or mis-
expansion of a manuscript 'y^e'.

97 **trip** (a) dance; (b) fall down (for sexual
intercourse)

98 **measures** dances (with a phallic pun:
Williams, p. 204)

100–1 **as much . . . courtesy** 'as much as to
say that you want to be prevented from
showing your courtly skill' (or perhaps
implying that he is refusing to dance out
of modesty)

101.1 ***They dance*** This terse phrase conceals
the fact that this is one of the central
events of the play in most performances.
Although Pericles and Thaisa have very
few lines in which to communicate their
dawning love (a problem exacerbated by

the impoverished text in this scene), they
can do so very effectively in what Oxford
calls 'a wordless ritual of courtship' (*TC*,
p. 558), through the traditional symbolism of the dance. See the Introduction,
pp. 23–4.

102 **Unclasp, unclasp** Q surely misplaces this
line before rather than after the dance.
The obvious point, as productions regularly demonstrate, is that Simonides
interrupts a dance in which Pericles
and Thaisa are becoming increasingly
engrossed in each other, and which is
becoming too intimate for his liking. If so,
the phrases before and after the dance
cannot be a complete verse line since it is
impossible to have a pentameter with a
dance in the middle of it: so this edition
treats them as two broken verse lines, of
which there are a large number in the first
half of the play, not necessarily attribut-
able to reporting.

105 **several** separate

109 **mark . . . you level at** target at which
you aim (an image from archery)

Therefore each one betake him to his rest; 110
Tomorrow all for speeding do their best.

Exeunt ⌈severally⌉

Sc. 8 *Enter Helicanus and Aeschines*

HELICANUS

No, Aeschines, know this of me:
Antiochus from incest lived not free,
For which the most high gods, not minding longer
To withhold the vengeance that they had in store
Due to this heinous capital offence, 5
Even in the height and pride of all his glory,
When he was seated in a chariot
Of an inestimable value, and
His daughter with him, both apparelled all in jewels,
A fire from heaven came and shrivelled up 10
Their bodies even to loathing, for they so stunk
That all those eyes adored them ere their fall
Scorn now their hands should give them burial.

AESCHINES

'Twas very strange.

HELICANUS   And yet but justice, for though
This king were great, his greatness was no guard 15
To bar heaven's shaft, but sin had his reward.

AESCHINES 'Tis very true.

Enter three Lords

---

111 **speeding** success (as wooers)

Sc. 8 This scene intrudes awkwardly into the Pentapolis sequence; for this reason it is often omitted entirely in modern performance. It is not missed: its information is repeated, more economically, in Gower's next chorus (Sc. 10.21–33); and Helicanus' opening speech, especially, is Wilkins at his most laborious, piling point upon point with little sense of dramatic shaping or climax, unless it has been very much mangled in the reporting.

3–13 The account of Antiochus seems to conflate that of two historical or biblical figures: Antiochus the Great himself, whose death by lightning is described in

Gower and Twine, and his son Antiochus IV who was riding in a chariot when he was struck down, and worms came out of his body, which 'no man could bear because of his stink' (2 Maccabees 9: 4–10).

3 **minding** intending

9 **both . . . jewels** Oxford inserts this phrase from Wilkins's narrative: it perhaps intensifies their self-glorious grandeur and so the extent of their fall.

12 **eyes** eyes that

16 **shaft** arrow
    his its

17.1 *three Lords* Q says '*two or three*', but there are speaking parts for three.

FIRST LORD

  See, not a man in private conference

  Or council has respect with him but he.

SECOND LORD

  It shall no longer grieve without reproof. 20

THIRD LORD

  And cursed be he that will not second it.

FIRST LORD

  Follow me, then.—Lord Helicane, a word.

HELICANUS

  With me? And welcome. Happy day, my lords.

FIRST LORD

  Know that our griefs are risen to the top,

  And now at length they overflow their banks. 25

HELICANUS

  Your griefs, for what? Wrong not your prince you love.

FIRST LORD

  Wrong not yourself then, noble Helicane,

  But if the prince do live, let us salute him

  Or know what ground's made happy by his step,

  And be resolved he lives to govern us, 30

  Or dead, give's cause to mourn his funeral

  And leave us to our free election.

SECOND LORD

  Whose death indeed's the strongest in our censure,

  And knowing this—kingdoms without a head,

  Like goodly buildings left without a roof, 35

  Soon fall to utter ruin—your noble self,

  That best know how to rule and how to reign,

  We thus submit unto as sovereign.

ALL ⌈*kneeling*⌉ Live, noble Helicane!

---

19 **respect** influence

20 **grieve** cause us grief

  reproof protest

24, 26 **griefs** grievances

28 **salute** greet

30 **resolved** reassured, persuaded

31 **give's** give us

33 **Whose . . . censure** the death of Pericles is the greatest likelihood, in our judgement

39 ***kneeling*** 'Some such referent seems desirable for Q's "thus"' in the previous line (*TC*, p. 569).

HELICANUS

By honour's cause, forbear your suffrages.   40
If that you love Prince Pericles, forbear.
⌈*The lords rise*⌉
Take I your wish I leap into the seas
Where's hourly trouble for a minute's ease,
But if I cannot win you to this love,
A twelvemonth longer then let me entreat you   45
Further to bear the absence of your king;
If in which time expired he not return,
I shall with agèd patience bear your yoke.
Go seek your noble prince like noble subjects,
And in your search spend your adventurous worth,   50
Whom if you find and win unto return,
You shall like diamonds sit about his crown.

FIRST LORD

To wisdom he's a fool that will not yield,
And since Lord Helicane enjoineth us,
We with our travels will endeavour us.   55
If in the world he live we'll seek him out;
If in his grave he rest, we'll find him there.

HELICANUS

Then you love us, we you, and we'll clasp hands.
When peers thus knit, a kingdom ever stands.   *Exeunt*

---

40 **By honour's cause** for the sake of honour
forbear your suffrages avoid electing (me)

42 **Take I** if I accept

44 **But . . . love** In Q this line comes after l.
48. Oxford comments that in its new position 'the line is a pivot between Helicanus'
outright rejection of their suffrages and
his compromise proposal of a postpone-
ment (during which Pericles will be
actively sought)' (*TC*, p. 569).

47 **not** does not

49 **seek your noble prince** Q's 'search like
nobles' makes poor metre and poor sense,
as Oxford comments (*TC*, p. 569), adopting an anonymous conjecture which at
least gives some sense and shape to the
line.

50 **spend . . . worth** exercise your worth as
adventurous knights

51 **Whom . . . return** and if you find Pericles
and persuade him to return

52 **like diamonds sit about his crown** The
image of the lords gathered like jewels
around their king's crown is, as Edwards
says, 'a mosaic of recollections' of Sc.
7.36 and 39, conflating Thaisa's 'diamonds' and Pericles' image of princes
gathered around a throne like stars
around the sun.

55 **endeavour us** attempt (to find Pericles)

56–7 In Q, these lines come much earlier,
between ll. 29 and 30, where they are
clearly misplaced, since the Lords then
anticipate advice that Helicanus has not
yet given. Here they follow naturally what
has gone before.

Sc. 8a *Enter Pericles and Gentlemen with lights*
FIRST GENTLEMAN
Here is your lodging, sir.
PERICLES   Pray leave me private.
Only for instant solace pleasure me
With some delightful instrument, with which,
And with my former practice, I intend
To pass away the tediousness of night,   5
Though slumbers were more fitting.
FIRST GENTLEMAN   Presently.
                    Exit First Gentleman

SECOND GENTLEMAN
Your will's obeyed in all things, for our master
Commanded you be disobeyed in nothing.
    Enter First Gentleman with a stringed instrument
PERICLES
I thank you. Now betake you to your pillows,
And to the nourishment of quiet sleep.   10
                    Exeunt Gentlemen

Sc. 8a This scene does not occur in Q, but is
wholly reconstructed from the verse
rhythms in Wilkins's prose narrative (see
Appendix B, Passage A). For a full discussion, see Introduction, pp. 40–1, where it
is suggested that by presenting Pericles as
expert warrior, dancer, and singer, he is
dramatized as the Renaissance universal
man, and that this helps to bind the
otherwise straggling Pentapolis sequence
together. This is even clearer if the
episode is placed before Sc. 8 rather
than after, where Wilkins places it. At
Stratford, Ontario in 1986, for example,
Pericles and the gentlemen ascended to
the balcony of the mock-Elizabethan
stage at the end of Sc. 7 and played
Oxford's reconstructed episode up there;
Pericles remained there while Sc. 8 was
played on the stage below, thus providing
a focus for its discussion about him, and
minimizing the clumsy intrusion of that
scene into the Pentapolis sequence. He
then descended to join Simonides at Sc.
9.19.1. This gave the Pentapolis sequence
ideal continuity and flow; but since this
edition's reconstruction is based on
Wilkins, I reluctantly follow Oxford's
example and use Wilkins's order.

0.1 *Gentlemen with lights* The gentlemen
are from Wilkins's account; at Sc. 7.104
Simonides calls for pages with lights, so
pages are a possible alternative. As Oxford
says, the lights 'usefully establish the continuity with the end of Sc. 7' (*TC*, p. 570),
a continuity that would be even better
established if this episode followed immediately after Sc. 7.
2–3 **pleasure me | With** allow me the plea-
sure of
4 **practice** exercise (of music) (*OED* 3)
6 **Presently** at once
8.1 *a stringed instrument* Wilkins's account
'refers to the "fingering" of the instrument, and Pericles sings while he plays (p.
513); in Twine it is a harp (p. 438)' (*TC*, p.
570). Perhaps it is a lute—at any rate, not
a bowed instrument.
9–10 **I thank ... sleep** In Wilkins, the other
knights 'betook themselves to their pillows, and to the nourishment of a quiet
sleep', on which Oxford draws: 'Some
formula of dismissal is needed; Pericles
is characteristically courteous; and the
lines emphasize, by contrast, his own
inability to sleep' (*TC*, p. 570).

Pericles plays and sings
Day—that hath still that sovereignty to draw back
The empire of the night, though for a while
In darkness she usurp—brings morning on.
I will go give his grace that salutation
Morning requires of me.   *Exit with instrument*   15

Sc. 9   *Enter King Simonides at one door reading of a letter,*
            the Knights enter ⌈at another door⌉ and meet him

FIRST KNIGHT
Good morrow to the good Simonides.

SIMONIDES
Knights, from my daughter this I let you know:
That for this twelvemonth she'll not undertake
A married life. Her reason to herself
Is only known, which from her none can get.   5

10.2 *Pericles plays and sings* Wilkins describes the beauty of Pericles' singing, but maddeningly provides no words for the song, as he does for Marina's at Sc. 21.68.2, usefully filling a lacuna in Q. Stratford, Ontario in 1986 used the first half of Marina's lyric for Marina herself, but the last eight lines for Pericles' song (see Appendix B, Passage D). These lines at least have some relevance to Pericles' situation, and using the same lyric had the merit of reinforcing the structural point that father and daughter sing at important moments in each half of the play.

11–15 **Day . . . me** Oxford takes these lines from the narration in Wilkins's account, since Pericles needs a motive to stop singing and to leave the stage.

11–13 **Day . . . usurp** Day and night are represented as rival monarchs: day has the *sovereignty* (power) to defeat and drive away night's usurping *darkness*.

14 **salutation** greeting

Sc. 9 The mainspring of this scene is Simonides' dissembling, opposing Pericles as a son-in-law while secretly approving him. But Wilkins's narrative expands his attack on Pericles in verse rhythms which many commentators have felt better represent what the original may have been like; more crucially from a dramatic

point of view, Wilkins provides Thaisa with an extended declaration of love for Pericles which she lacks in Q. Oxford's reconstruction, substantially followed here, incorporates this extra material. Oxford adjusts Q to accommodate the new material, and sometimes to improve the metre. See Appendixes A and B. Some of these alterations are discussed in the commentary, but for a full account see *TC*, pp. 570–1, and for a discussion of the advantages and disadvantages of this reconstructed episode, see Introduction, p. 41.

0.1 *reading of a letter* The apparently curious circumstance that Thaisa needs to communicate with Simonides by letter in the same house derives from Wilkins's condensing, in both play and narrative, a passage in both Gower and Twine where the King instructs the rival suitors: 'write your names every one severally in a piece of paper, and what jointure you will make, and I will send the writings to my daughter, that she may choose him whom she best liketh of' (Twine, p. 440); his daughter then replies in the same way. But see the note to l. 34.

5 **none can** Oxford's replacement of Q's 'by no means can I' restores the metre: Q's phrase anticipates 'by no means' in l. 7.

SECOND KNIGHT

May we not have access to her, my lord?

SIMONIDES

Faith, by no means. It is impossible,

She hath so strictly tied her to her chamber.

One twelve moons more she'll wear Diana's livery.

This by the eye of Cynthia hath she vowed,   10

And on her virgin honour will not break it.

THIRD KNIGHT

Loath to bid farewell, we take our leaves.

Exeunt Knights

SIMONIDES

So, they are well dispatched. Now to my daughter's
      letter.

She tells me here she'll wed the stranger knight,

Or never more to view nor day nor light.   15

I like that well. Nay, how absolute she's in't,

Not minding whether I dislike or no!

Mistress, 'tis well, I do commend your choice,

And will no longer have it be delayed.

      Enter Pericles

Soft, here he comes. I must dissemble that   20

In show, I have determined on in heart.

---

6 **have** Q's 'get' clumsily repeats l. 5; as
Maxwell says, 'have access' is the normal
idiom in both Shakespeare and Wilkins.
Access is stressed on the second syllable.

7–8 **It is . . . chamber** Q (see Appendix A, ll.
977–8) 'creates insoluble metrical and
lineation problems as it stands, easily
resolved by transposition of the floating
phrase " 'tis impossible" ' (*TC*, p. 570).

8 **tied her** confined herself

9 **One . . . more** another year; but the use
of *twelve moons* rather than the 'twelvemonth' of l. 3 leads naturally into the
reference to Diana, goddess of the moon.
  wear Diana's livery retain the clothes of
a servant of Diana, goddess of chastity
(i.e. remain a virgin)

10 **eye of Cynthia** *Cynthia* is another name
for Diana, so this presumably means the
moon, though elsewhere celestial eyes are
the stars (Sc. 1.116).

10–11 **hath . . . it** It is sometimes argued that

since Thaisa appears to make a vow of
chastity that she subsequently breaks, her
later misfortunes are Diana's punishment
for a broken vow; but surely this is merely
Simonides' invention to get rid of her
unwanted suitors.

15 **nor . . . nor** neither . . . nor. An emphatic
double negative, frequently used in the
period (Abbott 406).

15–16 Between these lines, Simonides says,
in Q: ''Tis well mistress, your choice
agrees with mine', omitted by Oxford
(and here) on the grounds that all its
elements are repeated elsewhere.

16 **absolute** positive, decisive

17 **minding** caring

20–1 **I must . . . heart** This phrase, from
Wilkins, expands and clarifies Q's cryptic
'I must dissemble it'.
  that | In show outwardly what

21 **determined** decided

PERICLES

All fortune to the good Simonides.

SIMONIDES

To you as much, sir. I am beholden to you

For your sweet music this last night. My ears,

I do protest, were never better fed   25

With such delightful pleasing harmony.

PERICLES

It is your grace's pleasure to commend,

Not my desert.

SIMONIDES   Sir, you are music's master.

PERICLES

The worst of all her scholars, my good lord.

SIMONIDES

Let me ask you one thing. What think you of my

daughter?   30

PERICLES

A most virtuous princess.

SIMONIDES   And she is fair, too, is she not?

PERICLES

As a fair day in summer: wondrous fair.

SIMONIDES

My daughter, sir, thinks very well of you;

So well indeed that you must be her master

And she will be your scholar; therefore look to it.   35

PERICLES

I am unworthy for her schoolmaster.

SIMONIDES

She thinks not so. Peruse this writing else.

He gives the letter to Pericles, who reads

PERICLES (*aside*)

What's here, a letter that she loves the knight of Tyre?

---

23 **beholden** indebted

32 **As . . . fair** Proverbial (Dent S966.1).

34 **master** schoolmaster. In the sources, he actually becomes her teacher for a time, but the play makes no further use of this. Frances Whistler suggests that Simonides' use of the letter may act as an echo of the riddle at Antioch; he pretends that it is about music teaching but then springs the letter's actual contents on him (leading to a nice double meaning in 'you must be her master'): this also explains why Pericles should instantly suspect a trap. See the note to l. 39.

35 **scholar** pupil

37 **else** (i.e. if you don't believe me)

'Tis the King's subtlety to have my life.
⌈*He prostrates himself at the King's feet*⌉
O seek not to entrap me, gracious lord,   40
A stranger and distressèd gentleman
That never aimed so high to love your daughter,
But bent all offices to honour her.
Never did thought of mine levy offence,
Nor never did my actions yet commence   45
A deed might gain her love or your displeasure.

SIMONIDES

Thou liest like a traitor.

PERICLES   Traitor?

SIMONIDES   Ay, traitor,
That thus disguised art stolen into my court
With witchcraft of thy actions to bewitch
The yielding spirit of my tender child.   50

PERICLES ⌈*rising*⌉

Who calls me traitor, unless it be the King,
Even in his bosom I will write the lie.

SIMONIDES (*aside*)

Now by the gods, I do applaud his courage.

PERICLES

My actions are as noble as my blood,
That never relished of a base descent.   55
I came unto your court in search of honour,

---

39 **'Tis . . . life** After his experiences with Antiochus, Pericles understandably judges Simonides by the same standards, a view that seems to be confirmed when Simonides turns on him.
subtlety cunning

39.1 **He . . . feet** From Wilkins's prose narrative (p. 515).

42 **to** as to (Abbott 281)

43 **bent all offices** devoted all my service

43–4 The three Q lines omitted between these two are repeated with greater power at ll. 47–50. See Appendix A, ll. 1019–21.

44 **levy** Probably used in the obsolete sense 'set up' (*OED v.* 3a), i.e. 'create'; but *OED v.* 7 gives two examples of the erroneous use of *levy* for 'level' (aim), from 1618 and 1634. This would sustain the archery imagery in ll. 42–3 ('aimed', 'bent'), but

not provide markedly clearer sense, so I retain Q.

46 **might** that might

51–2 **Who . . . lie** 'The transposition of the opening phrases of [Q's] two lines [Appendix A, ll. 1028–9] yields a much more intelligible and speakable sense' (*TC*, p. 571) and Wilkins's 'even in his bosom he would write the lie' is much more vivid than Q's 'Even in his throat . . . I return the lie'.

54 **blood** ancestry. Q's 'thoughts' does not lead properly into the next line.

55 **relished** showed a trace

56 **in search of honour** Wilkins's phrase is preferable, since Q's 'for honour's cause' echoes Sc. 8.40, and is probably a memorial substitution by the reporter.

And not to be a rebel to your state;
And he that otherwise accounts of me,
This sword shall prove he's honour's enemy.

SIMONIDES

I shall prove otherwise, since both your practice   60
And her consent therein is evident
There, by my daughter's hand, as she can witness.

        Enter Thaisa

PERICLES (*to Thaisa*)

Then as you are as virtuous as fair,
By what you hope of heaven or desire
By your best wishes here i'th' world fulfilled,   65
Resolve your angry father if my tongue
Did e'er solicit, or my hand subscribe
To any syllable made love to you.

THAISA Why, sir, say if you had,
Who takes offence at that would make me glad?   70

SIMONIDES

How, minion, are you so peremptory?
(*Aside*) I am glad on't.—Is this a fit match for you?
A straggling Theseus, born we know not where,
One that hath neither blood nor merit

---

57 **rebel to your state** Q's 'her state' (i.e.
honour's) makes sense, in which case the
phrase is metaphorical, but *your state*,
yielding a simple statement of fact, is supported by Wilkins's narrative: Pericles
'came into his court in search of honour,
and not to be a rebel to his state' (p. 515).

60–2 **I . . . witness** Q's 'here comes my
daughter, she can witness it' is a transparent echo of the cue for Desdemona's
first entry at *Othello* 1.3.169, 'Here comes
the lady. Let her witness it', suggesting
that the reporter is replacing the lines
from Wilkins's narrative with another
line he knew (see Introduction, p. 78).

60 **practice** deceit, treachery

62 **by . . . hand** written in her own handwriting
witness confirm

66 **Resolve** assure

68 **made** that made (which Q reads). The
omission of 'that' restores the metre, in a
style which is characteristic of the first
half of the play.

69–70 **Why . . . glad** Since *had* and *glad* are
an obvious rhyme, a phrase must be miss-

ing from l. 69. Wilkins's narrative is no
help here.

70 **that** what

71 **minion** impudent girl (more vivid than
Q's 'mistress')
peremptory self-willed

72, 100 *Aside* These two asides are marked in
Q; the others in the text are all editorial.

72–96 These lines are reconstructed from
Wilkins's narrative (see Appendix B, Passage B); they replace Q's 'with all my
heart' (Appendix A, l. 1046).

73 **A . . . where** Plutarch's Life of the Athenian hero Theseus, in North's translation,
was a source for *A Midsummer Night's
Dream*, and many commentators have
thought Shakespeare the author of this
vivid line, reported by Wilkins in his narrative; but Wilkins was capable of striking
lines, and we should beware of assuming
that *any* good line in the play is inevitably
by Shakespeare. But see the note to l.
89.
straggling wandering

74 **blood** aristocratic ancestry

For thee to hope for, or himself to challenge   75
Of thy perfections e'en the least allowance.
THAISA (*kneeling*)
    Suppose his birth were base, when that his life
    Shows that he is not so, yet he hath virtue,
    The very ground of all nobility,
    Enough to make him noble. I entreat you   80
    To remember that I am in love,
    The power of which love cannot be confined
    By the power of your will. Most royal father,
    What with my pen I have in secret written
    With my tongue now I openly confirm,   85
    Which is I have no life but in his love,
    Nor any being but in joying of his worth.
SIMONIDES
    Equals to equals, good to good is joined.
    This not being so, the bavin of your mind
    In rashness kindled must again be quenched,   90
    Or purchase our displeasure. And for you, sir,
    First learn to know I banish you my court,
    And yet I scorn our rage should stoop so low.
    For your ambition, sir, I'll have your life.
THAISA (*to Pericles*)
    For every drop of blood he sheds of yours   95
    He'll draw another from his only child.
SIMONIDES
    I'll tame you, yea, I'll bring you in subjection.
    Will you, not having my consent,
    Bestow your love and your affections
    Upon a stranger?—(*aside*) who for aught I know   100
    May be, nor can I think the contrary,
    As great in blood as I myself.

75–6 **himself . . . allowance** that would
    qualify him to claim even the slightest
    share of your perfections
77–87 These lines give Thaisa her only direct
    statement of her love for Pericles: they
    can have great impact in performance.
78–9 **virtue . . . nobility** Compare Marlowe's
    Tamburlaine, Part One, 5.1.188–90, where
    the base-born hero vows to show that 'for
    all my birth . . . virtue solely is the sum

of glory | And fashions men with true
    nobility'.
89 **bavin** blazing-up (i.e. her passionate dec-
    laration). *Bavin* is brushwood, and is also
    used figuratively at *1 Henry IV* 3.2.61–2:
    'rash bavin wits, | Soon kindled and soon
    burnt' (*OED sb.* 1c).
97 From this point, the Quarto provides the
    basic text once again.
100 **aught** anything (to the contrary)

Therefore hear you, mistress: either frame your will to
    mine—
And you, sir, hear you—either be ruled by me,
Or I shall make you
      ⌈*He claps their hands together*⌉
               man and wife.   105
Nay, come, your hands and lips must seal it too,
    Pericles and Thaisa kiss
And being joined, I'll thus your hopes destroy,
    ⌈*He parts them*⌉
And for your further grief—God give you joy.
What, are you pleased?

THAISA   Yes, (*to Pericles*) if you love me, sir.

PERICLES

Even as my life my blood that fosters it.   110

SIMONIDES

What, are you both agreed?

PERICLES *and* THAISA   Yes, if't please your majesty.

SIMONIDES

It pleaseth me so well that I will see you wed,
Then with what haste you can, get you to bed.   *Exeunt*

Sc. 10 *Enter Gower*

GOWER

      Now sleep y-slackèd hath the rout,
      No din but snores the house about,
      Made louder by the o'erfed breast
      Of this most pompous marriage feast.

---

103 **frame** accommodate
105, 106.1 The two stage directions derive
from Wilkins's narrative: 'he clapped
them hand in hand, while they as
lovingly joined lip to lip' (p. 516).
107–9 **I'll . . . pleased** Having just joined
them, he threatens to part them again,
only to explain that this *further grief* is to
wish them happiness. No wonder he asks
if they are *pleased*: they must both be
thoroughly bewildered by now.
110 **Even . . . it** as my life loves the blood that
nourishes it
112–13 **wed / bed** This rhyme concludes
Wilkins's *Miseries*, which also achieves a

happy ending for a marriage in unlikely
circumstances.
Sc. 10.1 **y-slackèd** laid to rest. The *y-* prefix
derives from Old and Middle English, and
is clearly used here as a conscious
archaism (Abbott 345).
    rout company
2 **the house about** Malone's inversion of Q's
'about the house' is required for the
rhyme.
3–4 **the o'er-fed . . . feast** The filled stomachs
of the feasters are transferred to the feast
itself.
4 **pompous** splendid, ceremonial

The cat with eyne of burning coal 5
Now couches fore the mouse's hole,
And crickets sing at the oven's mouth
All the blither for their drouth.
Hymen hath brought the bride to bed,
Where by the loss of maidenhead 10
A babe is moulded. Be attent,
And time that is so briefly spent
With your fine fancies quaintly eche.
What's dumb in show, I'll plain with speech.

    Dumb show. Enter Pericles and Simonides at one door
    with attendants. A messenger meets them, kneels, and
    gives Pericles a letter. Pericles shows it Simonides; the
    lords kneel to him. ⌈*Pericles knights the messenger.*⌉
    Then enter Thaisa with child, with Lychorida, a nurse.
    The King shows her the letter. She rejoices. She and
    Pericles take leave of her father and depart with
    Lychorida at one door; Simonides ⌈*and attendants*⌉
    depart at another

By many a dern and painful perch 15
Of Pericles the care-full search,
By the four opposing coigns
Which the world together joins,
Is made with all due diligence
That horse and sail and high expense 20
Can stead the quest. At last from Tyre

---

5 **eyne** eyes (an archaic plural, thought apt for Gower as a medieval poet)
  of burning coal i.e. glowing
6 **couches** sits
8 **blither** happier
  drouth dryness (probably intended as another archaism, though it survived in regional dialects: *OED* 1a)
9 **Hymen** god of marriage
11 **attent** attentive
13 **fancies** imagination
  quaintly skilfully
  eche fill out. Another probable archaism, though it is used by Portia at *Merchant* 3.2.23 and the Chorus at *Henry V* 3.0.35, neither with apparent archaic intent.
14 **dumb in show** (playing on the term 'dumb show', which he is about to introduce)

14 **plain** explain
14.4 *Pericles . . . messenger* This is transferred from the earlier dumb show (Sc. 5.16.4), where the news the messenger brings hardly merits such an elaborate reward, whereas the news this one brings does. This probably reflects a reporter's confusion of one dumb show with another.
15 **dern** dark, wild
  painful laborious
  perch measure of land
16 **Of** for
17 **opposing coigns** opposite corners (the biblical 'four corners of the world' (Isaiah 11: 12))
21 **stead** assist

Fame answering the most strange enquire,
To th' court of King Simonides
Are letters brought, the tenor these:
Antiochus and his daughter dead,   25
The men of Tyrus on the head
Of Helicanus would set on
The crown of Tyre, but he will none.
The mutiny there he hastes t'appease,
Says to 'em if King Pericles   30
Come not home in twice six moons
He, obedient to their dooms,
Will take the crown. The sum of this
Brought hither to Pentapolis
Y-ravishèd the regions round,   35
And everyone with claps can sound
'Our heir-apparent is a king!
Who dreamt, who thought of such a thing?'
Brief he must hence depart to Tyre;
His queen with child makes her desire—   40
Which who shall cross?—along to go.
Omit we all their dole and woe.
Lychorida her nurse she takes,
And so to sea. Their vessel shakes
On Neptune's billow. Half the flood   45
Hath their keel cut, but fortune's mood

22 **Fame** rumour
   the . . . enquire Probably 'the most distant enquiries' (i.e. they learnt by rumour
   that Pericles was at Pentapolis)
24 **tenor** theme, subject-matter
28 **will none** will have none of it, refuses it
29 **The mutiny . . . appease** *Mutiny* is a
   strong word for the mild opposition we
   have been shown in Sc. 8, but that is
   also what it is called in Wilkins's narrative, where Helicanus 'appeased the stub-
   born mutiny of the Tyrians' (p. 518), a
   phrase which also supports Steevens's
   emendation of Q's 'oppress'. Compare
   Travels Sc. vi.18–19: 'made them muti-
   nous, | Which to appease they put to sea
   again'.
31 **twice six moons** within twelve months.
   For the phrasing, compare Sc. 9.9.
32 **dooms** judgements

35 **Y-ravishèd** enraptured.   Another
   archaism: see l. 1 and note.
36 **claps** applause
   can began to. Another archaism: 'a
   Middle English variant of "gan" (=
   began), frequent in Spenser', who often
   uses archaisms (Maxwell).
   sound say, proclaim (*OED v.*[1] 10)
37 **heir-apparent**—because as Thaisa's husband he will inherit the kingdom
39 **Brief** in brief (or perhaps 'in a short time')
41 **cross** argue with
42 **dole** sorrow
45 **Neptune** god of the sea
   billow wave
45–6 **Half . . . cut** literally, 'their ship has cut
   through half the sea' (i.e. they have completed half of their journey)
46 **keel** The base timber of a ship (the part
   used to represent the whole).

Varies again. The grizzled north
Disgorges such a tempest forth
That as a duck for life that dives,
So up and down the poor ship drives.   50
The lady shrieks, and well-anear
Does fall in travail with her fear,
And what ensues in this fell storm
Shall for itself itself perform;
I nill relate; action may   55
Conveniently the rest convey,
Which might not what by me is told.
In your imagination hold
This stage the ship, upon whose deck
The sea-tossed Pericles appears to speke.   *Exit*   60

Sc. 11 ⌈*Thunder and lightning.*⌉ *Enter Pericles a-shipboard*
PERICLES

Thou god of this great vast rebuke these surges
Which wash both heaven and hell; and thou that hast

---

47 **grizzled** horrible, grisly
   north north wind (bringer of storms)
51 **The lady** (Thaisa)
   well-anear alas. 'An old north-country
   word' (Onions); compare 'welladay'
   (Sc. 5.62).
52 **travail** labour
53 **fell** ferocious
55 **nill** will not (Middle English: another
   archaism)
56 **Conveniently** appropriately
   convey express
57 **Which . . . told** which is not the case
   for the narrative I have related so far
   (Edwards)
58 **hold** assume
60 This is an iambic (ten-syllable) line, not
   an octosyllabic one, easing the audience
   back into the 'regular' rhythm of the
   main action (compare Sc. 1.41–2).
   speke This obsolete form of 'speak' is
   appropriate to the style of Gower's
   speeches, but doesn't affect the pronunciation: 'deck/speke' is another assonantal
   rhyme.
Sc. 11 Most commentators recognize that
   the language of this scene is different in
   kind from anything in the preceding
   scenes, evident even through the report-

ing, whose numerous errors need to be
corrected. For further discussion, see
Introduction, pp. 41–3.
0.1 ***Thunder and lightning*** See the note to
   Sc. 5.40.1.
   a-shipboard on board ship
1–2 **Thou . . . thou** Pericles first addresses
   Neptune, god of the sea, then Aeolus, god
   of the winds. The first *Thou* is Rowe's
   emendation of Q's 'The', perhaps a misreading of a manuscript 'ye'. 'The' makes
   sense: 'may Neptune rebuke . . .', but the
   dramatic logic of addressing one god after
   another seems to me decisively to support
   Rowe. *Thou* is not a mere synonym for
   'you': in Shakespeare's day 'you' was the
   polite form, *thou* familiar or abusive
   (Abbott 231): Pericles is not being mealy-
   mouthed with the gods, and maybe
   they repay him with fourteen years of
   suffering.
1 **vast** i.e. the sea, seen as a desolate
   expanse. The adjective is (characteristically of Shakespeare) also used as a noun
   at *Winter's Tale* 1.1.29–30, 'shook hands
   as over a vast', though there it does not
   specifically refer to the sea.
1–3 **rebuke . . . brass** These lines combine
   the classical and the Christian in a man-

153

Upon the winds command, bind them in brass,
Having called them from the deep. O still
Thy deaf'ning dreadful thunders, gently quench   5
Thy nimble sulphurous flashes.—O ho, Lychorida!
How does my queen?—Thou stormest venomously.
Wilt thou spit all thyself? The seaman's whistle
Is as a whisper in the ears of death,
Unheard.—Lychorida!—Lucina, O   10
Divinest patroness, and midwife gentle
To those that cry by night, convey thy deity
Aboard our dancing boat, make swift the pangs
Of my queen's travails!—Now, Lychorida.
    Enter Lychorida with a baby

LYCHORIDA

Here is a thing too young for such a place,   15
Who if it had conceit, would die, as I
Am like to do. Take in your arms this piece
Of your dead queen.

PERICLES   How, how, Lychorida?

---

ner typical of the Renaissance. The classical god of the winds was Aeolus, whose island, according to Homer's *Odyssey* 10.3–4, was surrounded by walls of brass (hence *bind them in brass* here); but the other phrasing evokes Christ calming the Sea of Galilee: he 'rebuked the wind and the waves', so that his disciples said 'Who is this that commandeth both the winds and water, and they obey him?' (Luke 8: 24–5).

4 **called** summoned
  the deep Both 'the sea' and 'the abyss or depth of space' (*OED sb.* 3a, c), as at *1 Henry IV* 3.1.51: 'I can call spirits from the vasty deep.'
  still quieten

6 **nimble** rapid (as at *History of Lear* Sc. 21 (4.7).32–3: 'nimble stroke | Of quick cross-lightning')
  sulphurous Sulphur was (wrongly) associated with thunder and lightning, because of its use in explosives, possibly

including those used to simulate these effects in the theatre. After his descent '*in thunder and lightning*' in *Cymbeline*, Jupiter's breath is said to be 'sulphurous to smell' (5.5.186.1, 209).

  ho Pericles probably summons Lychorida; but perhaps Q's 'how' is correct, the first of two urgent enquiries: 'how . . . How does my queen?'

8 **spit** (i.e. spit out): 'a tremendous image of the storm's whole being coming out of its mouth in the act of spitting' (Frances Whistler)

8–10 **The . . . Unheard** The storm is so noisy that the *whistle* with which the ship's master gives instructions to the crew is as inaudible as a *whisper* would be to a dead person.

10 **Lucina** Diana in her role as goddess of childbirth. See Sc. 1.51 and note.
14 **travails** labour
  Now (i.e. what is the news?)
16 **conceit** understanding
17 **like** likely

LYCHORIDA

    Patience, good sir, do not assist the storm.

    Here's all that is left living of your queen,   20

    A little daughter. For the sake of it

    Be manly, and take comfort.

PERICLES   O you gods!

    Why do you make us love your goodly gifts,

    And snatch them straight away? We here below

    Recall not what we give, and therein may   25

    Use honour with you.

LYCHORIDA   Patience, good sir,

    Even for this charge.

       She gives him the baby

PERICLES   Now mild may be thy life,

    For a more blusterous birth had never babe;

    Quiet and gentle thy conditions, for

    Thou art the rudeliest welcome to this world   30

    That ever was prince's child; happy what follows.

    Thou hast as chiding a nativity

    As fire, air, water, earth, and heaven can make

    To herald thee from the womb, poor inch of nature.

    Even at the first thy loss is more than can   35

    Thy partage quit with all thou canst find here.

    Now the good gods throw their best eyes upon't.

       Enter ⌈the Master⌉ and a Sailor

19 **do not assist the storm** (by raging your-self). The phrase also occurs in the open-ing storm scene of *The Tempest*, 1.1.13, but there it means that the passengers are getting in the way of the ship's crew.

25 **Recall** take back
    therein in that respect

26 **Use honour with you** deserve honour at your hands (or perhaps, more accus-ingly, 'compete with you in behaving honourably')

27 **charge** i.e. the child who is now your responsibility

29 **conditions** way of life (*OED sb.* 9a)

31 **happy what follows** may what follows be happy

33 **make** provide

34 **herald . . . womb** announce your birth
    poor inch of nature tiny natural creature. The phrase is introduced from Wilkins's narrative (p. 519).

35 **Even . . . first** at the very beginning (of your life)
    loss (i.e. of your mother)

36 **Thy partage quit** your share of life can compensate for. As Edwards says, Q's 'portage' is probably a misreading of *partage* (*OED sb.* 2); but 'portage' (sailor's cargo: *OED sb.*[1] 4) could be correct, inter-preted as Schanzer does: 'all that you are going to possess in the course of the voyage of life'.

37 **best** most favourable

37.1 *the Master and a Sailor* Wilkins's nar-rative speaks of 'the Master' (p. 520), Q merely of '*two sailors*'. Perhaps Q's '1 Sailor' in speech-prefixes is intended to suggest the Master, but that distinction seems to collapse at ll. 69–74 (see the note to ll. 72, 74).

⌈MASTER⌉ What courage, sir? God save you.

PERICLES

Courage enough, I do not fear the flaw;
It hath done to me its worst. Yet for the love   40
Of this poor infant, this fresh new seafarer,
I would it would be quiet.

⌈MASTER⌉ (*calling*) Slack the bow-lines, there.—Thou wilt
not, wilt thou? Blow, and split thyself.

SAILOR But searoom, an the brine and cloudy billow kiss   45
the moon, I care not.

⌈MASTER⌉ (*to Pericles*) Sir, your queen must overboard. The
sea works high, the wind is loud, and will not lie till the
ship be cleared of the dead.

PERICLES

That's but your superstition.   50

⌈MASTER⌉ Pardon us, sir; with us at sea it hath been still
observed, and we are strong in custom. Therefore briefly
yield 'er, for she must overboard straight.

PERICLES

As you think meet. Most wretched queen!

LYCHORIDA   Here she lies, sir.

---

38 **What courage, sir?** This must be a question, as in Q, not an exclamation, as in Oxford, in order to motivate Pericles' answer 'Courage enough'.

39 **flaw** squall, gust of wind

40 **its worst** Oxford's emendation of Q's 'the worst'; *TC* suggests that 'its worst' is the standard phrase in Shakespeare, citing examples, and that 'Q could arise from assimilation to the second half of the line' (p. 572).

43 **Slack** slacken
bow-lines ropes for steadying the sails in a strong wind (Edwards)

43-4 **Thou . . . thyself** Presumably addressed to the storm, not to the sailors.

44-5 **Blow . . . searoom** Compare *Tempest* 1.1.7: 'Blow till thou burst thy wind, if room enough', where 'if room enough' means 'so long as there is enough open sea, without the danger of drifting on to the rocks', which is what *But searoom* also means here.

45 **an** if

48 **works high** rages

48 **lie** subside

48-9 **till . . . dead** 'The belief that a dead body brought harm to a ship was widespread and long-lasting' (Edwards).

50 **but** merely. 'Whether or not the sailors were intended to speak verse in this passage [as in Q, after a fashion; prose in Oxford and this edition], Pericles clearly should, and the addition [*but*] strengthens both sense and metre' (*TC*, p. 572).

51 **still** always

52 **are strong in custom** adhere strongly to our customs (*OED*, *strong*, *a.* 13j)
briefly quickly

53 **yield . . . straight** The phrase *for she must overboard straight* is part of Pericles' speech in Q; the obvious dislocation implies a crowded manuscript, so *'er* may not be a colloquial contraction but merely an abbreviation, and should perhaps be emended to 'her', as many editors and actors, following Q4, have done.

53, 58 **straight** immediately

54 **meet** fit

She ⌐draws the curtain and⌐ reveals the body of Thaisa
⌐in a bed. Pericles gives Lychorida the baby⌐
PERICLES (*to Thaisa*)

A terrible childbed hast thou had, my dear,   55
No light, no fire. Th'unfriendly elements
Forgot thee utterly, nor have I time
To give thee hallowed to thy grave, but straight
Must cast thee, scarcely coffined, in the ooze,
Where for a monument upon thy bones   60
And aye-remaining lamps, the belching whale
And humming water must o'erwhelm thy corpse,
Lying with simple shells.—O Lychorida,
Bid Nestor bring me spices, ink, and paper,
My casket and my jewels, and bid Nicander   65
Bring me the satin coffer. Lay the babe
Upon the pillow. Hie thee whiles I say
A priestly farewell to her. Suddenly, woman.
    Exit Lychorida
⌐SAILOR⌐ Sir, we have a chest beneath the hatches caulked
and bitumed ready.   70

54.1 *draws the curtain* Lychorida probably
revealed Thaisa by drawing back the
curtain across the 'discovery space', a
recess at the back of the Elizabethan and
Jacobean stage. But it is inconceivable
that Pericles should have addressed a
speech so emotionally intense and
intimate as that at ll. 55–63 to her right up
there, where neither of them could be
seen by some of the audience at the Globe.
Like Arviragus and Guiderius when delivering their speeches to the apparently
dead Fidele at *Cymbeline* 4.2.219–82,
which bear several resemblances to this
one in sense, rhythm, and language, Pericles and Thaisa need to be as close to the
audience as possible. So either Thaisa is
lying on a bed which was '*put forth*' on to
the main stage, as at *2 Henry VI* 3.2.146.2
(by sailors); or Pericles, having given the
baby to Lychorida (who at ll. 66–7 placed
it on the bed in the discovery space), carried her on to the main part of the stage
himself, where he could direct his speech
both to her and to the majority of the
audience. Perhaps the latter is implied by
the last line of the scene, 'I'll bring the
body presently'.

55 **childbed** labour (*OED* 1)
58 **hallowed** i.e. with the benefit of a religious funeral
59 **in the ooze** in the mud of the sea-bed.
Steevens's emendation of Q's 'in oare' is
supported by *Tempest* 3.3.100, 'my son
i'th' ooze is bedded', and by *Cymbeline*
4.2.205–30: see Introduction, p. 43.
60 **for** instead of
61 **aye-remaining** ever-burning
belching spouting (as at *Troilus* 5.5.23)
62 **humming** booming
64 **spices** (to anoint the body; see Sc. 12.63)
paper Q's 'taper' may be correct, giving
Pericles some light to write by.
66 **satin coffer** satin-lined chest, from which,
perhaps, Pericles takes 'the cloth of
state in which . . . she was afterwards
shrouded' (Steevens)
67 **Hie thee** hurry away
whiles while
68 **priestly farewell** i.e. silent prayer
Suddenly immediately
69 **hatches** trapdoors on the deck of a ship,
leading below
69–70 **caulked and bitumed** sealed and
made watertight with bitumen (pitch)

PERICLES

    I thank thee. ⌈*To the Master*⌉ Mariner, say, what coast is
      this?

⌈MASTER⌉

    We are near Tarsus.

PERICLES   Thither, gentle mariner,

    Alter thy course from Tyre. When canst thou reach it?

⌈MASTER⌉

    By break of day, if the wind cease.

PERICLES   O make for Tarsus.

    There will I visit Cleon, for the babe   75
    Cannot hold out to Tyrus. There I'll leave it
    At careful nursing. Go thy ways, good mariner.
    I'll bring the body presently.

                    ⌈*Exit Master at one door and Sailor*
                      beneath the hatches. Exit Pericles
                      with Thaisa, closing the curtains⌉

Sc. 12 *Enter Lord Cerimon with two servants*

CERIMON

    Philemon, ho!

        Enter Philemon

PHILEMON   Doth my lord call?

CERIMON

    Get fire and meat for these poor men.   ⌈*Exit Philemon*⌉
    'T'as been a turbulent and stormy night.

FIRST SERVANT

    I have been in many, but such a night as this

72, 74 **MASTER** These speeches are given in Q
  to '2 Sailor', like 69–70; but it seems likelier that Pericles would consult the Master
  about what direction the ship is to take.
72 **Thither** [go] in that direction
76 **Tyrus** Tyre
77 **Go thy ways** i.e. go about it
78 **presently** at once
78.2 **beneath the hatches** Since *hatches* are
  trapdoors on a ship (see note to l. 69), perhaps the Sailor made his exit by way of
  the actual trapdoor in Elizabethan and
  Jacobean stages.
Sc. 12.0.1–9 **Enter . . . servants** Editors have
  made heavy weather of the opening of

this scene, but Q makes perfect sense as it
stands. Cerimon enters with two servants—*these poor men* (l. 2)—who have
been sent to him through the storm by
their respective masters for his medical
aid. For the first, he can do nothing (ll.
6–8); to the second servant, he gives a
prescription for the apothecary, which
may or may not *work* (l. 9). He instructs
his servant Philemon to give them hospitality before sending them out again.
They are obviously not shipwreck victims,
nor are any required by the scene.

Till now I ne'er endured.   5
CERIMON (*to First Servant*)
  Your master will be dead ere you return.
  There's nothing can be ministered in nature
  That can recover him. ⌈*To Second Servant*⌉ Give this to the
    pothecary
  And tell me how it works.   ⌈*Exeunt servants*⌉
      Enter two Gentlemen
FIRST GENTLEMAN   Good morrow.
SECOND GENTLEMAN
  Good morrow to your lordship.
CERIMON   Gentlemen,   10
  Why do you stir so early?
FIRST GENTLEMAN   Sir,
  Our lodgings, standing bleak upon the sea,
  Shook as the earth did quake.
  The very principals did seem to rend
  And all to topple. Pure surprise and fear   15
  Made me to quit the house.
SECOND GENTLEMAN
  That is the cause we trouble you so early;
  'Tis not our husbandry.
CERIMON   O, you say well.
FIRST GENTLEMAN
  But I much marvel that your lordship should,
  Having rich tire about you, at these early hours   20
  Shake off the golden slumber of repose. 'Tis most
    strange,

6–8 **Your . . . him** For a discussion of this
  important detail, see Introduction, p. 44.
7–8 **There's . . . him** no medicine derived
  from nature can cure him
  7 **in nature** Q has 'to nature', which Oxford
  says probably anticipates 'to' in the next
  line. At any rate, *in* makes much better
  sense, coming from one who emphasizes
  that he 'can speak of the disturbances |
  That nature works, and of her cures'
  (ll. 34–5).
  8 **pothecary** Abbreviated form of 'apothecary', similar to modern dispensing
  chemist.
12 **bleak upon** exposed to

13 **as** as if
14 **principals** principal rafters
15 **all** the whole house (Abbott 28)
  Pure sheer
18 **husbandry** zeal for work
20 **tire** Probably an abbreviated form of
  'attire': 'equipment, accoutrement,
  outfit' (*tire, sb.*[1] 1). The word evokes
  Cerimon's wealth in general, not specifically the trappings of his bed as Onions
  suggests, presumably arguing from the
  context of shaking 'off the golden
  slumber of repose' (l. 21).

Nature should be so conversant with pain,
Being thereto not compelled.
CERIMON   I held it ever
Virtue and cunning were endowments greater
Than nobleness and riches. Careless heirs   25
May the two latter darken and dispend,
But immortality attends the former,
Making a man a god. 'Tis known I ever
Have studied physic, through which secret art,
By turning o'er authorities, I have,   30
Together with my practice, made familiar
To me and to my aid the blest infusions
That dwells in vegetives, in metals, stones,
And so can speak of the disturbances
That nature works, and of her cures, which doth give
me   35
A more content and cause of true delight
Than to be thirsty after tottering honour,

22 **conversant with** accustomed to. *Conversant* is stressed on the first syllable.
pain labour
23 **held it ever** have always believed. Malone's emendation of Q's 'hold' is surely required by (or at least leads more naturally to) 'were' in the next line.
24 **cunning** knowledge
endowments gifts, capacities 'with which a person is endowed by nature or fortune' (*OED* 4). This antedates *OED*'s other examples of this sense, which include *Cymbeline* 1.4.5.
25 **nobleness** rank
25–6 **Careless heirs . . . dispend** At *Cymbeline* 4.2.227–8, in an episode which has much in common with this and the preceding scene (see the Introduction, p. 43), there is criticism of 'Those rich-left heirs that let their fathers lie | Without a monument'.
26 **darken** disgrace, dishonour (the nobleness of l. 25)
dispend spend (*OED v. Obs.* or *arch.*). Wilkins's *dispend* is likelier to be correct than Q's 'expend': 'although Shakespeare uses "expend" three times else-

where, none of the parallels involves material possessions; *dispend* alliterates with "darken", and is the rarer word' (*TC*, p. 573); and *dispend* occurs frequently in John Gower's *Confessio Amantis*, Shakespeare's principal source.
28 **ever** always
29 **physic** medicine
secret not available to public knowledge
30 **turning o'er authorities** reading learnèd writers
31 **my practice** putting the 'authorities' to practical tests
32 **my aid** to assist me in healing
blest infusions beneficial medicinal properties
33 **That . . . stones** Compare Friar Laurence at *Romeo* 2.2.15–16, who speaks of 'the powerful grace that lies | In plants, herbs, stones'.
vegetives plants
36 **more** greater (Abbott 17)
and cause and (a greater) cause (Oxford's emendation for Q's meaningless 'in course')
37 **tottering honour** unstable reputation

Or tie my treasure up in silken bags
To please the fool and death.
SECOND GENTLEMAN   Your honour has
    Through Ephesus poured forth your charity,   40
    And hundreds call themselves your creatures who by
        you
    Have been restored. And not alone your knowledge,
    Your personal pain, but even your purse still open
    Hath built Lord Cerimon such strong renown
    As time shall never—   45
        Enter ⌈Philemon and one or⌉ two with a chest
⌈PHILEMON⌉ So, lift there.
CERIMON What's that?
⌈PHILEMON⌉ Sir, even now
    The sea tossed up upon our shore this chest.
    'Tis off some wreck.
CERIMON   Set't down, let's look upon't.   50
SECOND GENTLEMAN
    'Tis like a coffin, sir.

---

38 **treasure** Q's 'pleasure' is almost certainly a slip, anticipating 'please' in the next line. Steevens's emendation is supported by a biblical passage urging the giving of alms: 'make you bags which wax not old, a treasure that can never fail in heaven' (Luke 12: 33), as Maxwell points out.

39 **To . . . death** just to please the fool who trusts in a wealth which will only be inherited by death in the end. (There may be an allusion to figures in the traditional Dance of Death.)

41 **call . . . creatures** acknowledge that they have been dependent on you (for life)

42 **not alone** not only. Oxford adds *alone* to make the sense clear.

43 **pain** labour
   still always

45 **never**—The sentence is obviously interrupted as the chest is carried on.

45.1–108 It is in this episode above all that we should heed Stanley Wells's advice, cited on p. 4 above, not to allow textual prob-

lems to distract from dramatic merits. The state of the text here involves a fair amount of emendation and relineation, necessarily discussed in the commentary. (It is often hard to be sure exactly what the lineation should be, partly because the verse has to accommodate a great deal of crucial stage business. For further discussion of this, and of the scene's theatrical impact, see Introduction, pp. 43–7.)

45.1 *Enter . . . chest* Oxford naturally interprets Q's '*two or three*' as Philemon, whom Cerimon names at the start of the scene, and two other servants carrying the chest. In Twine's account, Cerimon's assistant plays an important role in the resuscitation of Thaisa (see Introduction, p. 14), and Wilkins specifies 'a servant of his' (p. 522).

46, 48, 53 **PHILEMON** Oxford gives these lines, allocated to an unnamed servant in Q, to Philemon; see previous note.

CERIMON   Whate'er it be,

   'Tis wondrous heavy.—Did the sea cast it up?

⌈PHILEMON⌉

   I never saw so huge a billow, sir,

   Or a more eager.

CERIMON   Wrench it open straight.

     The others start to work

   If the sea's stomach be o'ercharged with gold   55

   'Tis by a good constraint of fortune that

   It belches upon us.

SECOND GENTLEMAN   'Tis so, my lord.

CERIMON

   How close 'tis caulked and bitumed!

     ⌈*They force the lid*⌉

                  Soft, it smells

   Most sweetly in my sense.

SECOND GENTLEMAN   A delicate odour.

CERIMON

   As ever hit my nostril. So, up with it.   60

     They take the lid off

52–3 **Did . . . sir** Q places this question and answer after 'bitumed' at l. 58. 'But Cerimon's incredulity is most naturally prompted by his recognition of the chest's weight. This recognition is followed in Q by the command "Wrench it open" (l. 54), a command pointlessly repeated at 58 [and so omitted there in Oxford and this edition]—a repetition most easily explained by the reporter's misplacement of Cerimon's question and the servant's answer. Moreover, "cast it up" seems at first an innocent synonym for "tossed up" (l. 49), but through the ambiguity of "cast" naturally initiates the vomiting imagery of 55–7' (*TC*, p. 574).

54 **Or a more eager** Oxford's emendation of Q's 'as tossed it upon shore', which is almost certainly the reporter's repetition of l. 49, draws upon Wilkins's narrative, where the chest is cast ashore 'by a more eager billow' (p. 521). This confirms Q's 'billow' in the previous line, but suggests an alternative for the repetition. Oxford comments that *eager* 'contributes to the developing imagery of sickness' (see the next note), citing several examples from Shakespeare's other works where eager-

ness is associated with sickness or indigestion (*TC*, p. 574).

55–7 **If . . . us** Despite his contempt for worldly riches, Cerimon is not above making a wry joke about acquiring them: the sea is personified as someone who has over-eaten, whose *stomach* is *o'ercharged*, to such an extent that he is forced (*constrained*) to *belch* and vomit; so if the chest thrown up by the sea contains gold, that is a stroke of luck (*good constraint of fortune*) for them. If Q's *constraint* is not an error, the sense is forced; but H. F. Brooks's conjecture (in Hoeniger), 'queasy fortune', adopted by Oxford, confuses the issue, since it is the sea's stomach that is 'queasy', not fortune's. I have made a simpler insertion to regularize the metre (see Appendix C).

58 **caulked and bitumed** See the note to Sc. 11.69–70.

   Soft wait a moment. 'Cerimon perceives there is something special about the chest' (Edwards).

58–60 **it smells . . . nostril** Compare *Antony* 2.2.219: 'A strange invisible perfume hits the sense'.

60 **up with it** (i.e. lift the lid)

O you most potent gods! What's here, a corpse?
SECOND GENTLEMAN
    Most strange.
CERIMON   Shrouded in cloth of state, and crowned,
Balmed and entreasured with full bags of spices.
A passport, too!
    He takes a paper from the chest
Apollo perfect me in the characters.   65
    'Here I give to understand,
    If e'er this coffin drives a-land,
    I, King Pericles, have lost
    This queen worth all our mundane cost.
    Who finds her, give her burying;   70
    She was the daughter of a king.
    Besides this treasure for a fee,
    The gods requite his charity.'
If thou liv'st, Pericles, thou hast a heart
That even cracks for woe. This chanced tonight.   75
SECOND GENTLEMAN
    Most likely, sir.
CERIMON   Nay, certainly tonight,
For look how fresh she looks. They were too rash
That threw her in the sea. Make a fire within.
Fetch hither all my boxes in my closet.   ⌈*Exit Philemon*⌉
Death may usurp on nature many hours,   80
And yet the fire of life kindle again
The o'erpressed spirits. I have heard

---

62 **cloth of state** material fit for a queen (literally, canopy for a chair of state, or throne)
   and crowned Inserted by Oxford from Wilkins's narrative: 'so crowned, so royally apparelled, so entreasured' (p. 522). It completes the trio of details of which Q mentions only two, and completes the verse line. See fig. 3.
63 **Balmed** embalmed, anointed with fragrant oil
64 **passport** letter of identification
65 **Apollo** (god of both healing and letters)
   perfect . . . characters enable me to understand what is written

67 **drives a-land** is driven ashore
69 **mundane cost** worldly wealth
70 **Who** whoever
75 **even** Q's 'ever' makes sense: 'forever'; but Wilkins's 'thou hast a body even drowned with woe' (p. 522) supports Q4's *even*.
   chanced happened
   tonight last night
77 **rash** Wilkins's 'condemning them for rashness' (p. 523) supports Malone's conjectural emendation of Q's 'rough'.
82 **o'erpressed** overcome
82–4 **I have heard . . . recoverèd** Edwards replaces these lines with Wilkins's version, which speaks of Egyptian doctors

163

Of an Egyptian that had nine hours lain dead
Who was by good appliances recoverèd.
    Enter ⌐Philemon⌐ with napkins and fire
Well said, well said, the fire and cloths.   85
The rough and woeful music that we have,
Cause it to sound, beseech you. The vial once more.
How thou stirr'st, thou block! The music there!
    Music sounds
I pray you give her air. Gentlemen,
This queen will live. Nature awakes, a warmth   90
Breathes out of her. She hath not been entranced
Above five hours. See how she 'gins to blow
Into life's flower again.

rather than an Egyptian patient; but as
Oxford tartly remarks, 'if the patient is
Egyptian, the doctor might be assumed
to be', adding that '*appliance* is a word
Shakespeare uses elsewhere in medical
contexts' (*TC*, p. 574).

85 **Well said** well done (as frequently in
Shakespeare)
86 **rough** At first sight, this seems unlikely in
the context: isn't something soothing
needed, as Wilkins suggests: 'command
some still music to sound' (p. 523)? But (a)
since *rough* is so unusual in this context,
it is unlikely to be a reporter's error,
as Edwards points out, and since the
reporter seems to have substituted
'rough' for 'rash' at l. 77 (see the note), he
must have got it from somewhere; (b) if
rough implies something actually stimu-
lating rather than soothing, it corresponds to another unusual expression
about music at Sc. 21.221, 'It nips me
unto listening', where Oxford also
emends Q, but where this edition retains
it. So perhaps, as Edwards suggests, *rough
and woeful music* suggests something 'very
eerie and unusual'.
87 **beseech** I ask, request (a polite standard
phrase)
vial phial containing medicine, as Wilkins
makes clear: 'pouring a precious liquor
into her mouth' (p. 522). Q's 'viol' was
probably suggested to the reporter or
compositor by the preceding reference to
music, which cannot have stopped so

soon to need the instruction 'once
more'—indeed, probably hadn't started
at all. See the next note.
88 **How . . . there** how slow you are (compare Sc. 5.57)—go and order the music.
Since he has to give the order twice, I have
assumed that the music does not sound
until after this line, rather than in the previous one, where editors usually place the
direction (Q does not have one at all).
block blockhead
89 **I . . . Gentlemen** This incomplete line
suggests a pause before *Gentlemen*, elo-
quently suggesting that Thaisa stirs into
life.
give her air i.e. don't 'crowd' her
89–93 **Gentlemen . . . again** I am not entirely persuaded that Steevens's relineation,
adopted here, as by most editors, is an
improvement on Q's (compare Appendix
A, ll. 1313–16), where *Nature . . . her* and
She . . . hours fall into natural blank verse
lines, and *See how . . . again* forms an
alexandrine, which beautifully catches
Thaisa's return to life by characteristically drawing upon the natural world
to express a natural event. On the other
hand, I concede that in Steevens's
arrangement the line endings throw
emphasis upon *warmth* (l. 90) and *blow*
(92), and that in Shakespeare's late verse
the sentence and line structure rarely
coincide. So, with misgivings, I follow
Steevens.
90–1 **Nature . . . her** For a change, in this
particular play, we have a choice of two

FIRST GENTLEMAN   The heavens
  Through you increase our wonder, and set up
  Your fame for ever.
CERIMON   She is alive. Behold,   95
  Her eyelids, cases to those heavenly jewels
  Which Pericles hath lost,
  Begin to part their fringes of bright gold.
  The diamonds of a most praisèd water
  Doth appear to make the world twice rich.—Live,   100
  And make us weep to hear your fate, fair creature,
  Rare as you seem to be.
        She moves
THAISA   O dear Diana,
  Where am I? Where's my lord? What world is this?
SECOND GENTLEMAN
  Is not this strange?
FIRST GENTLEMAN   Most rare.
CERIMON   Hush, my gentle neighbours.
  Lend me your hands. To the next chamber bear her.   105
  Get linen. Now this matter must be looked to,
  For her relapse is mortal. Come, come,
  And Aesculapius guide us.
                    They carry her away. Exeunt

---

good readings, though both are emendations of Q's 'Nature awakes a warmth
breath out of her'. Steevens's reading is
followed here, but Q2's also makes good
sense: 'Nature awakes a warm breath out
of her.' Both stress that Thaisa's revival is
a natural, not a supernatural, process.
91 **entranced** in a trance (swoon)
92 **blow** blossom

94 **set** Q's 'sets' is possible Jacobean grammar (Abbott 333), but, as Maxwell says, is
awkward after 'increase'.
98 **fringes** eyelashes (as at *Tempest* 1.2.411:
'The fringèd curtains of thine eye')
99 **water** lustre
100 **twice** (by the eyelids, and the eyes)

102, 104 **Rare** A favourite word with Shakespeare to express exceptional qualities in a
character, used no fewer than six times to
describe the hero or heroine in *Cymbeline*.
The First Gentleman at l. 104 uses it to
describe the exceptional nature of what
he has just seen.
102 **Diana** As she revives, Thaisa invokes the
presiding deity of the play.
103 **Where . . . this** Shakespeare borrows
this line from Gower's *Confessio Amantis*
ll. 1214–15 since it so perfectly catches
Thaisa's sense of disorientation as she
recovers consciousness.
107 **is mortal** would be fatal
108 **Aesculapius** The classical god of
healing.

Sc. 13 *Enter Pericles at Tarsus, with Cleon and Dionyza, and*
            Lychorida with a baby

PERICLES

    Most honoured Cleon, I must needs be gone.

    My twelve months are expired, and Tyrus stands

    In a litigious peace. You and your lady

    Take from my heart all thankfulness. The gods

    Make up the rest upon you!

CLEON   Your strokes of fortune,   5

    Though they hurt you mortally, yet glance

    Full woundingly on us.

DIONYZA   O your sweet queen!

    That the strict fates had pleased you had brought her
       hither

    To have blessed mine eyes with her!

PERICLES   We cannot but obey

    The powers above us. Should I rage and roar   10

    As doth the sea she lies in, yet the end

    Must be as 'tis. My gentle babe Marina,

    Whom for she was born at sea I have named so,

    Here I charge your charity withal, and leave her

    The infant of your care, beseeching you   15

    To give her princely training, that she may be

    Mannered as she is born.

CLEON   Fear not, my lord, but think

Sc. **13.2 My . . . expired** This refers to Sc.
10.21–33, where Helicanus informs Pericles by letter that he will agree to take the
crown if the lords have not found Pericles
within a year. An audience is unlikely to
remember this detail, and it is probably
just a convenient way to launch Pericles'
departure from Tarsus.

3 **litigious peace** 'Peace ridden with
conflict' is virtually an oxymoron. *Litigious* strictly speaking refers to law-suits,
litigation, but became more generally
used for 'fond of disputes, contentious'
(*OED a.* 1a).

4 **Take** receive

5 **Make . . . you** compensate you where my
gratitude is insufficient

5–7 **Your . . . us** although you bear the full
onslaught of fortune's blows, those that
glance off you wound us (i.e. we share
your grief)

8 **strict** stern (i.e. adverse)

10 **Should I** even if I should

12–13 **Marina . . . so** At the first mention of
the name in the play, its significance is
explained. It corresponds to other significant names for heroines in Shakespeare's
late plays: Innogen in *Cymbeline*, with the
connotations of 'innocence', disguises
herself as 'Fidele', of whom it is said 'Thy
name well fits thy faith, thy faith thy
name' (4.2.383); Perdita in *The Winter's
Tale* is so named because 'counted lost for
ever' (3.3.31–3); and Miranda in *The Tempest* is 'Indeed the top of admiration'
(3.1.38).

14 **charge . . . withal** entrust to your charity

15 **beseeching** requesting

17 **Mannered . . . born** educated as becomes
a princess

Your grace that fed my country with your corn—
For which the people's prayers still fall upon you—
Must in your child be thought on. If neglection   20
Should therein make me vile, the common body
By you relieved would force me to my duty.
But if to that my nature need a spur,
The gods revenge it upon me and mine
To the end of generation.

PERICLES   I believe you.   25
Your honour and your goodness teach me to't
Without your vows.—Till she be married, madam,
By bright Diana, whom we honour all,
Unscissored shall this hair of mine remain,
Though I show ill in't. So I take my leave.   30
Good madam, make me blessèd in your care
In bringing up my child.

DIONYZA   I have one myself,
Who shall not be more dear to my respect
Than yours, my lord.

PERICLES   Madam, my thanks and prayers.

CLEON

We'll bring your grace e'en to the edge o'th' shore,   35
Then give you up to the masted Neptune and
The gentlest winds of heaven.

20 **neglection** neglect
21 **common body** people
23 **that** (i.e. that duty)
25 **To . . . generation** till the human race
ceases to exist
26 **to't** to believe it
27 **Without your vows** i.e. I don't need you to
swear in order to believe you
28 **bright** This might refer specifically to
Diana in her role as goddess of the moon,
or be a term of general praise: shining,
glorious.
Diana The goddess is frequently invoked
in this section of the play (Sc. 11.10,
Sc. 12.102, Sc. 16.140), preparing
for her eventual appearance at Sc.
21.225.2.
29 **Unscissored** Steevens's emendation of

Q's 'unsistered' is confirmed by Wilkins:
'his head should grow unscissored'
(p. 524). Shaheen says that 'this
custom may have originated with Scrip-
ture', citing Numbers 6: 5: 'the razor
shall not come upon his head'. For the
repetition of this, see Sc. 18.27–8 and
note.
30 **show ill** Theobald's conjectured emendation of Q's 'show will' is supported
by Wilkins: 'himself in all uncomely'
(p. 524).
31 **blessèd** fortunate
your care the care you show
33 **to my respect** in my esteem
36 **masted Neptune** i.e. ship-bearing sea. Q's
'masked' might be correct: 'deceptively
calm' (Maxwell, who cites *Arcadia* 2.7:

PERICLES

    I will embrace your offer.—Come, dearest madam.—
    O no tears, Lychorida, no tears.
    Look to your little mistress, on whose grace   40
    You may depend hereafter.—Come, my lord.   *Exeunt*

Sc. 14 *Enter Cerimon and Thaisa*

CERIMON

    Madam, this letter and some certain jewels
    Lay with you in your coffer, which are all
    At your command. Know you the character?

THAISA

    It is my lord's. That I was shipped at sea
    I well remember, even on my eaning time,   5
    But whether there delivered, by the holy gods
    I cannot rightly say. But since King Pericles,
    My wedded lord, I ne'er shall see again,
    A vestal livery will I take me to,
    And never more have joy.   10

CERIMON

    Madam, if this you purpose as ye speak,

'with so smooth and smiling a face as if Neptune had as then learned falsely to fawn on princes' (p. 260)). Against it, Oxford objects that Cleon 'has no reason to hint darkly that the sea is less friendly than it seems; nor does any such foreboding serve a dramatic purpose—for Pericles' voyage from Tarsus is, atypically, uneventful', and proposes *masted*. *OED*'s first citation in this sense is from 1627, but 'Shakespeare uses the noun eleven times', and 'the conjectured error could be aural or palaeographical' (*TC*, p. 575).

40 **grace** favour

Sc. 14.2 coffer chest (*OED sb.* 1)

  3 **character** handwriting

  4 **shipped** on a ship

  5 **even on** just at

    eaning time time of delivery. *Eaning* is a term used for the breeding of sheep, and, as Jackson says, its 'figurative extension to human birth would be characteristic of the country-bred Shakespeare' (p. 186), who uses it to suggest especial tenderness,

as at Henry VI's longing for a shepherd's life: 'So many weeks ere the poor fools [the sheep] will ean', where 'fools' is a term of endearment (*3 Henry VI* 2.5.36).

7–8 **since . . . again** Editors (and reviewers) have sometimes wondered why she should think this; but it seems quite natural that she should believe herself to be the survivor of a wreck (see Sc. 12.50: 'off some wreck'). John Gower says that 'she supposeth | Hir lord be dreint [drowned]' (ll. 1246–7), Wilkins 'supposing her kingly husband to be shipwrecked' (p. 523). Perhaps a version of Wilkins's line could be stitched into the scene after l. 8 in performance.

  8 **My wedded lord** Perhaps an echo of the Marriage Service: 'Wilt thou have this man to thy wedded husband?'

  9 **vestal livery** uniform appropriate to vestal virgins, priestesses in the temple of Vesta, a virgin goddess, in Rome. Romeo refers to the *vestal livery* of the moon (2.1.50).

11 **purpose** intend

Diana's temple is not distant far,
Where till your date expire you may abide.
Moreover, if you please a niece of mine
Shall there attend you.   15

THAISA

My recompense is thanks, that's all,
Yet my good will is great, though the gift small.   *Exeunt*

Sc. 15 *Enter Gower*

GOWER

Imagine Pericles arrived at Tyre,
Welcomed and settled to his own desire.
His woeful queen we leave at Ephesus,
Unto Diana there's a votaress.
Now to Marina bend your mind,   5
Whom our fast-growing scene must find
At Tarsus, and by Cleon trained
In music's letters; who hath gained
Of education all the grace,
Which makes her both the heart and place   10
Of general wonder. But alack,
That monster envy, oft the wrack

---

12 **Diana's temple** The temple of Diana at Ephesus was one of the seven wonders of the ancient world. It, and Ephesus, were familiar to Elizabethan and Jacobean audiences from the Bible, especially the Acts of the Apostles 19: 27–8, alluding to the 'magnificence' of 'the temple of the great goddess Diana . . . which all Asia and the world worshippeth. . . . Great is Diana of the Ephesians.'

13 **date** term of life

Sc. **15**.1–4 Gower begins his speech in iambics, perhaps to ease the audience out of the blank verse in which the main action has been taking place, as he seems to have eased them into it at Sc. 10.59–60. As he introduces a new and important character, Marina, at l. 5, he slips back into his usual octosyllabic rhythm.

4 **there's** Either 'there as' or 'there she is'; but perhaps it is simpler in performance to follow Malone and read 'there'.
votaress nun

6 **fast-growing** (because fourteen years have passed and the baby Marina of Sc. 11 and 13 has grown up)

8 **music's letters** the study of music. This is often emended to 'music, letters', i.e. that Marina was taught about literature as well as music, which may be what was intended; but later in the play her skills in needlework are stressed as well as music, but not literary ones, except at ll. 27–9; and her skill in singing is dramatically important in the climactic scene with her father (Sc. 21.68.2).

9 **Of . . . grace** all the accomplishments that education could provide

10 **heart and place** centre and focus

12, 37 **envy** 'Though the modern sense is in place, the commoner Shakespearian meaning "ill-will, malice" is also present' (Maxwell).

12 **oft** often
wrack ruin

Of earnèd praise, Marina's life
Seeks to take off by treason's knife,
And in this kind: our Cleon has   15
One daughter, and a full-grown lass
Even ripe for marriage-rite. This maid
Hight Philoten, and it is said
For certain in our story she
Would ever with Marina be,   20
Be't when she weaved the sleided silk
With fingers long, small, white as milk;
Or when she would with sharp nee'le wound

---

13 **earnèd** justified

14 **treason** treachery

15-16 **And . . . lass** These lines in Q (see
Appendix A, 1406-7) raise two difficulties. If *in this kind* refers to something that
Cleon 'hath', it must be an attempt to
introduce his daughter Philoten, involving the forced interpretation 'the same
category (as Marina)' (H. F. Brooks in
Hoeniger). Secondly, the couplet does not
rhyme, in a rhyming passage. The first
problem is simply solved by Maxwell, who
interprets *in this kind* as 'in the following
way', so that the rest of Gower's speech
explains how and why 'envy' tries to take
Marina's life. The second requires more
adjustment. Malone adopted Steevens's
conjecture and reversed 'our Cleon hath'
and 'full grown wench' to provide the
rhyme 'Cleon/grown', but this involves
the grotesque pronunciation 'Clee-*own*'
rather than the normal *Cleon*. Oxford
adopts Schanzer's proposal (in Hoeniger)
of *has* for Q's 'hath', which Shakespeare
increasingly uses in his later work, and
lass for 'wench'; '*lass* is strongly associated with Shakespeare's late work', most
strikingly when Cleopatra is called 'lass
unparalleled' (*Antony* 5.2.310); and Q's
'wench' 'would be an easy substitution'
(*TC*, p. 575).

18 **Hight** was called. The past tense of the
Middle English 'hoten', this is another
of Gower's archaisms (*OED v.*[1] *arch.*).
Shakespeare elsewhere uses it in connec-

tion with the old-fashioned extravagances
of Don Armado (*Love's Labour's Lost*
1.1.168, 249) and for the old-fashioned
idiom of the play-within-the-play at
Dream 5.1.138: 'This grizzly beast, which
"Lion" hight by name.'

18 **Philoten** The name comes from Gower's
Confessio Amantis l. 1345, and presumably
draws on the common Greek prefix meaning 'dear, beloved', perhaps chosen by
Cleon to express his affection for his
daughter. It is stressed on the first
syllable.

20 **ever** always

21 **Be't** whether it was

she Malone's emendation of Q's 'they' is
needed since, though there is no reason
why both Marina and Philoten shouldn't
work at the embroidery, the next eight
lines concentrate exclusively on Marina's
qualities.

sleided separated out into threads for use
in embroidery (*OED, sleave-silk, Obs.*).
OED, sleided, says that this is an irregular
variant of 'sleaved', citing only this pas-
sage and *A Lover's Complaint* l. 48; but
'Sleyd silke' also occurs in the Folio text of
Troilus (5.1.28 / TLN 2898), where the
Quarto text has 'sleiue silke'.

22 **small** slender, delicate

23 **nee'le** needle (which Q reads; Maxwell
adopts the common Elizabethan variant,
which occurs in Q at Sc. 20.5, and which
fits the metre in both cases)

The cambric which she made more sound
By hurting it, or when to th' lute   25
She sung, and made the night bird mute
That still records with moan; or when
She would with rich and constant pen
Vail to her mistress Dian. Still
This Philoten contends in skill   30
With absolute Marina; so
With the dove of Paphos might the crow
Vie feathers white. Marina gets
All praises which are paid as debts,
And not as given. This so darks   35
In Philoten all graceful marks
That Cleon's wife with envy rare
A present murder does prepare
For good Marina, that her daughter
Might stand peerless by this slaughter.   40

24 **cambric** fine white linen
   more sound stronger (reinforced by her sewing)
26–7 **the night bird . . . moan** The *night bird* is the nightingale; it *records* (remembers) *with moan* because, in classical mythology, the nightingale was the princess Philomel transformed, after being raped by her brother-in-law Tereus, who tore out her tongue to prevent her revealing his crime (Ovid, *Metamorphoses* 6.424–674). The story was a favourite with Shakespeare: he alludes to it, for example, throughout *Titus Andronicus* as a parallel to that play's events, and at *Cymbeline* 2.2.44–6.
27–9 **when . . . Dian** The general sense seems to be that Marina writes (poems?) in praise of her patron goddess, Diana. See the following notes.
28 **rich** eloquent (as at *Cymbeline* 2.3.17: 'rich words' and Sonnet 84.2: 'rich praise')
   constant consistent, loyal (as at Sonnet 105.7, where the poet's exclusive praise of the same person is 'to constancy confined')
29 **Vail** do homage (literally 'bow', as at Sc. 7.42)

29 **her mistress Dian** Marina dedicates herself to the goddess as her mother has done in the previous scene.
30 **contends** competes
31 **absolute** perfect
32 **dove of Paphos** White doves drew the chariot of Venus, goddess of love; Paphos in Cyprus was dedicated to Venus, who was thought to have risen from the sea close to the town. Compare *Venus* ll. 1190–3 and *Tempest* 4.1.92–4. Venus is rather surprisingly evoked in a passage extolling a character who is dedicated to Venus' rival Diana.
33 **Vie** compete (i.e. it would be as absurd for the black crow to compete with the white dove in having white feathers as for Philoten to compete in perfection with Marina). The comparison was proverbial (Dent B435).
34 **debts** (i.e. what is naturally owed to her)
35 **given** (as compliments)
   darks darkens, puts in the shade
37 **rare** exceptional
38 **present** immediate
   murder Q's 'murderer' makes sense, but probably anticipates l. 52. Oxford compares *Hamlet* 4.3.67: 'The present death of Hamlet'.

The sooner her vile thoughts to stead
Lychorida, our nurse, is dead,
And cursèd Dionyza hath
The pregnant instrument of wrath
Pressed for this blow. The unborn event   45
I do commend to your content,
Only I carry wingèd Time
Post on the lame feet of my rhyme,
Which never could I so convey
Unless your thoughts went on my way.   50
⌈*Enter Dionyza with Leonine*⌉
Dionyza does appear,
With Leonine, a murderer.   *Exit*

DIONYZA

Thy oath remember, thou hast sworn to do't.
'Tis but a blow, which never shall be known.
Thou canst not do a thing in the world so soon   55
To yield thee so much profit. Let not conscience,

---

41 **stead** assist

42–3 Between these lines, Oxford adds the
direction '*A tomb is revealed*' because it 'is
clearly required later', in ll. 66 and 68 (*TC*,
p. 575). But that requirement depends
upon emendations made by Oxford in
both lines, which this edition does not follow; nor, therefore, does it follow Oxford
in introducing an unnecessary piece of
scenery.

44 **pregnant** apt to be influenced, ready (*OED
a.*² 3d)

45 **Pressed** forced into service (*OED v.*² 2d).
This interestingly qualifies the sense of
pregnant in the previous line (see the
note). Leonine is willing and not willing,
as the dialogue subsequently makes clear.
unborn event outcome

46 **content** pleasure (in watching the play)

47–8 **Only . . . rhyme** 'my narrative [goes]
faster than time, in spite of my halting
verses' (Edwards)

48 **Post** post-haste (an adverb derived from
the sixteenth-century custom of station-
ing horsemen along the post-roads to
carry messages as swiftly as possible)

49–50 **Which . . . way** which I could not
express unless your imaginations helped
me. Compare the Chorus at *Henry V* Pro-

logue 23: 'Piece out our imperfections
with your thoughts'.

50.1 *Enter . . . Leonine* Q places this direction
after Gower's exit, but this edition follows
Oxford, in order to emphasize the easy
interweaving of Gower's narratives with
the action proper. Compare Sc. 1.39.1, Sc.
5.38.1, and the note to Sc. 1.40.

Leonine Shakespeare transfers this name
from the brothel-keeper in Gower's original, who remains nameless in the play.
The name means 'lion-like', and is one of
several similarly-derived names in the late
plays: the Leonatus family in *Cymbeline*,
and Leontes in *The Winter's Tale*.

53–151 Q prints this scene as prose, with,
as Maxwell says, 'a few half-hearted
attempts' at the verse in which the original was obviously written (see Appendix
A, ll. 1445–1541). Earlier editors, especially Rowe and Malone, have attempted
to restore the verse, though some incomplete lines remain. It is, however, possible
that some of these reflect dramatically
deliberate pauses: see the note to ll.
101–15.

55 **a thing** anything
   soon quickly

56–9 **Let not . . . melt thee** In the passage

Which is but cold, or flaming love thy bosom
Enslave too nicely, nor let pity, which
Even women have cast off, melt thee; but be
A soldier to thy purpose.

LEONINE   I will do't;   60
But yet she is a goodly creature.

DIONYZA

The fitter then the gods should have her.
Here she comes weeping for her only nurse's death.
Thou art resolved?

LEONINE   I am resolved.
                Enter Marina with a basket of flowers

MARINA

No, I will rob Tellus of her weed   65

---

as amended here (see the next note),
Dionyza urges Leonine not to be influenced by conscience, love, or pity. These
three motivations occur together at *3
Henry VI* 5.6.68: 'I that have neither pity,
love, nor fear'.

57–8 **or flaming . . . nicely** Q's 'in flaming,
thy love bosom, enflame too nicely' is
obviously confused nonsense. I have not
adopted Oxford's emendation 'or fanning
love thy bosom | Unflame too nicely'
because it doesn't seem to me to make
very good sense (see the extended discussion at *TC*, pp. 575–6), but have preferred
Deighton's emendation, which provides a
characteristically Shakespearian contrast
with the preceding phrase: 'Don't let
either cold conscience or hot love (for
Marina) influence you'. Oxford objects
that *Enslave* is not recorded by *OED* before
1643, and it is true that Shakespeare does-
n't use it elsewhere; but as the Oxford
editors say in support of their own
emendation, Shakespeare was a great
coiner of words, and Deighton's has the
merit of simplicity and comprehensibility.

58 **nicely** scrupulously

60 **A soldier to** i.e. courageously resolved to
carry out. Compare *Cymbeline* 3.4.183–4:
'This attempt | I am soldier to'.

61–2 **she is . . . her** This exchange, especially
the ironic reply, recalls that between Lady
Anne and Richard III about Henry VI: 'O
he was gentle, mild, and virtuous. | The
fitter for the King of Heaven that hath

him' (*Richard III* (Q) 1.2.104–5).

63 **only nurse's** Q has 'only mistress'. It is
just possible that 'mistress' is correct,
though *OED*'s latest example of the
meaning 'a woman who has charge of a
child or young person' is from *c.* 1400 (*sb.*
3), and since it refers to Lychorida, it is
probably best to assume a misreading of
'nurse's'. I retain *only* with reluctance. If
correct, it must express Marina's high
regard for Lychorida: 'the only one to be
counted, reckoned, or considered' (*OED a.*
5); but I find this forced, and think that
Percy's conjecture 'old', adopted by
Steevens, is probably preferable in performance, though it makes an irregular line
still less regular. *Only nurse* occurs at
Romeo 1.3.69, but there the context gives
it a precise meaning which is irrelevant
here.

65–9 This flower-strewing passage has af-
finities, both in language and rhythm,
with Perdita's distribution of flowers at
Winter's Tale 4.4.103–27 and especially
Arviragus's promise to 'sweeten' Fidele's
grave with flowers 'Whilst summer lasts'
at *Cymbeline* 4.2.219–30.

65 **No** This probably has the force of 'Nay'
used, as often in Shakespeare, as an intensifier rather than a contradiction; or perhaps it implies 'Do not doubt that', since
the speech is addressed to the dead
Lychorida.
Tellus goddess of the earth
weed garment, covering (i.e. the flowers)

To strew thy green with flowers. The yellows, blues,
The purple violets and marigolds
Shall as a carpet hang upon thy grave
While summer days doth last. Ay me, poor maid,
Born in a tempest when my mother died,   70
This world to me is but a ceaseless storm
Whirring me from my friends.

DIONYZA

How now Marina, why do you keep alone?
How chance my daughter is not with you?
Do not consume your blood with sorrowing.   75
Have you a nurse of me. Lord, how your favour
Is changed with this unprofitable woe!
Give me your flowers. Come, o'er the sea-marge walk

---

66 **green** i.e. the turf covering Lychorida's
grave, as at *Tempest* 4.1.83: 'short-
grassed green'

67 **violets, marigolds** Both recur in Perdita's
flower speeches at *Winter's Tale* 4.4.105,
120.

68 **carpet** Editors say that this means 'tapes-
try', but the normal modern meaning is
supported | *Richard II* 3.3.48–9: 'we
march | Upon the grassy carpet of this
plain.'

   grave Oxford emends to 'tomb', partly
to avoid repetition from l. 66, where the
editors follow F3 in emending 'green' to
'grave'; but since 'green' makes perfect
sense, I retain Q in both lines. In any case,
if the actor of Marina was the principal
reporter, as Oxford persuasively argues,
he is unlikely to have misremembered his
opening lines.

69 **days doth** For the plural subject and singular verb, see the note to Sc. 1.115–16.

71 **but** only

   ceaseless Q's 'lasting' makes sense, but
may be a reporter's echo of 'last' at l. 69,
whose accuracy is confirmed by the parallel with *Cymbeline* mentioned in the note
to ll. 65–9. Oxford's emendation is discussed in *TC*, p. 576. Either reading makes
the point that Marina feels a victim of per-
petual storms, just as her father had been,
at the point where she takes over from
him as the centre of dramatic interest.

72 **Whirring** 'to carry or hurry along . . .
with a rushing or vibratory sound' (*OED*,
whirr, *v.* 1b)

73 **How now** what is the matter? (a common
catch-phrase)
   keep remain

75 **consume . . . sorrowing** Sorrow, and
especially sighing, was thought to draw
drops of blood from the heart; compare
Romeo 3.5.59, 'Dry sorrow drinks our
blood', and *2 Henry VI* 3.2.61: 'blood-
consuming sighs'.

76 **Have . . . me** let me be your nurse
   favour appearance

78–81 Oxford introduces several emendations and transpositions in these lines
(compare Appendix A, ll. 1469–72),
partly to provide more acceptable verse
(for supporting evidence, see *TC*, pp.
576–7). I have taken the process a little
further in l. 78. See the next note.

78 **Come . . . walk** As Oxford says, the line's
metrical irregularity in Q is 'easily recti-
fied' by transposing *Come* from the start of
the line. Such interjections are easily misplaced or inserted in reported texts (and
Dionyza uses 'Come' repeatedly in the
scene). Theobald conjectured 'o'er the sea
margin', for Q's meaningless 'ere the sea
mar it'; this is supported by *Dream* 2.1.85,
'the beachèd margin of the sea', and, as
Hoeniger notes, still more by the combination of 'sea-marge' and 'air' at *Tempest*
4.1.69–70. Influenced by the latter, I suggest that this line flows better if we read
marge rather than 'margin', and place
walk at the end of this line rather than, as
Oxford does, at the start of the next.

With Leonine. The air is piercing there,
And quick; it sharps the stomach. Come, Leonine,   80
Take her by the arm. Walk with her.
MARINA   No, I pray you,
I'll not bereave you of your servant.
DIONYZA   Come, come,
I love the King your father and yourself
With more than foreign heart. We every day
Expect him here. When he shall come and find   85
Our paragon to all reports thus blasted,
He will repent the breadth of his great voyage,
Blame both my lord and me, that we have taken
No care to your best courses. Go, I pray you,
Walk and be cheerful once again; resume   90
That excellent complexion which did steal
The eyes of young and old. Care not for me.
I can go home alone.
MARINA   Well, I will go,
But truly I have no desire to it.
DIONYZA
Nay, I know 'tis good for you. Walk half an hour,   95
Leonine, at the least; remember
What I have said.
LEONINE   I warrant you, madam.

79–80 **The air . . . stomach** Of Q's 'the air is
quick there, | And it pierces and sharpens
the stomach' Oxford says: 'Although the
air might be piercing, and might sharpen
the appetite, it does not "pierce the stomach". Q's line is also, for Shakespeare,
metrically impossible. The reporter might
easily transpose the two attributes, result-
ing in metrical confusion in two adjacent
lines' (*TC*, p. 577).

80 **quick** keen. Compare 'how quick and
fresh art thou' at *Twelfth Night* 1.1.9,
another context involving the breeze, the
sea, and appetite.
sharps the stomach sharpens the appetite
82 **bereave** deprive
84 **With . . . heart** i.e. as if we were relatives,
rather than strangers

86 **paragon to all reports** 'i.e. one who was
worthy of all the praise she received'
(Maxwell)
blasted withered
87 **breadth . . . voyage** i.e. that he went on
such a long journey (and so has been so
long away)
89 **to . . . courses** of what was best for you
94 Oxford's *truly* for Q's 'yet' creates a normal iambic line.
95 **Nay** Of Q's 'Come, come' Oxford says:
'Dionyza has already used the same interjection four times in her last two speeches'
(*TC*, p. 577); some of those, too, are probably the work of the reporter. For the
force of *Nay* here, see the note to 'No' at
l. 65.
97 **warrant** promise, guarantee

DIONYZA (*to Marina*)

    I'll leave you, my sweet lady, for a while.

    Pray you walk softly, do not heat your blood.

    What, I must have care of you.

MARINA   My thanks, sweet madam.   100

                              Exit Dionyza

    Is this wind westerly that blows?

LEONINE   South-west.

MARINA

    When I was born the wind was north.

LEONINE   Was't so?

MARINA

    My father, as nurse says, did never fear,

    But cried 'Good seamen' to the mariners,

    Galling his kingly hands with haling ropes,   105

    And clasping to the mast, endured a sea

    That almost burst the deck.

LEONINE When was this?

MARINA When I was born.

    Never was waves nor wind more violent,   110

    And from the ladder tackle washes off

    A canvas-climber. 'Ha!' says one, 'wolt out?'

    And with a dropping industry they skip

---

99 **softly** gently

101–15 Anne Barton writes of this episode: 'These two people may be placed, formally, in the attitude of conversation' but neither 'is really listening to the other. Arbitrarily sealed off in separate worlds, they talk at but not really to each other' ('Shakespeare and the Limits of Language', *SS 24* (Cambridge, 1971), 19–30; p. 29). In re-creating Scene 11 through Marina's eyes and imagination fourteen years later, the episode further emphasizes, not just the link between Pericles and Marina, but that she is taking over from him as the centre of the play (see the second note to l. 71). Leonine, however, has no interest in her story: he is simply awaiting his opportunity to strike.

102 **wind was north** See Sc. 10.47 and second note.

103 **says** Malone altered this to 'said', but Marina shows the natural human tendency to think of the newly-dead as still alive.

104 '**Good seamen**' (i.e. he encouraged them, as Alonso does at *Tempest* 1.1.8: 'Good Boatswain, have care')
    mariners Q has 'sailors', 'an easy unmetrical memorial substitution' (*TC*, p. 577).

105 **Galling** chafing
    haling pulling on (presumably to steady the wind-swept sails: *OED v.*[1])

106 **clasping** clinging

111 **ladder tackle** rope ladder in the ship's rigging

112 **canvas-climber** sailor climbing the rigging to trim the sails
    one (of the crew)
    '**wolt out?**' 'Are you leaving us?' As Ridley says, a brutally humorous remark to the sailor who has just been 'washed off' the rigging into the sea.
    wolt Colloquial construction of 'will you' (*OED*, *will*, *v.*[1] A.3).

113 **dropping** dripping wet (*OED ppl. a.* 1b)

From stem to stern. The boatswain whistles, and
The master calls and trebles their confusion.   115
LEONINE Come, say your prayers.
MARINA What mean you?
LEONINE
If you require a little space for prayer
I grant it. Pray, but be not tedious, for
The gods are quick of ear, and I am sworn   120
To do my work with haste.
MARINA   Why will you kill me?
LEONINE
To satisfy my lady.
MARINA   Why would she have me killed?
Now, as I can remember, by my troth
I never did her hurt in all my life.
I never spake bad word, nor did ill turn   125
To any living creature. Believe me, la,
I never killed a mouse nor hurt a fly.
I trod upon a worm against my will,
But I wept for it. How have I offended
Wherein my death might yield her any profit   130

---

114 **From . . . stern** from one end of the ship
to the other
118–19 **If . . . it** In Twine (p. 454), the
equivalent of Marina asks for time to
pray, which is granted; by making the ini-
tiative come from the murderer himself,
Shakespeare adds an additional touch to
the characterization of Leonine as a
reluctant murderer.
119 **be not tedious** don't take too long
120 **of ear** to hear (prayers)
123 **as** as far as
    by my troth by my faith (a mild oath)
126 **la** An emphatic exclamation, roughly
implying 'Yes indeed'. It is spelled both *la*
and 'law' (as in Q here), and though *OED*
lists these under separate headings, there
is little if any distinction in meaning.
Shakespeare uses it as an indication of
simplicity, frequently so used by Slender
in *Merry Wives*, or affectation, as when
Berowne uses it at *Love's Labour's Lost*
5.2.414 in the very act of renouncing
affectation. The rhyme in the latter con-

text requires the mannered pronunciation 'law'; I have modernized to *la* here
because the context is obviously one of
simplicity, and to avoid any hint of mincing affectation (see the next note).
127–9 **I never . . . it** This is a very curious
passage, to put it mildly. The aim seems to
be to express Marina's innocence, but its
sheer banality suggests instead simple-
mindedness, at complete odds with a
character celebrated for her accomplishments. Shakespeare was a master of simple, direct expression—at Sc. 21.201, for
example, or Sc. 21.127–9 and the comparable lines from *Twelfth Night* cited in the
Introduction, p. 12, or Marina's opening
speech in this scene, and the parallel from
Cymbeline cited in the note; and what
Maxwell calls the 'mincing fatuousness'
of these lines doesn't sound like Wilkins
either. Is it possible that the reporter
(probably the actor of Marina; see Introduction, pp. 78–9) was embroidering, or
introducing lines from another play?

Or my life imply her any danger?
LEONINE   My commission
Is not to reason of the deed, but do't.
MARINA
You will not do't for all the world, I hope.
You are well favoured, and your looks foreshow
You have a gentle heart. I saw you lately   135
When you caught hurt in parting two that fought.
Good sooth, it showed well in you. Do so now.
Your lady seeks my life. Come you between,
And save poor me, the weaker.
LEONINE ⌈*drawing his sword*⌉   I am sworn,
And will dispatch.   140
          Enter Pirates
FIRST PIRATE Hold, villain.
          Leonine runs away
SECOND PIRATE A prize, a prize.
THIRD PIRATE Half-part, mates, half-part. Come, let's have
her aboard suddenly.   *Exeunt Pirates* ⌈*carrying*⌉ *Marina*
          Leonine ⌈*steals back*⌉
LEONINE
These roguing thieves serve the great pirate Valdes.   145
An they have seized Marina, let her go.
There's no hope she'll return. I'll swear she's dead

134 **well favoured** good-looking (a hint for
      casting?)
      foreshow demonstrate, indicate
136 **caught hurt** received an injury
      in . . . fought Leonine is being character-
      ized as a peace-maker, like Benvolio at
      Romeo 1.1.61–6.
137 **Good sooth** truly (literally 'in good
      truth', a mild oath like 'by my troth' at
      l. 123)
138 **between** (us)
140 **dispatch** act (i.e. kill)
140.1 *Enter Pirates* This entrance has been
      variously staged: at Stratford-upon-Avon
      in 1958, for example, the pirates entered
      swiftly but silently a few lines earlier and
      threw themselves on the ground, watch-
      ing until they intervened to save Marina,
      while at the Swan Theatre there in 1989,

they abseiled down to the stage from the
gallery.
143 **Half-part** let's go shares. This could
      mean, as Leonine assumes at l. 149, that
      they all want to have intercourse with
      her, or that they will share the profit from
      selling her to the brothel in the next
      scene.
      have carry
144 **suddenly** immediately
144.1 *steals back* From Wilkins's narrative:
      'he secretly stole back' (p. 529).
145 **Valdes** Perhaps an allusion to the
      Spaniard Don Pedro de Valdes, referred to
      in Dekker's *The Whore of Babylon* (1607—
      i.e. roughly contemporary with *Pericles*).
146 **An** since
147 **hope** i.e. fear, risk

And thrown into the sea; but I'll see further.
Perhaps they will but please themselves upon her,
Not carry her aboard. If she remain,   150
Whom they have ravished must by me be slain.   *Exit*

Sc. 16 *Enter the three bawds: the Pander, his wife the Bawd,*
        and their man Bolt

PANDER Bolt.

BOLT Sir.

PANDER Search the market narrowly. Mytilene is full of
gallants. We lost too much money this mart by being too
wenchless.   5

BAWD We were never so much out of creatures. We have
but poor three, and they can do no more than they can
do, and they with continual action are even as good as
rotten.

PANDER Therefore let's have fresh ones, whate'er we pay for   10
them. If there be not a conscience to be used in every
trade, we shall never prosper.

---

149 **please themselves upon** have intercourse
with

Sc. 16 For a discussion of the characterful,
colloquial prose of this scene and of
Sc. 19, see Introduction, pp. 47–9.

0.1 Oxford begins its stage-direction with the
location indicator '*A brothel sign*', but
as elsewhere I am reluctant to impose
'scenery' on the text, especially since the
dialogue makes it so clear where we are.
bawds Used for procurers or brothel-
owners of either sex, though 'the Bawd'
as distinct from the Pander and Bolt is
clearly a woman.
Pander Sexual procurer or go-between
(derived from the name of a classical
character who brought Troilus and
Cressida together: see *Troilus* 3.2.198–
200)

0.2 *man* servant
Bolt This name is Shakespeare's
invention; it does not even occur in
Wilkins's narrative, where he is simply
called 'a leno' (pimp) in the list of characters. (Surprisingly, *OED* has no entry for
'leno' in this sense, although it also occurs
in the Quarto text of *Henry V* 4.5.13.)
Since Bolt is clearly a 'significant' name,
playing on the phallic shape suggested

by the two meanings 'arrow' and 'locking
device', and since both these meanings
survive in modern English, Q's spelling
'Boult' is accordingly modernized.

3 **narrowly** carefully
Mytilene A city on the island of Lesbos off
the west coast of Turkey.

4 **gallants** fashionable young-men-about-
town
mart market-day. The point is that when
people come into town for the market,
they may be expected to call in at the
brothel while they are there: so being 'too
wenchless' is a serious problem. The main
action of Shakespeare's other play drawing upon the Apollonius of Tyre story,
The Comedy of Errors, takes place in and
around the *mart* at Ephesus.

6 **out of . . . creatures** short of prostitutes

7 **but poor three** only a miserable trio

8 **with continual action** The three prostitutes have to service all the clients.

8–9 **even . . . rotten** as if they were infected
with venereal disease. This probably
implies that they are so worn out with
continual action that they are as useless as
if they were completely diseased. But see
ll. 18–23 and notes.

11–12 **If . . . trade** i.e. if one does not con-

179

BAWD Thou sayst true. 'Tis not our bringing up of poor
    bastards—as I think I have brought up some eleven—

BOLT Ay, to eleven, and brought them down again. But   15
    shall I search the market?

BAWD What else, man? The stuff we have, a strong wind
    will blow it to pieces, they are so pitifully sodden.

PANDER Thou sayst true. They're too unwholesome, o'
    conscience. The poor Transylvanian is dead that lay with   20
    the little baggage.

BOLT Ay, she quickly pooped him, she made him roast meat
    for worms. But I'll go search the market.   *Exit*

PANDER Three or four thousand chequins were as pretty a
    proportion to live quietly, and so give over.   25

BAWD Why to give over, I pray you? Is it a shame to get
    when we are old?

PANDER O, our credit comes not in like the commodity, nor
    the commodity wages not with the danger. Therefore if in
    our youths we could pick up some pretty estate, 'twere   30
    not amiss to keep our door hatched. Besides, the sore

---

scientiously offer good quality. I don't
understand why some editors attack the
Pander's 'twisted' idea of *conscience* here:
why is it wrong to give value for money?

13–14 **bringing . . . bastards** (one of the
hazards of the trade at a time of primitive
contraception)

15 **to . . . again** Bolt picks up the Bawd's
point about bringing up eleven bastards
by pointing out that they were brought up
to eleven years of age and then made
prostitutes themselves.

18 **blow it to pieces** make them fall apart with
syphilis (Williams, p. 274)
    sodden over-boiled (through being treated
in the sweating tub used to cope with
venereal diseases); so the 'poor three' of
ll. 7–9 are not just as good as rotten: they
are rotten.

19 **unwholesome** diseased

19–20 **o' conscience** I must admit, to tell the
truth (literally 'on my conscience': the
Pander returns to his theme at l. 11)

20 **Transylvanian** Transylvania was part of
modern Hungary. The brothel clearly has
an international clientele, which Bolt

hopes at ll. 107–8 Marina's presence will
increase.

21 **baggage** prostitute

22–3 **pooped . . . worms** infected and so
killed him. Syphilis was incurable in the
Jacobean period, and since the onset of
the Aids epidemic, we have become more
attuned to the darker element of these
scenes in modern performance.

22 **roast** 'Frequently used to indicate a poxed
condition' (Williams, p. 261).

24 **chequins** (Italian *zecchini*: gold coins)

24–5 **as pretty a proportion** a good fortune

25 **to live quietly** (on)
    give over retire

26 **get** earn

28–9 **credit . . . danger** reputation does not
accumulate like profit, nor does the profit
equal (compensate for?) the risk

30 **in our youths** Presumably this means
'now, while we are still able to earn',
rather than implying that the Bawd and
Pander are young people.
    estate fortune

30–1 **'twere not amiss** it wouldn't be a bad
idea

31 **keep . . . hatched** i.e. stay closed for

terms we stand upon with the gods will be strong with us
for giving o'er.

BAWD Come, other sorts offend as well as we.

PANDER As well as we? Ay, and better too; we offend worse.   35
Neither is our profession any mystery, it's no calling. But
here comes Bolt.

Enter Bolt with the Pirates and Marina

BOLT ⌈*to the Pirates*⌉ Come your ways, my masters, you say
she's a virgin?

A PIRATE O sir, we doubt it not.   40

BOLT (*to Pander*) Master, I have gone through for this piece
you see. If you like her, so; if not, I have lost my earnest.

BAWD Bolt, has she any qualities?

BOLT She has a good face, speaks well, and has excellent
good clothes. There's no farther necessity of qualities can   45
make her be refused.

BAWD What's her price, Bolt?

BOLT I cannot be bated one doit of a thousand pieces.

PANDER (*to Pirates*) Well, follow me, my masters, you shall
have your money presently. (*To Bawd*) Wife, take her in,   50

---

business. A *hatch* was the lower part of a
larger door; once the customer was vetted
through the open upper half, the *hatch*
was opened to admit him to the brothel
itself.
  sore ill

32 **strong with** a strong inducement to
34 **sorts** kinds of people
34–5 **as well as we** The Bawd means 'in addition to us'; the Pander takes *well* in an
evaluative sense.
36 **mystery** Oxford emends Q's 'trade' on the
grounds that there is insufficient distinction between 'profession' and 'trade',
though Maxwell's gloss on 'trade' as 'a
recognized business or occupation' perhaps supplies that distinction. *Mystery*,
borrowed from *Othello* 4.2.32, where it
is applied to a bawd, and *Measure*
4.2.27–39, where it is applied to an executioner, is rather a drastic emendation, but
it catches the humour of the Pander's
tone: he wants his profession to be a *calling*, a vocation like education or the
priesthood. This evokes the proverb
'Everyone must walk (labour) in his own
calling' (Dent C23), ultimately deriving

from the biblical 'Let every man abide in
the same vocation wherein he was called'
(1 Corinthians 7: 20). Into this high-
minded context *mystery* fits well.
38 **Come your ways** come along (a standard
catch-phrase, much used by Bolt, as at
Sc.19.175, 180, 201, and 246).
41 **gone through** bargained (*OED v.* 91)
  piece of flesh, i.e. girl (as at *Twelfth Night*
1.5.25–6: 'as witty a piece of Eve's flesh')
42 **so** well and good
  earnest money put down as a deposit
43 **qualities** accomplishments
45–6 **necessity . . . refused** 'A compressed
way of saying "no other requisite
qualities which she can be refused for
not possessing"' (Maxwell).
48 **be bated** get the price reduced
  one doit of (i.e. a penny less than)
  doit (small coin of little value)
  thousand pieces Some Panders have
howled in shock at such expense, no
doubt seeing the prospect of their retirement (ll. 25–33) receding into the distance. But business is business, and so the
Pander agrees to pay up in the next lines.
50 **presently** immediately

instruct her what she has to do, that she may not be raw
in her entertainment.   *Exeunt Pander and Pirates*

BAWD Bolt, take you the marks of her, the colour of her
hair, complexion, height, her age, with warrant of her
virginity, and cry 'He that will give most shall have   55
her first'. Such a maidenhead were no cheap thing if men
were as they have been. Get this done as I command you.

BOLT Performance shall follow.   *Exit*

MARINA
Alack that Leonine was so slack, so slow.
He should have struck, not spoke; or that these pirates,   60
Not enough barbarous, had but o'erboard thrown me
For to seek my mother.

BAWD Why lament you, pretty one?

MARINA That I am pretty.

BAWD Come, the gods have done their part in you.   65

MARINA I accuse them not.

BAWD You are light into my hands, where you are like to
live.

MARINA The more my fault
To scape his hands where I was like to die.   70

BAWD Ay, and you shall live in pleasure.

MARINA No.

BAWD Yes indeed shall you, and taste gentlemen of all
fashions. You shall fare well. You shall have the difference
of all complexions. What, do you stop your ears?   75

MARINA Are you a woman?

BAWD What would you have me be an I be not a woman?

MARINA An honest woman, or not a woman.

BAWD Marry, whip the gosling! I think I shall have

---

51 **raw** inexperienced

52 **entertainment** (of customers)

53 **marks** description

54 **warrant** guarantee (perhaps with the
secondary sense that virginity is a *warrant*
against infection)

56 **were no cheap thing** (i.e. will fetch a high
price)

58 **Performance shall follow** it shall be done

65 **done . . . you** i.e. done well by you.
Proverbial (Dent G188).

67 **are light** have fallen (*OED v.*[1] 10e)

67, 70 **like** likely

69 **fault** misfortune

73 **taste** have intercourse with (as at *Othello*
3.3.351: 'tasted her sweet body', and
Cymbeline 2.4.57: 'tasted her in bed')

74–5 **difference . . . complexions** men of different appearances

79 **Marry** See the note to Sc. 5.146.
whip the gosling A contemptuous catch-
phrase, meaning roughly 'confound the
little fool!'
whip doesn't have the literal meaning, as
sometimes suggested in performance. See
the next note.

something to do with you. Come, you're a young foolish   80
sapling, and must be bowed as I would have you.

MARINA The gods defend me!

BAWD If it please the gods to defend you by men, then men
must comfort you, men must feed you, men must stir you
up.   85

Enter Bolt

Bolt's returned. Now sir, hast thou cried her through the
market?

BOLT I have cried her almost to the number of her hairs. I
have drawn her picture with my voice.

BAWD And I prithee tell me, how dost thou find the   90
inclination of the people, especially of the younger sort?

BOLT Faith, they listened to me as they would have
hearkened to their fathers' testament. There was a
Spaniard's mouth watered as he went to bed to her very
description.   95

BAWD We shall have him here tomorrow with his best ruff
on.

BOLT Tonight, tonight. But mistress, do you know the
French knight that cowers i' the hams?

BAWD Who, Monsieur Veroles?   100

---

80 **something to do** some trouble. I think the
Bawd's tone is complaining rather than
aggressive, though actresses have sometimes interpreted *something to do* as 'I shall
have to have you sexually myself'; at this
point the Bawd seems more concerned
with persuasion than coercion.

81 **sapling** young, inexperienced person
(*OED* 2), literally a young tree, that can be
more easily *bowed*, influenced. Proverbial:
'Best to bend while it is a twig' (Dent
T632).

83 **by men** by the means of men

83–5 **men . . . stir you up** This phrase most
simply demonstrates the defects of Q:
after *men must comfort, men must feed*, the
third phrase should obviously be *men
must stir*, as in Q4, not 'men stir', as in Q1.
There is no reason for anyone to print,
or any actress to speak, Q's obviously
un-rhythmical version.

84 **feed** gratify sexually (Williams, p. 122)

84–5 **stir you up** arouse you

86, 88 **cried** advertised verbally

88 **to . . . hairs** to the point of numbering the
hairs on her head

92, 122 **Faith** Literally 'in faith', an emphatic
phrase; roughly 'indeed'.

93 **testament** will (to see what he had left
them)

96 **ruff** starched linen collar, fashionable in
the Elizabethan and Jacobean period

99 **cowers . . . hams** walks in a crooked
(bow-legged?) manner (a symptom of
venereal disease)
i' This very common abbreviation is
'a weakened form of IN *prep*. before a
consonant' (*OED*).
hams thighs

100 **Veroles** Q has 'Verollus', but a 'French
knight' should have a French-sounding
name: *vérole* means 'pox'.

BOLT Ay, he. He offered to cut a caper at the proclamation, but he made a groan at it, and swore he would see her tomorrow.

BAWD Well, well, as for him, he brought his disease hither; here he does but repair it. I know he will come in our shadow to scatter his crowns of the sun.   105

BOLT Well, if we had of every nation a traveller, we should lodge them all with this sign.

BAWD (*to Marina*) Pray you, come hither a while. You have fortunes coming upon you. Mark me, you must seem to do that fearfully which you commit willingly, to despise profit where you have most gain. To weep that you live as ye do makes pity in your lovers. Seldom but that pity begets you a good opinion, and that opinion a mere profit.   110

MARINA I understand you not.   115

BOLT (*to Bawd*) O take her home, mistress, take her home. These blushes of hers must be quenched with some present practice.

BAWD Thou sayst true, i' faith, so they must, for your bride goes to that with shame which is her way to go with warrant.   120

BOLT Faith, some do and some do not. But mistress, if I have bargained for the joint—

---

101 **offered** attempted
   cut a caper perform a rhythmic leap into the air, beating the feet together. But see the next note.
102 **made a groan** (presumably because, since he *cowered i' the hams* (l. 99), he couldn't manage the *caper* (see previous line) properly, and it caused him pain; or perhaps he groaned in ecstasy at the thought of Marina)
104–5 **he brought . . . repair it** he was diseased before he ever came to this brothel; here he merely renews his disease
105–6 **our shadow** the shade of our house
106 **scatter his crowns** liberally spend his money
   crowns of the sun (a) French coins current in England; (b) the baldness that was a symptom of syphilis
108 **lodge . . . sign** accommodate them all under this inn (or brothel) sign
   sign i.e. the description I have given of Marina

109 **hither a while** over here for a moment
112–13 **as ye do** (i.e. by prostitution)
113 **makes** encourages
114 **begets** creates for
   mere clear
116 **take her home** i.e. make her understand what she has to do (as at *1 Henry IV* 2.5.465–6: 'I would your grace would take me with you. Whom means your grace?')
118 **present practice** immediate (sexual) activity
119 **your** colloquial use: 'that which you know of'
120 **shame** modesty, reluctance
120–1 **which . . . warrant** to which she is entitled
122 **some do . . . not** Bolt wryly acknowledges that there is no generalizing about sexual habits.
122–6 **But . . . deny it** Wilkins's version of this exchange comes later, after the Lysimachus/Marina episode in Sc. 19,

---

BAWD Thou mayst cut a morsel off the spit.

BOLT I may so?   125

BAWD Who should deny it? (*To Marina*) Come, young one, I
like the manner of your garments well.

BOLT Ay, by my faith, they shall not be changed yet.

BAWD (*giving him money*) Bolt, spend thou that in the town.
Report what a sojourner we have. You'll lose nothing by   130
custom. When nature framed this piece she meant thee a
good turn, therefore say what a paragon she is, and thou
reap'st the harvest out of thine own setting forth.

BOLT I warrant you, mistress, thunder shall not so awake
the beds of eels as my giving out her beauty stirs up the   135
lewdly inclined. I'll bring home some tonight.   ⌈*Exit*⌉

where it arguably makes better sense. For
Bolt to ask to have Marina, and for the
Bawd to agree, seems bad business sense,
since they can presumably charge more
for a virgin; but after Marina has turned
the governor of the town, as well as other
clients, away from the brothel, Bolt and
the Bawd agree that the only solution is
that he shall ravish her, 'and make the
rest malleable' (Sc. 19.191–2); as Wilkins
says in his narrative at that point: 'there
was no way to bring her unto their bow,
but by having her ravished . . . where-
upon . . . they gave her up to the Pander
[= Bolt] who first agreed for her, saying
that he that had bargained for the whole
joint . . . was fittest . . . to cut a morsel
from off the spit' (p. 537). On the other
hand, since the Bawd's later phrase in this
scene 'You'll lose nothing by custom' (ll.
130–1) might refer back to this exchange,
and since it is not incontrovertibly misplaced (Wilkins might be in error), I
retain it at this point.

123–4 **joint . . . morsel . . . spit**   Marina's
body is seen as a *joint* of meat roasting
on a *spit*, of which Bolt like the brothel
customers can have his share.

125 **I may so?** I think, with Deighton and
Maxwell, that this phrase works better as
a request for confirmation than as a statement, giving the Bawd more to respond to
in her reply.

127 **manner** fashion

128 **changed** i.e. she will not be forced to
exchange her (presumably rich) clothes
for the standard dress of a prostitute

130 **sojourner** guest or lodger, an obvious
euphemism. *OED* 2 gives only two other
examples of this usage, from 1623 and
1660.

130–1 **You'll . . . custom** i.e. because he will
get his share of the takings (and perhaps
will not *lose* his opportunity to have
Marina just because the customers have
her too)

131 **framed** shaped, created
piece See the second note to l. 41; perhaps
also 'masterpiece', especially in view of
'paragon' in the next line.

132 **good turn** In addition to the obvious
modern sense, there may be a sexual
allusion: compare *Antony* 2.5.58–9: 'For
what good turn?—For the best turn i'th'
bed.'
paragon embodiment of perfection

133 **reap'st . . . setting forth** This is Oxford's
emendation of Q's 'hast the harvest out
of thine own report'. *Reap'st the harvest*
is a natural phrase for which there are
frequent parallels in Shakespeare,
whereas there are none for 'hast the
harvest', 'and "report" suspiciously
repeats the previous sentence' (*TC*, p.
578).

134–6 **thunder . . . inclined** Thunder was
supposed to arouse eels from the mud: an
apt phallic image for *stir*ring up the *lewdly
inclined*.

BAWD Come your ways, follow me.

MARINA

If fires be hot, knives sharp, or waters deep,
Untied I still my virgin knot will keep.
Diana aid my purpose!   140

BAWD What have we to do with Diana? Pray you, will you
go with me?   *Exeunt*

Sc. 17 *Enter Cleon and Dionyza* ⌈*in mourning garments*⌉

DIONYZA

Why, are you foolish? Can it be undone?

CLEON

O Dionyza, such a piece of slaughter
The sun and moon ne'er looked upon.

DIONYZA

I think you'll turn a child again.

CLEON

Were I chief lord of all this spacious world,   5
I'd give it to undo the deed. A lady
Much less in blood than virtue, yet a princess
To equal any single crown o'th' earth

---

138 **fires . . . knives . . . waters** Othello also
evokes these means of death to express
the intensity of his torment, interestingly
in a context mentioning Diana (*Othello*
3.3.391–5), as Marina does to express the
intensity of her passionate resolution.

140–1 **Diana . . . Diana** For a discussion of
this exchange, see Introduction, p. 49.

142 **me** Since Bolt has been sent into the
town, only the Bawd is left with Marina,
so Oxford emends Q's 'us', while also suggesting that *with me* might be omitted
altogether. *Will you go* is a common exit
line in Shakespeare. Q's 'us' might be
a colloquialism for 'me', as perhaps at
Coriolanus 5.3.207: 'Come, enter with us.'

Sc. 17 Editors compare this conversation to
that between Macbeth and Lady Macbeth
(*Macbeth* 2.2.14–72)—though it hardly
seems to enhance this flimsy scene to
make it stand the push of such a comparison—and, more reasonably, to that
between Gonoril and her husband

Albany (*History of Lear*, Sc. 16 (4.2),
where Gonoril derides Albany as 'a moral
fool'; see the note to l. 25.

0.1 *mourning garments* Suggested by l. 43:
'And yet we mourn.'

5 **spacious world** This phrase also occurs at
History of Justine (1606), probably by
George Wilkins, p. 102v.

7 **Much . . . virtue** Although Marina was
'great' in her ancestry, she was even
greater on account of her virtue. See
the next note.

7–9 **a princess . . . compare** i.e. Marina was
a princess who could justly rank with any
mortal ruler, however eminent. Compare
Giacomo's praise both of Innogen herself
and of her royal status at *Cymbeline*
1.6.120–2: 'A lady | So fair, and fastened
to an empery | Would make the great'st
king double'.

8 **crown o'th' earth** For the phrase, compare *Antony* 4.16.65: 'The crown o'th'
earth doth melt.'

I'th' justice of compare. O villain Leonine,
Whom thou hast poisoned too,   10
If thou hadst drunk to him 't'ad been a kindness
Becoming well thy fact. What canst thou say
When noble Pericles shall demand his child?

DIONYZA

That she is dead. Nurses are not the fates.
To foster is not ever to preserve.   15
She died at night. I'll say so. Who can cross it,
Unless you play the pious innocent
And for an honest attribute, cry out
'She died by foul play'?

CLEON   O, go to. Well, well,
Of all the faults beneath the heavens, the gods   20
Do like this worst.

DIONYZA   Be one of those that thinks
The petty wrens of Tarsus will fly hence
And open this to Pericles. I do shame
To think of what a noble strain you are,
And of how cowed a spirit.

CLEON   To such proceeding   25

---

9 **I'th' . . . compare** in a fair comparison.
Hoeniger says that *of compare* 'is an
unusual expression', but it also occurs
at Sonnet 21.5: 'Making a couplement
of proud compare'.

11 **drunk to him** toasted him (in the poison of
l. 10); or perhaps 'drunk the poison
instead of him'

12 **Becoming** appropriate to
fact (evil) deed (the usual meaning in the
sixteenth and seventeenth centuries (*OED*
1c))

14–15 **Nurses . . . preserve** i.e. a nurse can
take care of someone's life, but not preserve it for ever; that is the work of fate.
Vaughan's emendation (see Appendix C)
of Q's punctuation (Appendix A, ll.
1701–2)—which so confused editors that
they constructed elaborate theories about
missing lines—emphasizes that sometimes even a text as corrupt as this one
can be simply corrected.

16 **cross** deny

17 **pious** This emendation of Q's 'impious' is
supported by Wilkins's narrative: 'if such

a pious innocent as yourself do not reveal
it' (p. 530).

18 **for an honest attribute** to be thought an
honest man

19 **go to** A common catch-phrase of
impatience, here expressing Cleon's
disapproval.

22–3 **The petty wrens . . . Pericles** This
alludes to the folklore tradition that birds
can reveal secret murders. Perhaps the
wren is chosen as the tell-tale because,
although tiny (*petty*), it has an astonish-
ingly loud song.

23 **open** reveal

24 **strain** origin, ancestry

25 **cowed** Although Q's 'coward' makes
sense, it is, as Oxford says, 'extrametrical
and commonplace' (*TC*, p. 578), whereas
cowed is supported by *Macbeth* 5.10.18: 'it
hath cowed my better part of man', and
History of Lear Sc. 16 (4.2). 12, where
Gonoril, also speaking of her husband,
refers to 'the cowish terror of his spirit'.

Whoever but his approbation added,
Though not his prime consent, he did not flow
From honourable sources.

DIONYZA   Be it so, then.
Yet none does know but you how she came dead,
Nor none can know, Leonine being gone.   30
She did distain my child, and stood between
Her and her fortunes. None would look on her,
But cast their gazes on Marina's face
Whilst ours was blurted at, and held a malkin
Not worth the time of day. It pierced me through,   35
And though you call my course unnatural,
You not your child well loving, yet I find
It greets me as an enterprise of kindness
Performed to your sole daughter.

CLEON Heavens forgive it.   40

DIONYZA And as for Pericles,
What should he say? We wept after her hearse,
And yet we mourn. Her monument
Is almost finished, and her epitaphs
In glittering golden characters express   45
A general praise to her and care in us,
At whose expense 'tis done.

CLEON   Thou art like the harpy,

26–7 **but . . . consent** merely gave his approval, even if not his consent in the first place (i.e. even if he was not the instigator of the crime)

27–8 **flow . . . sources** derive from an honourable family. Cleon is responding to Dionyza's jibe about his 'noble strain' (l. 24) by saying that it would not be noble to agree to or approve the murder of Marina. Some editors retain Q's 'courses' and gloss 'tributary streams', but Dyce's *sources*, following *flow*, is supported by *All's Well* 2.1.138–9: 'great floods have flown | From simple sources'.

31 **distain** cast a stain upon, overshadow (a sense distinct from Q's 'disdain', which cannot be right: there is no suggestion in play or sources that Marina scorned Philoten)

34 **blurted at** derided
   malkin slut (a diminutive of 'Moll')

35 **Not . . . day** not worth a 'good day'

38 **greets** presents itself

43 **yet** still

44 **epitaphs** It was customary to affix more than one epitaph to tombs (Deighton).

45 **characters** letters

47, 50 **Thou, Ye** Cleon uses the abusive *Thou*, Dionyza the coolly polite *ye*.

47 **harpy** A mythological creature with a beautiful woman's face but with the claws of a bird of prey. It is an image of deception: while it smiles with its angel's face, it seizes its victim with its talons. The repetition of *with* is probably intended to reflect this double aspect, so unlike Oxford I have not emended *with* in l. 49, though it might be a reporter's slip. The comparison is apt for the duplicity of Dionyza, and is similarly used in *The Tempest* 3.3, where Ariel appears as a harpy to accuse Prospero's enemies at the climax of what at first seems an inviting banquet.

Which to betray, dost with thine angel's face,
Seize with thine eagle's talons.

DIONYZA

Ye're like one that superstitiously   50
Do swear to th' gods that winter kills the flies,
But yet I know you'll do as I advise.   *Exeunt*

Sc. 18 *Enter Gower*

GOWER

Thus time we waste, and long leagues make we short,
Sail seas in cockles, have an wish but for't,
Making to take imagination
From bourn to bourn, region to region.
By you being pardoned, we commit no crime   5
To use one language in each several clime
Where our scenes seem to live. I do beseech you
To learn of me, who stand i'th' gaps to teach you

---

50 **Ye're** you are

50–1 An obscure and possibly corrupt passage. It must be a response to Cleon's
accusing Dionyza of deception, so it probably implies 'if we / you are
superstitious in your simple-minded reverence for the gods, which merely
amounts to stating the obvious'. She then
adds that despite his protests he will not
act upon them but will conceal what
Dionyza has done.

Sc. **18.**1–7 There are two curious features
of this passage. Although in some of his
earlier speeches Gower has occasionally
slipped ten-syllable lines into his basic
eight-syllable verse, this is the first speech
to be wholly in pentameters; and Gower's
apology for using the same language in
each of the countries visited seems to be
made rather late in the play. Perhaps it
was originally planned to occur in one of
Gower's earlier speeches, where productions sometimes re-position it, though
of course to do that underlines the discrepancy from Gower's 'normal' verse
structure.

1–2 **Thus . . . for't** The general sense is 'we
can pass quickly over time and long dis-

tances if only we wish to do so'.

1 **waste** consume, use up (as at Sc. 1.16)
leagues A *league* is a distance of about
three miles.

2 **cockles** Either 'cockle-shells' (*OED sb.*² 2)
or more likely 'small boats', though if so
this line antedates *OED*'s earliest citation
of this sense, from 1648 (*sb.*² 3).
an if (we)

3 **Making** proceeding

4 **bourn** frontier

5 **By . . . pardoned** if you will allow us to
we commit no crime Time, the Chorus in
The Winter's Tale, makes a similar appeal
to the audience as he transports them
over a 'wide gap' of time: 'Impute it not a
crime . . . that I slide | O'er sixteen years'
(4.1.4–7). See the note to l. 8.

6 **clime** country (*OED* 2)

7 **scenes seem** Q's 'scenes seems' may
be acceptable as seventeenth-century
grammar (see the note to Sc. 1.115–16),
but is unacceptable as a tongue-twister, so
either 'scenes' or 'seems' needs to be
emended. Maxwell reads 'scene seems',
glossing 'scene' as 'dramatic performance' and citing Onions: 'the most
frequent Shakespearian sense', and

The stages of our story: Pericles
Is now again thwarting the wayward seas,   10
Attended on by many a lord and knight,
To see his daughter, all his life's delight.
Old Helicanus goes along. Behind
Is left to govern, if you bear in mind,
Old Aeschines, whom Helicanus late   15
Advanced in Tyre to great and high estate.
Well sailing ships and bounteous winds have brought
This king to Tarsus—think his pilot thought;
So with his steerage shall your thoughts go on—
To fetch his daughter home, who first is gone.   20
Like motes and shadows see them move a while;
Your ears unto your eyes I'll reconcile.

> *Dumb show. Enter Pericles at one door with all his*
> *train, Cleon and Dionyza ⌈in mourning garments⌉ at*
> *the other. Cleon ⌈draws the curtain and⌉ shows Pericles*
> *the tomb, whereat Pericles makes lamentation, puts on*
> *sack-cloth, and in a mighty passion departs, followed by*
> *his train. Cleon and Dionyza depart at the other door*

probably the sense at l. 42 of this speech. But Q4 reads 'scenes seem', taking 'scenes' as 'scenic units' which is also frequent in Shakespeare, as at *Hamlet* 2.2.442: 'an excellent play, well digested [organized] in the scenes', and this seems to me to follow more naturally from the preceding references to 'regions' and 'climes'.

live take place

8 **stand i'th' gaps** bridging the gaps between scenes, and also perhaps reinforcing the idea of carrying the audience across long distances of space and time in ll. 1–2; the 'wide gap' of time occurs at *Winter's Tale* 4.1.7 and 5.3.155.

10 **thwarting** (a) crossing; (b) opposing
   wayward untoward, i.e. hostile (*OED a.* 1b)

14 **if . . . mind** if you remember. Edwards objects that 'we have heard nothing of this', but it is probably dramatic shorthand to remind the audience who

Aeschines is, and that he has been associated with Helicanus in governing Tyre.

15 **late** recently

18–19 **think . . . go on** if you imagine that he is carried to Tarsus, you can arrive there by the same means

18 **pilot** (steering Pericles' ship)

19 **steerage** course his ship takes

20 **first is gone** has left already

21 **motes** particles of dust in a sunbeam (Onions). *Mote*, meaning 'particle', is frequent in Shakespeare.
   shadows spirits, illusions. The use of *shadows* for actors or dramatic characters (*OED sb.* 6b) occurs at *Dream* 5.1.210, 'The best in this kind are but shadows', and at the start of Puck's epilogue: 'If we shadows have offended'.

22 **I'll reconcile** (by explaining what you see)

22.3–4 *draws . . . tomb* The tomb was presumably placed in the 'discovery space' at the back of Elizabethan and

See how belief may suffer by foul show.
This borrowed passion stands for true-owed woe,
And Pericles, in sorrow all devoured,   25
With sighs shot through, and biggest tears
   o'ershowered,
Leaves Tarsus, and again embarks. He swears
Never to wash his face nor cut his hairs.
He puts on sack-cloth, and to sea. He bears
A tempest which his mortal vessel tears,   30
And yet he rides it out. Now please you wit
The epitaph is for Marina writ
By wicked Dionyza.
     He reads Marina's epitaph on the tomb
   'The fairest, chastest, and most best lies here,
   Who withered in her spring of year.   35
   In nature's garden, though by growth a bud,
    She was the chiefest flower: she was good.'

Jacobean stages, which Cleon reveals by drawing back the curtain that concealed it.

22.5 **sack-cloth** coarse material used for making sacks. Putting it on was a biblical sign of mourning, as at Genesis 37: 34, when Jacob put on sack-cloth believing his son Joseph to be dead.
passion display of grief

23 **how . . . show** how Pericles may be tricked into believing something false by hypocrisy

24 **borrowed** assumed (unlike Pericles' genuine grief at l. 22.5)
stands is substituted
true-owed woe grief that should genuinely be shown (for having Marina killed). This anonymous but brilliant emendation of Q's meaningless 'true old woe' not only restores sense, but, as with the emendations at Sc. 2.10 and 91 (see the notes) help the actor to 'focus' the line. Compare *A Lover's Complaint* l. 327, where hypocritical weeping is called 'borrowed motion seeming owed'.

25 **in sorrow all devoured** eaten up with sorrow

27–8 **He swears . . . hairs** It is curious

that Pericles should swear not to cut his hair when he has already done so at Sc. 13.29 (see note). The repetition probably derives from textual confusion, especially since in Wilkins the vow is not repeated: there, Pericles only 'apparels himself in sack-cloth' (p. 540). In performance, the oath about hair-cutting should presumably be omitted at Sc. 13 or here.

29–31 **He bears . . . out** The physical tempests which have assailed him in the past now become a metaphor for his internal condition.

29 **bears** carries (inside)

30 **vessel** body

31 **rides it out** survives (as a ship does at sea)—though presumably only in the sense of staying alive, in view of his comatose state in Sc. 21
wit understand

32 **is** that is

34–7 **'The fairest . . . good.'** This is the version of Marina's epitaph given in Wilkins's narrative. For Q's longer version, see Appendix A, ll. 1778–87, which has been justifiably attacked as 'a shocking piece of fustian' (Maxwell) and 'drivel' (Hoeniger). Oxford comments that the version given by Wilkins is 'superior,

No visor does become black villainy
So well as soft and tender flattery.
Let Pericles believe his daughter's dead   40
And bear his courses to be orderèd
By Lady Fortune, while our scene must play
His daughter's woe and heavy welladay
In her unholy service. Patience then,
And think you now are all in Mytilene.   *Exit*   45

Sc. 19 *Enter two Gentlemen*

FIRST GENTLEMAN Did you ever hear the like?

SECOND GENTLEMAN No, nor never shall do in such a place
as this, she being once gone.

FIRST GENTLEMAN But to have divinity preached there— did
you ever dream of such a thing?   5

SECOND GENTLEMAN No, no. Come, I am for no more bawdy
houses. Shall's go hear the vestals sing?

FIRST GENTLEMAN I'll do anything now that is virtuous, but
I am out of the road of rutting for ever.   *Exeunt*
    Enter Pander, Bawd, and Bolt

PANDER Well, I had rather than twice the worth of her she   10
had ne'er come here.

poetically and dramatically' and argues
that it either 'represents Shakespeare's
revised text' or that it is 'a revision (or
alternative)' by Wilkins (*TC*, p. 579).
Either way, it seems preferable to print,
and for actors to speak, sense rather than
nonsense. Rudolph Walker, delivering
Wilkins's lines with touching simplicity
at Stratford-upon-Avon in 1989, fully
justified their use.

35–6 **her spring of year, by growth a bud**
These phrases emphasize Marina's
youth.

38–9 **No . . . flattery** Proverbial: 'A well-
favoured vizor will hide her ill-favoured
face' (Dent V92).

38 **visor** mask

41 **bear . . . orderèd** allow his fate to be
arranged

43 **welladay** grief, lamentation (*OED sb.* B)

44 **unholy service** (as a prostitute)

Sc. **19**.1–9 Editors usually treat these lines as
a separate scene, but having the gentlemen leave the brothel 'converted' by
Marina, just before the brothel-keepers
arrive, provides a piquant illustration of
their complaints that Marina is ruining
their business (ll. 20–1, 26–7).

7 **Shall's** shall we
  vestals vestal virgins (see the note to Sc.
  14.9). The abruptness and extremity of
  their conversion, going from prostitutes
  to priestesses, always draws a laugh in
  performance, whether or not it was
  intended. It probably was.

9 **road of rutting** habit (literally 'way') of
  fornication. *Rutting* is normally used of
  the annual mating of animals, especially
  deer, and its choice perhaps reflects
  the gentlemen's new-found distaste for
  whoring.

BAWD Fie, fie upon her, she's able to freeze the god Priapus
and undo the whole of generation. We must either get
her ravished or be rid of her. When she should do for
clients her fitment and do me the kindness of our   15
profession, she has me her quirks, her reasons, her
master reasons, her prayers, her knees, that she would
make a puritan of the devil if he should cheapen a kiss of
her.

BOLT Faith, I must ravish her, or she'll disfurnish us of all   20
our cavalleria and make our swearers priests.

PANDER Now the pox upon her green-sickness for me.

BAWD Faith, there's no way to be rid on't but by the way to
the pox.

Enter Lysimachus

---

12 **Fie, fie** John Florio in his Italian/English
dictionary, *A World of Words* (1598), glosses this 'an interjection of . . . reproving'
(p. 242).
  freeze . . . Priapus even make the
classical god of lechery and fertility cold.
A hint for this may have come from
Twine, who says that Marina was forced
to venerate a golden idol of Priapus which
had 'a mighty member, unproportionable
to the body, always erected' (p. 456);
responding to this hint, and to the Bawd's
instructions at Sc. 16.53–6, Terry Hands
at Stratford-upon-Avon in 1969 had Marina paraded around the stage on a wagon
in front of a statue of Priapus, and finally
impaled on the effigy's erection.

13 **the whole of generation** Q's 'a whole
[= entire] generation' makes sense, but
Maxwell's conjecture, drawing on the
phrasing of Sc. 13.25, is, as Oxford says,
'much more appropriate, especially as a
suitably hyperbolic companion to the first
half of the sentence; it also permits a
Shakespearian pun on *whole* (= 'hole',
'vagina')' (*TC*, p. 579).

15 **fitment** duty, what is fitting (as a prostitute). This is *OED*'s only example of *fitment* in this sense, though the word
occurs in a related sense at *Cymbeline*
5.6.410–11: ''twas a fitment for │ The
purpose I then followed', as *OED* notes.

15, 16 **me** Examples of the so-called 'ethic
dative' in which *me* originally meant 'for

me' (as its use in the first line may actually mean, balanced against 'for clients').
By Shakespeare's time it had become little
more than an intensifier, by which the
speaker drew attention to himself or, as
here, herself.

15 **kindness** 'natural acts of goodness'
(Edwards)

16 **quirks** peculiarities (*OED sb.*[1] 4a), 'little
ways'—like objecting to forced inter-
course with strange men for the financial
advantage of others

17 **master** main, principal (Onions)
  knees i.e. kneeling to plead with the Bawd

18 **cheapen** bargain for (*OED v.* 1)

20 **disfurnish** deprive, rob

21 **cavalleria** Italian for 'body of gentlemen,
knights', and so 'our young customers'
(the 'gallants' of Sc. 16.4): Q's
'Ca[v]alereea' is a guide to pronunciation.
  swearers those who swear by us, believe
in us

22, 24 **pox** A standard catch-phrase ('a
plague'), which the Bawd takes literally
('syphilis') in her reply.

22 **green-sickness** 'chlorosis, an anaemic
disease affecting girls about the age of
puberty', whose 'natural remedy', intercourse, is indicated in the next speech
(Williams, pp. 146, 243).
  for me as far as I'm concerned

23 **on** of

Here comes the Lord Lysimachus, disguised.   25

BOLT We should have both lord and loon if the peevish
baggage would but give way to customers.

LYSIMACHUS How now, how a dozen of virginities?

BAWD Now the gods to-bless your honour!

BOLT I am glad to see your honour in good health.   30

LYSIMACHUS You may so. 'Tis the better for you that your
resorters stand upon sound legs. How now, wholesome
iniquity have you, that a man may deal withal and defy
the surgeon?

BAWD We have here one, sir, if she would—but there never   35
came her like in Mytilene.

LYSIMACHUS If she'd do the deed of darkness, thou wouldst
say.

BAWD Your honour knows what 'tis to say well enough.

---

25 **Lysimachus** The name does not occur in the principal sources of the story, but was probably suggested by Plutarch's *Life of Demetrius* (see the note to Sc. 3.4–7), or by Wilkins's *History of Justine* (see the Introduction, pp. 6 and 17). It is stressed on the first and fourth syllables.
disguised For a discussion of Lysimachus' behaviour, and of the entire episode, see Introduction, pp. 49–52.

26 **loon** man of low birth, peasant (*OED sb.*[1] 2, which makes it clear that 'lord and loon' was a common phrase; the sense overlaps with *OED* 3, 'a boor, lout, clown' (i.e. countryman))

26, 173 **peevish** perverse

27 **but** only
customers Oxford reads 'custom' (i.e. follow normal behaviour) in order to facilitate an elaborate triple pun (*TC*, p. 580), but Q seems adequate.

28 **how** how much for (as at *2 Henry IV* 3.2.47–50: 'How a score of ewes now? . . . A score of good ewes may be worth ten pounds.')

29 **to-bless** bless entirely (Onions). But although *OED* records several uses of *to-* as an intensive (*prefix*[2] 2), it does not list this one, and the phrase may simply be an abbreviation for 'I pray the gods to bless . . .'

32 **resorters** regular customers (those who *resort* to you)
sound legs i.e. healthy ones, not crooked as a result of venereal disease, as at Sc. 16.99.
How now This repetition of Lysimachus' opening phrase (l. 28) may be due to the reporter, but could be a deliberate indication of Lysimachus' colloquial casualness with the brothel-keepers.

32–4 **wholesome . . . surgeon** have you got a healthy prostitute that a man can have intercourse with without catching a disease and so needing the doctor

33 **iniquity** Literally 'sin', i.e. a prostitute.
deal Slang for 'have intercourse' (Williams, p. 92).
withal with (an emphatic form (Abbott 196), in keeping with Lysimachus' tone)

37 **deed of darkness** sexual act. Q5's *deed* for Q1's 'deeds' 'gives what was evidently the standard form' (Maxwell, citing Jonson's *The Devil is an Ass* 5.6.50, 'a deed of darkness', and *History of Lear* Sc. 11 (3.4).78: 'did the act of darkness'). Wilkins, however, has 'deeds of darkness' at *Miseries*, l. 1479.

39 **what 'tis to say** what I'm trying to say (another phrase indicating the familiarity that exists between the Bawd and her customer)

LYSIMACHUS Well, call forth, call forth.   ⌈*Exit Pander*⌉   40
BOLT For flesh and blood, sir, white and red, you shall see a
    rose. And she were a rose indeed, if she had but—
LYSIMACHUS What, prithee?
BOLT O sir, I can be modest.
LYSIMACHUS That dignifies the renown of a bawd no less   45
    than it gives a good report to a member to be chaste.
        ⌈*Enter Pander with Marina*⌉
BAWD Here comes that which grows to the stalk, never
    plucked yet, I can assure you. Is she not a fair creature?
LYSIMACHUS Faith, she would serve after a long voyage at
    sea. Well, there's for you, leave us.   50
        ⌈*He pays the Bawd*⌉
BAWD I beseech your honour give me leave: a word, and I'll
    have done presently.
LYSIMACHUS I beseech you, do.

40 **call forth, call forth** produce her. The
brisk, impatient repetition (compare ll.
50, 102) makes Lysimachus' attitude
plain: he hasn't come to the brothel
for small talk.

41 **white and red** A standard phrase of the
period to describe female beauty, as at
Love's Labour's Lost 1.2.87: 'My love is
most immaculate white and red.'

42 **if she had but**—a thorn. 'The innuendo is
clearer in the Elizabethan form of the
proverb' (Edwards): 'No rose without
a prickle' (Dent R182), i.e. Marina is sexually inexperienced.

45-6 **That . . . chaste** A difficult sentence.
Presumably it parallels two kinds of
praise: modesty gives a bawd a good reputation, just as it praises [something else]
for being chaste. The problem is what that
something or someone is. Q's 'a number'
makes a kind of sense, presumably ironical: perhaps 'many people who do not
deserve such praise'. Oxford proposes
'noble' on the assumption that Lysimachus compares his own hypocrisy
to Bolt's, and the censor demanded a
change (*TC*, p. 580). I suggest that 'number' is a simple reporter's or compositor's
error for 'member' (of the community, as
at *Love's Labour's Lost* 4.1.41, *Measure*
5.1.235), thus permitting the punning

sense 'penis', ironically praised for being
chaste, i.e. not erect (compare the quotation from Twine given in the note to l. 12).
This would fit Lysimachus' flippantly suggestive tone: modesty is equally irrelevant
to a *bawd* and to a *member*. The same
word-play occurs in the opening lines of
The Insatiate Countess (1.1.1–4), begun by
John Marston in 1607–8, and so exactly
contemporary with *Pericles*.

47 **grows to** is an integral part of. The Bawd
picks up Bolt's comparison of Marina to a
rose at l. 42.

49-50 **she . . . sea** An oddly offhand remark,
which seems to belittle Marina, since after
a long voyage at sea almost any woman
would serve; is Lysimachus concealing
his attraction from the Bawd, perhaps
even to reduce the cost? Later in Wilkins's
account of the episode Lysimachus sus-
pects that the Bawd wants 'to draw him to
a more large expense' (see Appendix B,
Passage C). But perhaps Lysimachus is
simply using his habitual flippant manner
to shut the Bawd up and get down to business, as the following brusque phrases
suggest.

51 **give me leave** permit me (to have a word
with Marina)

52 **have done presently** be finished soon

53 **I . . . do** i.e. go ahead

BAWD (*aside to Marina*) First, I would have you note this is
an honourable man.   55

MARINA I desire to find him so, that I may honourably
know him.

BAWD Next, he's the governor of this country, and a man
whom I am bound to.

MARINA If he govern the country you are bound to him   60
indeed, but how honourable he is in that, I know not.

BAWD Pray you, without any more virginal fencing, will
you use him kindly? He will line your apron with gold.

MARINA What he will do graciously I will thankfully
receive.   65

LYSIMACHUS (*to Bawd*) Ha' you done?

BAWD My lord, she's not paced yet. You must take some
pains to work her to your manège. (*To Bolt and Pander*)
Come, we will leave his honour and hers together. Go thy
ways.   *Exeunt Pander, Bawd, and Bolt*   70

LYSIMACHUS Now pretty one, how long have you been at
this trade?

MARINA What trade, sir?

56–7 **honourably know** Oxford emends Q's
  'worthily note' which the editors find
  'sensible but feeble. Marina picks up on
  "honourable", saying that she will
  "know" him virtuously (not carnally).
  The reporter repeated the wrong word
  ("note" instead of "honourabl(y)")' (*TC*,
  p. 580). This emendation also usefully
  begins the many references to 'honour'
  and 'honourable' throughout the rest of
  the scene.

59, 60 **bound . . . bound** The Bawd uses the
  word in the sense 'obliged to' (because
  Lysimachus is a regular customer),
  Marina in the sense 'subject to'.

61 **how . . . I know not** Marina speaks more
  truly than she realizes; she herself will
  have a hard job bringing Lysimachus to
  genuinely *honourable* behaviour during
  the course of the scene.

62 **virginal fencing** verbal quibbling about
  her virginity (i.e. converting customers
  such as those we have seen leaving the
  brothel at the start of the scene). The
  Bawd probably also chooses *fencing*
  because Marina has just been doing this
  with the word 'honourable' and she

foresees trouble ahead, correctly.

63 **line** fill (as if lining a garment)
  apron 'This item of dress . . . is specifically associated with whores' (Williams,
  p. 28). At *Timon* 4.3.135–6, Timon tells
  two whores 'Hold up, you sluts, | Your
  aprons mountant': they must raise
  their skirts (a) to catch the gold he gives
  them and (b) to earn more gold by doing
  so.

64 **graciously** kindly (perhaps turning the
  Bawd's sexual use of *kindly* in the previous line to a more acceptable sense)

67–8 **paced . . . manège** broken in . . . con-
  trol. These are technical expressions
  from the training of horses.

69 **hers** Oxford's emendation of Q's 'her' permits a pun on 'honour' which is entirely
  in keeping with the word-play already
  established at ll. 55–6 and 61.

69–70 **Go thy ways** come along

71–91 Oxford coaxes these lines into verse,
  involving extensive emendation, but
  despite the presence of some verse
  rhythms I have no doubt that they are
  prose, as Q prints them, and for an obvious dramatic reason: Lysimachus is con-

LYSIMACHUS Why, I cannot name it but I shall offend.

MARINA I cannot be offended with my trade, please you to   75
name it.

LYSIMACHUS How long have you been of this profession?

MARINA E'er since I can remember.

LYSIMACHUS Did you go to't so young? Were you a gamester
at five, or at seven?   80

MARINA Earlier too, sir, if now I be one.

LYSIMACHUS Why, the house you dwell in proclaims you to
be a creature of sale.

MARINA Do you know this house to be a place of such resort
and will come into it? I hear say you're of honourable   85
parts, and are the governor of this place.

LYSIMACHUS Why, hath your principal made known unto
you who I am?

MARINA Who is my principal?

LYSIMACHUS Why, your herb-woman, she that sets seeds   90
and roots of shame and iniquity.

⌈*Marina weeps*⌉

tinuing both his tone, and the attitude
that represents, from the previous lines:
he is making small-talk with a prostitute.
He has no interest whatever in Marina as
a person. But after its equivalent of l. 91,
Q indents the rest of Lysimachus' speech,
as if a new one were beginning, though
without repeating the speech-prefix. Perhaps, as Oxford suggests, something is
missing, but at any rate there is a 'change
of direction' as Lysimachus attempts to
force her to submit by pulling rank on her.
This abuse of his authority gives her the
cue for her impassioned response; and as
the scene intensifies so it moves into verse,
perhaps signalled by that 'paragraph'
indent in Q. To introduce verse before this
point spoils the impact of this dramatic
transition.

72, 75 **trade** Lysimachus means 'prostitution', Marina 'virginity'.

74, 82, 87, 90 **Why** These repetitions might
be the inventions of a reporter, but they
could also be intended as a mannerism, a
kind of verbal 'tic', perhaps expressing
exasperation as Marina refuses to engage
in small talk.

74 **I . . . offend** This mercilessly exposes Lysimachus' double standards: it's all right to
visit a brothel and use prostitutes, but bad
form to admit that that is what you're
doing; and Marina in her reply refuses to
let him get away with it.

79 **gamester** prostitute (as at *All's Well*
5.3.191, where Bertram tries to discredit
Diana by calling her 'a common gamester
to the camp')

86 **parts** qualities

87 **principal** employer

90 **herb-woman** woman who sells herbs. It
doesn't seem to have been a slang term
for 'bawd' as the context might lead us
to expect, but simply to prepare for the
idea of sowing vices that follows.
sets plants

91.1 **Marina weeps** Oxford inserts this to
'prompt Lysimachus' change of direction'
(*TC*, p. 581; see note to ll. 71–91); compare Wilkins's narrative: 'the Governor
suspecting these tears but to be some
new cunning . . . now began to be more
rough with her' (Appendix B, Passage
C). This is what Lysimachus does in his
next lines, moving into verse in the
process.

LYSIMACHUS

　O, you've heard something of my power, and so
　Stand off aloof for a more serious wooing.
　But pretty one, I do protest to thee
　I am the governor, whose authority　　　　　　　　　　95
　Can wink at blemishes, or on faults look friendly,
　Or my displeasure punish at my pleasure,
　From which displeasure all thy beauty shall
　Not privilege thee, nor my affection
　Which hath drawn me to this place abate,　　　　　　　100
　If thou with further lingering withstand me.
　Come, bring me to some private place. Come, come.

MARINA

　My lord, I entreat you but to hear me.

---

93 **off aloof** remote, playing hard to get. Oxford inserts *off* to improve the metre, citing *1 Henry VI* 4.4.21: 'Keep off aloof'.

94–101 These lines combine Q's 'but I protest to thee, pretty one, my authority shall not see thee, or else look friendly upon thee' with the verse 'fossils' in Wilkins's more extensive version of the speech in his prose narrative (Appendix B, Passage C), where the 'switch in mid-sentence into direct address strikingly suggests that Wilkins here echoes a dramatic text' (*TC*, p. 581). Lysimachus' threat to use (and so abuse) his authority to force Marina is much more blatant in Wilkins than in Q, prompting her extended reply.

94–5 **I do protest . . . the governor** Not a pointless repetition of something that Marina has revealed that she already knows (l. 86), but an emphatic assertion of his power.

94 **protest** assert, solemnly declare (*OED v.* 1; compare *Hamlet* 3.2.219: 'The lady protests too much')
　　thee As his behaviour becomes more threatening Lysimachus moves from the polite Elizabethan and Jacobean form 'you' to the abusive or familiar *thee* and 'thou', which he continues to use even after Marina has won him over, presumably then using the words for intimate rather than aggressive effect (assuming that the reporter is transmitting the text accurately). See the note to *thy* at l. 152.

96 **wink at blemishes** ignore moral shortcomings

96 **on faults look friendly** Oxford's emendation of Q's 'look friendly upon thee' is based upon the editors' view that Q's very abbreviated scene was the result of censorship of the much longer version that Wilkins's narrative reports: 'an uncontroversial specific ("thee")' replaces 'a dangerous generalization' about a governor's power (see the Introduction, pp. 79–80).

97 **displeasure/pleasure** The symmetry of the line serves to emphasize his blatant threat to abuse his power.

99–100 **nor . . . abate** nor modify the intensity of the sexual urge which has brought me here. These lines prepare very well for the brusque, no-nonsense urgency of l. 102, which in turn spurs Marina into her extended argument against his abuse of authority.

103–56 Except for ll. 109–11 and 149–50, from Q, this episode is reconstructed from the verse rhythms in Wilkins's prose narrative (given in Appendix B, Passage C), replacing the very brief passage in Q, in which Marina says next to nothing to justify Lysimachus' praise at ll. 149–50, and Lysimachus himself asserts (or pretends) that he came to the brothel 'with no ill intent', at complete odds with his tone and behaviour earlier in the scene. For Q's version, see Appendix A, ll. 1890–1912; and for a full discussion, see Introduction, pp. 49–52.

If as you say you are the governor,
Let not authority which teaches you   105
To govern others be the means
To make you misgovern much yourself.
If you were born to honour show it now;
If put upon you, make the judgement good
That thought you worthy of it.
LYSIMACHUS   How's this?   110
How's this? Some more, be sage.
MARINA   What reason's in
Your justice, who hath power over all,
To undo any? If you take from me
Mine honour, you are like him that makes
A gap into forbidden ground, whom after   115
Too many enter, and you are guilty
Of all their evils. My life is yet unspotted,
My chastity unstainèd even in thought.
Then if your violence deface this building,
The workmanship of heaven, made up for good,   120
And not for exercise of sin's intemperance,

---

104 **If . . . governor** Again, as at ll. 94–5, not a mere repetition of something Marina already knows, but a reply to his own reference to his power, leading in the next lines to her criticism of his abusing it.

105–17 **Let not authority . . . evils** Marina's criticism of the abuse of authority recalls Isabella's at *Measure* 2.2.109–40.

106 This is the first of several eight-syllable lines (e.g. ll. 110, 127), but these are not uncommon in Shakespeare's work.

108–11 **If . . . sage** These lines follow Q, rather than Wilkins's more laborious version. Oxford detaches Lysimachus' line and places it later in their reconstruction (after 'give them maintenance', l. 133 in this edition). But this seems much too late in the course of Marina's arguments for Lysimachus to be speaking to her 'with a sneer', as Malone rightly interprets *be sage*; he should surely be responding to her eloquence by then. So I have assumed that Lysimachus' line follows immediately on Marina's speech, as in Q.

108 **honour** honourable position, high rank
show demonstrate

109 **If put upon you** i.e. if your high rank was conferred upon you (with the implication 'through merit rather than inheritance')
make . . . good justify

111 **sage** wise (ironical)

112 **who hath** you who have

113 **undo any** ruin anyone

114–15 **like him . . . forbidden ground** Compare Angelo at *Measure* 2.2.175–7, just after Isabella's criticisms of authority mentioned in the note to ll. 105–17: 'Having waste ground enough, | Shall we desire to raze the sanctuary, | And pitch our evils there?'

115 **whom after** after whom

117 **unspotted** free from sin

119 **building** 'Shakespeare often uses this word of the human frame (*Macbeth* 2.3.68, etc.); it retained a strong verbal sense, as "a thing built" (*OED*), which leads naturally into the religious image of the next line' (*TC*, p. 581).

121 **intemperance** excessive indulgence

You kill your honour, abuse your justice,
And impoverish me.

LYSIMACHUS   Why, this house
Wherein thou liv'st is a receptacle
Of all men's sins, and nurse of wickedness.   125
How canst thou then be otherwise than naught
That liv'st in it?

MARINA   My yet good lord,
If there be fire before me, must I fly
There straight and burn myself? Suppose this house—
Which too too many feel such houses are—   130
Should be the doctor's patrimony and
The surgeon's feeding, follows it that I
Must needs infect myself to give them maintenance?
O my good lord, kill me but not deflower me,
Punish me how you please but spare my chastity,   135
And since 'tis all the dowry that the gods have given
And men have left me, do not take it from me.
Make me your servant, I willingly obey you,
Make me your bondmaid, I'll account it freedom.

123–7 **Why . . . in it** Oxford does not include
these lines in its reconstruction because
they, and Marina's reply (see Appendix B,
Passage C), appear to be a misplaced
report of ll. 82–3 above, from Q. But as
Oxford also says, Lysimachus' speech
could be a development and intensifica-
tion of his brief earlier speech, and in any
case Lysimachus needs *some* reaction to
Marina's accusations, so I include the
lines.

126 **otherwise than naught** anything other
than worthless

127 **My yet good lord** The verse line created
here is an eight-syllable one, permitting a
pause after this evocative phrase to
emphasize it: Marina varies the standard
respectful 'My good lord' by adding *yet*:
he is a *good lord* to his subject so long as he
doesn't take unfair advantage of her.

130 **too too** 'The iteration of *too* is characteristic of Shakespeare (seven occurrences,
including "too too oft" and "too too
much"; it does not appear elsewhere in
Painful Adventures or in *Miseries*' (*TC*, p.
582), and so is likely to reflect a genuinely

Shakespearian emphasis rather than a
Wilkinsian repetition.

feel i.e. discover through bitter experience
(as with the blinded Gloucester in *King
Lear*: 'I see it feelingly' (*History of Lear*
Sc. 20 (4.6.)144))

131 **patrimony** due inheritance (here, what
the doctor will earn from treating diseases
caught in brothels)

132 **feeding** living (as with the doctor in the
previous line)

134–48 **O my good lord . . . should be** Oxford
does not use this passage from Wilkins in
its reconstruction, instead inserting some
lines from Q's version (Appendix A, ll.
1893–9: 'How's this . . . purer air'). I
think, however, that if one follows
Wilkins's version of the scene it is preferable to include the bulk of it, rather than
to use some passages and not others.
Though in performance not all the material will necessarily be used, it seems desirable to provide a reconstruction of most of
the scene, so that performers can choose
for themselves what they need.

139 **bondmaid** female slave

Let me be the worst that is called vile;   140
So I may still live honest, I am content.
Or if you think't too blest a happiness
To have me stay so, let me even now,
⌈*She kneels*⌉
Now in this minute die, and I'll account
My death more happy far than was my birth.   145
LYSIMACHUS ⌈*lifting her up*⌉
Now surely this is virtue's image, nay,
Virtue herself sent down from heaven a while
To reign on earth and teach us what we should be!—
I did not think thou couldst have spoke so well,
Ne'er dreamt thou couldst.   150
I hither came with thoughts intemperate,
Foul and deformed, the which thy pains
So well hath laved that they are now white.
I came here meaning but to pay the price,
A piece of gold for thy virginity;   155
Here's twenty to relieve thine honesty.
Persever still in that clear way thou goest,
And the gods strengthen thee.
MARINA The good gods preserve you!
LYSIMACHUS Now to me   160

143.1 *She kneels* From Wilkins: 'which
words, being spoken upon her knees'.
150 The broken verse line suggests a pause
for stage business. I suggest lifting her up
(from Wilkins), or perhaps wiping the
tears from her eyes (also from Wilkins),
or both.
152, 155, 156 **thy, thine** Lysimachus in
Wilkins vacillates between 'thy' and
'your' to no apparent purpose; in Q after l.
94 he uses only *thy* to Marina (see the
note to *thee* there); so Wilkins's 'your' in
these lines has been modified accordingly.
153 **laved** washed. Shakespeare uses the
word three times elsewhere, including
OED's first recorded figurative use at *Macbeth* 3.2.34 (*TC*, p. 582).
156 **Here's** Oxford's emendation of Wilkins's
'now give you' in fact reverts to Q's wording: 'Hold, here's gold for thee' (*TC*,
p. 582).
157–9 These lines are basically from Q.

157 **Persever** (stressed on the second syllable,
as usual in Shakespeare)
still always
clear virtuous
160 **Now to me** This broken verse line
replaces Q's 'For me be you thoughten,
that I came with no ill intent, for to me',
which of course presents a different interpretation of Lysimachus' behaviour from
that given in Wilkins's narrative, in this
reconstruction, and in most performances. For a full discussion, see the
Introduction, pp. 49–52. Quite apart from
appearing to contradict the tone of all
Lysimachus' early speeches even in Q's
own version, the phrase 'be you thought-
en' is suspicious: 'you' suddenly crops up
when Lysimachus has been using 'thee'
and 'thou' consistently; and 'thoughten'
seems to belong with the would-be
archaisms ending in 'en' in Gower's
speeches (see Sc. 5.20, 24, 28, 35 and

The very doors and windows savour vilely.
Fare thee well. Thou art a piece of virtue,
The best wrought up that ever nature made,
And I doubt not thy training hath been noble.
A curse upon him, die he like a thief,   165
That robs thee of thy honour. Hold, here's more gold.
If thou dost hear from me, it shall be for thy good.
⌈*As Lysimachus leaves, he reveals Bolt standing ready
at the door*⌉

BOLT I beseech your honour, one piece for me.

LYSIMACHUS

Avaunt, thou damnèd doorkeeper!
Thy house, but for this virgin that doth prop it,   170
Would sink and overwhelm thee. Away.   *Exit*

BOLT How's this? We must take another course with you. If
your peevish chastity, which is not worth a breakfast in
the cheapest country under the cope, shall undo a whole
household, let me be gelded like a spaniel. Come your   175
ways.

---

notes) but sounds very odd coming from
Lysimachus. On the other hand, Oxford's
omission of the whole of Q's phrase,
resuming at 'The very doors and windows' in the next line, seems rather
abrupt; so I propose an isolated compromise phrase based on Q, which might
be played as a man trying to adjust to his
surroundings in terms of the conversion
he has undergone.

161 From this point, this edition is once again
based on Q, apart from l. 163, which is
from Wilkins: see *TC* for the numerous
Shakespearian parallels for its component
parts (p. 583).
    savour smell
162 **piece** specimen, example (*OED sb.* 8b)
163 **wrought up** created
165 **die he** may he die
166 **honour** As Oxford says, it is hard to see
how Marina can be robbed of her 'goodness' (Q's reading), while Wilkins's later
phrase 'rob me of mine honour' (p. 538)
supports the emendation.
    Hold, here's more gold Transferred by
Oxford from after 'noble' (l. 164) in Q for
metrical reasons: see *TC*, p. 583.

167.1–2 *As . . . door* Q provides no entry for
Bolt, nor should he be given one, as in
most editions. What clearly happened
was that as Lysimachus opened one of the
two doors set into the back wall of the
Jacobean stage to leave, he revealed Bolt,
waiting outside, '*standing ready at the
door*', as Wilkins has it (p. 537).
168 **piece** (of gold)
169 **Avaunt** begone
    doorkeeper Panders and bawds were
often called doorkeepers: Bolt has just
been revealed carrying out this function.
170, 171 **Thy, thee** Q's 'Your' and 'you' are
almost certainly wrong: having used the
thy and *thee* forms to Marina since l. 94,
Lysimachus is most unlikely in his fury to
use the polite ones to Bolt, especially after
using 'thou' in the previous line, and
Wilkins's 'thou hast a house here' confirms this (p. 537).
174 **cope** canopy, i.e. sky (*OED sb.*[1] 7a), as at
Hamlet 2.2.301–2: 'This most excellent
canopy the air'
    undo ruin
175 **gelded** castrated

MARINA Whither would you have me?

BOLT I must have your maidenhead taken off, or the
common executioner shall do it. We'll have no more
gentlemen driven away. Come your ways, I say.   180
 Enter Bawd

BAWD How now, what's the matter?

BOLT Worse and worse, mistress, she has here spoken holy
words to the Lord Lysimachus.

BAWD O, abominable!

BOLT She makes our profession as it were to stink afore the   185
face of the gods.

BAWD Marry, hang her up for ever!

BOLT The nobleman would have dealt with her like a
nobleman, and she sent him away as cold as a snowball,
saying his prayers, too.   190

BAWD Bolt, take her away, use her at thy pleasure, crack the
glass of her virginity, and make the rest malleable.

177–8 **Whither . . . off** These lines anticipate
ll. 202–3 (Marina's are almost identical),
so there may be some confusion on the
part of the reporter.

177 **Whither . . . me** what do you want of me
(literally 'where are you taking me?')

179 **executioner shall do** Oxford emends Q's
'hangman shall execute' to make clear
the pun on 'maidenhead' (as at *Romeo*
1.1.22–4: 'I will cut off their heads. | The
heads of the maids? | Ay, the heads of the
maids, or their maidenheads'), since
the head should be cut off rather than
hanged. 'Hangman' was probably caught
from l. 224 where it 'seems clearly
correct' (*TC*, p. 583).

 do it. We'll Between these sentences Q
has 'Come your way', where 'way'
should probably be 'ways' (the line is very
tightly set). Oxford says that this catch-
phrase occurs 'three times in five lines
here, and nine times in the brothel
scenes', so omits this occurrence (*TC*, p.
583), partly to avoid disrupting the
continuity of Bolt's thought. And see
Introduction, p. 74.

180.1 *Enter Bawd* Q says 'Bawds', which
could include the Pander, but Q gives him
no lines, so Oxford gives him the Bawd's

speech at ll. 191–2. At first sight, Wilkins
appears to support Q: 'the whole swarm
of bawds . . . rushing in hastily upon'
Marina (p. 537); but Wilkins presents a
somewhat different version of the inci-
dent, since they take away the gold that
Lysimachus has given her (or some of it),
and I am reluctant to deprive the Bawd of
her speech without stronger evidence. So
I omit the Pander from the scene, since he
has nothing to do.

184 **O, abominable!** The Bawd's shocked
reaction at the thought of speaking 'holy
words' to Lysimachus is another irre-
sistibly comic moment.

188–9 **like a nobleman** i.e. rewarded
her, perhaps with a reference to a nobleman's sexual prowess too, especially after
'dealt with': compare 'deal withal' at l.
33.

191–2 **crack the glass** 'The image seems
to be of a glass vessel, rigid and brittle'
(Edwards), and so appropriate to the
Bawd's attitude to Marina's virginity.
Compare the proverb 'A woman and a
glass are ever in danger' (Dent W646).
See *TC*, p. 583 for a discussion of Oxford's
emendation 'ice' for *glass*, which also
makes good sense.

BOLT An if she were a thornier piece of ground than she is,
    she shall be ploughed.

MARINA Hark, hark, you gods!   195

BAWD She conjures, away with her. Would she had never
    come within my doors.—Marry, hang you!—She's born
    to undo us.—Will you not go the way of womenkind?
    Marry come up, my dish of chastity with rosemary and
    bays.   *Exit*   200

BOLT Come mistress, come your ways with me.

MARINA Whither wilt thou have me?

BOLT To take from you the jewel you hold so dear.

MARINA Prithee, tell me one thing first.

BOLT Come now, your one thing.   205

MARINA What canst thou wish thine enemy to be?

BOLT Why, I could wish him to be my master, or rather my
    mistress.

MARINA
Neither of these can be so bad as thou art,
Since they do better thee in their command.   210
Thou hold'st a place for which the pained'st fiend
Of hell would not in reputation change,
Thou damnèd doorkeeper to every coistrel

---

193 **An if** A more emphatic version of 'if',
'even if'.

194 **ploughed** Sexual slang for 'penetrated',
a cruder version of 'makes | A gap into
forbidden ground' at ll. 114–15. Compare
Antony 2.2.235: 'He ploughed her, and
she cropped.'

196 **conjures** 'uses magic to invoke supernatural aid' (Edwards)

199 **Marry come up** A common proverbial
phrase (Dent M699.2) deriding a person's
pretentiousness (*OED*, *marry*, *int.* d),
a contempt continued in her mockery
of Marina's chastity in the next
phrase.

199–200 **my dish . . . bays** Rosemary and
bay-leaves were used to garnish special
dishes, for example at Christmas, so this is
'a gibe at Marina's ostentatious virtue'
(Schanzer).

202 **Whither . . . me** See the note to l.
177.

204–5 **one thing** Marina begins to argue;

Bolt turns her phrase to its sexual sense,
'vagina', keeping to the point.

206 **What . . . be** i.e. what is the worst thing
you could wish upon your enemy?

207 **be** (like). Bolt's reply is rather surprising,
since there has been no hint of dissension
between him and his employers. His
remark is needed, of course, to cue
Marina's attack on him.

210 **better thee in their command** They
are literally *better* because they are his
'superiors'.

211–17, 222–7 For a discussion of Marina's
language here, and Bolt's reply, see Introduction, p. 53.

211 **pained'st** most tormented

212 **change** exchange

213 **doorkeeper** See the second note to l. 169.
coistrel knave (literally 'groom' (*OED* 1)),
an abusive term used by Shakespeare at
Twelfth Night 1.3.38 and *2 Henry VI*
3.1.381.

That comes enquiring for his Tib.
To the choleric fisting of every rogue   215
Thy ear is liable. Thy food is such
As hath been belched on by infected lungs.
BOLT What would you have me do? Go to the wars, would
    you, where a man may serve seven years for the loss of a
    leg, and have not money enough in the end to buy him a   220
    wooden one?
MARINA
Do anything but this thou dost. Empty
Old receptacles or common sewers of filth,
Serve by indenture to the public hangman—
Any of these ways are better yet than this.   225
For what thou professest a baboon, could he speak,
Would own a name too dear. Here's gold for thee.
If that thy master would make gain by me,
Proclaim that I can sing, weave, sew, and dance,
With other virtues which I'll keep from boast,   230
And I will undertake all these to teach.
I doubt not but this populous city will
Yield many scholars.
BOLT But can you teach all this you speak of?
MARINA
Prove that I cannot, take me home again   235

214 **Tib** 'Probably short for Isabel' (Maxwell),
    a common term in the period for 'whore'.
215–16 **To . . . liable** you are likely to be
    boxed on the ears by every angry
    customer
219 **seven years** Often used simply to mean 'a
    long time' (*OED*, *seven*, *a.* 1d).
    for Literally 'in return for', i.e. all he
    would get as a reward for seven years'
    service is the loss of a leg.
224 **by indenture** as an apprentice. A pimp
    serves an executioner at *Measure*
    4.2.1–58.
    public Oxford emends Q's 'common'
    because it has probably been caught from
    the line above, or from Q's 'common
    hangman' at l. 179, or both.
225 **better yet** I reverse Q's 'yet better' to
    achieve a more fluent rhythm.
226 **thou professest** you do as an occupation

227 **own . . . dear** think it was too good a
    name (i.e. even a baboon would consider
    it beneath him to do your job—even
    though baboons were thought to be par-
    ticularly lecherous: compare *Kinsmen*
    3.5.134, where it has a 'long tail and eke
    [also] long tool')
    dear. Here's Between these sentences Q
    has 'that the gods would safely deliver me
    from this place', which Oxford eliminates
    as a reporter's unmetrical echo of Mari-
    na's truncated speech given at Appendix
    A, ll. 1896–7; certainly Marina seems at
    this point to be relying on more worldly
    solutions, as she gives Bolt money in the
    next phrase.
228 **make gain** profit
230 **virtues** accomplishments
233 **scholars** pupils
235 **Prove** if you find

And prostitute me to the basest groom
That doth frequent your house.

BOLT Well, I will see what I can do for thee. If I can place
thee, I will.

MARINA But amongst honest women.   240

BOLT Faith, my acquaintance lies little amongst them; but
since my master and mistress hath bought you, there's
no going but by their consent. Therefore I will make them
acquainted with your purpose, and I doubt not but I shall
find them tractable enough. Come, I'll do for thee what I   245
can. Come your ways.   *Exeunt*

Sc. 20 *Enter Gower*

GOWER

Marina thus the brothel scapes, and chances
   Into an honest house, our story says.
She sings like one immortal, and she dances
   As goddess-like to her admirèd lays.
Deep clerks she dumbs, and with her nee'le composes   5
   Nature's own shape of bud, bird, branch, or berry,
That even her art sisters the natural roses.
   Her inkle, silk, twin with the rubied cherry,

---

236 **basest groom** lowest menial. A *groom* did
not necessarily work with horses, though
he often did; the word is usually disparag-
ing in Shakespeare, as at *2 Henry VI*
2.1.197: 'meanest groom'.

244 **purpose** proposition

245 **tractable** co-operative

Sc. 20 This speech of Gower's offers a further
variation on his original octosyllabic couplets, as it is in quatrains.

1 **scapes** Abbreviated form of 'escapes',
common until the end of the seventeenth
century (*OED v.*[1] 1).

3–4 **she dances . . . lays** she sings and
dances at the same time, as if she were a
goddess

4 **goddess-like** The phrase is also used of
other heroines in Shakespeare's late
plays: Innogen (*Cymbeline* 3.2.8) and
Perdita (*Winter's Tale* 4.4.10).
lays songs

5 **Deep . . . dumbs** she reduces men of

learning to silence
nee'le needle. See the note to Sc. 15.23.

7 **That . . . roses** so that her art even equals
the real roses
sisters equals (as if her art and the real
roses were as identical as sisters). This is
an example of Shakespeare's favourite
technique of using one part of speech for
another, here a noun as a verb. Compare
'a sist'ring vale' at *A Lover's Complaint* l. 2,
antedating *OED*'s first reference, which is
to this line.

8 **Her . . . cherry** her linen thread (*inkle*)
and the silk on which she embroiders
with it, equals the red cherry
twin with resemble closely.
rubied coloured red like a ruby. Another
example of Shakespeare using one part of
speech for another, as in 'sisters' at l. 7,
compressing 'like a ruby' into a single
word. This is the first work to use *rubied* as
an adjective (*OED a.*).

That pupils lacks she none of noble race,
    Who pour their bounty on her, and her gain   10
She gives the cursèd Bawd. Here we her place,
    And to her father turn our thoughts again
Where we left him on the sea. Waves there him tossed,
    Whence, driven tofore the winds, he is arrived
Here where his daughter dwells, and on this coast   15
    Suppose him now at anchor. The city strived
God Neptune's annual feast to keep, from whence
    Lysimachus our Tyrian ship espies,
His banners sable, trimmed with rich expense;
    And to him in his barge with fervour hies.   20
In your supposing once more put your sight;
    Of heavy Pericles think this the barque,
Where what is done in action, more if might,
    Shall be discovered. Please you sit and hark.   *Exit*

Sc. 21 *Enter Helicanus; to him two Sailors, ⌈one of Tyre, the*
        other of Mytilene⌉
SAILOR OF TYRE (*to Sailor of Mytilene*)
    Lord Helicanus can resolve you, sir.

---

9 **That . . . none** (because they want to
learn her skills in embroidery)
race birth

13 **Waves there him tossed** Q's 'we there him
left' pointlessly repeats the first half of the
line, and doesn't rhyme.

14 **tofore** This line echoes John Gower's
original: 'tofore the wynde thei drive'
(l. 1615); Q's '"before" for the rare
"tofore" would be an easy substitution
for any compositor' (*TC*, p. 584).

16 **strived** went to great trouble, outdid itself

17 **Neptune's annual feast** Celebrated on 23
July (Hoeniger).

19 **His** its
banners sable Pericles' ship is flying black
flags in mourning for Marina.

20 **him** it
hies hurries

21 **supposing** imagination

22 **Of . . . barque** imagine that this stage is
the deck of Pericles' ship. Compare Sc.
10.58–60. It is clearly important that
such a climactic episode as the reunion of

Pericles and Marina should occupy the
whole stage.
heavy sorrowful

23–4 **Where . . . discovered** 'where the stage
action, which would show more if it
could, will reveal what happens' (Norton)

Sc. 21.0.1–54 'Even by its own standards, Q
makes a mess of the action and dialogue
of the first portion of this scene, which is
full of short speeches and complicated
comings and goings—a nightmare for
a reporter' (*TC*, p. 585)—especially if, as
Oxford conjectures, the reporter was the
actor playing Marina, who was offstage,
and may have been changing his cos-
tume, during it. It is noticeable that Q
becomes more fluent (and even manages
some verse layout, though not for long)
when Marina appears. Editions which
simply follow Q usually raise problems in
rehearsal, and for that reason the episode
is often truncated. The Oxford editors
attempt to clarify both the text, consider-
ably emended (compare Appendix A, ll.

(*To Helicanus*) There is a barge put off from Mytilene.

In it, Lysimachus, the governor,

Who craves to come aboard. What is your will?

HELICANUS That he have his.

⌐*Exit Sailor of Mytilene*⌐

Call up some gentlemen.   5

⌐SAILOR OF TYRE⌐

Ho, my lord calls!

Enter two or three Gentlemen

FIRST GENTLEMAN   What is your lordship's pleasure?

HELICANUS

Gentlemen, some of worth would come aboard.

I pray you, greet him fairly.

Enter Lysimachus ⌐*with the Sailor and Lords of*
Mytilene⌐

⌐SAILOR OF MYTILENE⌐ (*to Lysimachus*)

This is the man that can in aught resolve you.

LYSIMACHUS (*to Helicanus*)

Hail, reverend sir; the gods preserve you!   10

HELICANUS

And you sir, to outlive the age I am,

And die as I would do.

2011–66), and the staging; they offer a full discussion at *TC*, pp. 584–6. This edition substantially follows Oxford, but modifies its stage directions, and occasionally restores Q where there did not seem an overwhelming need to emend.

0.1 *Enter Helicanus* Oxford brings him on 'above', but I see no need for this (or indeed to use an upper level until the end of the scene, so that the descent of Diana comes as even more of a surprise); surely Helicanus entered at one of the two doors at the back of the Jacobean stage and the two sailors at the other, as was the convention when characters enter, meeting.

1 **resolve** answer

2 **put off** sailed from

5 **Call up** summon. It surely doesn't necessarily mean 'call from below', any more than it does at *Hamlet* 4.1.37, 'we'll call up our wisest friends', though Oxford

assumes that it does by having the Gentlemen enter at l. 6 '*from below the stage*'. It would surely be very cramped for *two or three Gentlemen* under the trap in the Jacobean stage, though I concede that an entry from there would help to emphasize that the main stage is the deck of the ship. But surely the Sailor from Mytilene leaves at one door, and the Gentlemen enter at the other.

6 **What . . . pleasure** Q has 'Doth your lordship call?' Hoeniger doubts that there were originally three speeches, all of them including 'call', so Oxford emends this one, taking a hint for the phrasing from *Cymbeline* 2.3.78: 'What's your lordship's pleasure?'

7 **some of worth** some nobleman (who)

8 **fairly** courteously

9 **in aught resolve** answer anything for

10 **reverend** i.e. worthy of respect (because of his age)

LYSIMACHUS   You wish me well.
  I am the governor of Mytilene;
  Being on shore, honouring of Neptune's triumphs,
  Seeing this goodly vessel ride before us,   15
  I made to it to know of whence you are.
HELICANUS
  Our vessel is of Tyre, in it our king,
  A man who for this three months hath not spoken
  To anyone, nor taken sustenance
  But to prorogue his grief.   20
LYSIMACHUS
  Upon what ground grew his distemperature?
HELICANUS
  'Twould be too tedious to tell it over,
  But the main grief springs from the precious loss
  Of a belovèd daughter and a wife.
LYSIMACHUS
  May we not see him?
HELICANUS   See him, sir, you may,   25
  But bootless is your sight. He will not speak
  To any.
LYSIMACHUS Let me yet obtain my wish.
HELICANUS
  Behold him.
       ⌈*Helicanus draws a curtain, revealing Pericles lying
       upon a couch*⌉

13 **I . . . Mytilene** Oxford moves this line from after l. 16, where Helicanus in Q asks 'First what is your place?' when he already knows it; it is natural for Lysimachus to begin his visit by identifying himself.
14 **triumphs** festivities
16 **of whence you are** where you come from
18 **this** the past
20 **But to prorogue** except to prolong
21 **distemperature** mental disturbance
22 **tell it over** Oxford emends Q's 'repeat' on the grounds that the line is short—'especially improbable here, since the next line is also short'—and that the phrase 'tedious to repeat' is probably a reporter's

memory of 'odious to repeat' (Sc. 4.31) (*TC*, p. 585).
23 **precious** Oxford inserts this word to regularize the line. It is a favourite of Shakespeare's, as *TC*'s examples show: the most telling parallel is at *Winter's Tale* 4.2.23–5: Leontes' 'loss of his most precious queen and children are even now to be afresh lamented'.
26 **bootless** useless
28 *Helicanus . . . couch* Pericles was presumably lying in the 'discovery space' at the back of the Jacobean stage, screened off by curtains. At some point before his scene with Marina begins, he must have been carried forward on to the main stage, since it is inconceivable that such a

This was a goodly person
Till the disaster of one mortal night
Drove him to this.   30

LYSIMACHUS (*to Pericles*)

Sir King, all hail. Hail, royal sir.

⌈*Pericles shrinks down upon his pillow*⌉

HELICANUS

It is in vain, he will not speak to you.

LORD OF MYTILENE

Sir, we have a maid in Mytilene I durst wager
Would win some words of him.

LYSIMACHUS   'Tis well bethought.

She questionless, with her sweet harmony   35
And other choice attractions, would alarm
And make a battery through his deafened ports,
Which now are midway stopped. She in all happy,

---

climactic episode should be confined to
the 'discovery space'. This is a tricky problem, since there is no obvious point at
which to do it, and since Pericles, for all
his comatose state, is a dangerous man,
as appears when he strikes Marina at l.
73. But there is no need for him to be
brought out during the ensuing conversation (indeed he would be in the way), so I
suggest that he be carried out at l. 68.1, to
listen to Marina's song.

28 **a goodly person** At *Tempest* 1.2.417–19,
Prospero uses the same phrase to describe
Ferdinand who, if he were not 'stained |
With grief' might be called 'A goodly
person'.

29 **of one mortal night** Oxford adopt's
Hoeniger's conjecture *of* for Q's 'that'
since it 'more plausibly specifies that the
disaster itself—not the madness—
occurred on one night (Thaisa's death,
leading to his separation from Marina
[and thence to her "death"])' (*TC*, p. 585).
mortal fatal

31.1 *Pericles . . . pillow* From Wilkins's 'he
shrunk himself down upon his pillow'
(p. 541).

33 **durst** dare

34 **of** from (often used interchangeably)

36 **alarm** awaken (literally 'call to arms'). My
emendation of Q's 'allure' slightly modifies Oxford's 'alarum' and makes the line
regular. *Alarm* and 'alarum' were 'differentiated spellings of the same word'
(Onions), and *alarm* is the spelling of all
Oxford's supporting examples (*TC*, p.
586). Were it not for the fact that *alarm*
leads so appropriately into another military expression, 'make a battery', in the
next line, 'allure' might be retained, since
with its sexual overtone it might seem
suited to Lysimachus. True, he is a *converted* whoremonger, but no-one changes
overnight, and his continuing interest in
Marina is clearly audible in his immediately preceding reference to her 'other
choice attractions'.

37 **make a battery** Literally 'assault with
artillery'. It occurs, with the 'alarm' of
the previous line, at *Venus* 424–6: 'To
love's alarms it will not ope the gate . . .
they make no batt'ry.'
ports eardrums (literally, portals, gates
under attack). Steevens's conjecture for
Q's 'parts' is supported by *Kinsmen*
5.3.10–12: 'thine ear . . . into whose port
| Ne'er entered wanton sound'.

38 **midway stopped** half closed
happy skilful

As the fairest of all, among her fellow maids
Dwells now i'th' leafy shelter that abuts   40
Against the island's side. Go fetch her hither.

⌈*Exit Lord*⌉

HELICANUS

Sure, all effectless; yet nothing we'll omit
That bears recovery's name. But since your kindness
We have stretched thus far, let us beseech you
That for our gold we may provision have,   45
Wherein we are not destitute for want,
But weary for the staleness.

LYSIMACHUS   O sir, a courtesy
Which if we should deny, the most just gods
For every graft would send a caterpillar,
And so inflict our province. Yet once more   50
Let me entreat to know at large the cause
Of your king's sorrow.

HELICANUS   Sit, sir. I will recount it.

⌈*Enter Lord with Marina and another maid*⌉

But see, I am prevented.

LYSIMACHUS

O here's the lady that I sent for.—
Welcome, fair one.—Is't not a goodly presence?   55

HELICANUS She's a gallant lady.

LYSIMACHUS

She's such a one that, were I well assured
Came of a gentle kind or noble stock, I'd wish

---

41 **Go . . . hither** Oxford supplies the instruction to fetch Marina that is missing in Q.

42 **all effectless** entirely useless

43 **bears recovery's name** i.e. might cure him

46 **Wherein** of which
for because of

47 **weary for the staleness** tired of lack of variety (Maxwell). They have been on board ship so long that the food has become monotonous.

49 **graft** grafted plant (*graft*ing was the cross-breeding of one plant with another, stronger variety)

50 **inflict** afflict (with famine, since the caterpillars will have eaten the grafted plants)

51 **at large** in detail

53 **prevented** forestalled

55 **presence** person

56 **gallant** excellent, fine

58 **gentle kind or noble stock** Both mean 'an aristocratic family', though Oxford sees a distinction between 'gentry *or* nobility' (*TC*, p. 586), and so alters Q's 'and' to *or*.

No better choice, and think me rarely wed.—
Fair one, all goodness that consists in bounty   60
Expect even here, where is a kingly patient;
If that thy prosperous and artificial feat
Can draw him but to answer thee in aught,
Thy sacred physic shall receive such pay
As thy desires can wish.

MARINA   Sir, I will use   65
My utmost skill in his recure, provided
That none but I and my companion maid
Be suffered to come near him.

⌈*Pericles' couch is put forth; the men stand aside*⌉
The Song

---

60 **all . . . bounty** every advantage that generosity can give (i.e. a generous reward)

62 **prosperous** able to achieve good results
artificial skilful (literally 'using artifice')
feat act, deed

63 **in aught** in anything (i.e. at all)

64 **physic** medicine. Does 'sacred' imply that
she will achieve something miraculous,
or perhaps that it is blessed by the gods,
and therefore holy?

66 **recure** recovery (which is Q's reading, but
which leads to a metrically awkward line.
'Maxwell objects that "recure" is not
found elsewhere as a substantive in
Shakespeare, but he uses it as a verb three
times (all verse, all in situations where
"recover" would fit the sense but not
the metre), [and] the substantive is
recorded until 1626 [*OED sb. Obs.*]' (*TC*, p.
586).)

67 **companion maid** Her only function in the
scene must be to provide vocal or instru-
mental accompaniment to Marina's
song.

68 **suffered** allowed

68.1–71.1 There are two staging difficulties
here. (a) Pericles' couch needs to be
moved out from the 'discovery space' at
the back of the stage on to the main stage
for his climactic scene with Marina; (b) it
is very awkward for anyone to remain on
stage during the Pericles/Marina dialogue
until they are called for at l. 169, even at

the back of the stage, especially since they
would surely intervene when Pericles
strikes Marina at l. 73. I therefore propose
a staging, and a rearrangement of Q, to
deal with both problems. In response to
Marina's insistence that she and her companion are left alone with Pericles, he is
carried out to them on the main stage,
while the others retreat to the back or
sides; after the song Lysimachus comes
forward, but then retreats, and after 'See,
she will speak to him', delivers the lines
that in Q follow l. 68, preceding the song.
This assumes that these lines were misplaced in reaction to Marina's insistence
on being left alone, a suggestion also
made in the New Cambridge edition
(see p. 3, n. 3). Then everyone follows
Lysimachus' instruction and departs,
leaving Pericles and Marina alone
together.

68.1 *put forth* A standard term in stage
directions of the period when large props
need to be moved on to the main stage
(see the note to Sc. 11.54.1), though here
editorial.

68.2 *The Song* No words are provided in Q,
but Wilkins includes some, taken from
Twine. They are perhaps no great work of
art, but they are better than nothing, and
they have often been used in modern performance. They are given in Appendix B,
Passage D.

LYSIMACHUS ⌈*coming forward*⌉
  Marked he your music?
MARINA   No, nor looked on us.
LYSIMACHUS ⌈*returning to the others*⌉
  See, she will speak to him. Come, let us leave her,   70
  And the gods make her prosperous.
      ⌈*Exeunt all but Pericles and Marina*⌉
MARINA
  Hail sir; my lord, lend ear.
PERICLES
  Hum, ha! ⌈*He strikes her*⌉
MARINA
  I am a maid,
  My lord, that ne'er before invited eyes,   75
  But have been gazed on like a comet. She speaks,
  My lord, that maybe hath endured a grief
  Might equal yours, if both were justly weighed.
  Though wayward fortune did malign my state,
  My derivation was from ancestors   80
  Who stood equivalent with mighty kings,
  But time hath rooted out my parentage,
  And to the world and awkward casualties
  Bound me in servitude. (*Aside*) I will desist.

---

73 **Hum . . . her** Q's *Hum, ha* presumably
represents an inarticulate cry of rage at
her persistence, as he strikes her, which
Wilkins confirms that he does (p. 543).
Editorial directions like '*pushing her back*'
are surely not strong enough; although
Pericles himself says 'When I did push
thee back' at l. 116, he may well be
attempting to minimize his earlier
ferocity.

74 The half-line here allows for a pause
before it, as Marina recovers from the
blow and tries to collect her thoughts.

75 **that . . . eyes** i.e. she didn't ask people to
look at her as she is now asking Pericles to

76 **like a comet** i.e. in amazement. Comets
were thought to be omens of major
events.

78 **Might** that might

78 **justly weighed** equally balanced in the
scales

78–9 Later in the scene Pericles quotes
Marina as saying she had 'been tossed
from wrong to injury' (l. 120); in his
abbreviated account of this scene Wilkins
makes her speak this line (p. 543), and
perhaps it should be inserted in the text at
this point. On the other hand, Marina
replies to Pericles 'Some such thing I said'
(l. 122), which may imply that Pericles'
line merely summarizes the drift of her
speech here, and that Wilkins misattrib-
utes Pericles' line to her in his report.

79 **wayward** hostile (as at Sc. 18.10), or fickle
did malign 'regarded with hatred'
(Maxwell)

83 **awkward casualties** adverse chances

But there is something glows upon my cheek,   85
And whispers in mine ear 'Stay till he speak.'
PERICLES
My fortunes, parentage, good parentage,
To equal mine? Was it not thus? What say you?
MARINA
I said if you did know my parentage,
My lord, you would not do me violence.   90
PERICLES
I do think so. Pray you, turn your eyes upon me.
You're like something that—what countrywoman?
Here of these shores?
MARINA   No, nor of any shores,
Yet I was mortally brought forth, and am
No other than I appear.   95
PERICLES
I am great with woe, and shall deliver weeping.
My dearest wife was like this maid, and such a one
My daughter might have been: my queen's square
   brows,
Her stature to an inch, as wand-like straight,
As silver-voiced, her eyes as jewel-like,   100
And cased as richly, in pace another Juno,
Who starves the ears she feeds, and makes them hungry
The more she gives them speech.—Where do you live?

85–6 **But . . . speak** As Marina resolves to stay, the verse clinches her resolution with a couplet. For the sake of regularity, Oxford emends Q's 'Go not' to *Stay* in the second line.

85 **something . . . cheek** See Introduction, p. 55.

92–3 **what . . . shores?** Pericles' questions recall those of Sebastian to Viola/Cesario at their reunion after shipwreck at the climax of *Twelfth Night*: 'What countryman? What name? What parentage?' (5.1.229). The technique of this scene, drawing out the truth by insistent questioning, develops and extends that of the *Twelfth Night* scene.

94 **mortally** as a mortal, by ordinary human birth (perhaps, as Maxwell suggests, with word-play on her birth having been *mortal*—fatal—to her mother)

96 **great** pregnant
   deliver (a) give birth (b) speak
98 **square brows** high and broad forehead
99 **stature** height
101 **cased** enclosed (i.e. by her eyelids, described as 'cases to those heavenly jewels' (compare the previous line) by Cerimon at Sc. 12.96)
   in pace another Juno Juno, queen of the classical gods, was traditionally recognized by her way of walking, as at *Tempest* 4.1.102: 'Great Juno comes; I know her by her gait', ultimately derived from Virgil (*Aeneid* 1.405).
102–3 **starves . . . speech** i.e. the more she says, the more they want to hear (as at *Antony* 2.2.243–4: 'she makes hungry | Where most she satisfies')

MARINA

  Where I am but a stranger. From the deck
  You may discern the place.

PERICLES   Where were you bred,   105
  And how achieved you these endowments which
  You make more rich to owe?

MARINA   If I should tell
  My history, it would seem like lies
  Disdained in the reporting.

PERICLES   Prithee speak.
  Falseness cannot come from thee, for thou look'st   110
  Modest as justice, and thou seem'st a palace
  For the crowned truth to dwell in. I will believe thee,
  And make my senses credit thy relation
  To points that seem impossible; thou show'st
  Like one I loved indeed. What were thy friends?   115
  Didst thou not say, when I did push thee back—
  Which was when I perceived thee—that thou cam'st
  From good descending?

MARINA   So indeed I did.

PERICLES

  Report thy parentage. I think thou said'st
  Thou hadst been tossed from wrong to injury,   120
  And that thou thoughts thy griefs might equal mine,
  If both were opened.

---

105 **bred** brought up

107 **to owe** by owning them

109 **Disdained** that would be scorned (i.e. in disbelief)

  in the reporting even as I spoke

111 **Modest as justice** Presumably because *justice* was represented as a woman, the classical goddess Astraea.

112 **crowned truth** Truth, which Marina represents, is personified as a monarch wearing a crown and living in the palace which is Marina herself.

113 **credit thy relation** trust your story

114 **To** even to

115 **friends** relatives

116–17 **when I . . . perceived thee** Pericles refers back to his striking Marina at l. 73; but *perceived* may imply more than merely

'saw', as Geraint Wyn Davies suggested when rehearsing Pericles at Stratford, Ontario in 1986: an instinctive level of perception achieved through the physical contact. This possibility is supported by *OED*, *perceive*, *v*. 3: 'to apprehend . . . through one of the senses'.

118 **descending** family descent

120 **from wrong to injury** from one wrong to another

121 **thoughts** Q's 'thou thoughts' where we should expect 'thou thought'st' is an example of the way in which 'in verbs ending with *t*, -*test* in the second person singular often becomes -*ts* for euphony' (Abbott 340).

122 **opened** revealed, made plain

MARINA   Some such thing I said,
And said no more but what my circumstance
Did warrant me was likely.
PERICLES   Tell thy story.
If thine considered prove the thousandth part   125
Of my endurance, thou art a man, and I
Have suffered like a girl. Yet thou dost look
Like patience gazing on kings' graves, and smiling
Extremity out of act. What were thy friends?
How lost thou them? Thy name, my most kind virgin?   130
Recount, I do beseech thee. Come, sit by me.
        She sits

MARINA
My name is Marina.
PERICLES   O I am mocked,
And thou by some incensèd god sent hither
To make the world to laugh at me.
MARINA   Patience, good sir,
Or here I'll cease.
PERICLES   Nay, I'll be patient.   135
Thou little know'st how thou dost startle me
To call thyself Marina.
MARINA   The name
Was given me by one that had some power:
My father, and a king.

---

123 **circumstance** detail of my life, evidence.
Q's 'thoughts' repeats l. 121 in a metrically short line, so Oxford emends with a
word that occurs at about the same point
in Wilkins's narrative: 'Pericles . . . by all
the circumstances . . . guessed she was
his child' (p. 544).
124 **warrant** assure
126 **my endurance** what I have endured
126–7 **thou . . . girl** you have endured with a
man's strength, while I have given in to
suffering as if I were a girl
127–9 **thou . . . act** For a discussion of these
evocative lines, see the Introduction, p.
56.
129 **What were thy friends?** By repeating his

question from l. 115, Pericles reverts to the
insistent questioning which forms the
structure of this scene.
131 **Recount** tell me
132 **My name is Marina** Oxford follows
Steevens in inserting 'sir' into Q's phrase,
presumably for metrical reasons, but I
think that the simplicity of this climactic
statement should not be disturbed.
133 **incensèd** enraged
134 **To . . . me** This recalls the phrasing of
the similar reunion between Lear and
Cordelia: 'Do not laugh at me, | For as I
am a man, I think this lady | To be my
child, Cordelia' (*History of Lear* Sc. 21
(4.7).65–7).

PERICLES   How, a king's daughter,
And called Marina?
MARINA   You said you would believe me,   140
But not to be a troubler of your peace,
I will end here.
PERICLES   But are you flesh and blood?
Have you a working pulse and are no fairy?
Motion as well? Speak on. Where were you born,
And wherefore called Marina?
MARINA   Called Marina   145
For I was born at sea.
PERICLES   At sea? What mother?
MARINA
My mother was the daughter of a king,
Who died when I was born, as my good nurse
Lychorida hath oft recounted weeping.
PERICLES
O, stop there a little! ⌈*Aside*⌉ This is the rarest dream   150
That e'er dull sleep did mock sad fools withal.
This cannot be my daughter, buried. Well.—
Where were you bred? I'll hear you more to th' bottom
Of your story, and never interrupt you.
MARINA
You'll scarce believe me, 'twere best I did give o'er.   155
PERICLES
I will believe you by the syllable
Of what you shall deliver. Yet give me leave.

---

143 **working** beating
　fairy spirit. (Pericles still fears he may be
　the victim of deception by supernatural
　powers.) Compare Lear's reaction to
　Cordelia: 'You're a spirit, I know. Where
　did you die?' (Sc. 21 (4.7).47).
144 **Motion as well** Q's 'Motion well' has
　provoked much debate, but Maxwell's
　solution works well: 'have you motion
　(movement) as well as a beating
　pulse?'
149 **recounted** Oxford's emendation for Q's
　'delivered' which appears to be a
　reporter's echo of l. 96, where it is inte-
　gral to the pregnancy metaphor.

151 **dull** Q4's emendation of Q1's 'dulled'
　seems right: it is the sleeper who is dulled,
　not sleep itself.
　withal with
152 **buried** who is buried
155 **You'll scarce believe me** Q's 'You scorn,
　believe me' makes sense if 'believe me'
　means 'I assure you', but Malone's emen-
　dation makes better sense: Pericles will
　not find her story credible. 'Scorne' is an
　easy misreading for 'scarce'.
156 **by the syllable** in every word (an
　emphatic reply to Marina's doubts in the
　previous line)
157 **give me leave** (to ask)

How came you in these parts? Where were you bred?

MARINA

The King my father did in Tarsus leave me,

Till cruel Cleon, with his wicked wife,   160

Did seek to murder me, and wooed a villain

To attempt the deed; who having drawn to do't,

A crew of pirates came and rescued me.

To Mytilene they brought me. But good sir,

What will you of me? Why do you weep? It may be   165

You think me an impostor. No, good faith,

I am the daughter to King Pericles,

If good King Pericles be.

PERICLES ⌈*rising*⌉ Ho, Helicanus!

    Enter Helicanus, Lysimachus, and attendants

HELICANUS Calls my lord?   170

PERICLES

Thou art a grave and noble councillor,

Most wise in general. Tell me if thou canst

What this maid is, or what is like to be,

That thus hath made me weep.

HELICANUS   I know not,

But here's the regent, sir, of Mytilene   175

Speaks nobly of her.

LYSIMACHUS   She would never tell

Her parentage. Being demanded that,

She would sit still and weep.

PERICLES

O Helicanus, strike me, honoured sir,

Give me a gash, put me to present pain,   180

Lest this great sea of joys rushing upon me

O'erbear the shores of my mortality

---

162 **drawn** (his sword)

165 **What will you of me?** 'What do you want of me?', which is what Q's 'Whither will you have me?' means; Oxford emends a phrase which Marina has already used twice before in her preceding scene (Sc. 19.177, 202), and which may therefore derive from a reporter.

168 **be** lives

173 **like** likely

175 **regent** ruler (*OED sb.* 1b)

176 **Speaks** who speaks

180–3 **Give me . . . sweetness**   These metaphorical lines powerfully evoke the sense of a man overwhelmed by unexpected happiness; see the Introduction, p. 56.

180 **present** immediate

182 **O'erbear** overwhelm
    mortality human condition

And drown me with their sweetness! (*To Marina*) O come
    hither,
Thou that begett'st him that did thee beget,
Thou that wast born at sea, buried at Tarsus,   185
And found at sea again!—O Helicanus,
Down on thy knees, thank the holy gods as loud
As thunder threatens us, this is Marina!
(*To Marina*) What was thy mother's name? Tell me but that,
For truth can never be confirmed enough,   190
Though doubts did ever sleep.
MARINA   First, sir, I pray,
What is your title?
PERICLES   I am Pericles
Of Tyre. But tell me now my drowned queen's name.
As in the rest thou hast been godlike perfect,
So prove but true in that, thou art my daughter,   195
The heir of kingdoms, and another life
To Pericles thy father.
MARINA ⌈*kneeling*⌉   Is it no more
To be your daughter than to say my mother's name?
Thaisa was my mother, who did end
The minute I began.   200
PERICLES
Now blessing on thee! Rise. Thou art my child.
    ⌈*Marina stands. He kisses her*⌉
  ⌈*To attendants*⌉ Give me fresh garments.—Mine own,
    Helicanus!

---

184 **Thou . . . beget** For the full significance and impact of this line, see the Introduction, p. 57.
begett'st i.e. gives new life to
189 **What . . . name** Even after the ecstasy of the preceding lines, he returns to factual questions again: he needs to be sure.
191 **Though . . . sleep** 'though all doubts were laid to rest' (Deighton)
194 **rest** Oxford deletes Q's 'you said': it clashes with the 'thou' used by Pericles to Marina consistently from l. 184, and results in an irregular line.
godlike perfect (a) as omniscient as if you were a god; (b) like a god in your perfection
195 **So . . . daughter** This is Oxford's propos-

al for a line probably missing in Q. *Prove but true* was suggested by *Twelfth Night* 3.4.367; 'thou art my daughter' provides the cue for Marina's reply at l. 198.
197–8 **Is it . . . name** is saying my mother's name the only thing I need to do to be acknowledged as your daughter
199–200 **who . . . began** Compare *Winter's Tale* 5.3.45: 'Dear Queen, that ended when I but began'.
201 After all the agonies, ecstasies, and questions, Pericles' acceptance of Marina is expressed with beautiful simplicity.
202 **fresh garments** Compare *History of Lear* Sc. 21 (4.7).20.
Mine own She is my own

Not dead at Tarsus, as she should have been
By savage Cleon. She shall tell thee all,
When thou shalt kneel and justify in knowledge   205
She is thy very princess. Who is this?

HELICANUS

Sir, 'tis the governor of Mytilene,
Who hearing of your melancholy state,
Did come to see you.

PERICLES (*to Lysimachus*) I embrace you, sir.—
Give me my robes.
⌈*He is attired in fresh robes*⌉
                              I am wild in my beholding.   210
O heavens bless my girl! But hark, what music?
Tell Helicanus, my Marina, tell him
O'er point by point, for yet he seems to doubt,
How sure you are my daughter. But what music?

HELICANUS My lord, I hear none.   215

PERICLES

None? The music of the spheres, list, my Marina.

LYSIMACHUS

It is not good to cross him, give him way.

PERICLES Rarest sounds, do ye not hear?

LYSIMACHUS Music, my lord? I hear.

PERICLES Most heavenly music.   220
It nips me unto listening, and thick slumber

---

203 **should have been** was intended to be
204 **By** at the hands of
205 **justify in knowledge** acknowledge through knowing the facts that
210 **wild in my beholding** 'ecstatic, almost delirious (*OED a.* 10) in what I see' seems to fit the intensity of the scene better than the prosaic 'unkempt in appearance'.
211 **hark, what music?** See the Introduction, p. 58, for a discussion as to whether or not the celestial music should be audible to the audience. Since there are strong arguments on both sides, and since Q does not specify music, this edition does not insert a direction for any, leaving the issue open. Helicanus and Lysimachus don't hear the music; it is clear from l. 217 that

Lysimachus' 'I hear' at l. 219 is spoken to humour Pericles. Whether Marina hears it is left ambiguous.
213 **point by point** detail by detail
214 **sure** certainly
216 **The music of the spheres** See Introduction, p. 58.
221 **nips** compels. Maxwell thinks this 'a vividly Shakespearian image for the keen attention the music provokes'; Oxford objects that *nips* suggests 'an irritant, whereas Pericles experiences rapture' (*TC*, p. 588), but this objection seems to me to miss the utterly Shakespearian (and especially late-Shakespearian) contribution of pain to ecstatic experiences, sharpening them by contrast.

Hangs upon mine eyelids. Let me rest.

    He sleeps

LYSIMACHUS

A pillow for his head. ⌈*To Marina and others*⌉ Companion
    friends,

If this but answer to my just belief

I'll well remember you. So leave him all.   225

           Exeunt all but Pericles

    Diana ⌈*descends from the heavens*⌉

DIANA

My temple stands in Ephesus. Hie thee thither,

    And do upon mine altar sacrifice.

There when my maiden priests are met together,

    At large discourse thy fortunes in this wise:

With a full voice before the people all,   230

    Reveal how thou at sea didst lose thy wife.

To mourn thy crosses, with thy daughter's, call

    And give them repetition to the life.

223–5 **Companion friends . . . him all** Q's speech has drawn editorial fire for both its alleged verbal and metrical defects. But Oxford shows that Shakespeare juxtaposes 'companion' and 'friend' often (*TC*, p. 588) and solves the lineation problem by moving *So leave him all* to the end of the speech, thus providing a strong exit line.

224 **but . . . belief** only turn out as I expect (i.e. that Marina is a princess, and so suitable to be my wife)

225 **remember** reward

225.2 *Diana . . . heavens* The many references to the play's presiding deity earlier have prepared for her eventual appearance, as Pericles' hearing the music of the spheres has prepared him to be receptive to the goddess. Her descent is a theatrical externalizing of his dream, as the descent of Jupiter at *Cymbeline* 5.5.186.1–207 is an externalizing of Posthumus's. And as with Jupiter, Diana was probably flown down from the area above the Jacobean stage known as 'the heavens', which usually housed flying apparatus operated by a winch. Characters descended seated in a chair or throne.

226 **My . . . Ephesus** See Sc. 14.12 and note. **Hie thee thither** hasten there

228 **maiden priests** vestal virgins. See Sc. 14.9 and note.

229–30 **At large . . . voice** Although Q prints Diana's speech in prose, it clearly falls into two quatrains and a concluding couplet—or would do so, were there not a line and a half obviously missing, supplied by Oxford here. The editors explain how they went about this in detail at *TC* p. 589. The rhyme *wise* with *sacrifice* occurs in Gower's next speech (ll. 11–12); *At large discourse thy fortunes* is parallelled at the climax of *The Comedy of Errors* where the Abbess at Ephesus, a character derived from the sources for *Pericles*, invites the other characters to 'hear at large discoursèd all our fortunes' (5.1.398); *With a full voice* has a parallel at e.g. *Henry V* 4.4.64.

229 **At large discourse** describe in detail **wise** manner

230 **full** loud

232 **crosses** misfortunes **call** declare

233 **give . . . life** recount them in lifelike detail (Maxwell)

Perform my bidding, or thou liv'st in woe;
　　Do't, and rest happy, by my silver bow.   235
Awake, and tell thy dream.
　　　　　　　　⌜*Diana ascends into the heavens*⌝

PERICLES

Celestial Dian, goddess argentine,
I will obey thee. (*Calling*) Helicanus!
　　　Enter Helicanus, Lysimachus, and Marina

HELICANUS   Sir?

PERICLES

My purpose was for Tarsus, there to strike
The inhospitable Cleon, but I am   240
For other service first. Toward Ephesus
Turn our blown sails. Eftsoons I'll tell thee why.
　　　　　　　　　　⌜*Exit Helicanus*⌝

Shall we refresh us, sir, upon your shore,
And give you gold for such provision
As our intents will need?

LYSIMACHUS   With all my heart, sir,   245
And when you come ashore I have a suit.

PERICLES

You shall prevail, were it to woo my daughter,
For it seems you have been noble towards her.

LYSIMACHUS

Sir, lend me your arm.

PERICLES   Come, my Marina.
　　　　　Exit Pericles supported by Lysimachus
　　　　　at one arm, and by Marina at the other

235　**rest** remain. Oxford supplies a word that
　　is missing in Q.
　　silver bow Diana was the goddess of hunt-
　　ing as well as chastity, and of the moon,
　　which may have suggested *silver*. At
　　Dream 1.1.9–10, the crescent moon is
　　compared to 'a silver bow | New bent in
　　heaven'. See the next note.

237　**argentine** silvery (*OED a.* 2). The adjec-
　　tive was probably suggested by 'argentea'
　　in Ovid's description of Diana (*Heroides*
　　18.71). In Samuel Daniel's masque *The
　　Vision of the Twelve Goddesses* (1604),

Diana wears 'a green mantle embroidered
with silver half moons' and has 'a bow
and a quiver' of arrows (ll. 75–6).

242　**blown** full, inflated
　　Eftsoons afterwards (*OED adv.* 3), an
　　archaism much used by Spenser, but not
　　otherwise by Shakespeare, who probably
　　borrowed it from Twine (pp. 426, 476).

245　**intents** purposes

246　**a** Q's 'another' is extrametrical, and
　　'Lysimachus has no other suit' (*TC*, p.
　　589).

Sc. 22 *Enter Gower*

GOWER

Now our sands are almost run;
More a little, and then dumb.
This my last boon give me,
For such kindness must relieve me,
That you aptly will suppose   5
What pageantry, what feats, what shows,
What minstrelsy and pretty din
The regent made in Mytilene
To greet the King. So well he thrived
That he is promised to be wived   10
To fair Marina, but in no wise
Till he had done his sacrifice
As Dian bade, whereto being bound
The interim, pray you, all confound.
In feathered briefness sails are filled,   15
And wishes fall out as they're willed.
At Ephesus the temple see
⌈*An altar, Thaisa and other vestals are revealed*;
Cerimon is present⌉
Our king, and all his company.
⌈*Enter Pericles, Marina, Lysimachus, Helicanus, with
attendants*⌉

Sc. 22.1 sands . . . run i.e. through an hour-glass (as at *Cymbeline* 3.2.72–3): 'the sands | That run i'th' clock's behalf')

2 **More . . . dumb** there is only a little more to say and then the story (and/or I) will be silent. F4's reading 'done' for 'dumb' would be tempting, were it not for the numerous assonantal rhymes in the early part of the play. But since those are a characteristic feature of Wilkins's style, either Shakespeare is imitating Wilkins here, or Wilkins wrote this speech.

3–4 **This . . . relieve me** Maxwell compares Prospero's epilogue in *The Tempest*, 'And my ending is despair | Unless I be relieved by prayer' (ll. 15–16), though Prospero's tone is darker and more serious.

5 **aptly will suppose** will readily imagine

6 **feats** activities

7 **pretty** pleasing

8 **regent** (Lysimachus)

9–10 **thrived . . . wived** A common prover-bial jingle: 'First thrive and then wive' (Dent T264).

11 **wise** way

12 **he** (Pericles)

13 **bade** commanded
whereto to which
being bound (he is) on his way

14 **The interim . . . confound** destroy (Schmidt), do away with the time between. As at Sc. 18.1–2, Gower carries the audience over an interval of time and space.

15 **feathered briefness** 'with the speed of a bird in flight' (Maxwell)

16 **as they're willed** as you want them to be

17.1–2, 18.1–2 There are no stage directions at all in Q; these are based on Oxford's, and are introduced during Gower's speech to emphasize the interweaving that is evident elsewhere (e.g. Sc. 1.39.1; Sc. 5.38.1; Sc. 15.50.1).

17.1–2 *An altar . . . present* Probably these

That he can hither come so soon
Is by your fancies' thankful doom.   *Exit*   20

PERICLES

Hail, Dian. To perform thy just command
I here confess myself the King of Tyre,
Who frighted from my country, did espouse
The fair Thaisa (*Thaisa starts*) at Pentapolis.
At sea in childbed died she, but brought forth   25
A maid child called Marina, who, O goddess,
Wears yet thy silver livery. She at Tarsus
Was nursed with Cleon, who at fourteen years
He sought to murder, but her better stars
Bore her to Mytilene, 'gainst whose shore riding   30
Her fortunes brought the maid aboard our barque,
Where by her own most clear remembrance, she
Made known herself my daughter.

THAISA   Voice and favour—

You are, you are—O royal Pericles!
          She falls

---

were '*revealed*' in the 'discovery space' at the back of the stage. Thaisa and Cerimon would then come out on to the main stage to participate in the scene.

19–20 **That . . . doom** Gower shares a genial joke with the audience as he reminds them that they must use their imaginations.

20 **fancies'** imagination's
  thankful doom judgement, for which we are grateful

21 **just** exact

23 **espouse** 'Metre requires an iambic synonym for [Q's] "wed" and Wilkins supplies one [at p.] 544' (*TC*, p. 590).

24 *Thaisa starts* This (obvious) stage direction is confirmed by Wilkins: 'Thaisa. At the naming of whom, she herself being by, could not choose but start' (pp. 544–5). Compare '*He starteth*' in the 1594 Quarto of *2 Henry VI* (4.1.32.1 in Oxford) when Suffolk hears the name of the man by whom it was prophesied he should die.

26 **who** Q's 'whom' was perhaps wrongly corrected instead of the 'who' in l. 28 (Maxwell), but see the note.

27 **Wears . . . livery** i.e. is still a virgin. See the second note to Sc. 9.9, and for *silver*, the note to *argentine* at Sc. 21.237.

28 **with** by
  who Sometimes altered, as by Oxford, to 'whom', but 'who' as an object is common in Shakespeare, as at *Hamlet* 2.2.197: 'Between who?'

30 **Bore** Oxford emends Q's 'brought' which 'suspiciously occurs three times in five lines, and this seems the least appropriate of the three occasions' (*TC*, p. 590), especially since 'Her fortunes brought' in the next line duplicates the sense of Q's 'her better stars brought her'.
  riding as we rode at anchor

31 **aboard our barque** Q has 'aboard us'. 'Q's line is a syllable short, and entails an idiom unparalleled in the canon' (*TC*, p. 590). Oxford's emendation uses an idiom from *Tempest* 1.2.144: 'they hurried us aboard a barque'; and Gower calls Pericles' ship a barque when introducing it (Sc. 20.22).

32 **remembrance** recollection (retelling her story)

33 **favour** appearance

PERICLES

What means the nun? She dies. Help, gentlemen!   35

CERIMON   Noble sir,

If you have told Diana's altar true,

This is your wife.

PERICLES   Reverend appearer, no.

I threw her overboard with these same arms.

CERIMON

Upon this coast, I warrant you.

PERICLES   'Tis most certain.   40

CERIMON

Look to the lady. O, she's but overjoyed.

Early one blustering morn this lady

Was thrown upon this shore. I oped the coffin,

Found there rich jewels, recovered her, and placed her

Here in Diana's temple.

PERICLES   May we see them?   45

CERIMON

Great sir, they shall be brought you to my house,

Whither I invite you. Look, Thaisa is

Recoverèd.

THAISA   O let me look upon him!

If he be none of mine, my sanctity

Will to my sense bend no licentious ear,   50

But curb it, spite of seeing. O my lord,

Are you not Pericles? Like him you spake,

Like him you are. Did you not name a tempest,

A birth and death?

PERICLES   The voice of dead Thaisa!   55

THAISA   That Thaisa

---

35 **nun** Collier's emendation of Q's absurd 'mum' is supported by Wilkins, who calls Thaisa a nun in this episode (p. 545). Q's reading is so preposterous that it is likelier to be a slip by the compositor than the reporter: m/n confusions abound, for example 'dumb Iohn' for 'Don John' in the Quarto of *Much Ado* at 2.1.77.2.

38 **appearer** one who appears, comes to one's notice (or perhaps *reverend appearer* is a linked phrase, meaning 'one who appears reverend', i.e. worthy of respect because old)

44 **recovered** revived

49–51 **If . . . seeing** if he is not my husband, my religious vocation will not indulge my sensual impulse, but curb it, despite appearances

Am I, supposèd dead and drowned.

PERICLES ⌜*taking Thaisa's hand*⌝
    Immortal Dian!

THAISA   Now I know you better.
    When we with tears parted Pentapolis,
    The King my father gave you such a ring.   60

PERICLES
    This, this! No more, you gods. Your present kindness
    Makes my past miseries sports; you shall do well
    That on the touching of her lips I may
    Melt, and no more be seen.—O come, be buried
    A second time within these arms.
            ⌜*They embrace and kiss*⌝

MARINA (*kneeling to Thaisa*)   My heart   65
    Leaps to be gone into my mother's bosom.

PERICLES
    Look who kneels here: flesh of thy flesh, Thaisa,
    Thy burden at the sea, and called Marina
    For she was yielded there.

THAISA ⌜*embracing Marina*⌝   Blest, and mine own!

HELICANUS ⌜*kneeling to Thaisa*⌝
    Hail madam, and my queen.

THAISA   I know you not.   70

PERICLES
    You have heard me say, when I did fly from Tyre,
    I left behind an ancient substitute.
    Can you remember what I called the man?
    I have named him oft.

THAISA ’Twas Helicanus then.   75

---

58 *taking Thaisa's hand* Oxford says that its
    conjectural direction 'explains her notic-
    ing the ring upon his finger' (*TC*, p. 590).
    Immortal Dian (be praised)
59 **parted** departed from
61 **No more** (because this happiness is as
    much as I can bear)
62–3 **shall . . . That** should . . . if
63–4 **I may . . . seen** Either 'that I may die in
    ecstasy at the moment of kissing her',
    recalling the interrelation of ecstatic plea-
    sure and pain at Sc. 21.179–83; or more

simply 'that I may become one with
    her'.
67 **flesh . . . flesh** A biblical echo: Adam calls
    Eve 'flesh of my flesh' at Genesis 2: 23.
69 **For** because
    yielded brought forth, born
    Blest I follow Q's spelling to make clear
    that this is a monosyllable; Thaisa's
    speech completes a regular blank verse
    line.
71 **fly** flee
72 **ancient** elderly

PERICLES Still confirmation.
    Embrace him, dear Thaisa; this is he.
    Now do I long to hear how you were found,
    How possibly preserved, and who to thank—
    Besides the gods—for this great miracle.   80
THAISA
    Lord Cerimon, my lord. This is the man
    Through whom the gods have shown their power, that
        can
    From first to last resolve you.
PERICLES (*to Cerimon*)   Reverend sir,
    The gods can have no mortal officer
    More like a god than you. Will you deliver   85
    How this dead queen re-lives?
CERIMON   I will, my lord.
    Beseech you, first go with me to my house,
    Where shall be shown you all was found with her,
    And told how in this temple she came placed,
    No needful thing omitted.
PERICLES   Pure Dian,   90
    I bless thee for thy vision, and will offer
    Nightly oblations to thee.—Thaisa,
    This prince, the fair betrothèd of your daughter,
    Shall marry her at Pentapolis.
    (*To Marina*) And now this ornament   95
    Makes me look dismal will I clip to form,
    And what this fourteen years no razor touched,
    To grace thy marriage day I'll beautify.

---

79 **possibly** by what possible means
83 **resolve you** answer all your questions
84 **mortal officer** human agent
85 **deliver** relate
88 **all** all that
89 **And told . . . placed** Oxford's reconstruction regularizes Q's line ('how she came placed here in the temple') by adding *And told*, and draws on Wilkins—'for in this temple was she placed to be a nun' (p. 545)—to emend a line whose similarity to ll. 44–5 suggests 'cross-contamination . . . by the reporter' (Brooks, cited in Hoeniger).
    came came to be

92 **Nightly oblations** evening prayers. Q's 'night oblations' means the same thing, but Maxwell's *Nightly* gives, as he says, 'a more natural expression, and, if the lineation is otherwise correct, restores metre'.
93 **fair** handsome. *OED a.* 1a shows that *fair* was applied to both men and women in the period.
95 **ornament** (his long hair and beard)
96 **Makes** which makes
    form proper shape
98 **beautify** Although Polonius criticizes 'beautified' as 'a vile phrase' at *Hamlet* 2.2.111, *beautify* does not seem to be used

THAISA

Lord Cerimon hath letters of good credit,
Sir, from Pentapolis: my father's dead.   100

PERICLES

Heaven make a star of him! Yet there, my queen,
We'll celebrate their nuptials, and ourselves
Will in that kingdom spend our following days.
Our son and daughter shall in Tyrus reign.—
Lord Cerimon, we do our longing stay   105
To hear the rest untold. Sir, lead's the way.   *Exeunt*
     Enter Gower

GOWER

In Antiochus and his daughter you have heard
Of monstrous lust the due and just reward;
In Pericles, his queen, and daughter seen,
Although assailed with fortune fierce and keen,   110
Virtue preserved from fell destruction's blast,
Led on by heaven, and crowned with joy at last.
In Helicanus may you well descry
A figure of truth, of faith, of loyalty.
In reverend Cerimon there well appears   115
The worth that learnèd charity aye wears.
For wicked Cleon and his wife, when fame

---

for critical effect elsewhere in the Shakespeare canon.

99 **good credit** trustworthiness
100 **from Pentapolis** Wilkins's account gives
this information when Pericles departs for
Tyre (p. 545). By inserting it, Oxford
'completes the verse line, picks up "at
Pentapolis" in the preceding speech . . .
and explains "there" in the following' line
(*TC*, p. 591).
101 **Heaven . . . him** 'The primary reference
is undoubtedly to the translation of Julius
Caesar's soul to a star at the end of Ovid's
Metamorphoses [Book 15.843–51]'
(Hoeniger).
Heaven Oxford adopts the *Heaven* of Q's
catchword rather than the 'Heavens' of
its text because 'Shakespeare overwhelm-
ingly prefers the singular' (*TC*, p. 591).
102 **their nuptials** the wedding of Marina
and Lysimachus

105 **do our longing stay** are curbing our
impatience (i.e. are impatient to hear the
rest)
106 **untold** that is untold
lead's the way For a similar phrase to
clear the stage, compare *Winter's Tale*
5.3.156: 'Hastily lead away.'
lead's lead us
107–24 Gower glances back over the play,
providing a 'moral' comment on each
character. It is sometimes staged as a kind
of tableau, the characters assembling as
he refers to them.
111 **fell** cruel
blast attack (literally 'icy wind', as at
Winter's Tale 4.4.111–12: 'blasts of
January | Would blow you through and
through')
113 **descry** see, observe
116 **aye** always
117 **wicked . . . wife** It would be fairer to the
facts to read 'Cleon and his wicked wife',

Had spread their cursèd deed to the honoured name
Of Pericles, to rage the city turn,
That him and his they in his palace burn.   120
The gods for murder seemèd so content
To punish that, although not done, but meant.
So on your patience evermore attending,
New joy wait on you. Here our play has ending.   *Exit*

since she instigated the murder; his guilt
lay only in concealing it. But the play, like
its sources, consistently gives Cleon a
rough ride and lays the blame specifically
on him.
fame report, rumour

118 **their** Q reads 'his', as usual laying
the blame for the planned murder on
Cleon. Q4's *their* at least spreads the
responsibility.
to against

119 **to . . . turn** the citizens became enraged.
Or perhaps ll. 117–19 mean 'when report
had spread the news of their attempted
murder, respect for Pericles' reputation
enraged the city'.

120 **his** his family

122 **although . . . meant**   although   the
intended crime was not carried out

123 **on . . . attending** Is this a polite request
for applause, as is customary in Shakespearian epilogues?

A DIPLOMATIC REPRINT OF THE FIRST QUARTO
OF *PERICLES* (1609)

The text and intoduction that follow, by Gary Taylor and MacD. P. Jackson, are
reprinted from *William Shakespeare, The Complete Works: Original Spelling Edition*,
General Editors: Stanley Wells and Gary Taylor (1986)

The text which follows reproduces as exactly as possible the uncorrected
state of the first edition of *Pericles*. It preserves the spelling, punctuation,
italicization, and capitalization of that edition; it also reproduces ligatures
and the use of 'vv' for 'ww'.

For ease of reference, each page is identified by a signature; as is normal
in quartos of the period, the original does not mark versos at all, or the final
recto of each sheet; nor does it provide a signature for the title-page ('A1').
Blank pages are not reproduced. Beside each signature reference we
identify the compositor believed to have set the page: X worked in the shop
of William White; Y and Z in the shop of Thomas Creede. For two pages
(F3, F4^v) the compositor is uncertain: it was either Y or a fourth workman.
In addition to this signature information, each type line is numbered
consecutively.

We do not reproduce the catchwords, which merely duplicate at the
bottom right of each page the first word on the next, except in the follow-
ing cases: *king.* (D3), *2.Sayl.* Sir (E2), *Cler.* I (E4^v), *Bawd.* (F4^v), *Cle.* (G1^v),
Gower. (G3, uncorrected state), golde, (G4^v), Hoe (H4^v), *Per.* Heauen (I3).

We do not preserve differences in type size or in the exact face of different
types. We have placed a space after all punctuation marks; the practice of
the original is erratic. We have tried to reproduce anomalies of spacing (or
the lack of it) between words and letters; but sometimes the original is
ambiguous. We have not attempted to indicate spacing around stage
directions, such as the use of blank lines above or below directions, or the
exact indentation of stage directions on the page. Nor do we preserve the
ornaments on the title-page and A2, or the ornamental letter which begins
the first word of Gower's first speech.

The reprint is based upon collation of the Bodleian copy, supplemented
by consultation of a facsimile of the Huntington copy, and of the published
record of press variants in all nine known copies.

A Diplomatic Reprint of
Pericles (1609)

THE LATE, A1 (X)
And much admired Play,
Called
Pericles, Prince
of Tyre. 5
With the true Relation of the whole Hiſtorie,
aduentures, and fortunes of the ſaid Prince:
As alſo,
The no leſſe ſtrange, and worthy accidents,
in the Birth and Life, of his Daughter 10
MARIANA.
As it hath been diuers and ſundry times acted by
his Maieſties Seruants, at the Globe on
the Banck-ſide.
By William Shakeſpeare. 15
Imprinted at London for *Henry Goſſon*, and are
to be ſold at the ſigne of the Sunne in
Pater-noſter row, &c.
I 6 O 9.

The Play of Pericles A2 (X)
Prince of Tyre. &c. 21
Enter Gower.

To ſing a Song that old was ſung,
From aſhes, auntient *Gower* is come,
Aſſuming mans infirmities, 25
To glad your eare, and pleaſe your eyes:
It hath been ſung at Feaſtiuals,
On Ember eues, and Holydayes:
And Lords and Ladyes in their liues,
Haue red it for reſtoratiues: 30
The purchaſe is to make men glorious,
Et bonum quo Antiquius eo melius:
If you, borne in thoſe latter times,
When Witts more ripe, accept my rimes;
And that to heare an old man ſing, 35

May to your Wifhes pleafure bring:
I life would wifh, and that I might
Wafte it for you, like Taper light.
This *Antioch*, then *Antiochus* the great,
Buylt vp this Citie, for his chiefeft Seat;   40
The fayreft in all *Syria*.
I tell you what mine Authors faye:
This King vnto him tooke a Peere,
Who dyed, and left a female heyre,
So buckfome, blith, and full of face,   45
As heauen had lent her all his grace:
With whom the Father liking tooke,
And her to Inceft did prouoke:
Bad child, worfe father, to intice his owne
To euill, fhould be done by none: A2v (X)
But cuftome what they did begin,   51
Was with long vfe, account'd no finne;
The beautie of this finfull Dame,
Made many Princes thither frame,
To feeke her as a bedfellow,   55
In maryage pleafures, playfellow:
Which to preuent, he made a Law,
To keepe her ftill, and men in awe:
That who fo askt her for his wife,
His Riddle tould, not loft his life: 60
So for her many of wight did die,
As yon grimme lookes do teftifie.
What now enfues, to the iudgement of your eye,
I giue my caufe, who beft can iuftifie.   *Exit.*
  Enter Antiochus, Prince Pericles, and followers.   65
 Anti. Young Prince of *Tyre*, you haue at large receiued
The danger of the taske you vndertake.
 Peri. I haue (*Antiochus*) and with a foule emboldned
With the glory of her prayfe, thinke death no hazard,
In this enterprife.   70
 Ant. Muficke bring in our daughter, clothed like a bride,
For embracements euen of *Ioue* himfelfe;
At whofe conception, till *Lucina* rained,
Nature this dowry gaue; to glad her prefence,
The Seanate houfe of Planets all did fit,   75
To knit in her, their beft perfections.
   Enter Antiochus daughter.
 Per. See where fhe comes, appareled like the Spring,

Graces her fubiects, and her thoughts the King,
Of euery Vertue giues renowne to men :   80
Her face the booke of prayfes, where is read,
Nothing but curious pleafures, as from thence,
Sorrow were euer racte, and teaftie wrath
Could neuer be her milde companion.
You Gods that made me man, and fway in loue ;   A3 (X)
That haue enflamde defire in my breaft,   86
To tafte the fruite of yon celeftiall tree,
(Or die in th'aduenture) be my helpes,
As I am fonne and feruant to your will,
To compaffe fuch a bondleffe happineffe.   90
    Anti. Prince *Pericles.*
    Peri. That would be fonne to great *Antiochus.*
    Ant. Before thee ftandes this faire *Hefperides*,
With golden fruite, but dangerous to be toucht :
For Death like Dragons heere affright thee hard :   95
Her fa ce like Heauen, inticeth thee to view
Her countleffe glory ; which defert muft gaine :
And which without defert, becaufe thine eye
Prefumes to reach, all the whole heape muft die :
Yon fometimes famous Princes, like thy felfe,   100
Drawne by report, aduentrous by defire,
Tell thee with fpeachleffe tongues, and femblance pale,
That without couering, faue yon field of Starres,
Heere they ftand Martyrs flaine in *Cupids* Warres :
And with dead cheekes, aduife thee to defift,   105
For going on deaths net, whom none refift.
    Per. Antiochus, I thanke thee, who hath taught,
My frayle mortalitie to know it felfe ;
And by thofe fearefull obiectes, to prepare
This body, like to them, to what I muft :   110
For Death remembered fhould be like a myrrour,
Who tels vs, life's but breath, to truft it errour :
Ile make my Will then, and as fickemen doe,
Who know the World, fee Heauen, but feeling woe,
Gripe not at earthly ioyes as earft they did ;   115
So I bequeath a happy peace to you,
And all good men, as euery Prince fhould doe ;
My ritches to the earth, from whence they came ;
But my vnfpotted fire of Loue, to you :
Thus ready for the way of life or death,   120
I wayte the fharpeft blow (*Antiochus*)

234

Scorning aduice; read the concluſion then: A3v (X)
Which read and not expounded, tis decreed,
As theſe before thee, thou thy ſelfe ſhalt bleed.
   Daugh. Of all ſayd yet, mayſt thou prooue proſperous,   125
Of all ſayd yet, I wiſh thee happineſſe.
   Peri. Like a bold Champion I aſſume the Liſtes,
Nor aske aduiſe of any other thought,
But faythfulneſſe and courage.

The Riddle.   130

> *I am no Viper, yet I feed*
> *On mothers fleſh which did me breed:*
> *I ſought a Huſband, in which labour,*
> *I found that kindneſſe in a Father;*
> *Hee's Father, Sonne, and Huſband milde;*   135
> *I, Mother, Wife; and yet his child:*
> *How they may be, and yet in two,*
> *As you will liue reſolue it you.*

Sharpe Phiſicke is the laſt: But ô you powers!
That giues heauen countleſſe eyes to view mens actes,   140
Why cloude they not their ſights perpetually,
If this be true, which makes me pale to read it?
Faire Glaſſe of light, I lou'd you, and could ſtill,
Were not this glorious Casket ſtor'd with ill:
But I muſt tell you, now my thoughts reuolt,   145
For hee's no man on whom perfections waite,
That knowing ſinne within, will touch the gate.
You are a faire Violl, and your ſenſe, the ſtringes;
Who finger'd to make man his lawfull muſicke,
Would draw Heauen downe, and all the Gods to harken: 150
But being playd vpon before your time,
Hell onely daunceth at ſo harſh a chime:
Good ſooth, I care not for you.
   Ant. Prince *Pericles,* touch not, vpon thy life;
For that's an Article within our Law,   155
As dangerous as the reſt: your time's expir'd,
Either expound now, or receiue your ſentence.
   Peri. Great King,   A4 (X)
Few loue to heare the ſinnes they loue to act,
T'would brayde your ſelfe too neare for me to tell it: 160
Who has a booke of all that Monarches doe,
Hee's more ſecure to keepe it ſhut, then ſhowne.
For Vice repeated, is like the wandring Wind,
Blowes duſt in others eyes to ſpread it ſelfe;

235

And yet the end of all is bought thus deare, 165
The breath is gone, and the fore eyes fee cleare:
To ftop the Ayre would hurt them, the blind Mole caftes
Copt hilles towards heauen, to tell the earth is throng'd
By mans opprefsion, and the poore Worme doth die for't:
Kinges are earths Gods; in vice, their law's their will: 170
And if *Ioue* ftray, who dares fay, *Ioue* doth ill:
It is enough you know, and it is fit;
What being more knowne, growes worfe, to fmother it.
All loue the Wombe that their firft beeing bred,
Then giue my tongue like leaue, to loue my head. (ning: 175
   Ant. Heauen, that I had thy head; he ha's found the mea-
But I will gloze with him. Young Prince of *Tyre*,
Though by the tenour of your ftrict edict,
Your expofition mifinterpreting,
We might proceed to counfell of your dayes; 180
Yet hope, fucceeding from fo faire a tree
As your faire felfe, doth tune vs otherwife;
Fourtie dayes longer we doe refpite you,
If by which time, our fecret be vndone,
This mercy fhewes, wee'le ioy in fuch a Sonne: 185
And vntill then, your entertaine fhall bee
As doth befit our honour and your worth.
                   Manet Pericles folus.
   Peri. How courtefie would feeme to couer finne,
When what is done, is like an hipocrite, 190
The which is good in nothing but in fight.
If it be true that I interpret falfe,
Then were it certaine you were not fo bad,
As with foule Inceft to abufe your foule:
Where now you both a Father and a Sonne, A4v (X)
By your vntimely clafpings with your Child, 196
(Which pleafures fittes a husband, not a father)
And fhee an eater of her Mothers flefh,
By the defiling of her Parents bed,
And both like Serpents are; who though they feed 200
On fweeteft Flowers, yet they Poyfon breed.
Antioch farewell, for Wifedome fees thofe men,
Blufh not in actions blacker then the night,
Will fhew no courfe to keepe them from the light:
One finne (I know) another doth prouoke; 205
Murther's as neere to Luft, as Flame to Smoake:
Poyfon and Treafon are the hands of Sinne,
I, and the targets to put off the fhame,

Then leaft my life be cropt, to keepe you cleare,
By flight, Ile fhun the danger which I feare.   *Exit.*   210
                Enter Antiochus.
    Anti. He hath found the meaning.
For which we meane to haue his head:
He muft not liue to trumpet foorth my infamie,
Nor tell the world *Antiochus* doth finne   215
In fuch a loathed manner:
And therefore inftantly this Prince muft die,
For by his fall, my honour muft keepe hie.
Who attends vs there?
                Enter Thaliard.   220
    Thali. Doth your highnes call?
    Antio. Thaliard, you are of our Chamber, *Thaliard,*
And our minde pertakes her priuat actions,
To your fecrecie; and for your faythfulnes,
We will aduaunce you, *Thaliard*:   225
Behold, heere's Poyfon, and heere's Gold:
Wee hate the Prince of *Tyre*, and thou muft kill him;
It fittes thee not to aske the reafon why?
Becaufe we bid it: fay, is it done?
    Thali. My Lord, tis done.   230
             Enter a Meffenger.   B1 (Y)
    Anti. Enough. Let your breath coole your felfe, telling
your hafte.
    Meff. My Lord, Prince *Pericles* is fled.
    Antin. As thou wilt liue flie after, and like an arrow fhot   235
from a well experienft Archer hits the marke his eye doth
leuell at: fo thou neuer returne vnleffe thou fay Prince *Pe-*
ricles is dead.
      Thal. My Lord, if I can get him within my Piftols
length, Ile make him fure enough, fo farewell to your   240
highneffe.
Thaliard adieu, till *Pericles* be dead,
My heart can lend no fuccour to my head.
         Enter Pericles with his Lords.
    Pe. Let none difturb vs, why fhold this châge of thoughts   245
The fad companion dull eyde melancholie,
By me fo vfde a gueft, as not an houre
In the dayes glorious walke or peacefull night,
The tombe where griefe ftould fleepe can breed me quiet,
Here pleafures court mine eies, and mine eies fhun them,   250
And daunger which I fearde is at *Antioch,*
Whofe arme feemes farre too fhort to hit me here,

Yet neither pleafures Art can ioy my fpirits,
Nor yet the others diftance comfort me,
Then it is thus, the paffions of the mind,   255
That haue their firft conception by mifdread,
Haue after nourifhment and life, by care
And what was firft but feare, what might be done,
Growes elder now, and cares it be not done.
And fo with me the great *Antiochus*,   260
Gainft whom I am too little to contend,
Since hee's fo great, can make his will his act,
Will thinke me fpeaking, though I fweare to filence,
Nor bootes it me to fay, I honour,
If he fufpect I may difhonour him.   265
And what may make him blufh in being knowne,   B1v(Y)
Heele ftop the courfe by which it might be knowne,
With hoftile forces heele ore-fpread the land,
And with the ftint of warre will looke fo huge,
Amazement fhall driue courage from the ftate,   270
Our men be vanquifht ere they doe refift,
And fubiects punifht that nere thought offence,
Which care of them, not pittie of my felfe,
Who once no more but as the tops of trees,
Which fence the rootes they grow by and defend them,   275
Makes both my bodie pine, and foule to languifh,
And punifh that before that he would punifh.
                    Enter all the Lords to Pericles.
  1. *Lord.* Ioy and all comfort in your facred breft.
  2. *Lord.* And keepe your mind till you returne to vs   280
peacefull and comfortable.
  Hel. Peace, peace, and giue experience tongue,
They doe abufe the King that flatter him,
For flatterie is the bellowes blowes vp finne,
The thing the which is flattered, but a fparke,   285
To which that fparke giues heate, and ftronger
Glowing, whereas reproofe obedient and in order,
Fits kings as they are men, for they may erre,
When *fignior* footh here does proclaime peace,
He flatters you, makes warre vpon your life.   290
Prince paadon me, or ftrike me if you pleafe,
I cannot be much lower then my knees.
  Per. All leaue vs elfe: but let your cares ore-looke,
What fhipping, and what ladings in our hauen,
And then returne to vs, *Hellicans* thou haft   295

238

Mooude vs, what feeſt thou in our lookes?

　Hel. An angrie brow, dread Lord.

　Per. If there be ſuch a dart in Princes frownes,
How durſt thy tongue moue anger to our face?

　Hel. How dares the plants looke vp to heauen,　　　　300
From whence they haue their nouriſhment?　　　　B2(Y)

　Per. Thou knoweſt I haue power to take thy life from

　Hel. I haue ground the Axe my ſelfe,　　　(thee.
Doe but you ſtrike the blowe.

　Per. Riſe, prethee riſe, ſit downe, thou art no flatterer, 305
I thanke thee fort, and heaue forbid
That kings ſhould let their eares heare their faults hid.
Fit Counſellor, and ſeruant for a Prince,
Who by thy wiſdome makes a Prince thy ſeruant,
What wouldſt thou haue me doe?　　　　310

　Hel. To beare with patience ſuch griefes as you your
ſelfe doe lay vpon your ſelfe.

　Per. Thou ſpeakſt like a Phyſition *Hellicanus,*
That miniſters a potion vnto me:
That thou wouldſt tremble to receiue thy ſelfe,　　　315
Attend me then, I went to *Antioch,*
Whereas thou knowſt againſt the face of death,
I ſought the purchaſe of a glorious beautie,
From whence an iſſue I might propogate,
Are armes to Princes, and bring ioies to ſubiects,　　320
Her face was to mine eye beyond all wonder,
The reſt harke in thine eare, as blacke as inceſt,
Which by my knowledge found, the ſinful father
Seemde not to ſtrike, but ſmooth, but thou knowſt this,
Tis time to feare when tyrants ſeemes to kiſſe.　　325
Which feare ſo grew in me I hither fled,
Vnder the couering of a carefull night,
Who ſeemd my good protector, and being here,
Bethought what was paſt, what might ſucceed,
I knew him tyrannous, and tyrants feare　　　330
Decreaſe not, but grow faſter then the yeares,
And ſhould he doo't, as no doubt he doth,
That I ſhould open to the liſtning ayre,
How many worthie Princes blouds were ſhed,
To keepe his bed of blackneſſe vnlayde ope,　　　1335
To lop that doubt, hee'le fill this land with armes,　　B2v(Y)
And make pretence of wrong that I haue done him,
When all for mine, if I may call offence,

Muſt feel wars blow, who ſpares not innocence,
Which loue to all of which thy ſelfe art one,   340
Who now reprou'dſt me fort.
 Hell. Alas ſir.
 Per. Drew ſleep out of mine eies, blood frõ my cheekes,
Muſings into my mind, with thouſand doubts
How I might ſtop this tempeſt ere it came,   345
And finding little comfort to relieue them,
I thought it princely charity to griue for them.
 Hell. Well my Lord, ſince you haue giuen mee leaue to
Freely will I ſpeake, *Antiochus* you feare,   (ſpeake,
And iuſtly too, I thinke you feare the tyrant,   350
Who either by publike warre, or priuat treaſon,
Will take away your life: therfore my Lord, go trauell for
a while, till that his rage and anger be forgot, or till the De-
ſtinies doe cut his threed of life: your rule direct to anie,
if to me, day ſerues not light more faithfull then Ile be.   355
 Per. I doe not doubt thy faith.
But ſhould he wrong my liberties in my abſence?
 Hel. Weele mingle our bloods togither in the earth,
From whence we had our being, and our birth.
 Per. Tyre I now looke from thee then, and to *Tharſus*   360
Intend my trauaile, where Ile heare from thee,
And by whoſe Letters Ile diſpoſe my ſelfe.
The care I had and haue of ſubiects good,
On thee I lay, whoſe wiſdomes ſtrength can beare it,
Ile take thy word, for faith not aske thine oath,   365
Who ſhuns not to breake one, will cracke both.
But in our orbs will liue ſo round, and ſafe,
That time of both this truth ſhall nere conuince,
Thou ſhewdſt a ſubiects ſhine, I a true Prince.   *Exit.*

Enter Thaliard ſolus.   B3 (Z)

  So this is *Tyre,* and this the Court, heere muſt I kill   371
King *Pericles,* and if I doe it not, I am ſure to be hang'd at
home: t'is daungerous.
  Well, I perceiue he was a wiſe fellowe, and had good
diſcretion, that beeing bid to aske what hee would of the   375
King, deſired he might knowe none of his ſecrets.
  Now doe I ſee hee had ſome reaſon for't: for if a
king bidde a man bee a villaine, hee's bound by the inden-
ture of his oath to bee one.
  Huſht, heere comes the Lords of *Tyre.*   380

240

Enter Hellicanus, Efcanes, with
other Lords.

Helli. You fhall not neede my fellow-Peers of *Tyre*,
further to queftion mee of your kings departure: his fea-
led Commiffion left in truft with mee, does fpeake fuffici- 385
ently hee's gone to trauaile.

Thaliard. How? the King gone?

Hell. If further yet you will be fatisfied, (why as it
were vnlicenfed of your loues) he would depart? Ile giue
fome light vnto you, beeing at *Antioch.*   390

Thal. What from *Antioch*?

Hell. Royall *Antiochus* on what caufe I knowe not,
tooke fome difpleafure at him, at leaft hee iudg'de fo: and
doubting left hee had err'de or finn'de, to fhewe his forrow,
hee'de correct himfelfe; fo puts himfelfe vnto the Ship- 395
mans toyle, with whome eache minute threatens life or
death.

Thaliard. Well, I perceiue I fhall not be hang'd now,
although I would, but fince hee's gone, the Kings feas
muft pleafe: hee fcap'te the Land to perifh at the Sea, I'le 400
prefent my felfe. Peace to the Lords of *Tyre.*

Lord *Thaliard* from *Antiochus* is welcome.   B3v (Z)

Thal. From him I come with meffage vnto princely
Pericles, but fince my landing, I haue vnderftood your Lord
has betake himfelfe to vnknowne trauailes, now meffage 405
muft returne from whence it came.

Hell. Wee haue no reafon to defire it, commended
to our maifter not to vs, yet ere you fhall depart, this wee
defire as friends to *Antioch* wee may feaft in *Tyre.*   *Exit.*

Enter Cleon the Gouernour of Tharfus, with   410
his wife and others.

Cleon. My *Dyoniza* fhall wee reft vs heere,
And by relating tales of others griefes,
See if t'will teach vs to forget our owne?

Dion. That were to blow at fire in hope to quench it, 415
For who digs hills becaufe they doe afpire?
Throwes downe one mountaine to caft vp a higher:
O my diftreffed Lord, euen fuch our griefes are,
Heere they are but felt, and feene with mifchiefs eyes,
But like to Groues, being topt, they higher rife.   420
Cleon. O *Dioniza.*
Who wanteth food, and will not fay hee wants it,
Or can conceale his hunger till hee famifh?

241

Our toungs and forrowes to found deepe:
Our woes into the aire, our eyes to weepe.   425
Till toungs feteh breath that may proclaime
Them louder, that if heauen flumber, while
Their creatures want, they may awake
Their helpers, to comfort them.
Ile then difcourfe our woes felt feuerall yeares,   430
And wanting breath to fpeake, helpe mee with teares.
       Dyoniza. Ile doe my beft Syr.   (ment,
       Cleon. This *Tharfus* ore which I haue the gouerne-
A Cittie on whom plentie held full hand:
For riches ftrew'de her felfe euen in her ftreetes,   435
Whofe towers bore heads fo high they kift the clowds,   B4 (Z)
And ftrangers nere beheld, but wondred at,
Whofe men and dames fo jetted and adorn'de,
Like one anothers glaffe to trim them by,
Their tables were ftor'de full to glad the fight,   440
And not fo much to feede on as delight,
All pouertie was fcor'nde, and pride fo great,
The name of helpe grewe odious to repeat.
       Dion. O t'is too true.
       Cle. But fee what heauen can doe by this our change, 445
Thefe mouthes who but of late, earth, fea, and ayre,
Were all too little to content and pleafe,
Although thy gaue their creatures in abundance,
As houfes are defil'de for want of vfe,
They are now ftaru'de for want of exercife,   450
Thofe pallats who not yet too fauers younger,
Muft haue inuentions to delight the taft,
Would now be glad of bread and beg for it,
Thofe mothers who to nouzell vp their babes,
Thought nought too curious, are readie now   455
To eat thofe little darlings whom they lou'de,
So fharpe are hungers teeth, that man and wife,
Drawe lots who firft fhall die, to lengthen life.
Heere ftands a Lord, and there a Ladie weeping:
Heere manie fincke, yet thofe which fee them fall,   460
Haue fcarce ftrength left to giue them buryall.
       Is not this true?
       Dion. Our cheekes and hollow eyes doe witneffe it.
       Cle. O let thofe Cities that of plenties cup,
And her profperities fo largely tafte,   465
With their fuperfluous riots heare thefe teares,
The miferie of *Tharfus* may be theirs.

Enter a Lord.

Lord. Wheres the Lord Gouernour?

Cle. Here, ſpeake out thy ſorrowes, which thee bringſt   470
in haſt, for comfort is too farre for vs to expect.   B4v (Z)

Lord. Wee haue deſcryed vpon our neighbouring
ſhore, a portlie ſaile of ſhips make hitherward.

Cleon. I thought as much.

One ſorrowe neuer comes but brings an heire,   475
That may ſucccede as his inheritor:
And ſo in ours, ſome neighbouring nation,
Taking aduantage of our miſerie,
That ſtuff't the hollow veſſels with their power,
To beat vs downe, the which are downe alreadie,   480
And make a conqueſt of vnhappie mee,
Whereas no glories got to ouercome.

Lord. That's the leaſt feare.

For by the ſemblance of their white flagges diſplayde, they
bring vs peace, and come to vs as fauourers, not as foes. 485

Cleon. Thou ſpeak'ſt like himnes vntuterd to repeat,
Who makes the faireſt ſhowe, meanes moſt deceipt.
But bring they what they will, and what they can,
What need wee leaue our grounds the loweſt?
And wee are halfe way there: Goe tell their Generall wee   490
attend him heere, to know for what he comes, and whence
he comes, and what he craues?

Lord. I goe my Lord.

Cleon. Welcome is peace, if he on peace confiſt,
If warres, wee are vnable to reſiſt.   495

Enter Pericles with attendants.

Per. Lord Gouernour, for ſo wee heare you are,
Let not our Ships and number of our men,
Be like a beacon fier'de, t'amaze your eyes,
Wee haue heard your miſeries as farre as *Tyre*,   500
And ſeene the deſolation of your ſtreets,
Nor come we to adde ſorrow to your teares,
But to relieue them of their heauy loade,
And theſe our Ships you happily may thinke,
Are like the Troian Horſe, was ſtuft within   C1(X)
With bloody veines expecting ouerthrow,   506
Are ſtor'd with Corne, to make your needie bread,
And giue them life, whom hunger-ſtaru'd halfe dead.

Omnes. The Gods of *Greece* protect you,
And wee'le pray for you.   510

Per. Ariſe I pray you, riſe; we do not looke for reuerence,
But for loue, and harborage for our ſelfe, our ſhips, & men.

Cleon. The which when any fhall not gratifie,
Or pay you with vnthankfulneffe in thought,
Be it our Wiues, our Children, or our felues,   515
The Curfe of heauen and men fucceed their euils:
Till when the which (I hope) fhall neare be feene:
Your Grace is welcome to our Towne and vs.
     Peri. Which welcome wee'le accept, feaft here awhile,
Vntill our Starres that frowne, lend vs a fmile.   *Exeunt.*   520

Enter Gower.

Heere haue you feene a mightie King,
His child I'wis to inceft bring:
A better Prince, and benigne Lord,
That Will proue awfull both in deed and word: 525
Be quiet then, as men fhould bee,
Till he hath paft necefsitie:
I'le fhew you thofe in troubles raigne;
Loofing a Mite, a Mountaine gaine:
The good in conuerfation,   530
To whom I giue my benizon:
Is ftill at *Tharftill*, where each man,
Thinkes all is writ, he fpoken can:
And to remember what he does,
Build his Statue to make him glorious: 535
But tidinges to the contrarie,
Are brought your eyes, what need fpeake I.

Dombe fhew.   C1v (X)

     Enter at one dore Pericles *talking with* Cleon, *all the traine
       with them: Enter at an other dore, a Gentleman with a*   540
       Letter to Pericles, Pericles *fhewes the Letter to* Cleon;
       Pericles *giues the Meffenger a reward, and Knights him:
       Exit* Pericles *at one dore, and* Cleon *at an other.*
Good *Helicon* that ftayde at home,
Not to eate Hony like a Drone,   545
From others labours; for though he ftriue
To killen bad, keepe good aliue:
And to fulfill his prince defire,
Sau'd one of all that haps in *Tyre*:
How *Thaliart* came full bent with finne,   550
And hid in Tent to murdred him;
And that in *Tharfis* was not beft,
Longer for him to make his reft:
He doing fo, put foorth to Seas;
Where when men been there's feldome eafe,   555

For now the Wind begins to blow,
Thunder aboue, and deepes below,
Makes ſuch vnquiet, that the Shippe,
Should houſe him ſafe; is wrackt and ſplit,
And he (good Prince) hauing all loſt,　　　　　　　560
By Waues, from coaſt to coaſt is toſt:
All periſhen of man of pelfe,
Ne ought eſcapend but himſelfe;
Till Fortune tir'd with doing bad,
Threw him a ſhore, to giue him glad:　　　　　　565
And heere he comes: what ſhall be next,
Pardon old *Gower*, this long's the text.
　　　　　　Enter Pericles wette.
　　Peri. Yet ceaſe your ire you angry Starres of heauen,
Wind, Raine, and Thunder, remember earthly man　　570
Is but a ſubſtaunce that muſt yeeld to you:
And I (as fits my nature) do obey you.
Alaſſe, the Seas hath caſt me on the Rocks,　　　　C2 (X)
Waſht me from ſhore to ſhore, and left my breath
Nothing to thinke on, but enſuing death:　　　　　575
Let it ſuffize the greatneſſe of your powers,
To haue bereft a Prince of all his fortunes;
And hauing throwne him from your watry graue,
Heere to haue death in peace, is all hee'le craue.
　　　　　　Enter three Fiſher-men.　　　　580
　　1. What, to pelch?
　　2. Ha, come and bring away theNets.
　　1. What Patch-breech, I ſay.
　　3. What ſay you Maiſter?
　　1. Looke how thou ſtirr'ſt now:　　　　　　585
Come away, or Ile fetch'th with a wanion.
　　3. Fayth Maiſter, I am thinking of the poore men,
That were caſt away before vs euen now.
　　1. Alaſſe poore ſoules, it grieued my heart to heare,
What pittifull cryes they made to vs, to helpe them,　590
When (welladay) we could ſcarce helpe our ſelues.
　　3. Nay Maiſter, ſayd not I as much,
When I ſaw the Porpas how he bounſt and tumbled?
They ſay they're halfe fiſh, halfe fleſh:
A plague on them, they nere come but I looke to be waſht.　595
Maiſter, I maruell how the Fiſhes liue in the Sea?
　　1. Why, as Men doe a-land;
The great ones eate vp the little ones:
I can compare our rich Miſers to nothing ſo fitly,

245

As to a Whale; a playes and tumbles,   600
Dryuing the poore Fry before him,
And at laſt, deuowre them all at a mouthfull:
Such Whales haue I heard on, a'th land,
Who neuer leaue gaping, till they ſwallow'd
The whole Pariſh, Church, Steeple, Belles and all.   605
    Peri. A prettie morall.
    3. But Maiſter, if I had been the Sexton,
I would haue been that day in the belfrie.
    2. Why, Man?
    1. Becauſe he ſhould haue ſwallowed mee too,   C2v (X)
And when I had been in his belly,   611
I would haue kept ſuch a iangling of the Belles,
That he ſhould neuer haue left,
Till he caſt Belles, Steeple, Church and Pariſh vp againe:
But if the good King *Simonides* were of my minde.   615
    Per. Simonides?
    3. We would purge the land of theſe Drones,
That robbe the Bee of her Hony.
    Per. How from the fenny ſubiect of the Sea,
Theſe Fiſhers tell the infirmities of men,   620
And from their watry empire recollect,
All that may men approue, or men detect.
Peace be at your labour, honeſt Fiſher-men.
    2. Honeſt good fellow what's that, if it be a day fits you
Search out of the Kalender, and no body looke after it? 625
    Peri. May ſee the Sea hath caſt vpon your coaſt:
    2. What a drunken Knaue was the Sea,
To caſt thee in our way?
    Per. A man whom both the Waters and the Winde,
In that vaſt Tennis-court, hath made the Ball   630
For them to play vpon, intreates you pittie him:
Hee askes of you, that neuer vs'd to begge.
    1. No friend, cannot you begge?
Heer's them in our countrey of *Greece*,
Gets more with begging, then we can doe with working.   635
    2. Canſt thou catch any Fiſhes then?
    Peri. I neuer practizde it.
    2. Nay then thou wilt ſtarue ſure: for heer's nothing to
be got now-adayes, vnleſſe thou canſt fiſh for't.
    Per. What I haue been, I haue forgot to know;   640
But what I am, want teaches me to thinke on:
A man throng'd vp with cold, my Veines are chill,
And haue no more of life then may ſuffize,

To giue my tongue that heat to aske your helpe:
Which if you fhall refufe, when I am dead,   645
For that I am a man, pray you fee me buried.

   1. Die, ke-tha; now Gods forbid't, and I haue a Gowne   C3(X)
heere, come put it on, keepe thee warme: now afore mee a
handfome fellow: Come, thou fhalt goe home, and wee'le
haue Flefh for all day, Fifh for fafting-dayes and more; or   650
Puddinges and Flap-iackes, and thou fhalt be welcome.

   Per. I thanke you fir.

   2. Harke you my friend: You fayd you could not beg?

   Per. I did but craue.

   2. But craue?   655

Then Ile turne Crauer too, and fo I fhall fcape whipping.

   Per. Why, are you Beggers whipt then?

   2. Oh not all, my friend, not all: for if all your Beggers
were whipt, I would wifh no better office, then to be Beadle:
But Maifter, Ile goe draw vp the Net.   660

   Per. How well this honeft mirth becomes their labour?

   1. Harke you fir; doe you know vvhere yee are?

   Per. Not well.

   1. Why Ile tell you, this I cald *Pantapoles*,
And our King, the good *Symonides*.   665

   Per. The good *Symonides*, doe you call him?

   1. I fir, and he deferues fo to be cal'd,
For his peaceable raigne, and good gouernement.

   Per. He is a happy King, fince he gaines from
His fubiects the name of good, by his gouernment.   670
How farre is his Court diftant from this fhore?

   1. Mary fir, halfe a dayes iourney: And Ile tell you,
He hath a faire Daughter, and to morrow is her birth-day,
And there are Princes and Knights come from all partes of
the World, to Iuft and Turney for her loue.   675

   Per. Were my fortunes equall to my defires,
I could wifh to make one there.

   1. O fir, things muft be as they may: and what a man can
not get, he may lawfully deale for his Wiues foule.

       Enter the two Fifher-men, drawing vp a Net.   680

   2. Helpe Maifter helpe; heere's a Fifh hanges in the Net,
Like a poore mans right in the law: t'will hardly come out.
Ha bots on't, tis come at laft; & tis turnd to a rufty Armour.

   Per. An Armour friends; I pary you let me fee it.   C3v(X)
Thankes Fortune, yeat that after all croffes,   685
Thou giueft me fomewhat to repaire my felfe:
And though it was mine owne part of my heritage,

Which my dead Father did bequeath to me,
With this ſtrict charge euen as he left his life,
Keepe it my *Perycles, it hath been a Shield*   690
Twixt me and death, and poynted to this brayſe,
For that it ſaued me, keepe it in like neceſsitie:
The which the Gods protect thee, Fame may defend thee:
It kept where I kept, I ſo dearely lou'd it,
Till the rough Seas, that ſpares not any man,   695
Tooke it in rage, though calm'd, haue giuen't againe:
I thanke thee for't, my ſhipwracke now's no ill,
Since I haue heere my Father gaue in his Will.
    1. What meane you ſir?
    Peri. To begge of you (kind friends) this Coate of worth, 700
For it was ſometime Target to a King;
I know it by this marke: he loued me dearely,
And for his ſake, I wiſh the hauing of it;
And that you'd guide me to your Soueraignes Court,
Where with it, I may appeare a Gentleman: 705
And if that euer my low fortune's better,
Ile pay your bounties; till then, reſt your debter.
    1. Why wilt thou turney for the Lady?
    Peri. Ile ſhew the vertue I haue borne in Armes.
    1. Why di'e take it: and the Gods giue thee good an't.   710
    2. I but harke you my friend, t'was wee that made vp
this Garment through the rough ſeames of the Waters:
there are certaine Condolements, certaine Vailes: I hope
ſir, if you thriue, you'le remember from whence you had
them.   715
    Peri. Beleeue't, I will:
By your furtherance I am cloth'd in Steele,
And ſpight of all the rupture of the Sea,
This Iewell holdes his buylding on my arme:
Vnto thy value I will mount my ſelfe   720
Vpon a Courſer, whoſe delight ſteps,   C4 (X)
Shall make the gazer ioy to ſee him tread;
Onely (my friend) I yet am vnprouided of a paire of Baſes.
    2. Wee'le ſure prouide, thou ſhalt haue
My beſt Gowne to make thee a paire;   725
And Ile bring thee to the Court my ſelfe.
    Peri. Then Honour be but a Goale to my Will,
This day Ile riſe, or elſe adde ill to ill.
       Enter Simonydes, with attendaunce, and Thaiſa.
    King. Are the Knights ready to begin the Tryumph?   730

248

1. *Lord.* They are my Leidge, and ſtay your comming,
To preſent them ſelues.

 King. Returne them, We are ready, & our daughter heere,
In honour of whoſe Birth, theſe Triumphs are,
Sits heere like Beauties child, whom Nature gat,   735
For men to ſee; and ſeeing, woonder at.

 Thai. It pleaſeth you (my royall Father) to expreſſe
My Commendations great, whoſe merit's leſſe.

 King. It's fit it ſhould be ſo, for Princes are
A modell which Heauen makes like to it ſelfe: 740
As Iewels looſe their glory, if neglected,
So Princes their Renownes, if not reſpected:
T'is now your honour (Daughter) to entertaine
The labour of each Knight, in his deuice.

  Thai. Which to preſerue mine honour, I'le performe. 745
      The firſt Knight paſſes by.

 King. Who is the firſt, that doth preferre himſelfe?

 Thai. A Knight of *Sparta* (my renowned father)
And the deuice he beares vpon his Shield,
Is a blacke Ethyope reaching at the Sunne: 750
The word: *Lux tua vita mihi.*

 King. He loues you well, that holdes his life of you.
      The ſecond Knight.
Who is the ſecond, that preſents himſelfe?

 Tha. A Prince of *Macedon* (my royall father)   C4v (X)
And the deuice he beares vpon his Shield,   756
Is an Armed Knight, that's conquered by a Lady:
The motto thus in Spaniſh. *Pue Per doleera kee per forſa.*

 3. *Knight. Kin.* And with the third?

 Thai. The third, of *Antioch*; and his deuice,   760
A wreath of Chiually: the word: *Me Pompey prouexit apex.*

 4. *Knight. Kin.* What is the fourth.

 Thai. A burning Torch that's turned vpſide downe;
The word: *Qui me alit me extinguit.*

 Kin. Which ſhewes that Beautie hath his power & will, 765
Which can as well enflame, as it can kill.

 5. *Knight. Thai.* The fift, an Hand enuironed with Clouds,
Holding out Gold, that's by the Touch-ſtone tride:
The motto thus: *Sic ſpectanda fides.*

 6. *Knight. Kin.* And what's the ſixt, and laſt; the which, 770
The knight himſelf with ſuch a graceful courteſie deliuered?

 Thai. Hee ſeemes to be a Stranger: but his Preſent is
A withered Branch, that's onely greene at top,
The motto: *In hac ſpe viuo.*

    Kin. A pretty morrall frō the deiected ſtate wherein he is, 775
He hopes by you, his fortunes yet may flouriſh.
    1. Lord. He had need meane better, then his outward ſhew
Can any way ſpeake in his iuſt commend:
For by his ruſtie outſide, he appeares,
To haue practis'd more the Whipſtocke, then the Launce. 780
    2. Lord. He well may be a Stranger, for he comes
To an honour'd tryumph, ſtrangly furniſht.
    3. Lord. And on ſet purpoſe let his Armour ruſt
Vntill this day, to ſcowre it in the duſt.
    Kin. Opinion's but a foole, that makes vs ſcan 785
The outward habit, by the inward man.
But ſtay, the Knights are comming,
We will with-draw into the Gallerie.
        Great ſhoutes, and all cry, the meane Knight.
          Enter the King and Knights from Tilting.   D1 (X)
    King. Knights, to ſay you're welcome, were ſuperfluous. 791
I place vpon the volume of your deedes,
As in a Title page, your worth in armes,
Were more then you expect, or more then's fit,
Since euery worth in ſhew commends it ſelfe: 795
Prepare for mirth, for mirth becomes a Feaſt.
You are Princes, and my gueſtes.
    Thai. But you my Knight and gueſt,
To whom this Wreath of victorie I giue,
And crowne you King of this dayes happineſſe. 800
    Peri. Tis more by Fortune (Lady) then my Merit.
    King. Call it by what you will, the day is your,
And here (I hope) is none that enuies it:
In framing an Artiſt, art hath thus decreed,
To make ſome good, but others to exceed, 805
And you are her labourd ſcholler: come Queene a th'feaſt,
For (Daughter) ſo you are; heere take your place:
Martiall the reſt, as they deſerue their grace.
    Knights. We are honour'd much by good *Symonides.*
    King. Your preſence glads our dayes, honour we loue, 810
For who hates honour, hates the Gods aboue.
    Marſhal. Sir, yonder is your place.
    Peri. Some other is more fit.
    1. Knight. Contend not ſir, for we are Gentlemen,
Haue neither in our hearts, nor outward eyes, 815
Enuies the great, nor ſhall the low deſpiſe.
    Peri. You are right courtious Knights.
    King. Sit ſir, ſit.

By *Ioue* (I wonder) that is King of thoughts,
Thefe Cates refift mee, hee not thought vpon.   820
   Tha. By *Iuno* (that is Queene of mariage)
All Viands that I eate do feeme vnfauery,
Wifhing him my meat: fure hee's a gallant Gentleman.
   Kin. Hee's but a countrie Gentleman: ha's done no more
Then other Knights haue done, ha's broken a Staffe,   825
Or fo; fo let it paffe.   D1v (X)
   Tha. To mee he feemes like Diamond, to Glaffe.
   Peri. You Kings to mee, like to my fathers picture,
Which tels in that glory once he was,
Had Princes fit like Starres about his Throane,   830
And hee the Sunne for them to reuerence;
None that beheld him, but like leffer lights,
Did vaile their Crownes to his fupremacie;
Where now his fonne like a Gloworme in the night,
The which hath Fire in darkneffe, none in light: 835
Whereby I fee that Time's the King of men,
Hee's both their Parent, and he is their Graue,
And giues them what he will, not what they craue.
   King. What, are you merry, Knights?
   Knights. Who can be other, in this royall prefence.   840
   King. Heere, with a Cup that's ftur'd vnto the brim,
As do you loue, fill to your Miftris lippes,
Wee drinke this health to you.
   Knights. We thanke your Grace.
   King. Yet paufe awhile, yon Knight doth fit too melan   845
As if the entertainemente in our Court,   (choly
Had not a fhew might counteruaile his worth:
Note it not you, *Thaifa.*
   Tha. What is't to me, my father?
   king. O attend my Daughter,   850
Princes in this, fhould liue like Gods aboue,
Who freely giue to euery one that come to honour them:
And Princes not doing fo, are like to Gnats,
Which make a found, but kild, are wondred at:
Therefore to make his entraunce more fweet,   855
Heere, fay wee drinke this ftanding boule of wine to him.
   Tha. Alas my Father, it befits not mee,
Vnto a ftranger Knight to be fo bold,
He may my profer take for an offence,
Since men take womens giftes for impudence.   860
   king. How? doe as I bid you, or you'le mooue me elfe.
   Tha. Now by the Gods, he could not pleafe me better.

 king. And furthermore tell him, we defire to know of him D2(X)
Of whence he is, his name, and Parentage?
 Tha. The King my father (fir) has drunke to you.   865
 Peri. I thanke him.
 Tha. Wifhing it fo much blood vnto your life.
 Peri. I thanke both him and you, and pledge him freely.
 Tha. And further, he defires to know of you,
Of whence you are, your name and parentage?   870
 Peri. A Gentleman of *Tyre*, my name *Pericles*,
My education beene in Artes and Armes:
Who looking for aduentures in the world,
Was by the rough Seas reft of Ships and men,
and after fhipwracke, driuen vpon this fhore.   875
 Tha. He thankes your Grace; names himfelfe *Pericles*,
A Gentleman of *Tyre*: who onely by misfortune of the feas,
Bereft of Shippes and Men, caft on this fhore.
 king. Now by the Gods, I pitty his misfortune,
And will awake him from his melancholy.   880
Come Gentlemen, we fit too long on trifles,
And wafte the time which lookes for other reuels:
Euen in your Armours as you are addreft,
Will well become a Souldiers daunce:
I will not haue excufe with faying this,   885
Lowd Muficke is too harfh for Ladyes heads,
Since they loue men in armes, as well as beds.
     They daunce.
So, this was well askt, t'was fo well perform'd.
Come fir, heer's a Lady that wants breathing too,   890
And I haue heard, you Knights of *Tyre*,
Are excellent in making Ladyes trippe;
And that their Meafures are as excellent.
 Peri. In thofe that practize them, they are (my Lord.)
 king. Oh that's as much, as you would be denyed   895
Of your faire courtefie: vnclafpe, vnclafpe.
     They daunce.
Thankes Gentlemen to all, all haue done well;
But you the beft: Pages and lights, to conduct
Thefe Knights vnto their feuerall Lodgings: D2v(X)
Yours fir, we haue giuen order be next our owne.   901
 Peri. I am at your Graces pleafure.
Princes, it is too late to talke of Loue,
And that's the marke I know, you leuell at:
Therefore each one betake him to his reft,   905
To morrow all for fpeeding do their beft:

Enter Hellicanus and Escanes.
Hell. No *Escanes*, know this of mee,
Antiochus from inceſt liued not free:
For which the moſt high Gods not minding,　　　910
Longer to with-hold the vengeance that
They had in ſtore, due to this heynous
Capitall offence, euen in the height and pride
Of all his glory, when he was ſeated in
A Chariot of an ineſtimable value, and his daughter　　　915
With him; a fire from heauen came and ſhriueld
Vp thoſe bodyes euen to lothing, for they ſo ſtounke,
That all thoſe eyes ador'd them, ere their fall,
Scorne now their hand ſhould giue them buriall.
　　Escanes. T'was very ſtrange.　　　920
　　Hell. And yet but iuſtice; for though this King were great,
His greatneſſe was no gard to barre heauens ſhaft,
But ſinne had his reward.
　　Escan. Tis very true.
　　　　　Enter two or three Lords.　　　925
　　1. Lord. See, not a man in priuate conference,
Or counſaile, ha's reſpect with him but hee.
　　2. Lord. It ſhall no longer grieue, without reprofe.
　　3. Lord. And curſt be he that will not ſecond it.
　　1. Lord. Follow me then: Lord *Hellicane*, a word.　　　930
　　Hell. With mee? and welcome happy day, my Lords.
　　1. Lord. Know, that our griefes are riſen to the top,
And now at length they ouer-flow their bankes.
　　Hell. Your griefes, for what?
Wrong not your Prince, you loue.　　　D3 (X)
　　1. Lord. Wrong not your ſelfe then, noble *Hellican*,　　　936
But if the Prince do liue, let vs ſalute him,
Or know what ground's made happy by his breath:
If in the world he liue, wee'le ſeeke him out:
If in his Graue he reſt, wee'le find him there,　　　940
And be reſolued he liues to gouerne vs:
Or dead, giue's cauſe to mourne his funerall,
And leaue vs to our free election.
　　2. Lord. Whoſe death in deed, the ſtrongeſt in our ſenſure,
And knowing this Kingdome is without a head,　　　945
Like goodly Buyldings left without a Roofe,
Soone fall to ruine: your noble ſelfe,
That beſt know how to rule, and how to raigne,
Wee thus ſubmit vnto our Soueraigne.
　　Omnes. Liue noble *Hellicane.*　　　950

Hell. Try honours caufe; forbeare your fuffrages:
If that you loue Prince *Pericles*, forbeare,
(Take I your wifh, I leape into the feas,
Where's howerly trouble, for a minuts eafe)
A twelue-month longer, let me intreat you   955
To forbeare the abfence of your King;
If in which time expir'd, he not returne,
I fhall with aged patience beare your yoake:
But if I cannot winne you to this loue,
Goe fearch like nobles, like noble fubiects,   960
And in your fearch, fpend your aduenturous worth,
Whom if you find, and winne vnto returne,
You fhall like Diamonds fit about his Crowne.
 1. Lord. To wifedome, hee's a foole, that will not yeeld:
And fince Lord *Hellicane* enioyneth vs,   965
We with our trauels will endeauour.
 Hell. Then you loue vs, we you, & wee'le clafpe hands:
When Peeres thus knit, a Kingdome euer ftands.
   Enter the King reading of a letter at one doore,
     the Knightes meete him.   970
 1. Knight. Good morrow to the good *Simonides.*
King. Knights, from my daughter this I let you know, D3v (X)
That for this twelue-month, fhee'le not vndertake
A maried life: her reafon to her felfe is onely knowne,
Which from her, by no meanes can I get.   975
 2. Knight. May we not get acceffe to her (my Lord?)
 king. Fayth, by no meanes, fhe hath fo ftrictly
Tyed her to her Chamber, that t'is impofsible:
One twelue Moones more fhee'le weare *Dianas* liuerie:
This by the eye of *Cinthya* hath fhe vowed,   980
And on her Virgin honour, will not breake it.
 3. knight. Loth to bid farewell, we take our leaues.
 king. So, they are well difpatcht:
Now to my daughters Letter; fhe telles me heere,
Shee'le wedde the ftranger Knight,   985
Or neuer more to view nor day nor light.
T'is well Miftris, your choyce agrees with mine:
I like that well: nay how abfolute fhe's in't,
Not minding whether I dislike or no.
Well, I do commend her choyce, and will no longer 990
Haue it be delayed: Soft, heere he comes,
I muft diffemble it.
    Enter Pericles.
 Peri. All fortune to the good *Symonides.*

King. To you as much: Sir, I am behoulding to you   995
For your ſweete Muſicke this laſt night:
I do proteſt, my eares were neuer better fedde
With ſuch delightfull pleaſing harmonie.
   Peri. It is your Graces pleaſure to commend,
Not my deſert.   1000
   king. Sir, you are Muſickes maiſter.
   Peri. The worſt of all her ſchollers (my good Lord.)
   king. Let me aske you one thing:
What do you thinke of my Daughter, ſir?
   Peri. A moſt vertuous Princeſſe.   1005
   king. And ſhe is faire too, is ſhe not?
   Peri. As a faire day in Sommer: woondrous faire.
   king. Sir, my Daughter thinkes very well of you,   D4(X)
I ſo well, that you muſt be her Maiſter,
And ſhe will be your Scholler; therefore looke to it.   1010
   Peri. I am vnworthy for her Scholemaiſter.
   king. She thinkes not ſo: peruſe this writing elſe.
   Per. What's here, a letter that ſhe loues the knight of *Tyre?*
T'is the Kings ſubtiltie to haue my life:
Oh ſeeke not to intrappe me, gracious Lord,   1015
A Stranger, and diſtreſſed Gentleman,
That neuer aymed ſo hie, to loue your Daughter,
But bent all offices to honour her.
   king. Thou haſt bewitcht my daughter,
And thou art a villaine.   1020
   Peri. By the Gods I haue not; neuer did thought
Of mine leuie offence; nor neuer did my actions
Yet commence a deed might gaine her loue,
Or your diſpleaſure.
   king. Traytor, thou lyeſt.   1025
   Peri. Traytor?
   king. I, traytor.
   Peri. Euen in his throat, vnleſſe it be the King,
That cals me Traytor, I returne the lye.
   king. Now by the Gods, I do applaude his courage.   1030
   Peri. My actions are as noble as my thoughts,
That neuer reliſht of a baſe diſcent:
I came vnto your Court for Honours cauſe,
And not to be a Rebell to her ſtate:
And he that otherwiſe accountes of mee,   1035
This Sword ſhall prooue, hee's Honours enemie.
   king. No? heere comes my Daughter, ſhe can witneſſe it.

Enter Thaifa.

Peri. Then as you are as vertuous, as faire,
Refolue your angry Father, if my tongue   1040
Did ere folicite, or my hand fubfcribe
To any fillable that made loue to you?
　Thai. Why fir, fay if you had, who takes offence?
At that, would make me glad?   D4v (X)
　King. Yea Miftris, are you fo peremptorie?   1045
I am glad on't with all my heart,
Ile tame you; Ile bring you in fubiection.   *Afide.*
Will you not, hauing my confent,
Beftow your loue and your affections,
Vpon a Stranger? who for ought I know,   1050
May be (nor can I thinke the contrary)   *Afide.*
As great in blood as I my felfe:
Therefore, heare you Miftris, either frame
Your will to mine: and you fir, heare you;
Either be rul'd by mee, or Ile make you,   1055
Man and wife: nay come, your hands,
And lippes muft feale it too: and being ioynd,
Ile thus your hopes deftroy, and for further griefe:
God giue you ioy; what are you both pleafed?
　Tha. Yes, if you loue me fir?   1060
　Peri. Euen as my life, my blood that fofters it.
　King. What are you both agreed?
　Ambo. Yes, if't pleafe your Maieftie.
　King. It pleafeth me fo well, that I will fee you wed,
And then with what hafte you can, get you to bed.   *Exeunt.*   1065

Enter Gower.

Now fleepe yflacked hath the rout,
No din but fnores about the houfe,
Made louder by the orefed breaft,
Of this moft pompous maryage Feaft: 1070
The Catte with eyne of burning cole,
Now coutches from the Moufes hole;
And Cricket fing at the Ouens mouth,
Are the blyther for their drouth:
Hymen hath brought the Bride to bed,   1075
Whereby the loffe of maydenhead,
A Babe is moulded: be attent,
And Time that is fo briefly fpent,   E1 (X)
With your fine fancies quaintly each,

What's dumbe in fhew, I'le plaine with fpeach.　　　1080
　Enter Pericles *and* Symonides *at one dore with attendantes,*
　　a Meffenger meetes them, kneeles and giues Pericles *a letter,*
　　Pericles *fhewes it* Symonides, *the Lords kneele to him;*
　　then enter Thayfa *with child, with* Lichorida *a nurfe,*
　　the King fhewes her the letter, fhe reioyces: fhe and Pericles 1085
　　take leaue of her father, and depart.
By many a dearne and painefull pearch
Of *Perycles* the carefull fearch,
By the fower oppofing Crignes,
Which the world togeather ioynes,　　　　　　　　1090
Is made with all due diligence,
That horfe and fayle and hie expence,
Can fteed the queft at laft from *Tyre*:
Fame anfwering the moft ftrange enquire,
To'th Court of King *Symonides*,　　　　　　　　　1095
Are Letters brought, the tenour thefe:
Antiochus and his daughter dead,
The men of *Tyrus*, on the head
Of *Helycanus* would fet on
The Crowne of *Tyre*, but he will none:　　　　　　1100
The mutanie, hee there haftes t'oppreffe,
Sayes to'em, if King *Pericles*
Come not home in twife fixe Moones,
He obedient to their doomes,
Will take the Crowne: the fumme of this,　　　　　1105
Brought hither to *Penlapolis*,
Iranyfhed the regions round,
And euery one with claps can found,
Our heyre apparant is a King:
Who dreampt? who thought of fuch a thing?　　　　1110
Briefe he muft hence depart to *Tyre*,
His Queene with child, makes her defire,
Which who fhall croffe along to goe,　　　　　　E1v (X)
Omit we all their dole and woe:
Lichorida her Nurfe fhe takes,　　　　　　　　　1115
And fo to Sea; their veffell fhakes,
On *Neptunes* billow, halfe the flood,
Hath their Keele cut: but fortune mou'd,
Varies againe, the grifled North
Difgorges fuch a tempeft forth,　　　　　　　　　1120
That as a Ducke for life that diues,
So vp and downe the poore Ship driues:
The Lady fhreekes, and wel-a-neare,

Do's fall in trauayle with her feare:
And what enfues in this fell ftorme,   1125
Shall for it felfe, it felfe performe:
I nill relate, action may
Conueniently the reft conuay;
Which might not? what by me is told,
In your imagination hold: 1130
This Stage, the Ship, vpon whofe Decke
The feas toft *Pericles* appeares to fpeake.

            Enter Pericles a Shipboard.

  Peri. The God of this great Vaft, rebuke thefe furges,
Which wafh both heauen and hell, and thou that haft   1135
Vpon the Windes commaund, bind them in Braffe;
Hauing call'd them from the deepe, ô ftill
Thy deafning dreadfull thunders, gently quench
Thy nimble fulphirous flafhes: ô How *Lychorida!*
How does my Queene? then ftorme venomoufly,   1140
Wilt thou fpeat all thy felfe? the fea-mans Whiftle
Is as a whifper in the eares of death,
Vnheard *Lychorida? Lucina*, oh!
Diuineft patrioneffe, and my wife gentle
To thofe that cry by night, conuey thy deitie   1145
Aboard our dauncing Boat, make fwift the pangues
Of my Queenes trauayles? now *Lychorida.*

            Enter Lychorida.   E2 (X)

  Lychor. Heere is a thing too young for fuch a place,
Who if it had conceit, would die, as I am like to doe: 1150
Take in your armes this peece of your dead Queene.

  Peri. How? how *Lychorida?*

  Lycho. Patience (good fir) do not afsift the ftorme,
Heer's all that is left liuing of your Queene;
A litle Daughter: for the fake of it,   1155
Be manly, and take comfort.

  Per. O you Gods!
Why do you make vs loue your goodly gyfts,
And fnatch them ftraight away? we heere below,
Recall not what we giue, and therein may   1160
Vfe honour with you.

  Lycho. Patience (good fir) euen for this charge.

  Per. Now mylde may be thy life,
For a more blufterous birth had neuer Babe:
Quiet and gentle thy conditions; for   1165
Thou art the rudelyeft welcome to this world,

That euer was Princes Child: happy what followes,
Thou haſt as chiding a natiuitie,
As Fire, Ayre, Water, Earth, and Heauen can make,
To harould thee from the wombe: 1170
Euen at the firſt, thy loſſe is more then can
Thy portage quit, with all thou canſt find heere:
Now the good Gods throw their beſt eyes vpon't.
     Enter two Saylers.
 1. Sayl. What courage ſir? God ſaue you.   1175
 Per. Courage enough, I do not feare the flaw,
It hath done to me the worſt: yet for the loue
Of this poore Infant, this freſh new ſea-farer,
I would it would be quiet.
 1. Sayl. Slake the bolins there; thou wilt not wilt thou: 1180
Blow and ſplit thy ſelfe.
 2. Sayl. But Sea-roome, and the brine and cloudy billow
Kiſſe the Moone, I care not.
 1. Sir your Queene muſt ouer board, the ſea workes hie,   E2v (X)
The Wind is lowd, and will not lie till the Ship   1185
Be cleard of the dead.
 Per. That's your ſuperſtition.
 1. Pardon vs, ſir; with vs at Sea it hath bin ſtill obſerued.
And we are ſtrong in eaſterne, therefore briefly yeeld'er,
 Per. As you thinke meet; for ſhe muſt ouer board ſtraight: 1190
Moſt wretched Queene
 Lychor. Heere ſhe lyes ſir.
 Peri. A terrible Child-bed haſt thou had (my deare,
No light, no fire, th'vnfriendly elements,
Forgot thee vtterly, nor haue I time   1195
To giue thee hallowd to thy graue, but ſtraight,
Muſt caſt thee ſcarcly Coffind, in oare,
Where for a monument vpon thy bones,
The ayre remayning lampes, the belching Whale,
And humming Water muſt orewelme thy corpes,   1200
Lying with ſimple ſhels: ô *Lychorida,*
Bid *Neſtor* bring me Spices, Incke, and Taper,
My Casket, and my Iewels; and bid *Nicander*
Bring me the Sattin Coffin: lay the Babe
Vpon the Pillow; hie thee whiles I ſay   1205
A prieſtly farewell to her: ſodainely, woman.
 2. Sir, we haue a Chiſt beneath the hatches,
Caulkt and bittumed ready.
 Peri. I thanke thee: Mariner ſay, what Coaſt is this?
 2. Wee are neere *Tharſus.*   1210

259

Peri. Thither gentle Mariner,
Alter thy courſe for *Tyre*: When canſt thou reach it?
  2. By breake of day, if the Wind ceaſe.
  Peri. O make for *Tharſus*,
There will I viſit *Cleon*, for the Babe   1215
Cannot hold out to *Tyrus*; there Ile leaue it
At carefull nurſing: goe thy wayes good Mariner,
Ile bring the body preſently.   *Exit.*
        Enter Lord Cerymon with a ſeruant.   E3 (X)
  Cery. Phylemon, hoe.   1220
          Enter Phylemon.
  Phyl. Doth my Lord call?
  Cery. Get Fire and meat for theſe poore men,
T'as been a turbulent and ſtormie night.
  Seru. I haue been in many; but ſuch a night as this,   1225
Till now, I neare endured.
  Cery. Your Maiſter will be dead ere you returne,
There's nothing can be miniſtred to Nature,
That can recouer him: giue this to the Pothecary,
And tell me how it workes.   1230
        Enter two Gentlemen.
  1. *Gent.* Good morrow.
  2. *Gent.* Good morrow to your Lordſhip,
  Cery. Gentlemen, why doe you ſtirre ſo early?
  1. *Gent.* Sir, our lodgings ſtanding bleake vpon the ſea, 1235
Shooke as the earth did quake:
The very principals did ſeeme to rend and all to topple:
Pure ſurprize and feare, made me to quite the houſe.
  2. *Gent.* That is the cauſe we trouble you ſo early,
T'is not our husbandry.   1240
  Cery. O you ſay well.
  1. *Gent.* But I much maruaile that your Lordſhip,
Hauing rich tire about you, ſhould at theſe early howers,
Shake off the golden ſlumber of repoſe; tis moſt ſtrange
Nature ſhould be ſo conuerſant with Paine,   1245
Being thereto not compelled.
  Cery. I hold it euer Vertue and Cunning,
Were endowments greater, then Nobleneſſe & Riches;
Careleſſe Heyres, may the two latter darken and expend;
But Immortalitie attendes the former,   1250
Making a man a god:
T'is knowne, I euer haue ſtudied Phyſicke:
Through which ſecret Art, by turning ore Authorities,

I haue togeather with my practize, made famyliar,   E3v (X)
To me and to my ayde, the bleſt infuſions that dwels   1255
In Vegetiues, in Mettals, Stones: and can ſpeake of the
Diſturbances that Nature works, and of her cures;
which doth giue me a more content in courſe of true delight
Then to be thirſty after tottering honour, or
Tie my pleaſure vp in ſilken Bagges,   1260
To pleaſe the Foole and Death.
    2. Gent. Your honour has through *Epheſus*,
Poured foorth your charitie, and hundreds call themſelues,
Your Creatures; who by you, haue been reſtored;
And not your knowledge, your perſonall payne,   1265
But euen your Purſe ſtill open, hath built Lord *Cerimon*,
Such ſtrong renowne, as time ſhall neuer.
                Enter two or three with a Chiſt.
    Seru. So, lift there.
    Cer. What's that?   1270
    Ser. Sir, euen now did the ſea toſſe vp vpon our ſhore
This Chiſt; tis of ſome wracke.
    Cer. Set't downe, let's looke vpon't.
    2. Gent. T'is like a Coffin, ſir.
    Cer. What ere it be, t'is woondrous heauie;   1275
Wrench it open ſtraight:
If the Seas ſtomacke be orecharg'd with Gold,
T'is a good conſtraint of Fortune it belches vpon vs.
    2. Gent. T'is ſo, my Lord.
    Cer. How cloſe tis caulkt & bottomed, did the ſea caſt it vp? 1280
    Ser. I neuer ſaw ſo huge a billow ſir, as toſt it vpon ſhore.
    Cer. Wrench it open ſoft; it ſmels moſt ſweetly in my ſenſe.
    2. Gent. A delicate Odour.
    Cer. As euer hit my noſtrill: ſo, vp with it.
Oh you moſt potent Gods! what's here, a Corſe?   1285
    2. Gent. Moſt ſtrange.
    Cer. Shrowded in Cloth of ſtate, balmed and entreaſured
with full bagges of Spices, a Paſport to *Apollo*, perfect mee
in the Characters:

    Heere I giue to vnderſtand,   E4(X)
    If ere this Coffin driues aland;   1291
    I King Pericles *haue loſt*
    This Queene, worth all our mundaine coſt:
    Who finds her, giue her burying,
    She was the Daughter of a King: 1295
    Beſides, this Treaſure for a fee,
    The Gods requit his charitie.

If thou liueſt *Pericles*, thou haſt a heart,
That euer cracks for woe, this chaunc'd to night.
2. Gent. Moſt likely ſir.   1300
Cer. Nay certainely to night, for looke how freſh ſhe looks
They were too rough, that threw her in the ſea.
Make a Fire within; fetch hither all my Boxes in my Cloſet,
Death may vſurpe on Nature many howers, and yet
The fire of life kindle againe the ore-preſt ſpirits: 1305
I heard of an *Egiptian* that had 9. howers lien dead,
Who was by good applyaunce recouered.
              Enter one with Napkins and Fire.
Well ſayd, well ſayd; the fire and clothes: the rough and
Wofull Muſick that we haue, cauſe it to ſound beſeech you: 1310
The Violl once more; how thou ſtirr'ſt thou blocke?
The Muſicke there: I pray you giue her ayre:
Gentlemen, this Queene will liue,
Nature awakes a warmth breath out of her;
She hath not been entranc'ſt aboue fiue howers: 1315
See how ſhe ginnes to blow into lifes flower againe.
     1. Gent. The Heauens, through you, encreaſe our wonder,
And ſets vp your fame for euer.
     Cer. She is aliue, behold her ey-lids,
Caſes to thoſe heauenly iewels which *Pericles* hath loſt,   1320
Begin to part their fringes of bright gold,
The Diamonds of a moſt prayſed water doth appeare,
To make the world twiſe rich, liue, and make vs weepe.
To heare your fate, faire creature, rare as you ſeeme to bee.
                         Shee moues.   1325
     Thai. O deare *Diana*, where am I? where's my Lord?
What world is this?   E4v (X)
     2. Gent. Is not this ſtrange?   *1. Gent.* Moſt rare.
     Ceri. Huſh (my gentle neighbours) lend me your hands,
To the next Chamber beare her: get linnen: 1330
Now this matter muſt be lookt to for her relapſe
Is mortall: come, come; and *Eſcelapius* guide vs.
                  They carry her away. Exeunt omnes.
          Enter Pericles, Atharſus, with Cleon and Dioniſa.
     Per. Moſt honor'd *Cleon*, I muſt needs be gone, my twelue 1335
months are expir'd, and *Tyrus* ſtandes in a litigious peace:
You and your Lady take from my heart all thankfulneſſe,
The Gods make vp the reſt vpon you.
     Cle. Your ſhakes of fortune, though they hant you mor-
Yet glaunce full wondringly on vs.   (tally   1340

Di. O your fweet Queene! that the ftrict fates had pleaf'd,
you had brought her hither to haue bleft mine eies with her.
    Per. We cannot but obey the powers aboue vs;
Could I rage and rore as doth the fea fhe lies in,
Yet the end muft be as tis: my gentle babe *Marina*,   1345
Whom, for fhe was borne at fea, I haue named fo,
Here I charge your charitie withall; leauing her
The infant of your care, befeeching you to giue her
Princely training, that fhe may be manere'd as fhe is borne.
    Cle. Feare not (my Lord) but thinke your Grace,   1350
That fed my Countrie with your Corne; for which,
The peoples prayers ftill fall vpon you, muft in your child
Be thought on, if neglection fhould therein make me vile,
The common body by you relieu'd,
Would force me to my duety: but if to that,   1355
My nature neede a fpurre, the Gods reuenge it
Vpon me and mine, to the end of generation.
    Per. I beleeue you, your honour and your goodnes,
Teach me too't without your vowes, till fhe be maried,
Madame, by bright *Diana*, whom we honour,   1360
All vnfifterd fhall this heyre of mine remayne,
Though I fhew will in't; fo I take my leaue:
Good Madame, make me bleffed in your care
In bringing vp my Child.
    Dion. I haue one my felfe, who fhall not be more deere   F1 (Y)
to my refpect then yours, my Lord.   1366
    Peri. Madam, my thanks and prayers.
    Cler. Weel bring your Grace ene to the edge ath fhore,
then giue you vp to the mask'd *Neptune*, and the gentleft
winds of heauen.   1370
    Peri. I will imbrace your offer, come deereft Madame,
O no teares *Licherida*, no teares, looke to your litle Miftris,
on whofe grace you may depend hereafter: come my
Lord.
                 Enter Cerimon, and Tharfa.   1375
    Cer. Madam, this Letter, and fome certaine Iewels,
Lay with you in your Coffer, which are at your command:
Know you the Charecter?
    Thar. It is my Lords, that I was fhipt at fea I well remem-
ber, euen on my learning time, but whether there deliue-   1380
red, by the holie gods I cannot rightly fay: but fince King
Pericles my wedded Lord, I nere fhall fee againe, a vaftall
liuerie will I take me to, and neuer more haue ioy.

Cler. Madam, if this you purpofe as ye fpeake,
Dianaes Temple is not diftant farre,   1385
Where you may abide till your date expire,
Moreouer if you pleafe a Neece of mine,
Shall there attend you.
    Thin. My recompence is thanks, thats all,
Yet my good will is great, though the gift fmall.   *Exit.* 1390
                 Enter Gower.
Imagine *Pericles* arriude at *Tyre*,
Welcomd and fetled to his owne defire:
His wofull Queene we leaue at *Ephefus*,
Vnto *Diana* ther's a Votariffe.   1395
Now to *Marina* bend your mind,   F1v (Y)
Whom our faft growing fcene muft finde
At *Tharfus*, and by *Cleon* traind
In Muficks letters, who hath gaind
Of education all the grace,   1400
Which makes hie both the art and place
Of generall wonder: but alacke
That monfter Enuie oft the wracke
Of earned praife, *Marinas* life
Seeke to take off by treafons knife,   1405
And in this kinde, our *Cleon* hath
One daughter and a full growne wench,
Euen right for marriage light: this Maid
Hight *Philoten*: and it is faid
For certaine in our ftorie, fhee   1410
Would euer with *Marina* bee.
Beet when they weaude the fleded filke,
With fingers long, fmall, white as milke,
Or when fhe would with fharpe needle wound,
The Cambricke which fhe made more found   1415
By hurting it or when too'th Lute
She fung, and made the night bed mute,
That ftill records with mone, or when
She would with rich and conftant pen,
Vaile to her Miftreffe *Dian* ftill,   1420
This *Phyloten* contends in skill
With abfolute *Marina*: fo
The Doue of *Paphos* might with the crow
Vie feathers white, *Marina* gets

All prayſes, which are paid as debts,   1425
And not as giuen, this ſo darkes
In *Phyloten* all gracefull markes,
That *Cleons* wife with Enuie rare,
A preſent murderer does prepare
For good *Marina*, that her daughter   1430
Might ſtand peerleſſe by this ſlaughter.   F2 (Y)
The ſooner her vile thoughts to ſtead,
Lichorida our nurſe is dead,
And curſed *Dioniza* hath
The pregnant inſtrument of wrath.   1435
Preſt for this blow, the vnborne euent,
I doe commend to your content,
Onely I carried winged Time,
Poſt one the lame feete of my rime,
Which neuer could I ſo conuey,   1440
Vnleſſe your thoughts went on my way,
Dioniza does appeare,
With *Leonine* a murtherer.   *Exit.*

        Enter Dioniza, with Leonine.

   Dion. Thy oath remember, thou haſt ſworne to doo't,   1445
tis but a blowe which neuer ſhall bee knowne, thou
canſt not doe a thing in the worlde ſo ſoone to yeelde
thee ſo much profite: let not conſcience which is but
cold, in flaming, thy loue boſome, enflame too nicelie,
nor let pittie which euen women haue caſt off, melt thee,   1450
but be a ſouldier to thy purpoſe.

   Leon. I will doo't, but yet ſhe is a goodly creature.

   Dion. The fitter then the Gods ſhould haue her.
Here ſhe comes weeping for her onely Miſtreſſe death,
Thou art reſolu'de.   1455

   Leon. I am reſolude.

      Enter Marina with a Basket of flowers.

   Mari. No: I will rob *Tellus* of her weede to ſtrowe
thy greene with Flowers, the yellowes, blewes, the purple
Violets, and Marigolds, ſhall as a Carpet hang vpon thy   1460
graue, while Sommer dayes doth laſt: Aye me poore maid,
borne in a tempeſt, when my mother dide, this world to me   F2v(Y)
is a laſting ſtorme, whirring me from my friends.

   Dion. How now *Marina*, why doe yow keep alone?
How chaunce my daughter is not with you?   1465
Doe not conſume your bloud with ſorrowing,
Haue you a nurſe of me? Lord how your fauours
Changd with this vnprofitable woe:

265

Come giue me your flowers, ere the fea marre it,
Walke with *Leonine*, the ayre is quicke there,   1470
And it perces and fharpens the ftomacke,
Come *Leonine* take her by the arme, walke with her.

    Mari. No I pray you, Ile not bereaue you of your feruāt.

    Dion. Come, come, I loue the king your father, and your
felfe, with more then forraine heart, wee euery day expect   1475
him here, when he fhall come and find our Paragon to all
reports thus blafted,
He will repent the breadth of his great voyage, blame both
my Lord and me, that we haue taken no care to your beft
courfes, go I pray you, walke and be chearfull once againe, 1480
referue that excellent eomplexion, which did fteale the
eyes of yong and old. Care not for me, I can goe home a-
lone.

    Mari. Well, I will goe, but yet I haue no defire too it.

    Dion. Come, come, I know tis good for you, walke halfe   1485
an houre *Leonine*, at the leaft, remember what I haue fed.

    Leon. I warrant you Madam.

    Dion. Ile leaue you my fweete Ladie, for a while, pray
walke foftly, doe not heate your bloud, what, I muft haue
care of you.   1490

    Mari. My thanks fweete Madame, Is this wind Wefterlie
that blowes?

    Leon. Southweft.

    Mari. When I was borne the wind was North.

    Leon. Waft fo?   1495

    Mari. My father, as nutfe fes, did neuer feare, but cryed
good fea-men to the Saylers, galling his kingly hands ha-   F3 (Y?)
ling ropes, and clafping to the Maft, endured a fea that almoft burft the decke.

    Leon. When was this?   1500

    Mari. When I was borne, neuer was waues nor winde
more violent, and from the ladder tackle, wafhes off a can-
uas clymer, ha fes one, wolt out? and with a dropping in-
duftrie they skip from fterne to fterne, the Boatfwaine
whiftles, and the Maifter calles and trebles their confufion. 1505

    Leon. Come fay your prayers.

    Mari. What meane you?

    Leon. If you require a little fpace for praier, I graunt it,
pray, but bee not tedious, for the Gods are quicke of eare,
and I am fworne to do my worke with hafte.   1510

    Mari. Why will you kill me?

    Leon. To fatisfie my Ladie.

Mari. Why would fhee haue mee kild now? as I can remember by my troth, I neuer did her hurt in all my life, I
neuer fpake bad worde, nor did ill turne to anie liuing crea-   1515
ture: Beleeue me law, I neuer killd a Moufe, nor hurt a Fly:
I trode vpon a worme againft my will, but I wept fort. How
haue I offended, wherein my death might yeeld her anie
profit, or my life imply her any danger?

Leon. My Commiffion is not to reafon of the deed, but   1520
doo't.

Mari. You will not doo't for all the world I hope: you
are well fauoured, and your lookes forefhew you haue a
gentle heart, I faw you latelie when you caught hurt in parting two that fought: good footh it fhewde well in you, do   1525
fo now, your Ladie feekes my lifeCome, you betweene, and
faue poore mee the weaker.

Leon. I am fworne and will difpatch.   *Enter Pirats.*

Pirat. 1. Hold villaine.

Pira. 2. A prize, a prize.   1530

Pirat. 3. Halfe part mates, halfe part. Come lets haue
her aboord fodainly.   F3v (Z)

Exit.

Enter Leonine.

Leon. Thefe rogueing theeues ferue the great Pyrate   1535
Valdes, and they haue feizd *Marina,* let her goe, ther's no
hope fhee will returne, Ile fweare fhees dead, and throwne
into the Sea, but ile fee further: perhappes they will but
pleafe themfelues vpon her, not carrie her aboord, if fhee
remaine   1540
Whome they haue rauifht, muft by mee be flaine.

Exit.

Enter the three Bawdes.

Pander. Boult.

Boult. Sir.   1545

Pander. Searche the market narrowely, *Mettelyne* is
full of gallants, wee loft too much much money this mart
by beeing too wenchleffe.

Bawd. Wee were neuer fo much out of Creatures, we
haue but poore three, and they can doe no more then they   1550
can doe, and they with continuall action, are euen as good
as rotten.

Pander. Therefore lets haue frefh ones what ere wee pay
for them, if there bee not a confcience to be vfde in euerie
trade, wee fhall neuer profper.   1555

Bawd. Thou fayſt true, tis not our bringing vp of poore baſtards, as I thinke, I haue brought vp ſome eleuen.

Boult. I to eleuen, and brought them downe againe, but ſhall I ſearche the market?

Bawde. What elſe man? the ſtuffe we haue, a ſtrong 1560 winde will blowe it to peeces, they are ſo pittifully ſodden.

Pandor. Thou fayeſt true, ther's two vnwholeſome a   F4 (Z) conſcience, the poore *Tranſiluanian* is dead that laye with the little baggadge.

Boult. I, ſhee quickly poupt him, ſhe made him roaſt- 1565 meate for wormes, but Ile goe ſearche the market.

Exit.

Pand. Three or foure thouſande Checkins were as prettie a proportion to liue quietly, and ſo giue ouer.

Bawd. Why, to giue ouer I pray you? Is it a ſhame to 1570 get when wee are olde?

Pand. Oh our credite comes not in like the commo-ditie, nor the commoditie wages not with the daunger: therefore if in our youthes we could picke vp ſome prettie eſtate, t'were not amiſſe to keepe our doore hatch't, beſides 1575 the ſore tearmes we ſtand vpon with the gods, wilbe ſtrong with vs for giuing ore.

Bawd. Come other ſorts offend as well as wee.

Pand. As well as wee, I, and better too, wee offende worſe, neither is our profeſſion any trade, It's no calling, 1580 but heere comes *Boult.*

Enter Boult with the Pirates and Marina.

Boult. Come your wayes my maiſters, you ſay ſhee's a virgin.

Sayler. O Sir, wee doubt it not.   1585

Boult. Maſter, I haue gone through for this peece you ſee, if you like her ſo, if not I haue loſt my earneſt.

Bawd. Boult, has ſhee anie qualities?

Boult. Shee has a good face, ſpeakes well, and has ex-cellent good cloathes: theres no farther neceſſitie of qua- 1590 lities can make her be refuz'd.

Bawd. What's her price *Boult?*

Boult. I cannot be bated one doit of a thouſand peeces.   F4v (Y?)

Pand. Well, follow me my maiſters, you ſhall haue your money preſenly, wife take her in, inſtruct her what ſhe has 1595 to doe, that ſhe may not be rawe in her entertainment.

Bawd. Boult, take you the markes of her, the colour of her haire, complexion, height, her age, with warrantof her virginitie, and crie; He that wil giue moſt ſhal haue her firſt,

fuch a maydenhead were no cheape thing, if men were as   1600
they haue beene: get this done as I command you.

   Boult. Performance fhall follow.   *Exit.*

  Mar. Alacke that *Leonine* was fo flacke, fo flow, he fhould
haue ftrooke, not fpoke, or that thefe Pirates, not enough
barbarous, had not oreboord throwne me, for to feeke my   1605
mother.

   Bawd. Why lament you prettie one?

  Mar. That I am prettie.

   Bawd. Come, the Gods haue done their part in you.

   Mar. I accufe them not.   1610

   Bawd. You are light into my hands, where you are like
to liue.

  Mar. The more my fault, to fcape his handes, where I
was to die.

   Bawd. I, and you fhall liue in peafure.   1615

  Mar. No.

   Bawd. Yes indeed fhall you, and tafte Gentlemen of all
fafhions, you fhall fare well, you fhall haue the difference of
all complexions, what doe you ftop your eares?

  Mar. Are you a woman?   1620

   Bawd. What would you haue mee be, and I bee not a
woman?

  Mar. An honeft woman, or not a woman.

   Bawd. Marie whip the Goffeling, I thinke I fhall haue
fomething to doe with you, come you'r a young foolifh   1625
fapling, and muft be bowed as I would haue you.

  Mar. The Gods defend me.

   Baud. If it pleafe the Gods to defend you by men, then   G1 (Y)
men muft comfort you, men muft feed you, men ftir you
vp: *Boults* returnd. Now fir, haft thou cride her through   1630
the Market?

   Boult. I haue cryde her almoft to the number of her
haires, I haue drawne her picture with my voice.

   Baud. And I prethee tell me, how doft thou find the inclination of the people, efpecially of the yonger fort?   1635

   Boult. Faith they liftened to mee, as they would haue
harkened to their fathers teftament, there was a Spaniards
mouth watred, and he went to bed to her verie defcription.

   Baud. We fhall haue him here to morrow with his beft
ruffe on.   1640

   Boult. To night, to night, but Miftreffe doe you knowe
the French knight, that cowres ethe hams?

   Baud. Who, *Mounfieur Verollus?*

Boult. I, he, he offered to cut a caper at the proclamation, but he made a groane at it, and fwore he would fee her   1645
to morrow.

Baud. Well, well, as for him, hee brought his difeafe hither, here he does but repaire it, I knowe hee will come in
our fhadow, to fcatter his crownes in the Sunne.

Boult. Well, if we had of euerie Nation a traueller, wee   1650
fhould lodge them with this figne.

Baud. Pray you come hither a while, you haue
Fortunes comming vppon you, marke mee, you muft
feeme to doe that fearefully, which you commit willingly, defpife profite, where you haue moft gaine, to weepe   1655
that you liue as yee doe, makes pittie in your Louers feldome, but that pittie begets you a good opinion, and that
opinion a meere profite.

Mari. I vnderftand you not.

Boult. O take her home Miftreffe, take her home, thefe   1660
blufhes of hers muft bee quencht with fome prefent
practife.

Mari. Thou fayeft true yfaith, fo they muft, for your   G1v(Y)
Bride goes to that with fhame, which is her way to goe with
warrant.   1665

Boult. Faith fome doe, and fome doe not, but Miftreffe
if I haue bargaind for the ioynt.

Baud. Thou maift cut a morfell off the fpit.

Boult. I may fo.

Baud. Who fhould denie it?   1670
Come young one, I like the manner of your garments
well.

Boult. I by my faith, they fhall not be changd yet.

Baud. Boult, fpend thou that in the towne: report what
a foiourner we haue, youle loofe nothing by cuftome.   1675
When Nature framde this peece, fhee meant thee a good
turne, therefore fay what a parragon fhe is, and thou haft
the harueft out of thine owne report.

Boult. I warrant you Miftreffe, thunder fhall not fo a-
wake the beds of Eeles, as my giuing out her beautie ftirs   1680
vp the lewdly enclined, Ile bring home fome to night.

Baud. Come your wayes, follow me.

Mari. If fires be hote, kniues fharpe, or waters deepe,
Vntide I ftill my virgin knot will keepe.
Diana ayde my purpofe.   1685

Baud. What haue we to doe with *Diana*, pray you will
you goe with vs?

Exit.
Enter Cleon, and Dioniza.

Dion. Why ere you foolifh, can it be vndone?   1690
Cleon. O *Dioniza*, fuch a peece of flaughter,
The Sunne and Moone nere lookt vpon.

Dion. I thinke youle turne a chidle agen.

Cleon. Were I chiefe Lord of all this fpacious world, Ide   G2 (Y)
giue it to vndo the deede. O Ladie much leffe in bloud then   1695
vertue, yet a Princes to equall any fingle Crowne ath earth-
ith Iuftice of compare, O villaine, *Leonine* whom thou haft
poifned too, if thou hadft drunke to him tad beene a
kindneffe becomming well thy face, what canft thou fay
when noble *Pericles* fhall demaund his child?   1700

Dion. That fhee is dead. Nurfes are not the fates to fo-
fter it, not euer to preferue, fhe dide at night, Ile fay fo, who
can croffe it vnleffe you play the impious Innocent, and
for an honeft attribute, crie out fhee dyde by foule
play.   1705

Cle. O goe too, well, well, of all the faults beneath the
heauens, the Gods doe like this worft.

Dion. Be one of thofe that thinkes the pettie wrens of
Tharfus will flie hence, and open this to *Pericles*, I do fhame
to thinke of what a noble ftraine you are, and of how co-   1710
ward a fpirit.

Cle. To fuch proceeding who euer but his approbation added, though not his prince confent, he did not flow
from honourable courfes.

Dion. Be it fo then, yet none does knowe but you   1715
how fhee came dead, nor none can knowe *Leonine* being
gone. Shee did difdaine my childe, and ftoode betweene
her and her fortunes: none woulde looke on her, but
caft their gazes on *Marianas* face, whileft ours was blurted at, and helde a Mawkin not worth the time of day.   1720
It pierft me thorow, and though you call my courfe vn-
naturall, you not your childe well louing, yet I finde it
greets mee as an enterprize of kindneffe performd to your
fole daughter.

Cle. Heauens forgiue it.   1725

Dion. And as for *Pericles*, what fhould hee fay, we wept
after her hearfe, & yet we mourne, her monument is almoft
finifhed, & her epitaphs in glittring goldēcharacters expres
a generrall prayfe to her, and care in vs at whofe expence   G2v (Y)
tis done.   1730

Cle. Thou art like the Harpie,
Which to betray, doeſt with thine Angells face ceaze with
thine Eagles talents.

Dion. Yere like one that fuperſticiouſly,
Doe ſweare too'th Gods, that Winter kills   1735
The Fliies, but yet I know, youle
doe as I aduiſe.

Gower. Thus time we waſte, & long leagues make ſhort,
Saile ſeas in Cockles, haue and wiſh but ſort,
Making to take our imagination,   1740
From bourne to bourne, region to region,
By you being pardoned we commit no crime,
To vſe one language, in each ſeuerall clime,
Where our ſceanes ſeemes to liue,
I doe beſeech you   1745
To learne of me who ſtand with gappes
To teach you.
The ſtages of our ſtorie *Pericles*
Is now againe thwarting thy wayward ſeas,
Attended on by many a Lord and Knight,   1750
To ſee his daughter all his liues delight.
Old *Helicanus* goes along behind,
Is left to gouerne it, you beare in mind.
Old *Eſcenes*, whom *Hellicanus* late
Aduancde in time to great and hie eſtate.   1755
Well ſayling ſhips, and bounteous winds
Haue brought
This king to *Tharſus*, thinke this Pilat thought
So with his ſterage, ſhall your thoughts grone
To fetch his daughter home, who firſt is gone   1760
Like moats and ſhadowes, ſee them
Moue a while,
Your eares vnto your eyes Ile reconcile.

Enter Pericles at one doore, with all his trayne, Cleon and Dio-   G3 (Z)
niza at the other. Cleon ſhewes Pericles the tombe, whereat Pe-   1765
ricles makes lamentation, puts on ſacke-cloth, and in a mighty
paſſion departs.

     Gowr. See how beleefe may ſuffer by fowle ſhowe,
This borrowed paſſion ſtands for true olde woe:
And *Pericles* in ſorrowe all deuour'd,   1770
With ſighes ſhot through, and biggeſt teares ore-ſhowr'd.
Leaues *Tharſus*, and againe imbarques, hee ſweares
Neuer to waſh his face, nor cut his hayres:
Hee put on ſack-cloth, and to Sea he beares,

A Tempeſt which his mortall veſſell teares.   1775
And yet hee rydes it out, Nowe pleaſe you wit:
The Epitaph is for *Marina* writ, by wicked *Dioniza*.
>   *The faireſt, ſweeteſt, and beſt lyes heere,*
>   *Who withered in her ſpring of yeare:*
>   *She was of Tyrus the Kings daughter,*   1780
>   *On whom fowle death hath made this ſlaughter.*
>   *Marina was ſhee call'd, and at her byrth,*
>   *Thetis being prowd, ſwallowed ſome part ath'earth:*
>   *Therefore the earth fearing to be ore-flowed,*
>   *Hath Thetis byrth-childe on the heauens beſtowed.*   1785
>   *Wherefore ſhe does and ſweares ſheele neuer ſtint,*
>   *Make raging Battery vpon ſhores of flint.*
No vizor does become blacke villanie,
So well as ſoft and tender flatterie:
Let *Pericles* beleeue his daughter's dead,   1790
And beare his courſes to be ordered;
By Lady *Fortune*, while our Steare muſt play,
His daughters woe and heauie welladay.
In her vnholie ſeruice: Patience then,
And thinke you now are all in *Mittelin*.   1795
>   *Exit.*

>   *Enter two Gentlemen.*
    1. *Gent.* Did you euer heare the like?
    2. *Gent.* No, nor neuer ſhall doe in ſuch a place as this,   G3v (Z)
ſhee beeing once gone.   1800
    1. But to haue diuinitie preach't there, did you euer
dreame of ſuch a thing?
    2. No, no, come, I am for no more bawdie houſes, ſhall's
goe heare the Veſtalls ſing?
    1. Ile doe any thing now that is vertuous, but I am out 1805
of the road of rutting for euer.   *Exit.*
>   *Enter Bawdes 3.*
    Pand. Well, I had rather then twice the worth of her
ſhee had nere come heere.
    Bawd. Fye, fye, vpon her, ſhee's able to freze the god 1810
Priapus, and vndoe a whole generation, we muſt either get
her rauiſhed, or be rid of her, when ſhe ſhould doe for Cly-
ents her fitment, and doe mee the kindeneſſe of our profeſſion, ſhee has me her quirks, her reaſons, her maſter reaſons, her prayers, her knees, that ſhee would make a *Puri-* 1815
taine of the diuell, if hee ſhould cheapen a kiſſe of her.
    Boult. Faith I muſt rauiſh her, or ſhee'le disfurniſh vs
of all our Caualereea, and make our ſwearers prieſts.

Pand. Now the poxe vpon her greene ficknes for mee.

Bawd. Faith ther's no way to be ridde on't but by the   1820
way to the pox. Here comes the Lord *Lyfimachus* difguifed.

Boult. Wee fhould haue both Lorde and Lowne, if the
peeuifh baggadge would but giue way to cuftomers.

Enter Lyfimachus.

Lyfim. How now, how a douzen of virginities?   1825

Bawd. Now the Gods to bleffe your Honour.

Boult. I am glad to fee your Honour in good health.

Li. You may, fo t'is the better for you that your re-
forters ftand vpon found legges, how now? wholfome iniquitie haue you, that a man may deale withall, and defie   1830
the Surgion?

Bawd. Wee haue heere one Sir, if fhee would, but
there neuer came her like in *Meteline.*   (fay.   G4 (Z)

Li. If fhee'd doe the deedes of darknes thou wouldft

Bawd. Your Honor knows what t'is to fay wel enough.   1835

Li. Well, call forth, call forth.

Boult. For flefh and bloud Sir, white and red, you fhall
fee a rofe, and fhe were a rofe indeed, if fhee had but.

Li. What prithi?

Boult. O Sir, I can be modeft.   1840

Li. That dignities the renowne of a Bawde, no leffe
then it giues a good report to a number to be chafte.

Bawd. Heere comes that which growes to the ftalke,
Neuer pluckt yet I can affure you.
Is fhee not a faire creature?   1845

Ly. Faith fhee would ferue after a long voyage at Sea,
Well theres for you, leaue vs.

Bawd. I befeeche your Honor giue me leaue a word,
And Ile haue done prefently.

Li. I befeech you doe.   1850

Bawd. Firft, I would haue you note, this is an Honor-
rable man.   (note him.

Mar. I defire to finde him fo, that I may worthilie

Bawd. Next hees the Gouernor of this countrey, and
a man whom I am bound too.   1855

Ma. If he gouerne the countrey you are bound to him
indeed, but how honorable hee is in that, I knowe not.

Bawd. Pray you without anie more virginall fencing,
will you vfe him kindly? he will lyne your apron with gold.

Ma. What hee will doe gratioufly, I will thankfully   1860
receiue.

Li. Ha you done?

274

Bawd. My Lord ſhees not pac'ſte yet, you muſt take
ſome paines to worke her to your mannage, come wee will
leaue his Honor, and her together, goe thy wayes.   (trade? 1865

    Li. Now prittie one, how long haue you beene at this
    Ma. What trade Sir?

    Li. Why, I cannot name but I ſhall offend.   (name it. G4v (Z)

    Ma. I cannot be offended with my trade, pleaſe you to
    Li. How long haue you bene of this profeſſion?   1870

    Ma. Ere ſince I can remember.

    Li. Did you goe too't ſo young, were you a gameſter
at fiue, or at ſeuen?

    Ma. Earlyer too Sir, if now I bee one.

    Ly. Why? the houſe you dwell in proclaimes you to 1875
be a Creature of ſale.

    Ma. Doe you knowe this houſe to be a place of ſuch
reſort, and will come intoo't? I heare ſay you're of honourable parts, and are the Gouernour of this place.

    Li. Why, hath your principall made knowne vnto 1880
you who I am?

    Ma. Who is my principall?

    Li. Why, your hearbe-woman, ſhe that ſets ſeeds and
rootes of ſhame and iniquitie.

    O you haue heard ſomething of my power, and ſo 1885
ſtand aloft for more ſerious wooing, but I proteſt to thee
prettie one, my authoritie ſhall not ſee thee, or elſe looke
friendly vpon thee, come bring me to ſome priuate place:
Come, come.

    Ma. If you were borne to honour, ſhew it now, if put 1890
vpon you, make the iudgement good, that thought you
worthie of it.

    Li. How's this? how's this? ſome more, be ſage.

    Mar. For me that am a maide, though moſt vngentle
Fortune haue plac't mee in this Stie, where ſince I came, 1895
diſeaſes haue beene ſolde deerer then Phiſicke, that the
gods would ſet me free from this vnhalowed place, though
they did chaunge mee to the meaneſt byrd that flyes i'th
purer ayre.

    Li. I did not thinke thou couldſt haue ſpoke ſo well, 1900
nere dremp't thou could'ſt, had I brought hither a cor-
rupted minde, thy ſpeeche had altered it, holde, heeres
golde for thee, perſeuer in that cleare way thou goeſt and   H1 (Z)
the gods ſtrengthen thee.

    Ma. The good Gods preſerue you.   1905

Li. For me be you thoughten, that I came with no ill
intent, for to me the very dores and windows fauor vilely,
fare thee well, thou art a peece of vertue, & I doubt not but
thy training hath bene noble, hold, heeres more golde for
thee, a curfe vpon him, die he like a theefe that robs thee of   1910
thy goodnes, if thou doeft heare from me it fhalbe for thy
good.

Boult. I befeeche your Honor one peece for me.

Li. Auaunt thou damned dore-keeper, your houfe but
for this virgin that doeth prop it, would fincke and ouer-   1915
whelme you. Away.

Boult. How's this? wee muft take another courfe with
you? if your peeuiſh chaftitie, which is not worth a breake-
faft in the cheapeft countrey vnder the coap, fhall vndoe a
whole houfhold, let me be gelded like a fpaniel, come your   1920

Ma. Whither would you haue mee?   (wayes.

Boult. I muft haue your mayden-head taken off, or the
cõmon hãg-man fhal execute it, come your way, weele haue
no more Gentlemen driuen away, come your wayes I fay.

                    Enter Bawdes.   1925

Bawd. How now, whats the matter?

Boult. Worfe and worfe miftris, fhee has heere fpoken
holie words to the Lord *Lifimachus.*

Bawd. O abhominable.

Boult. He makes our profeffion as it were to ftincke a-   1930
fore the face of the gods.

Bawd. Marie hang her vp for euer.

Boult. The Noble man would haue dealt with her like
a Noble man, and fhee fent him away as colde as a Snowe-
ball, faying his prayers too.   1935

Bawd. Boult take her away, vfe her at thy pleafure, crack
the glaffe of her virginitie, and make the reft maliable.

Boult. And if fhee were a thornyer peece of ground   H1v (Z)
then fhee is, fhee fhall be plowed.

Ma. Harke, harke you Gods.   1940

Bawd. She coniures, away with her, would fhe had neuer come within my doores, Marrie hang you: fhees borne
to vndoe vs, will you not goe the way of wemen-kinde?
Marry come vp my difh of chaftitie with rofemary & baies.

Boult. Come miftris, come your way with mee.   1945

Ma. Whither wilt thou haue mee?

Boult. To take from you the Iewell you hold fo deere.

Ma. Prithee tell mee one thing firft.

Boult. Come now your one thing.

Ma. What canſt thou wiſh thine enemie to be.   1950
   Boult. Why, I could wiſh him to bee my maſter, or rather my miſtris.
   Ma. Neither of theſe are ſo bad as thou art, ſince they
doe better thee in their command, thou hold'ſt a place for
which the painedſt feende of hell would not in reputation 1955
change: Thou art the damned doore-keeper to euery cu-
ſterell that comes enquiring for his Tib. To the cholerike
fiſting of euery rogue, thy eare is lyable, thy foode is ſuch
as hath beene belch't on by infected lungs.
   Bo. What wold you haue me do? go to the wars, wold you? 1960
wher a man may ſerue 7. yeers for the loſſe of a leg, & haue
not money enough in the end to buy him a woodden one?
   Ma. Doe any thing but this thou doeſt, emptie olde receptacles, or common-ſhores of filthe, ſerue by indenture,
to the common hang-man, anie of theſe wayes are yet 1965
better then this: for what thou profeſſeſt, a Baboone could
he ſpeak, would owne a name too deere, that the gods wold
ſafely deliuer me from this place: here, heers gold for thee,
if that thy maſter would gaine by me, proclaime that I can
ſing, weaue, ſow, & dance, with other vertues, which Ile keep 1970
from boaſt, and will vndertake all theſe to teache. I doubt
not but this populous Cittie will yeelde manie ſchollers.
   Boult. But can you teache all this you ſpeake of?   H2 (Z)
   Ma. Prooue that I cannot, take mee home againe,
And proſtitute mee to the baſeſt groome that doeth fre- 1975
quent your houſe.
   Boult. Well I will ſee what I can doe for thee: if I can
place thee I will.
   Ma. But amongſt honeſt woman.
   Boult. Faith my acquaintance lies little amongſt them, 1980
But ſince my maſter and miſtris hath bought you, theres
no going but by their conſent: therefore I will make them
acquainted with your purpoſe, and I doubt not but I ſhall
finde them tractable enough. Come, Ile doe for thee what
I can, come your wayes.   *Exeunt.*   1985
                    Enter Gower.
   Marina thus the Brothell ſcapes, and chaunces
   Into an *Honeſt-houſe* our Storie ſayes:
   Shee ſings like one immortall, and ſhee daunces
   As Goddeſſe-like to her admired layes.   (ſes, 1990
   Deepe clearks ſhe dumb's, and with her neele compo-
   Natures owne ſhape, of budde, bird, branche, or berry.
   That euen her art ſiſters the naturall Roſes

Her Inckle, Silke Twine, with the rubied Cherrie,
That puples lackes fhe none of noble race,   1995
Who powre their bountie on her: and her gaine
She giues the curfed Bawd, here wee her place,
And to hir Father turne our thoughts againe,
Where wee left him on the Sea, wee there him left,
Where driuen before the windes, hee is arriu'de   2000
Heere where his daughter dwels, and on this coaft,
Suppofe him now at *Anchor*: the Citie ftriu'de
God *Neptunes Annuall* feaft to keepe, from whence
Lyfimachus our *Tyrian* Shippe efpies,
His banners Sable, trim'd with rich expence,   2005
And to him in his Barge with former hyes,   H2v (Z)
In your fuppofing once more put your fight,
Of heauy *Pericles*, thinke this his Barke:
Where what is done in action, more if might
Shalbe difcouerd, pleafe you fit and harke.   *Exit.* 2010
         Enter Helicanus, to him 2. Saylers.

1. *Say.* Where is Lord *Helicanus*? hee can refolue you,
O here he is Sir, there is a barge put off from *Metaline*, and
in it is *Lyfimachus* the Gouernour, who craues to come a-
boord, what is your will?   2015

Helly. That hee haue his, call vp fome Gentlemen.
2. *Say.* Ho Gentlemen, my Lord calls.
         Enter two or three Gentlemen.

1. *Gent.* Doeth your Lordfhip call?

Helli. Gentlemen there is fome of worth would come 2020
aboord, I pray greet him fairely.
         Enter Lyfimachus.

Hell. Sir, this is the man that can in ought you would
refolue you.

Lyf. Hayle reuerent Syr, the Gods preferue you.   2025

Hell. And you to out-liue the age I am, and die as I
would doe.

Li. You wifh mee well, beeing on fhore, honoring of
Neptunes triumphs, feeing this goodly veffell ride before
vs, I made to it, to knowe of whence you are.   2030

Hell. Firft what is your place?

Ly. I am the Gouernour of this place you lie before.

Hell. Syr our veffell is of *Tyre*, in it the King, a man,
who for this three moneths hath not fpoken to anie one,
nor taken fuftenance, but to prorogue his griefe.   2035

Li. Vpon what ground is his diftemperature?

Hell Twould be too tedious to repeat, but the mayne
griefe fprings frō the loffe of a beloued daughter & a wife.

Li. May wee not fee him?

Hell. You may, but bootleffe. Is your fight, fee will not   H3 (Y)
fpeake to any, yet let me obtaine my wifh.   2041

Lyf. Behold him, this was a goodly perfon.

Hell. Till the difafter that one mortall wight droue him
to this.

Lyf. Sir King all haile, the Gods preferue you, haile 2045
royall fir.

Hell. It is in vaine, he will not fpeake to you.

Lord. Sir we haue a maid in *Metiliue*, I durft wager would
win fome words of him.

Lyf. Tis well bethought, fhe queftionleffe with her fweet 2050
harmonie, and other chofen attractions, would allure and
make a battrie through his defend parts, which now are
midway ftopt, fhee is all happie as the faireft of all, and her
fellow maides, now vpon the leauie fhelter that abutts a-
gainft the Iflands fide.   2055

Hell. Sure all effectleffe, yet nothing weele omit that
beares recoueries name. But fince your kindneffe wee haue
ftretcht thus farre, let vs befeech you, that for our golde
we may prouifion haue, wherein we are not deftitute for
want, but wearie for the ftaleneffe.   2060

Lyf. O fir, a curtefie, which if we fhould denie, the moft
iuft God for euery graffe would fend a Caterpillar, and fo
inflict our Prouince: yet once more let mee intreate to
knowe at large the caufe of your kings forrow.

Holl. Sit fir, I will recount it to you, but fee I am pre- 2065
uented.

Lyf. O hee'rs the Ladie that I fent for,
Welcome faire one, ift not a goodly prefent?

Hell. Shee's a gallant Ladie.

Lyf. Shee's fuch a one, that were I well affurde   2070
Came of a gentle kinde, and noble ftocke, I do wifh
No better choife, and thinke me rarely to wed,
Faire on all goodneffe that confifts in beautie,
Expect euen here, where is a kingly patient,
If that thy profperous and artificiall fate,   H3v (Y)
Can draw him but to anfwere thee in ought,   2076
Thy facred Phyficke fhall receiue fuch pay,
As thy defires can wifh.

Mar. Sir I willvſe my vtmoſt skill in his recouerie, pro-
uided that none but I and my companion maid be ſuffered 2080
to come neere him.

Lyſ. Come, let vs leaue her, and the Gods make her proſperous.   *The Song.*

Lyſ. Marke he your Muſicke?

Mar. No nor lookt on vs.   2085

Lyſ. See ſhe will ſpeake to him.

Mar. Haile ſir, my Lord lend eare.

Per. Hum, ha.

Mar. I am a maid, my Lorde, that nere before inuited
eyes, but haue beene gazed on like a Comet: She ſpeaks 2090
my Lord, that may be, hath endured a griefe might equall
yours, if both were iuſtly wayde, though wayward fortune
did maligne my ſtate, my deriuation was from anceſtors,
who ſtood equiuolent with mightie Kings, but time hath
rooted out my parentage, and to the world, and augward 2095
caſualties, bound me in ſeruitude, I will deſiſt, but there is
ſomething glowes vpon my cheek, and whiſpers in mine
eare, go not till he ſpeake.

Per. My fortunes, parentage, good parentage, to equall
mine, was it not thus, what ſay you?   2100

Mari. I ſed my Lord, if you did know my parentage,
you would not do me violence.

Per. I do thinke ſo, pray you turne your eyes vpon me,
your like ſomething that, what Countrey women heare of
theſe ſhewes?   2105

Mar. No, nor of any ſhewes, yet I was mortally brought
forth, and am no other then I appeare.

Per. I am great with woe, and ſhall deliuer weeping: my
deareſt wife was like this maid, and ſucha one my daughter might haue beene: My Queenes ſquare browes, her   H4 (Y)
ſtature to an inch, as wandlike-ſtraight, as ſiluer voyſt, 2111
her eyes as Iewell-like, and caſte as richly, in pace an o-
ther *Iuno.* Who ſtarues the eares ſhee feedes, and makes
them hungrie, the more ſhe giues them ſpeech, Where doe
you liue?   2115

Mar. Where I am but a ſtraunger from the decke, you
may diſcerne the place.

Per. Where were you bred? and how atchieu'd you theſe
indowments which you make more rich to owe?

Mar. If I ſhould tell my hyſtorie, it would ſeeme like 2120
lies diſdaind in the reporting.

Per. Prethee fpeake, falfneffe cannot come from thee,
for thou lookeft modeft as iuftice, & thou feemeft a *Pallas*
for the crownd truth to dwell in, I wil beleeue thee & make
fenfes credit thy relation, to points that feeme impoffible, 2125
for thou lookeft like one I loued indeede: what were thy
friends? didft thou not ftay when I did pufh thee backe,
which was when I perceiu'd thee that thou camft from
good difcending.   *Mar.* So indeed I did.

Per. Report thy parentage, I think thou faidft thou hadft 2130
beene toft from wrong to iniurie, and that thou thoughts
thy griefs might equall mine, if both were opened.

Mar. Some fuch thing I fed, and fed no more, but what
my thoughts did warrant me was likely.

Per. Tell thy ftorie, if thine confidered proue the thou- 2135
fand part of my enduraunce, thou art a man, and I haue
fuffered like a girle, yet thou doeft looke like patience,
gazing on Kings graues, and fmiling extremitie out of
act, what were thy friends? howe loft thou thy name,
my moft kinde Virgin? recount I doe befeech thee, Come 2140
fit by mee.

Mar. My name is *Marina.*

Per. Oh I am mockt, and thou by fome infenced God
fent hither to make the world to laugh at me.

Mar. Patience good fir: or here Ile ceafe.   H4 v(Y)

Per. Nay Ile be patient: thou little knowft howe thou 2146
doeft ftartle me to call thy felfe *Marina.*

Mar. The name was giuen mee by one that had fome
power, my father, and a King.

Per. How, a Kings daughter, and cald *Marina?*   2150

        Mar. You fed you would beleeue me, but not to bee a
troubler of your peace, I will end here.

Per. But are you flefh and bloud?
Haue you a working pulfe, and are no Fairie?
Motion well, fpeake on, where were you borne?   2155
And wherefore calld *Marina?*

Mar. Calld *Marina,* for I was borne at fea.

Plr. At fea, what mother?

Mar. My mother was the daughter of a King, who died
the minute I was borne, as my good Nurfe *Licherida* hath 2160
oft deliuered weeping.

Per. O ftop there a little, this is the rareft dreame
That ere duld fleepe did mocke fad fooles withall,
This cannot be my daughter, buried, well, where were you
bred? Ile heare you more too'th bottome of your ftorie, 2165
and neuer interrupt you.

Mar. You fcorne, beleeue me twere beft I did giue ore.

Per. I will beleeue you by the fyllable of what you fhall deliuer, yet giue me leaue, how came you in thefe parts? where were you bred?   2170

Mar. The King my father did in *Tharfus* leaue me,
Till cruel *Cleon* with his wicked wife,
Did feeke to murther me: and hauing wooed a villaine,
To attempt it, who hauing drawne to doo't,
A crew of Pirats came and refcued me,   2175
Brought me to *Metaline*,
But good fir whither wil you haue me? why doe you weep?
It may be you thinke mee an impofture, no good fayth: I
am the dsughter to King *Pericles*, if good king *Pericles* be.

Hell. Hoe, *Hellicanus?*   I1(Y)

Hel. Calls my Lord.   2181

Per. Thou art a graue and noble Counfeller,
Moft wife in generall, tell me if thou canft, what this mayde
is, or what is like to bee, that thus hath made mee
weepe.   2185

Hel. I know not, but heres the Regent fir of *Metaline*,
fpeakes nobly of her.

Lyf. She neuer would tell her parentage,
Being demaunded, that fhe would fit ftill and weepe.

Per. Oh *Hellicanus*, ftrike me honored fir, giue mee a   2190
gafh, put me to prefent paine, leaft this great fea of ioyes ru-
fhing vpon me, ore-beare the fhores of my mortalitie, and
drowne me with their fweetneffe: Oh come hither,
thou that begetft him that did thee beget,
Thou that waft borne at fea, buried at *Tharfus*,   2195
And found at fea agen, O *Hellicanus*,
Downe on thy knees, thanke the holie Gods as loud
As thunder threatens vs, this is *Marina*.
What was thy mothers name? tell me, but that
for truth can neuer be confirm'd inough,   2200
Though doubts did euer fleepe.

Mar. Frift fir, I pray what is your title?

Per. I am *Pericles* of *Tyre*, but tell mee now my
Drownd Queenes name, as in the reft you fayd,
Thou haft beene God-like perfit, the heir of kingdomes,   2205
And an other like to *Pericles* thy father.

Ma. Is it no more to be your daughter, then to fay, my
mothers name was *Thaifa*, *Thaifa* was my mother, who did
end the minute I began.

Pe. Now blelling on thee, rile th'art my child. 2210
Giue me frelh garments, mine owne *Hellicanus*, lhee is not
dead at *Tharlus* as lhee lhould haue beene by lauage *Cleon*,
lhe lhall tell thee all, when thou lhalt kneele, and iultifie in
knowledge, lhe is thy verie Princes, who is this?

Hel. Sir, tis the gouernor of *Metaline*, who hearing of I₁v(Y)
your melancholie ltate, did come to lee you. 2216

Per. I embrace you, giue me my robes.
I am wilde in my beholding, O heauens blelle my girle,
But harke what Mulicke tell, *Hellicanus* my *Marina*,
Tell him ore point by point, for yet he leemes to doat. 2220
How lure you are my daughter, but what mulicke?

Hel My Lord I heare none.

Per. None, the Mulicke of the *Spheres*, lift my *Marina*.

Lyl. It is not good to crolle him, giue him way.

Per. Rarelt lounds, do ye not heare? 2225

Lyl. Mulicke my Lord? I heare.

Per. Molt heauenly Mulicke.
It nips me vnto liltning, and thicke llumber
Hangs vpon mine eyes, let me relt.

Lyl. A Pillow for his head, lo leaue him all. 2230
Well my companion friends, if this but anlwere to my iult
beliefe, Ile well remember you.

Diana.

Dia. My Temple ltands in *Ephelus*,
Hie thee thither, and doe vppon mine Altar lacrifice, 2235
There when my maiden prielts are met together before the
people all, reueale how thou at lea didlt loole thy wife, to
mourne thy crolles with thy daughters, call, & giue them
repetition to the like, or performe my bidding, or thou li-
uelt in woe: doo't, and happie, by my liluer bow, awake and 2240
tell thy dreame.

Per. Celeltiall *Dian*, Goddelle *Argentine*.
I will obey thee *Hellicanus*.   *Hell.* Sir.

Per. My purpole was for *Tharlus*, there to ltrike,
The inholpitable *Cleon*, but I am for other leruice firlt, 2245
Toward *Ephelus* turne our blowne layles,
Eftloones Ile tell thee why, lhall we refrelh vs lir vpon your
lhore, and giue you golde for luch prouilion as our in-
tents will neede.

Lyl Sir, with all my heart, and when you come a lhore, I2(Y)
I haue another lleight. 2251

Per. You lhall preuaile were it to wooe my daughter, for
it leemes you haue beene noble towards her.

Lyf. Sir, lend me your arme.

Per. Come my *Marina*. 2255

          Exeunt.

  Gower. Now our fands are almoſt run,

More a little, and then dum.

This my laſt boone giue mee,

For fuch kindneſſe muſt relieue mee: 2260

That you aptly will fuppofe,

What pageantry, what feats, what ſhowes,

What minſtrelſie, and prettie din,

The Regent made in *Metalin*.

To greet the King, fo he thriued, 2265

That he is promiſde to be wiued

To faire *Marina*, but in no wife,

Till he had done his facrifice.

As *Dian* bad, whereto being bound,

The *Interim* pray, you all confound. 2270

In fetherd briefenes fayles are fild,

And wiſhes fall out as they'r wild,

At *Epheſus* the Temple fee,

Our King and all his companie.

That he can hither come fo foone, 2275

Is by your fancies thankfull doome.

  Per. Haile *Dian*, to performe thy iuſt commaund,

I here confeſſe my felfe the King of *Tyre*,

Who frighted from my countrey did wed at *Pentapolis*, the

faire *Thaiſa*, at Sea in childbed died ſhe, but brought forth a 2280

Mayd child calld *Marina* whom O Goddeſſe wears yet thy

filuer liuerey, ſhee at *Tharſus* was nurſt with *Cleon*, who at

fourteene yeares he fought to murder, but her better ſtars

brought her to *Meteline*, gainſt whoſe ſhore ryding, her   I2v(Z)

Fortunes brought the mayde aboord vs, where by her 2285

owne moſt cleere remembrance, ſhee made knowne her

felfe my Daughter.

    Th. Voyce and fauour, you are, you are, O royall

Pericles.

    Per. What meanes the mum? ſhee die's, helpe Gen- 2290

tlemen.

    Ceri. Noble Sir, if you haue tolde *Dianaes* Altar

true, this is your wife?

    Per. Reuerent appearer no, I threwe her ouer-boord

with thefe verie armes. 2295

    Ce. Vpon this coaſt, I warrant you.

    Pe. T'is moſt certaine.

Cer. Looke to the Ladie, O fhee's but ouer-joyde,
Earlie in bluftering morne this Ladie was throwne vpon
this fhore.   2300

I op't the coffin, found there rich Iewells, recouered her, and plac'fte her heere in *Dianaes* temple.

Per. May we fee them?

Cer. Great Sir, they fhalbe brought you to my houfe,
whither I inuite you, looke *Thaifa* is recouered.   2305

Th. O let me looke if hee be none of mine, my fan-
ctitie will to my fenfe bende no licentious eare, but curbe
it fpight of feeing: O my Lord are you not *Pericles*? like
him you fpake, like him you are, did you not name a tempeft, a birth, and death?   2310

Per. The voyce of dead *Thaifa*.

Th. That *Thaifa* am I, fuppofed dead and drownd.

Per. I mortall *Dian*.

Th. Now I knowe you better, when wee with teares
parted *Pentapolis*, the king my father gaue you fuch a ring. 2315

Per. This, this, no more, you gods, your prefent kinde-
nes makes my paft miferies fports, you fhall doe well that
on the touching of her lips I may melt, and no more be
feene, O come, be buried a fecond time within thefe armes.   I3 (Z)

Ma. My heart leaps to be gone into my mothers bo- 2320
fome.

Per. Looke who kneeles here, flefh of thy flefh *Thaifa*,
thy burden at the Sea, and call'd *Marina*, for fhe was yeel-
ded there.

Th. Bleft, and mine owne.   2325

Hell. Hayle Madame, and my Queene.

Th. I knowe you not.

Hell. You haue heard mee fay when I did flie from
Tyre, I left behind an ancient fubftitute, can you remember what I call'd the man, I haue nam'de him oft.   2330

Th. T'was *Hellicanus* then.

Per. Still confirmation, imbrace him deere *Thaifa*, this
is hee, now doe I long to heare how you were found? how
poffiblie preferued? and who to thanke (befides the gods)
for this great miracle?   2335

Th. Lord *Cerimon*, my Lord, this man through whom
the Gods haue fhowne their power, that can from firft to
laft refolue you.

Per. Reuerent Syr, the gods can haue no mortall officer
more like a god then you, will you deliuer how this dead 2340
Queene reliues?

Cer. I will my Lord, befeech you firft, goe with mee
to my houfe, where fhall be fhowne you all was found with
her. How fhee came plac'fte heere in the Temple, no
needfulll thing omitted.   2345

Per. Pure *Dian* bleffe thee for thy vifion, and will offer
night oblations to thee *Thaifa*, this Prince, the faire betro-
thed of your daughter, fhall marrie her at *Pentapolis*, and
now this ornament makes mee looke difmall, will I clip to
forme, and what this fourteene yeeres no razer touch't, to 2350
grace thy marridge-day, Ile beautifie.

Th. Lord *Cerimon* hath letters of good credit. Sir,
my father's dead.

Per. Heauens make a Starre of him, yet there my   I3v (Z)
Queene, wee'le celebrate their Nuptialls, and our felues 2355
will in that kingdome fpend our following daies, our fonne
and daughter fhall in *Tyrus* raigne.

Lord *Cerimon* wee doe our longing ftay,
To heare the reft vntolde, Sir lead's the way.
                    FINIS.   2360
                    Gower.

In *Antiochus* and his daughter you haue heard
Of monftrous luft, the due and iuft reward:
In *Pericles* his Queene and Daughter feene,
Although affayl'de with *Fortune* fierce and keene.   2365

   Vertue preferd from fell deftructions blaft,
   Lead on by heauen, and crown'd with ioy at laft.

In *Helycanus* may you well defcrie,
A figure of trueth, of faith, of loyaltie:
In reuerend *Cerimon* there well appeares,   2370
The worth that learned charitie aye weares.

   For wicked *Cleon* and his wife, when Fame
   Had fpred his curfed deede, the honor'd name

Of *Pericles*, to rage the Cittie turne,
That him and his they in his Pallace burne: 2375
The gods for murder feemde fo content,
To punifh, although not done, but meant.

   So on your Patience euermore attending,
   New ioy wayte on you, heere our play has ending.
                    FINIS.   2380

PASSAGES FROM WILKINS'S *PAINFUL ADVENTURES OF PERICLES*

THIS appendix includes extracts from Wilkins's prose narrative which form the basis for the longer passages of reconstruction in the text of this edition. Shorter passages are given in the Introduction, p. 77, and at the relevant places in the Commentary. The text is modernized from that given in Geoffrey Bullough's *Narrative and Dramatic Sources of Shakespeare*.

A. PERICLES PLAYS AND SINGS (compare Scene 8a)

Whereas all the other princes upon their coming to their lodgings betook themselves to their pillows and to the nourishment of a quiet sleep, [Pericles] of the gentlemen that attended him—for it is to be noted that, upon the grace that the King had bestowed on him, there was of his officers toward him no attendance wanting—he desired that he might be left private, only that for his instant solace they would pleasure him with some delightful instrument, with which, and his former practice, he intended to pass away the tediousness of the night instead of more fitting slumbers.

His will was presently obeyed in all things, since their master had commanded he should be disobeyed in nothing. The instrument is brought him, and as he had formerly wished, the chamber is disfurnished of any other company but himself, where presently he began to compel such heavenly voices from the senseless workmanship, as if Apollo himself had now been fingering on it, and as if the whole synod of the gods had placed their deities round about him of purpose to have been delighted with his skill, and to have given praises to the excellency of his art; nor was this sound only the ravisher of all hearers, but from his own clear breast he sent such cheerful notes, which by him were made up so answerable to the other's sound, that they seemed one only consort of music. . . . [Simonides] was so satisfied to hear him thus express his excellence that he accounted his court happy to entertain so worthy a guest, and himself more happy in his acquaintance. But day, that hath still that sovereignty to draw back the empire of the night, though a while she in darkness usurp, brought the morning on, and . . . even in the instant came in Pericles to give his grace that salutation which the morning required of him.

(Bullough, pp. 512–14)

B. SIMONIDES, PERICLES, AND THAISA (compare Sc. 9.71–96)

'How, minion', quoth her father . . . 'is this a fit match for you? A straggling Theseus born we know not where, one that hath neither blood nor
merit for thee to hope for, or himself to challenge even the least allowance
of thy perfections?', when she, humbling her princely knees before her
father, besought him to consider that, suppose his birth were base—when
his life showed him not to be so—yet he had virtue, which is the very
ground of all nobility, enough to make him noble. She entreated him to
remember that she was in love, the power of which love was not to be confined by the power of his will. 'And my most royal father', quoth she, 'what
with my pen I have in secret written unto you, with my tongue now I openly confirm, which is that I have no life but in his love, neither any being but
in the enjoying of his worth.' 'But daughter', quoth Simonides, 'equals to
equals, good to good is joined. This not being so, the bavin of your mind, in
rashness kindled, must again be quenched, or purchase our displeasure.
And for you, sir', speaking to Prince Pericles, 'first learn to know I banish
you my court, and yet scorning that our kingly enragement should stoop
so low, for that your ambition, sir, I'll have your life.' 'Be constant', quoth
Thaisa. 'For every drop of blood he sheds of yours, he shall draw another
from his only child.'

(Bullough, p. 516)

C. LYSIMACHUS AND MARINA (compare Sc. 19.94–167)

But the Governor, suspecting these tears but to be some new cunning
which her matron the Bawd had instructed her in, to draw him to a more
large expense, he as freely told her so; and now began to be more rough
with her, urging her that he was the Governor, whose authority could
wink at those blemishes herself and that sinful house could cast upon her,
or his displeasure punish at his own pleasure, 'which displeasure of mine,
thy beauty shall not privilege thee from, nor my affection, which hath
drawn me unto this place, abate, if thou with further lingering withstand
me'. By which words, she understanding him to be as confident in evil as
she was constant in good, she entreated him but to be heard, and thus she
began.

'If as you say, my lord, you are the Governor, let not your authority,
which should teach you to rule others, be the means to make you misgovern yourself. If the eminence of your place came unto you by descent and
the royalty of your blood, let not your life prove your birth a bastard. If it
were thrown upon you by opinion, make good that opinion was the cause
to make you great. What reason is there in your justice, who hath power
over all, to undo any? If you take from me mine honour, you are like him
that makes a gap into forbidden ground, after whom too many enter, and

you are guilty of all their evils. My life is yet unspotted, my chastity unstained in thought. Then if your violence deface this building, the workmanship of heaven, made up for good, and not to be the exercise of sin's intemperance, you do kill your own honour, abuse your own justice, and impoverish me.'

'Why', quoth Lysimachus, 'this house wherein thou livest is even the receptacle of all men's sins, and nurse of wickedness; and how canst thou then be otherwise than naught, that livest in it?' 'It is not good', answered Marina, 'when you that are the Governor, who should live well, the better to be bold to punish evil, do know that there is such a roof, and yet come under it. Is there a necessity, my yet good lord, if there be fire before me, that I must straight then thither fly and burn myself? Or if suppose this house—which too too many feel such houses are—should be the doctor's patrimony and surgeon's feeding, follows it therefore that I must needs infect myself to give them maintenance? O my good lord, kill me but not deflower me, punish me how you please so you spare my chastity, and since it is all the dowry that both the gods have given and men have left to me, do not you take it from me. Make me your servant, I will willingly obey you; make me your bondwoman, I will account it freedom; let me be the worst that is called vile, so I may still live honest I am content. Or if you think it is too blessed a happiness to have me so, let me even now, now in this minute die, and I'll account my death more happy than my birth.'

With which words, being spoken upon her knees, while her eyes were the glasses that carried the water of her mishap, the good gentlewoman being moved, he lift her up with his hands, and even then embraced her in his heart, saying aside, 'Now surely this is virtue's image, or rather virtue's self, sent down from heaven a while to reign on earth, to teach us what we should be. So instead of willing her to dry her eyes, he wiped the wet himself off, and could have found in his heart with modest thoughts to have kissed her, but that he feared the offer would offend her. This only he said: 'Lady, for such your virtues are, a far more worthy style your beauty challenges, and no way less your beauty can promise me that you are, I hither came with thoughts intemperate, foul and deformed, the which your pains so well hath laved that they are now white. Continue still to all so, and for my part, who hither came but to have paid the price, a piece of gold for your virginity, now give you twenty to relieve your honesty. It shall become you still to be even as you are, a piece of goodness, the best wrought up that ever nature made; and if that any shall enforce you ill, if you but send to me, I am your friend.' With which promise, leaving her presence, she most humbly thanked the gods for the preservation of her chastity and the reformation of his mind.

(Bullough, pp. 535–6)

D. MARINA'S SONG (Sc. 21.68.2)

Amongst the harlots foul I walk
    Yet harlot none am I ;
The rose amongst the thorns doth grow
    And is not hurt thereby.
The thief that stole me, sure I think
    Is slain before this time.
A bawd me bought, yet am I not
    Defiled by fleshly crime.
Nothing were pleasanter to me
    Than parents mine to know ;
I am the issue of a king,
    My blood from kings doth flow.
In time the heavens may mend my state
    And send a better day,
For sorrow adds unto our griefs
    But helps not any way.
Show gladness in your countenance,
    Cast up your cheerful eyes ;
That God remains, that once of naught
    Created earth and skies.

(Bullough, pp. 542–3)

ATTRIBUTION OF EMENDATIONS

THIS list records the first editor to introduce each emendation of the Quarto text. (Parentheses indicate the first scholar to propose each emendation.) Unlisted changes are from the Oxford *Complete Works*. Where an emendation is supported by Wilkins's prose narrative, this is indicated by '*P.A.*'.

Sc. 1.	6	holy-ales] MALONE (Farmer; Theobald); Holydayes Q
	11	these] Q2; those QI
	21	fere] MALONE (Theobald); Peere Q
	29	By] MALONE; But Q
	39	a wight] F3; of wight Q
	48.1	*Music*] MALONE; *not in* Q
	50	Fit for th'] OXFORD (Elze); For Q
	54	In . . . knit] OXFORD; To knit . . . perfections Q; Their best perfections in her to knit (*conj.* Steevens)
	65	the] Q3; th' QI
	67	boundless] ROWE bondlesse Q
	83	From] MALONE; For Q
	99	ANTIOCHUS] MALONE; *not in* Q
	99.1	*angrily . . . riddle*] HOENIGER, *after P.A.*; *not in* Q
	154	our] F3; your Q
	156	cancel] F3; counsell Q
	170	you're] F3; you Q
	171	uncomely] MAXWELL (Delius, *conj. from P.A.*); vntimely Q
	204	*Exit*] MALONE 2; *not in* Q
	211	*Exit*] DYCE; *not in* Q
	212	ANTIOCHUS] Q4; *not in* QI
	213.1	*Exit*] Q2; *not in* QI
Sc. 2.	1	*Exeunt Lords* ALEXANDER; *not in* Q
	3	Be my] DYCE; By me Q
	7	feared's] DYCE 2 (W. S. Walker); fearde is Q
	20	honour him] ROWE; honour Q
	25	th'ostent] MALONE (Tyrwhitt); the stint Q
	30	am] STEEVENS (Farmer); once Q
	33.1	*among them old Helicanus*] DYCE (*subs.*; old *P.A.*); *not in* Q
	46	wind] EDWARDS (Steevens); sparke Q
	49	a] MALONE; *not in* Q
	55	*Exeunt Lords*] MALONE 2; *not in* Q
		Helicanus] Q2; *Hellicans* QI

	56	movèd] MALONE; Mooude Q
	63	you but] Q4; but you Q1
	70	you] STEEVENS; you your selfe Q
	75	Where as] Q2; Whereas Q1
	88	me] ROWE; *not in* Q
	89	fears] F4; feare Q
	91	doubt] MALONE (Steevens); doo't Q
		doubt no] OXFORD (*conj.* Brooks); no Q
	105	grieve] Q5; griue for Q1
	113	Or] STEEVENS; or till the Q
	126	sure crack] F3; cracke Q
	127	we'll] MALONE; will Q
	129.1	*Exeunt*] ROWE; *Exit* Q
Sc. 3.	11	question] STEEVENS; question mee Q
	21	lest that he] STEEVENS; lest hee Q
	27	King's ears it] WHITE (Dyce); Kings seas Q
	28	on the seas] STEEVENS (Malone, Percy); at the Sea Q
	30	HELICANUS] Q4; *not in* Q1
	34	betook] Q2; betake Q1
	35	Now my] EDWARDS; now Q1; my Q4
	39	*Exeunt*] Q2; *Exit* Q1
Sc. 4.	8	they're] ROWE; they are Q
	15	lungs] MALONE (Steevens); toungs Q
	17	helps] MALONE; helpers Q
	23	the] Q3; her Q1
	34	Those] DYCE 2; These Q
	36	they] Q2; thy Q1
	39	two summers] STEEVENS (Mason, Theobald), *P.A.*; too sauers Q
	54	heed] COLLIER 2; heare Q
	57	thou] Q4; thee Q1
	66	Hath] ROWE 3; That Q
		these] MALONE (Steevens); the Q
	68	men] MALONE; mee Q
	75	fear] Q4; leaue Q1
	79	*Exit*] MALONE 2; *not in* Q
	81.1	*the Lord again, conducting*] HOENIGER (*subs.*); *not in* Q
	88	hearts] HUDSON 2 (W. S. Walker); teares Q
	92	importing] OXFORD (Deighton); expecting Q
Sc. 5.	4	Prove] STEEVENS; That Will proue Q
	11	Tarsus] Q4; *Tharstill* Q1
	12	speken] GRANT WHITE; spoken Q
	19	for that] OXFORD (Richard Proudfoot); for though Q

	22	Sent word] OXFORD; Sau'd one Q; Sends word STEEVENS (Theobald), *P.A.*
	27	deeming] OXFORD (Wilson); doing Q
	40	*Exit*] MALONE; *not in* Q
	52	What ho] MALONE (Tyrwhitt); What, to Q
	58	fetch thee] Q4; fetch'th QI
	72	devours] F4; deuowre Q
	79	MASTER] This edition; 2. (i.e. SECOND FISHERMAN) Q
	80	THIRD] Q4; I. QI
	94	scratch't] SINGER 2; Search Q; scratch it MALONE 2 (Steevens)
	117	pray] Q4; pray you QI
	122	holidays] MALONE; all day Q
		moreo'er] MALONE (Farmer); more; or Q
	130	all your] Q4; you QI
	134	*Exit . . . Fisherman*] MALONE (*subs.*); *not in* Q
	138	is] Q2; I QI
	143–4	from his subjects | He gains] STEEVENS; he gaines from | His subiects Q
	160	thy] DELIUS (Theobald), *P.A.*; *not in* Q
	161	losses] OXFORD (Elze); selfe Q
	173	in's] Q4; in his QI
	193	rapture] ROWE 2, *P.A.*; rupture Q
	196	delightsome] OXFORD; delight Q; delightfull F3
	203	equal] MAXWELL (Staunton); a Goale Q
	204	*Exeunt*] ROWE; *not in* Q
Sc. 6.	4	daughter] MALONE; daughter heere Q
	7	*Exit one*] *Exit a Lord* MALONE; *not in* Q
	13	renown] MALONE; Renownes Q
	16.1–3	*richly . . . Thaisa*] MALONE (*subs.*), *P.A.*; *not in* Q
	27	*Piuè . . . forza*] HOENIGER (Hertzberg, *conj. in* Maxwell); *Pue Per doleera kee per forsa* Q
	29	what's] Q4; with QI
	31	*pompae*] STEEVENS (Theobald), *P.A.*; *Pompey* Q
	34	with] This edition; bearing OXFORD; *not in* Q
	37	this] OXFORD (Maxwell); his Q
	45	delivereth] OXFORD (Maxwell); deliuered Q
	48	In . . . live] This edition (*P.A.*); A pretty morrall Q
	60	for] SCHANZER (anon. *conj. in* Cambridge); by Q
	62.1	*Exeunt*] ROWE; *not in* Q
Sc. 7.	0.1.	*A . . . in*] MALONE (A Banquet prepared), *P.A.*; *not in* Q
	3	To] F4; I Q
	12	yours] Q3; your QI

	14	artists] STEEVENS (Malone); an Artist Q
	16	You are] OXFORD; And you are Q1; And you Q4; And you're MALONE
	25	Envied] SISSON (Vaughan); Enuies Q
	27	gods] This edition (Oxford); thoughts Q
	28	distaste] OXFORD (Collier 2); resist Q
		but] DYCE (Mason); not Q
	37	Yon] Q2; You Q1
	38	me] Q4; *not in* Q1
		what] EDWARDS; that Q
	43	son's] MALONE; sonne Q
		a] STEEVENS; like a Q
	50	stored] MALONE (Steevens); stur'd Q
	51	you do] Q4; do you Q1
	62	entertain] DYCE 2 (W. S. Walker); entraunce Q
	63	bear] OXFORD (Wilson); say wee drinke Q
	70	further] MALONE; furthermore Q
		know] MALONE; know of him Q
	83	whom sour misfortune] This edition; who onely by misfortune of the seas Q
	93.1	*The Knights*] MALONE; *They* Q
	95	Come] OXFORD (Elze); Come sir Q
	96	sir] OXFORD (Brooks); *not in* Q
	106	should] MAXWELL (Wilson), *P.A.*; *not in* Q
	108	SIMONIDES] KING Q4; *not in* Q1
	111.1	*Exeunt* MALONE; *not in* Q
Sc. 8.	11	Their] STEEVENS; those Q
	33	death indeed's] OXFORD (Brooks); death in deed Q; death's indeed MALONE
	34	this—kingdoms] MAXWELL; this Kingdome is Q
	40	By] ALEXANDER (Theobald); Try Q
	45	longer then let me] OXFORD; longer, let me Q; longer, let me then STEEVENS
	46	Further to bear] EDWARDS (Hoeniger); To forbeare Q
	55	us] GLOBE; *not in* Q
	59	*Exeunt*] ROWE; *not in* Q
Sc. 9.	6	have] MAXWELL (W. S. Walker); get Q
	12.1	*Exeunt Knights*] ROWE; *not in* Q
	24–5	night. My ears, | I do protest,] STEEVENS; night: | I do protest, my eares Q
	30	think you of my daughter] OXFORD; do you thinke of my Daughter, sir Q; do you think, sir, of | My daughter STEEVENS

33	My daughter, sir] MALONE; Sir, my Daughter Q
47–50	traitor, | That . . . child] EDWARDS (*after P.A.*); traytor Q
49	With] OXFORD; With the *P.A.*; *not in* Q
56	in search of honour] OXFORD (Wilson), *P.A.*; for Honours cause Q
57	your] HUDSON (W. S. Walker); her Q
105	I shall] OXFORD; Ile Q; I will STEEVENS
113	Then] MALONE; And then Q
Sc. 10.2	the house about] MALONE; about the house Q
6	fore] STEEVENS (Malone); from Q
7	crickets] ROWE 2; Cricket Q
8	All] DELIUS; Are Q
10	Where by] Q2; Whereby Q1
14.1	*Dumb show*] Q5; *not in* Q1
14.7–9	*with . . . another*] MALONE (*subs.*); *not in* Q
17	coigns] ROWE 3; Crignes Q
29	mutiny there he] STEEVENS; mutanie, hee there Q
	appease] STEEVENS, *P.A.*; oppresse Q
46	fortune's mood] MALONE (Steevens, Theobald); fortune mou'd Q
60	sea] ROWE 2; seas Q
	Exit] Q5; *not in* Q1
Sc. 11.1	Thou] ROWE; The Q
7	Thou] MALONE; then Q
	stormest] DYCE; storme Q
11	midwife] MALONE (Steevens); my wife Q
14.1	*with a baby*] *with an infant* STEEVENS; *not in* Q
34	poor inch of nature] HOENIGER (Collier), *from P.A.*; *not in* Q
36	partage] OXFORD (Edwards); portage Q
52	custom] SINGER (Boswell); easterne Q
53	'er] Q1; her Q4
	for . . . straight] MALONE; *after* 'meet', l. 54, *in* Q
54.1–2	*She . . . reveals the body of Thaisa*] EDWARDS; *not in* Q
59	the ooze] STEEVENS; oare Q
61	And] STEEVENS; The Q
	aye] STEEVENS (Malone); ayre Q; e'er GLOBE
64	paper] Q2; Taper Q1
66	coffer] MALONE; Coffin Q
68.1	*Exit Lychorida*] MALONE 2; *not in* Q
73	from] MAXWELL (Collier 2), *P.A.*; for Q
78.1–3	*Exit . . . curtains*] *Exeunt* ROWE; *Exit* Q
Sc. 12.2	*Exit Philemon*] HOENIGER; *not in* Q
9	*Exeunt servants*] HOENIGER (*subs.*); *not in* Q

23	held] MALONE (Theobald); hold Q
34	so] OXFORD; *not in* Q; I MALONE
38	treasure] STEEVENS; pleasure Q
56	by] OXFORD (Hoeniger); *not in* Q
	that] This edition; *not in* Q
58	bitumed] MALONE (Theobald); bottomed Q
75	even] Q4, *P.A.*; euer Q1
77	rash] OXFORD (Malone), *P.A.*; rough Q
82	have heard] MALONE; heard Q
84	appliances] DYCE; applyaunce Q
88.1	*Music*] HOENIGER; *not in* Q
90–1	warmth | Breathes] STEEVENS; warmth breath Q1; warme breath Q2
94	set] MALONE; sets Q
Sc. 13.0.1–2	*and . . . baby*] *and Lychorida with Marina in her arms* DYCE; *not in* Q
5	strokes] ROUND; shakes Q; shafts STEEVENS
6	hurt] STEEVENS; hant Q
7	woundingly] DEIGHTON (Schmidt, Kinnear); wondringly Q
14	and leave] STEEVENS; leauing Q
28	honour all] MALONE; honour, | All Q
29	Unscissored] STEEVENS, *P.A.*; vnsisterd Q
30	show ill] SINGER 2 (Theobald); shew will Q
35	CLEON] Q4; *Cler.* Q1
41	*Exeunt*] ROWE; *not in* Q
Sc. 14.5	eaning] F3; learning Q
11	CERIMON] Q6; *Cler.* Q1
16	THAISA] Q4; *Thin.* Q1
17	*Exeunt*] ROWE; *Exit* Q
Sc. 15.10	her] MALONE (Steevens); hie Q
	heart] MALONE (Steevens); art Q
14	Seeks] ROWE; Seeke Q
15–16	has . . . lass] OXFORD (*conj.* Schanzer *in* Hoeniger); hath . . . wench Q
17	ripe] Q2; right Q1
	rite] COLLIER 2; light Q
21	she] MALONE; they Q
23	nee'le] MAXWELL; needle Q
26	bird] MALONE (Theobald); bed Q
32	With the] STEEVENS (Mason); The Q
	might] STEEVENS (Mason); might with Q
38	murder] OXFORD (W. S. Walker); murderer Q
47	carry] STEEVENS; carried Q

57	or] DEIGHTON; in Q
	love thy] SINGER; thy loue Q
58	Enslave] DEIGHTON; enflame Q
63	nurse's] STEEVENS (Theobald, Percy); Mistresse Q
76–7	favour | Is changed] SCHANZER; fauours | Changd Q
78	o'er] OXFORD (Theobald); ere Q
	marge] This edition; marre it Q
90	resume] MAXWELL (Wilson); reserue Q
99	Pray you] MALONE; pray Q
100.1	*Exit Dionyza*] MALONE; *not in* Q
105	with] MALONE; *not in* Q
114	stem] MALONE; sterne Q
129	for it] Q4; fort Q1
141.1	*Leonine runs away*] MALONE; *not in* Q
144	*Exeunt . . . Marina*] MALONE (*subs.*); *Exit* Q
147	she'll] MALONE; shee will Q
Sc. 16.0.1–2	*the Pander . . . Bolt*] F3 (*subs.*); *not in* Q
4	too much] Q2; too much much Q1
19	They're too] MALONE; ther's two Q
40	A PIRATE] ROWE (*subs.*); *Sayler.* Q
52	*Exeunt . . . Pirates*] MALONE; *not in* Q
61	but] MALONE; not Q
70	like] Q4; *not in* Q1
84	must stir] Q4; stir Q1
85.1.	*Enter Bolt*] Q4; *not in* Q1
100	Veroles] MALONE; *Verollus* Q
106	of] EDWARDS (W. S. Walker); in Q
111	to despise] MALONE; despise Q
119	BAWD] F3; *Mari.* Q
142	*Exeunt*] F3; *Exit* Q
Sc. 17.1	are] Q4; ere Q1
6	A] MAXWELL (Delius); O Q
12	fact] SINGER 2; face Q
14–15	fates. | To foster is] MAXWELL (Vaughan); fates to foster it Q
17	pious] COLLIER (Mason), *P.A.*; impious Q
25	cowed] STEEVENS; coward Q
27	prime] DYCE; prince Q
28	sources] DYCE; courses Q
31	distain] SINGER (Steevens); disdaine Q
33	Marina's] Q2; *Marianas* Q1
52	*Exeunt*] ROWE; *not in* Q
Sc. 18.0.1	*Enter Gower*] Q4; *not in* Q1
1	make we] OXFORD (Maxwell); make Q

3	take] HUDSON 2; take our Q
7	scenes seem] Q4; sceanes seemes Q1; scene seems MAXWELL
8	i'th'] MAXWELL (Bullen); with Q1; i'the MALONE
10	the] Q2; thy Q1
14	govern, if] OXFORD (Maxwell); gouerne it, Q
16	Tyre] SCHANZER (W. S. Walker); time Q
18	his] MALONE; this Q
19	go on] MAXWELL (Malone); grone Q
22.1	*Dumb show*] MALONE; *not in* Q
24	owed] MAXWELL (anon. *conj. in* Cambridge); olde Q
29	puts] MALONE; put Q
33.1	*He . . . tomb*] MALONE (*subs.*); *not in* Q
42	scene] MALONE 2; Steare Q

Sc. 19.9	*Exeunt*] F3; *Exit* Q
13	the whole of] OXFORD (Maxwell); a whole Q
37	deed] Q5; deedes Q1
45	dignifies] Q4; dignities Q1
46	member] This edition; number Q
46.1	*Enter Pander with Marina*] OXFORD; *Enter Marina* Q4; *not in* Q1
50.1	*He pays the Bawd*] EDWARDS (*subs.*); *not in* Q
70	*Exeunt . . . Bolt*] MALONE (*subs.*); *not in* Q; *Exit Bawd* Q4
74	name it] EDWARDS; name Q; name't F3
93	aloof] ROWE; aloft Q
94	But . . . thee] This edition; but I protest to thee prettie one Q
	95–101, 103–7, 111–48, 151–6, 163] *from P.A.* (see Appendix B, Passage C)
157	Persever still] STEEVENS; perseuer Q
160	Now] This edition; for Q
170	Thy] This edition; your Q
171	thee] This edition; you Q
	Exit] ROWE; *not in* Q
180.1	*Bawd*] ROWE; *Bawdes* Q
185	She] ROWE; He Q
200	*Exit*] Q4; *not in* Q1
228	make gain] HUDSON 2; gaine Q
231	I will] ROWE; will Q
240	women] Q4; woman Q1

Sc. 20.14	Whence] STEEVENS; Where Q
20	fervour] Qb; former Qa
22	the] MALONE; his Q

Sc. 21.1	SAILOR OF TYRE] MALONE (*subs.*); *1. Say.* Q
6	SAILOR OF TYRE] MALONE (*subs.*); *2. Say.* Q
8	you] Q6; *not in* Q1
9	SAILOR OF MYTILENE] OXFORD; *Hell.* Qa; *1. Say.* Qb
11	sir] MALONE 2; *not in* Q
27	any.	LYSIMACHUS] Q4; any, Q1
28	HELICANUS] Q4; *Lys.* Q1
	Helicanus . . . couch] EDWARDS; *not in* Q; *Pericles discovered* MALONE
28–9	person	Till] Q4; person.	*Hell.* Till Q1
29	of] OXFORD (Hoeniger); that Q
	night] MALONE; wight Q
36	choice] STEEVENS; chosen Q
	alarm] This edition; alarum OXFORD; allure Q
37	ports] MAXWELL (Steevens); parts Q
41.1	*Exit Lord*] MALONE; *not in* Q
48	gods] DYCE (W. S. Walker); God Q
52	it] STEEVENS; it to you Q
52.1	*Enter . . . maid*] MALONE (*subs.*); *not in* Q
55	presence] MALONE; present Q
58	I'd] Q4; I do Q1
59	wed] Q4; to wed Q1
60	bounty] MALONE (Steevens); beautie Q
66	recure] HUDSON 2 (W. S. Walker); recouerie Q
69	Marked] Q4; Marke Q1
70–1	Come . . . prosperous] NEW CAMBRIDGE; *after* l. 68 *in* Q
92	countrywoman] Q6; Countrey women Q1
93	shores . . . shores] MALONE (Charlemont); shewes . . . shewes Q
113	my senses] Q4; senses Q1
116	say] MALONE; stay Q
130	thou them? Thy] MALONE; thou thy Q
144	Motion as well?] MAXWELL; Motion well, Q
151	dull] Q4; duld Q1
155	You'll scarce believe me] MALONE; You scorne, beleeue me Q
169	PERICLES Ho] Q4; *Hell.* Hoe Q1
176	would never] STEEVENS; neuer would Q
194	rest] SINGER; rest you sayd Q
196	life] STEEVENS (Mason); like Q
198	name] OXFORD (Brooks); name was *Thaisa* Q
201	Thou art] Q4; th'art Q1
203	Not] STEEVENS; shee is not Q

209	sir] STEEVENS; *not in* Q
213	doubt] MALONE; doat Q
222	eyelids] STEEVENS; eyes Q
222.1	*He sleeps*] MALONE (*subs.*); *not in* Q
225.1	*Exeunt . . . Pericles*] MALONE (*subs.*); *not in* Q
225.2	*Diana descends from the heavens*] OXFORD; *Diana.* Q; *Diana appearing to Pericles asleep* ROWE
233	life] MALONE (Charlemont); like Q
234	Perform] MALONE; or performe Q
236.1	*Diana . . . heavens*] OXFORD; *not in* Q; *Diana disappears* MALONE
238	*Enter . . . Marina*] MALONE (*subs.*); *not in* Q
245	With . . . sir] STEEVENS; Sir, with all my heart Q
246	suit] MALONE; sleight Q
Sc. 22.0.1	*Enter Gower*] Q4; *not in* Q1
9	well] OXFORD (Brooks); *not in* Q
18.1–2	*Enter . . . attendants*] Q4 (*subs.*); *not in* Q1
20	*Exit*] Q4; *not in* Q1
24	The fair Thaisa at Pentapolis] MALONE; at *Pentapolis*, the faire *Thaisa* Q
26	who] F4; whom Q
35	nun] COLLIER 2; mum Q
42	one] STEEVENS (Malone); in Q
48	upon him] MALONE; *not in* Q
58	Immortal] Q4; I mortall Q1
71	PERICLES] Q4; *Hell.* Q1
91	I] MALONE; *not in* Q
92	Nightly] MAXWELL; night Q
106	*Exeunt*] Q4; *not in* Q1
106.1	*Enter*] Q4; *not in* Q1
111	preserved] TONSON; preferd Q
118	their] Q4; his Q1
	deed to the] MAXWELL (Collier 2); deede, the Q
122	that] OXFORD; *not in* Q; them MALONE
124	*Exit*] MALONE; *not in* Q

INDEX

THIS is a selective guide to the Commentary and the Introduction, though it does not duplicate the section headings of the latter. Characters in the play are only listed if their names are discussed. Asterisks identify entries which supplement the information given in *OED*.

The Oxford World's Classics Website

www.worldsclassics.co.uk

- Information about new titles
- Explore the full range of Oxford World's Classics
- Links to other literary sites and the main OUP webpage
- Imaginative competitions, with bookish prizes
- Peruse the Oxford World's Classics Magazine
- Articles by editors
- Extracts from Introductions
- A forum for discussion and feedback on the series
- Special information for teachers and lecturers

www.worldsclassics.co.uk

American Literature

British and Irish Literature

Children's Literature

Classics and Ancient Literature

Colonial Literature

Eastern Literature

European Literature

History

Medieval Literature

Oxford English Drama

Poetry

Philosophy

Politics

Religion

The Oxford Shakespeare

A complete list of Oxford Paperbacks, including Oxford World's Classics, Oxford Shakespeare, Oxford Drama, and Oxford Paperback Reference, is available in the UK from the Academic Division Publicity Department, Oxford University Press, Great Clarendon Street, Oxford OX2 6DP.

In the USA, complete lists are available from the Paperbacks Marketing Manager, Oxford University Press, 198 Madison Avenue, New York, NY 10016.

Oxford Paperbacks are available from all good bookshops. In case of difficulty, customers in the UK can order direct from Oxford University Press Bookshop, Freepost, 116 High Street, Oxford OX1 4BR, enclosing full payment. Please add 10 per cent of published price for postage and packing.